The Gospel in the Dock

The Gospel in the Dock

Is the Gospel of Jesus Christ Good for the
Church, Humanity, and the World?

Bryan M. Christman

RESOURCE *Publications* • Eugene, Oregon

THE GOSPEL IN THE DOCK
Is the Gospel of Jesus Christ Good for the Church, Humanity, and the World?

Copyright © 2021 Bryan M. Christman. All rights reserved. Except for brief quotations in critical publications or reviews, no part of this book may be reproduced in any manner without prior written permission from the publisher. Write: Permissions, Wipf and Stock Publishers, 199 W. 8th Ave., Suite 3, Eugene, OR 97401.

Resource Publications
An Imprint of Wipf and Stock Publishers
199 W. 8th Ave., Suite 3
Eugene, OR 97401

www.wipfandstock.com

PAPERBACK ISBN: 978-1-7252-7724-3
HARDCOVER ISBN: 978-1-7252-7725-0
EBOOK ISBN: 978-1-7252-7726-7

08/05/21

Unless otherwise indicated, all Scripture quotations are from the ESV® Bible (The Holy Bible, English Standard Version®), copyright © 2001 by Crossway, a publishing ministry of Good News Publishers. Used by permission. All rights reserved.

Scripture quotations marked NLV are taken from the New Life Version, copyright © 1969 and 2003. Used by permission of Barbour Publishing, Inc., Uhrichsville, Ohio 44683. All rights reserved.

Scripture quotations marked NLT are taken from the Holy Bible, New Living Translation, copyright © 1996, 2004, 2015 by Tyndale House Foundation. Used by permission of Tyndale House Publishers, Inc., Carol Stream, Illinois 60188. All rights reserved.

Scripture quotations marked NRSV are from the New Revised Standard Version Bible, copyright © 1989 the Division of Christian Education of the National Council of the Churches of Christ in the United States of America. Used by permission. All rights reserved.

Then some of the scribes and Pharisees answered him, saying, "Teacher, we wish to see a sign from you." But he answered them, "An evil and adulterous generation seeks for a sign, but no sign will be given to it except the sign of the prophet Jonah. For just as Jonah was three days and three nights in the belly of the great fish, so will the Son of Man be three days and three nights in the heart of the earth.

—MATTHEW 12:38–39

And you shall call his name Isaac (*he laughs*).

—GENESIS 17:19

Contents

Tables — ix
Acknowledgements — xi
Abbreviations — xiii

Introduction: *"The Gospel in the Dock"* — 1
Excursus: *God and the Way of Force* — 25
1. Evangel: *The Primal Gospel* — 34
2. Rehabilitating the Gospel — 49
3. Evangelism: *The Stewardship of the Gospel* — 91
4. Rehabilitating the Stewardship of the Gospel — 107
5. Evangelizers: *The Stewards of the Gospel* — 160
6. Rehabilitating the Stewards of the Gospel — 171
Conclusion: *"God's Purification of Means"* — 252
Unscientific Exegetical Postscript: *Is there a "Dark Side" of the Gospel?* — 266
Epilogue: *"The Beginning of the End of Adversaries"* — 337

Bibliography — 345
Index — 361

Tables

Table 1. The Sign of the Prophet Jonah | 79

Table 2. A basic overview of "the prosecution of evangelism" in Chapters 3–6 | 95

Table 3. Is the Gospel Conditional or Unconditional? | 131

Table 4. The Place of Decision in Conditional and Unconditional Salvation | 136

Table 5. The Relation of Gospel Doctrine to Gospel Culture | 186

Table 6. Mediated and Non-Mediated Communities | 201

Table 7. Characteristics of Mediated and Non-Mediated Communities | 202

Table 8. Dynamics and Results of Mediated and Immediate Communities | 203

Table 9. Sin as the Doorway to the Gospel Community | 226

Table 10. God's Purification of Means in the Sign of Jonah | 262

Table 11. The Exclusivist vs. Biblical Views of the Gospel, History, and Condemnation | 273

Acknowledgements

My greatest debt of gratitude is to C. S. Lewis. It came to pass that over four decades ago, as I made my way through the dis-enchanted wilderness of the world, I happened upon a magical wardrobe. It pulled this rejector of Christianity into the world of Narnia and "Aslan." That great Lion was "on the move" and followed me as I left the wardrobe, soon pouncing upon me as the living Christ. Humanly speaking, apart from Lewis's re-enchanting "spell" of Narnia, and the subsequent mentorship received through many of his other books, this book would never have been written.

I also acknowledge the magnitude of influence the late Christian musician/gospel evangelist Keith Green had upon me and this book. He had written a powerful two-part critique on the modern gospel which mirrored what I was seeing in our early Fundamentalist/Evangelical church experience. This launched me into the decades-long struggle with many of the false gospels discussed in these pages. Fortunately, along the way I found others who greatly influenced my path. Chief among them, in roughly the order in which I "met" them were, George Eldon Ladd, Geerhardus Vos, Herman Ridderbos, Blaise Pascal, Dietrich Bonhoeffer, Lesslie Newbigin, Soren Kierkegaard, James K. A. Smith, Merold Westphal, and Simone Weil.

I also am grateful for those in the realm of "regular" life who have enabled or contributed in various ways to this book. I am most thankful for my wife Debbi who for the last two years has patiently supported my writing which required me to neglect many other things. The crumbling home in which we humbly abide will attest to her love and grace. Our son Justin has also helped me with this book in many invaluable ways, chief of which has been to amiably participate in countless hours of discussion of the form and content of the book. I also thank my mom for her support, along with our entire family, church family, and friends for providing the "landed" quality of my life that has enabled writing from an invaluable sense of "home" that strangers and pilgrims cannot take for granted.

I would like to thank Stanley and Barbara Yake for the gift of several hundred volumes in philosophy, ethics, and theology. Though I received these books in the midst of this process and could not take advantage of most of them, many were perused and made "contributions" to these pages. I express my thanks for the encouragement I received for this project early on from Dr. Keith Dow and from Kori Frazier Morgan. I would also like to thank the baker's dozen of friends who through several Facebook discussions provided invaluable feedback and advice for the formulation of the book's all-important cover blurb: Roger D. Allen, JoAnna Barrera, Josh Barrera, Tony Barrera, Jessica Biette, Bill Clarke, Mike Ernest, R. I. Hardesty, Cynthia Mulford, Angela Alaimo O'Donnell, Jennifer Ratliff, Fernanda Rossini, and Adam Stoddard. I also acknowledge my thanks to all those at Wipf and Stock who have graciously helped this first-time author.

Lastly, I give thanks for those who read any or all of these pages, and trust that they may point them further toward the author of the gospel, for their good and God's praise.

Abbreviations

BC	Before Christ	Jas	James
Col	Colossians	Jer	Jeremiah
Cor	Corinthians	KJV	King James Version
CUP	Concluding Unscientific Postscript, *Soren Kierkegaard's Writings*	Matt	Matthew
		Mic	Micah
		Nah	Nahum
Deut	Deuteronomy	NLV	New Life Version
Eccl	Ecclesiastes	NLT	New Living Translation
Eph	Ephesians	NRSV	New Revised Standard Version
ESV	English Standard Version		
Exod	Exodus	NT	New Testament
Ezek	Ezekiel	OT	Old Testament
FSE	For Self-Examination, *Soren Kierkegaard's Writings*	Pet	Peter
		Phil	Philippians
		Prov	Proverbs
Gal	Galatians	Ps	Psalms
Gen	Genesis	Rev	Revelation
Hag	Haggai	Rom	Romans
Heb	Hebrews	Song	Song of Songs
Hos	Hosea	Thess	Thessalonians
Isa	Isaiah	Tim	Timothy

Introduction

"The Gospel in the Dock"

> And they said to one another, "Come, let us cast lots, that we may know on whose account this evil has come upon us." So they cast lots, and the lot fell on Jonah. So they picked up Jonah and hurled him into the sea, and the sea ceased from its raging.
>
> —JONAH 1:7, 15

"The Prosecution's Opening Statement in Humankind vs. The Gospel of Jesus Christ"

Bailiff: "Please rise. The World Court of the City of Man, Joint Civil and Criminal Division, is now in session, the Honorable *Judge Will T. Power* presiding."[1]

Judge: "Everyone but the jury may be seated. *Mr. Steward*, please swear in the jury."[2]

Bailiff: "Please raise your right hand. Do you solemnly swear or affirm that you will truly listen to this case and render a true verdict and a fair sentence as to this defendant?"

Jury: "I do".

Bailiff: "You may be seated."

---

1. Obviously personifying Friedrich Nietzsche's concept of "the will to power," to be discussed below.

2. We will see that "stewardship" is the chief vocation of human beings as created by God, and that participating in a trial of the gospel is not fulfilling that vocation.

Judge: "Members of the jury, your duty will be to determine whether the defendant is guilty or not guilty based only on facts and evidence provided in this case. The prosecution has the burden of proving the guilt of the defendant beyond a reasonable doubt. This burden remains on the prosecution through the trial. The prosecution must prove that a crime was committed, and that the defendant committed the crime. However, if you are not satisfied of the defendant's guilt to that extent, then reasonable doubt exists, and the defendant must be found not guilty. Mr. Steward, what is today's case?"

Bailiff: "Your Honor, today's case is 'The State of Humankind versus The Gospel of Jesus Christ.'"

Judge: "Is the prosecution ready?"

Prosecuting Attorneys: "Yes, Your Honor."

Judge: "Is the defense ready?"

Defense Attorneys: "Yes, Your Honor."

Judge: "The prosecution may begin with its opening statement."

Pilate H. Cain: "Your Honorable Judge Will T. Power, ladies and gentlemen of the jury, my name is Pilate H. Cain.[3] My esteemed colleagues and I are representing The State of Humankind against this allegedly good news of *Jesus Christ* in this trial of the millennia. We intend to prove beyond reasonable doubt that this gospel is guilty of both civil and criminal crimes against humankind. This gospel is of course infamously known by its three main perpetrators: the gospel of Jesus Christ himself; the practice of propagating said gospel, otherwise known as evangelism; and the persons of said practice, otherwise known as evangelizers. Our witnesses will not be limited to the twelve apostolic glory-seekers but will include many in history who have been victims of our diabolical defendants. My opening argument will present five allegedly historical reports which together represent a microcosm of the entire lengthy deliberation to follow. I will briefly present each incident, provide some historical context, and then make a point or two regarding its damning significance for our case.

---

3. We combine Cain from Genesis, the middle initial H for some modern "flavor," and the Roman Pilate, who interrogated Jesus and reluctantly sentenced him to death, at the request of the mob the religious leaders of Israel riled up. Of course, the composite person is inspired by C. S. Lewis's "Screwtape," an "elderly retired devil," who pens letters of advice and instruction to "a young devil who has just started work" on his first human "patient." Lewis, *Screwtape Letters*, xviii. (For more on our inspiration see in our Conclusion: "On Pilate H. Cain as Prosecutor.")

The First Incident: The Report of Isaiah

> How beautiful upon the mountains are the feet of him who brings good news, who publishes peace, who brings good news of happiness, who publishes salvation, who says to Zion, "Your God reigns" (Isa 52:7).

The first report is from the ancient Israelite prophet Isaiah, who graphically depicts the gospel as "good news." His description of the beauty of the feet of those traveling over mountains with "good news" indicates what the defendants claim should be our response to their "gospel." The statement derives from ancient times when a city's watchmen waited for traveling heralds bearing news of a victory which would signify liberation for the people. Thus, this gospel is claimed to signify the good news of God's *victorious liberation of all of humanity and the world*. It's a big claim, and on the face of it, simply "too good to be true."[4] But Isaiah's words are repeated by several other prophets and apostles in the Bible and are in some way, shape or form, the core message of the whole. That this obviously preposterous claim is even made is *the primary reason* the defendants are "in the dock" of this court. They are the true antagonists in this case, though they claim innocence and question the justness of this eminently just trial. Even I admit it's a terrible pity that they force us to try them. In the words of a former eminent gospel prosecutor who, unlike myself, was tragically "taken in" by them, "They are simple old souls most of them—just like children. They have no knowledge of modern science and would believe anything they were told."[5]

The Second Incident: Jonah and the Ancient Mariners

> And they said to one another, "Come, let us cast lots, that we may know on whose account this evil has come upon us." So they cast lots, and the lot fell on Jonah. So they picked up Jonah and hurled him into the sea, and the sea ceased from its raging (Jonah 1:7, 15).

---

4. Ferry, *Brief History of Thought*, 11.

5. Lewis, *The Pilgrim's Regress*, 35. Mr. Enlightenment also says, "I am a man of the world . . . do I look as if I was easily taken in?"

The second report is from another ancient, and even by the Bible's own *questionable* standards, an admittedly scandalous Israelite prophet named Jonah. He is on a boat in a violent storm at sea with some heathen mariners. In this case we don't see them viewing Jonah's feet which carried him from afar as beautiful, but as needing to tread water when they hurl him overboard, since on his account the dangerous storm had come upon *them*. This quite simply counters the view that the evangelizers of this gospel, like Jonah, should find the joyful reception that Isaiah claimed was normal. So also, in our times, these pesky gospellers with their strange ancient fables are about as helpful to our sophisticated modern problems as useless Jonah was to these expert sailors. The casting of lots (or drawing of straws) then and now, seems to point to these gospellers as part of the problem, and definitely not part of the solution. So, I admit that sometimes they have been cast overboard from the world, so to speak, to restore the normal calm of humanity that Jonah and his kind interrupt. Of course, the subsequent calm following Jonah's plunge was claimed to have some mysterious and greater "gospel" significance by Jesus of Nazareth, who was of course the chief instigator beneath this whole conspiracy against our established order. At any rate, what we constantly see with all those connected to this "gospel" is that they first disrupt the world by telling us how evil we are and then oh-so *conveniently* claiming to have the *only* solution. History continually demonstrates that "the lot" falls on these "snake-oil salesmen." Their trumped-up cure for imaginary ailments is the real problem. Therefore, we deal with them and their "gospel-cure" accordingly, to uphold our superlative social order. And that is why these perpetrators require a once and for all time verdict, to lay to rest and finally move beyond this embarrassing regression of evolutionary childhood, to the glorious destiny we are so rationally and self-sacrificially creating for all who will submit to our humble and beneficent wisdom.

The Third Incident: The Supposed Paradise of Irenaeus

"The Church has been planted as a paradisus in this world."[6]

The third incident is more recent by a number of centuries, and brings us, ha, ha, oh, pardon my lack of composure at the laughable

---

6. Brock and Parker, *Saving Paradise*, 84.

"contemporaneity" of this supposed "gospel," all the way up to the second century after Christ! The prominent early-church Bishop named Irenaeus declared that "the church was planted as a *paradisus* (or paradise) in the world." Whether some believed him at the time seems irrelevant since it now seems glaringly obvious that the only reply to such an *extravagant* claim is that the church has manifestly been *anything but* a "paradise" in the world. *Where* is this paradise? Show it to us! That is all we ask! Some today, known as the "new atheists," have now bravely declared themselves to be "anti-theists," and have the courage to say that the world would better become a paradise *without* the gospel or *any* "religion" for that matter, with their constantly disrupting the otherwise inevitable progress of humanity toward a *real* paradise. Depending on the verdict, our just and liberating proceedings may finally acquit some in history who courageously ensured that the only "paradise" these gospellers would enjoy was in the "sweet by and by," since our world intends to be a "swamp" to any *this-worldly* "planting" of a paradise.[7]

The Fourth Incident: Orual and Psyche, Two Pagan Sisters

> "Have done with it, Psyche," I said sharply. "Where is this god? Where the palace is? Nowhere—in your fancy. Where is he? Show him to me? What is he like? She looked a little aside and spoke, lower than ever but very clear, and as if all that had yet passed between us were of no account beside the gravity of what she was now saying. "Oh, Orual," she said, "not even I have seen him—yet. He comes to me only in the holy darkness."[8]

The fourth report comes from a supposed historical record of the lives of an honorable Queen and her childlike sister, made known by the puzzlingly popular twentieth-century Christian author C. S. Lewis, who to

---

7. "Why does the song of the exhausted Mokichi, bound to the stake gnaw constantly at my heart:

'We're on our way, we're on our way,
We're on our way to the temple of Paradise.' . . .

'Father, you were not defeated by me.' The Lord of Chikugo looked straight into the ashes of the brazier as he spoke. 'You were defeated by this swamp of Japan.'" Endo, *Silence*, 63, 199.

8. Lewis, *Till We Have Faces*, 122–23.

most seemed a culturally anachronistic dinosaur.[9] This, once again, *archaic* story is from the dank dark of history, and this time from a wholly uncivilized land with ravenous mountain gods receiving human sacrifices to boot. In fact, Psyche was "offered up" to the god as the "obviously" logical thing to do to appease the plague fallen upon the people, just as Jonah was *so primitively* sacrificed to the storm God. But rather than being consumed by this "god," Psyche claimed to have become his betrothed, and lived in his glorious palace. Of course, when Orual visits her delusional sister, clothed in rags in the wilderness, she asks her, "Where is this god? Where the palace is? Nowhere—in your fancy." And then Psyche lets go the real shocker: "Oh, Orual," she said, "not even I have seen him—yet. He comes to me only in the holy darkness." These accused persons of the gospel: Isaiah, Jonah, Irenaeus, Psyche, along with the gospel's multitudes of rather boring and less colorful characters, all hold in common such obviously deranged claims! And so, we conclude that the reasonable people of the world have done well to place them and their gospel in the dock, but we must render the well-deserved verdict: guilty! In regard to a few minor individual cases that were already settled out of court through the death penalty, the defense repeatedly claims that of them the world was not worthy.[10] But the prosecution counter-replies that they were obviously not worthy of *our* world.

The Fifth Incident: Cain and Abel, the First Two Brothers

> By faith Abel offered to God a more acceptable sacrifice than Cain, through which he was commended as righteous, God commending him by accepting his gifts. And through his faith, though he died, he still speaks (Hebrews 11:4).

The final incident to be considered in this opening argument is from the supposed story of the first two brothers at the very dawn of humanity, although the defense will say from the dawn of inhumanity.[11] The story tells of Abel, the first entry in the Bible's list of those supposedly "not worthy of the world." Cain killed Abel because Abel's "sacrifice" was accepted by God while Cain's was not. The story does not explicitly state why God

---

9. Lewis's own self-description. See Lewis, *Selected Essays*, 13–14.
10. See Heb 11:38.
11. See Gen 4:1–17.

"regarded" the one's sacrifice but not the other's. Many centuries later the unnamed author of an early Christian writing called "The Letter to the Hebrews" wrote that Abel offered his "by faith," which made the difference to God. Well regardless of that, it certainly made the difference to Cain, because these two brothers pursued radically different way of life. And what if the wrong way of idle busybodies took hold from the very beginning? Even the gospel's apostle Paul warned against violating such basic community standards![12] And *that* was Cain's concern! So far, we have only reported this incident according to the bare facts. But the Bible slants this report in such a way that Cain can barely receive a fair hearing. For the fact is that the "pious" but useless "way of faith," versus the practical way of the hardworking Cain who went on to gloriously build the first fortress-city, is a very slim reed to build a life on, let alone set the foundation for the society of humankind to come! The real truth is that Cain has been grossly misrepresented by those who wrote the "history." We all know how that story goes!

I submit that the accused trio of the gospel, evangelism and its evangelizers, constantly agitate the world with their outrageous and dangerous claims of a God who through a crucified peasant has provided salvation for all of humanity, planted the church as a paradise in the world and other such rot, and has capped it all off with a flimsy "way of faith" for humankind's progress! Is it not self-evident that the "lot" falls on the lot of them, these sleeping stowaway Jonahs and "goody two shoes" lazy Abels. Why this waste of life? "What use is this?"[13] Anyone of sound mind can see that their useless lives make them more like the *enemies of humanity* than the bearers of its good news. This so-called "gospel" is either fanatically loved or sensibly hated, and that such a dangerous catalyst even exists in our cultured society is reason enough to proceed "in force," with this trial. After the defense presents its pathetically underwhelming case, we will begin to consider the merest sampling of the infinite remainder of inglorious crimes against humanity, perpetuated by the gospel and its co-conspirators, all of which invariably further indict the accursed, I mean, the accused, in the dock before us. For if all their crimes were recorded "I suppose that the world itself could not contain the books that would

---

12. See 2 Thess 2:6–12.

13. Tillich, *The New Being*, 48. (From Tillich's sermon, "Holy Waste" which aims at our utilitarianism.)

be written."[14] For the damning sum of our delicious argument is that they have altogether "thrown everything off balance." [15]

"The Gospel in the Dock"

This exaggerated, satirical mock-trial was presented to introduce the subject of this book, the gospel in the dock. Hereafter the "trial" will be pursued through *non-fictional* means, until a revisit to the court at the end.[16] The subtitle, "Is the Gospel of Jesus Christ Good for the Church, Humanity, and the World" is the underlying question we seek to answer "yes" to, throughout these pages. Our presumption that humanity generally does not see the gospel as good is probably not scandalous. But the implication that the Church herself often relates to the gospel as though it is *not* good is probably scandalous. Nevertheless, the church often places the gospel "in the dock" and thereby puts itself there also. Of course, this is a lose-lose situation for the gospel.

The title "The Gospel in the Dock" is derived from the essay "God in the Dock" by one of the twentieth century's most well-known Christian authors, C. S. Lewis, which will be more explicitly discussed below.[17]

Just above, the reader may have noted the mentions of "faithful" Abel and of proceeding "in force" with the "trial." This is because both *faith and force* underly each of the incidents above, and were personified respectively by Psyche and Orual, Abel and Cain. Therefore faith, and force need to be adequately introduced as the foundation of everything to follow in this book. Faith most simply signifies placing one's trust in God rather than in one's self. Force obviously implies an action, but what the action expresses is the opposite of trust in God. Force therefore signifies one's "will to power" which relies on one's self, rather than God. For the most part faith and the will to power will be the terms most often used, and always signify the opposite ways in relation to self and God.

---

14. John 21:25.

15. The voice of the serial killer "misfit" in O'Connor's "A Good Man is Hard to Find." O'Connor, *Complete Stories*, 131–32.

16. The argument of Pilate H. Cain was inspired by, *The Screwtape Letters*, by C. S. Lewis. Therefore, we attempted a few Lewis inspired arguments. Ad hominem argument was discussed by Lewis in the essay "Bulverism," in Lewis, *God in the Dock*, 271–77. He discussed "chronological snobbery" in Lewis, *Surprised by Joy*, 207–8.

17. Lewis, *God in the Dock*.

There is a proper use of the will as part of the creational gift of human being. Thus, it also requires an act of the will to choose to follow the way of faith. But the usage in this book will generally always signify an improper use of the will. The main difference derives from how the self relates to itself and to God. Faith wills to trust in God and therefore does not rely on self. This also enters into what it means to love God, since the trust is in response to God's love. But the one exercising the will to power relies on self, signifying the rejection of God's love, and the "fall" to self-love. Therefore, the will to power derives from self-love, but faith derives from the love of God. We also at this point can bring in a simple definition of the gospel as the way of faith that God, in love, provided for the good of humanity. But self-love and the rejection of faith and God turn into a hatred of the God of love and the gospel of faith.

Now, returning to the courtroom scene above, we will draw out some of the traits of faith and love, and the will to power and the hateful rejection of God in what was presented.

Irenaeus was one who loved the church and saw it as a paradise in the world. But many hearing his words hate the gospel since the church appeared to *not* be a paradise to them.

"Psyche" loved the God she had never seen, much to the chagrin of her sister the Queen who represents our "deposed royalty" in its autonomous human authority.[18] For "Orual" hates the "god of the great mountain" who has "thrown everything of balance." This "god" has deluded her sister, offended her reason and especially her will to power. For he calls into question Orual's love for *her* Psyche, who as common-folk humanity represents the to-be pitied *subject* of "Royal" Orual's self-serving and controlling "love."

In Cain we see the biblical beginning of the human *lineage* of explicit hatred of the way of faith exhibited by his murder of his brother Abel. Thus, he represents humanity which rejects God's way to the point of violence against those of faith, and more generally at any who stand in the way of self-love and the will to power. Of course, the hatred of the way of faith was implicit in Adam and Eve. Thus, in the courtroom scene, Pilate H. Cain glorifies Cain's way as the proper and utilitarian way of realistic personal and societal progress which is *ironically* thought to be hindered by the *dead weight* of vaporous Abel, the progenitor of the

---

18. Pascal, *Pensees*, #398.

impractical line of humanity living in faith.[19] Cain is important because he represents the link that connects *individual* self-love/will to power to the *collective* self-love/will to power. O'Donovan summarizes this for us:

> "Two loves made two cities," wrote Augustine in a famous and much-quoted passage of the *City of God*. "Self-love to despite of God made the earthly city, love of God to despite of self the heavenly."[20]

Jonah, who we will see much more of throughout this book, will be our chief representative of those with a conflicted love/hate relationship to the gospel, and in a sense straddles both cities, standing with one foot in each. Thus, following the lead of the Book of Jonah, he is our chief personification of the evangelizers of the gospel, on whose account the gospel is often "in the dock."

Thus, we will see that characters throughout this book will represent much more than only themselves, which is of course the biblical "usage" of many characters in the Scriptures so that we learn of the fruits of the ways of faith and the willful sins of humankind through them (1 Cor 10:11).

On that note we can explicitly introduce the broader worldview that makes sense of the characters and conflicts we have already considered and of those to follow. This larger picture is simply the biblical/creational context in which humankind always lives in *some* relation to God, as that living is expressed toward self, others, and the created world itself: whether in faith or force, the self-love to despite of God ironically leading to self-destruction, or the love of God to despite of self but counterintuitively leading to salvation (Mark 8:34–36).

---

19. The biblical Abel was likely not as Pilate H. Cain described him but was certainly not perfect. He may have been more like the schemer/supplanter/wrestler Jacob, which gave rise to the ire of Esau. But Abel nevertheless represents the way of faith. His name means "vapor" and epitomizes the quality of life that points to the necessity of faith in light of the vaporous nature of life, as the book of Ecclesiastes teaches. Perhaps the difference is that Abel's "line" wrestles with God and men in "fear and trembling" while Cain's "line" wrestles in "pride and prejudice." See Meyers, *A Table in the Mist*, 39–45.

20. O'Donovan, *Problem of Self-Love*, 93.

God as the Eternal Mystery and the Perpetual Gospel Way of Faith

Whatever view one has of Genesis, it seems that its main purpose is to present the fact that a relationship with God has always "required" faith, and that a "fall" from that faith is the reason for the manifold ills of humankind. Faith was not a "solution" added by God after the fall but was needed from the beginning of God's creation of beings with free volition.

This necessity seems evident in the fact that *faith in God* was necessary to "pass the test" of obedience regarding the "forbidden fruit" in Eden, and that *suspicion of God* was able to find root because of God's mysterious character. One could argue that God was only mystery to them because they were so "young" and had not yet grown in relation to God, and that if they passed the test, they would not have needed it afterwards. Their "youngness" was certainly true, and God meant for them to grow in wisdom through faith. But that probably did not mean that they would soon or possibly ever be able to know God fully, and in a sense a childlike faith was likely meant to be perpetual as Jesus taught (Matt 18:3). What was important for human life was not the infallible human interpretation of providence, or the unrevealed eventualities of eternity, but rather living by faith under the present mysteries of existence where finite humans were called to grow by embracing the faith relation to God. John Macquarie writes something especially relevant to the account in Genesis wherein death is not yet in view, which is typically held to be the supreme cause of human anxiety:

> Tillich talked about the shock of non-being, the realization that one will cease to exist. I think myself that more primordial than the shock of non-being is the shock of being.[21]

Thus, in the face of the shock of existence, the only alternative to faith was to seek to grow independently from relation to God, by grasping for our own *reasonable* "knowledge of good and evil" that would conceivably make us "like God." Stating that intention so baldly seems to reveal its folly, but its repeated attempt in every life seems to verify it as our chosen way. And so, ironically, the trade of faith for a supposed "pure reason" resulted in the many forms of *death* in relation to God, self, and others that Gen 2:15—3:24 narrates.

---

21. Macquarrie, *Two Worlds Are Ours*, 25.

The entire Bible variously and constantly re-narrates the necessity of the faith relation to God in light of the challenge life invariably presents. Shoemaker notes how this was boldly punctuated very near the beginning of the story of Abraham, the father of faith (Rom 4:16):

> Blessing in the ancient world was understood as good fortune already received: crops, flocks, and babies; health, wealth, and success. Abraham and Sarah begin a new kind of spiritual history—a people of faith who act in trust of a promise spoken but not realized, of a blessing promised but not yet here. It is faith as delayed gratification. Abraham and Sarah rose and went as God called them to do. When they arrived at the new land, it was in the midst of a drought. The land of promise was a land of famine.[22]

What may not be obvious in the "test" of "the fruit of the tree of the knowledge of good and evil" is that it portrays how the gospel's way of faith was presented to them. In the face of God as mystery, "the good news" (the essential meaning of the word gospel) to them was that through faith humans could "be fruitful and multiply" in a proper relation to God and the entire creation (Gen 1:28). Genesis swiftly moves on to declare this perpetual gospel largely by demonstrating the tragic consequences of "the alternative way" which we will now introduce more fully.

The Alternate "Gospel Way" of Humankind: The Will to Power

The alternate way is to have faith in a different gospel that is not the gospel, for it is to have faith in oneself and in force. As we will see, faith in oneself can coexist with the notion of faith in God because the standard human "technique" for the mastery of life is the autonomous will to power which even attempts the mastery of God for one's own purposes. Martin Buber interpreted Israel's quest to know the name of God as a quest for this "magical" power. Merold Westphal discusses Buber's view of that quest and God's answer to it, saying,

> Accordingly, he interprets the famous answer of Exodus 3:14 not as "I am who I am" but as the promise "I shall be there" with

---

22. Shoemaker, *GodStories*, 37. Abraham and Sarah thus embody a new Adam and Eve.

the meaning "you do not need to conjure Me, but you cannot conjure Me either."[23]

Humankind's grasping for mastery over the mystery of life and even over God, is revealed as *the quest* that arises from the very beginning. Genesis seems to satirically present the misguided but perpetual question of humankind: "How will we live, by *faith* in this mysterious unseen God who has already provided life itself, and *every* fruit tree for our flourishing, or by *fixating* on the *one* deprivation, the *one* fruit of the tree of knowledge of good and evil, and asking why are we prohibited from knowing what we want to?"

This satirical re-telling of the unspoken question reveals the choice between the way of faith and the way of sight which necessitates an illicit grasping after knowledge for the sake of power. The alternative way seeks to overcome the "unjust" deprivation by grasping after what it mistakes as God's *whole* nature: sheer unmitigated power and complete self-determination based in God's complete knowledge. We will see later that the mysterious God's whole nature *wisely* includes the *weakness* of self-limitation and that such practical wisdom and humility is the secret power of the gospel precisely because it was the way of Christ (1 Cor 1:25; Phil 2:6). But the alternative way seeks mastery according to the "knowledge" and "power" it mistakenly conceives of as unlimited in its conception of "the whole God" and so seeks "to be like God" with that complete knowledge and power. The *need* to grasp reveals not only the impossibility of the quest, but also the foolishness of ignorantly lifting the lid to admit the Pandora's Box of the manifold forms of sin and death. For Genesis satirically reveals the disaster of anxiety-laden, knowledge-lacking, power-grasping finite beings, struggling within their emotional, intellectual, and volitional capacities, and yet seeking therefrom to resolve the mysteries of God and the problems of existence.[24] An interesting observation of Annie Dillard seems to fittingly illustrate the irony of humankind's "will to power" quest for mastery:

> An infant who has just learned to hold his head up has a frank and forthright way of gazing about him in bewilderment. He

---

23. As cited in Westphal, *Overcoming Onto-Theology*, 26.

24. Allan Hugh Cole Jr. writes that "anxiety relates to one's standing before God in some form or fashion, including how one understands and approaches one's finitude, freedom, and potential for sin. As such, anxiety has to do with the core of personhood, with *who one is*. Cole, *Be Not Anxious*, 90.

hasn't the faintest clue where he is, and he aims to learn. In a couple of years, what he will have learned instead is how to fake it: he'll have the cocksure air of a squatter who has come to feel he owns the place. Some unwonted, taught pride diverts us from our original intent, which is to explore the neighborhood, view the landscape, to discover at least where it is that we have been so startlingly been set down, if we can't learn why.[25]

Dillard wonders why our creational limitations don't simply lead us to a childlike humble exploration of where we are in the awesome mysteries of creation and before the inscrutably mysterious God, rather than the prideful attempted "mastery" of both through achieving (or faking) the "God's eye view" of knowing the "why" of everything. Where does this inclination come from? Is the mysterious serpent that answer or merely a setting of the question back a bit further into the unanswerable why? Perhaps the question simply arises from the contingencies and capabilities of the amphibious spirit/flesh creature we simply are.[26] To be human thus seems to require encountering the serpent's temptation for *answers*, and *a way*, to *overcome* the discomfiting mystery. But to be human is to also encounter the provision, possibility, and soul-prosperity of faith and relation to our Creator in the face of that mystery, and finding ourselves *conficere*, or "put together" in the place that God declared to be "good."[27] Humankind lives in relation to the one way or the other, in the way of Abel or the way of Cain, in faith or in the will to power, in relation to God, self, creation, and one another. Our "life together" exists in the complex and clash of the two ways. This conflict is what leads to the gospel's way of faith being perennially "in the dock." We now need return more specifically to our proper subject of the gospel in the dock and look a bit more closely at the prophet Jonah who personifies the problem that largely contributes to the need for this book and others like it.[28] That problem is the reality of the tragic shortcomings of

25. Dillard, *Pilgrim at Tinker Creek*, 12.

26. Screwtape observes that humans are "amphibians" in Letter 8. Lewis, *The Screwtape Letters*, 45.

27. See Rigney, *The Things of Earth*, 79.

28. Of course, consideration of Jonah raises a host of questions about his story which this book has, and needs to have, little interest in. For the most part I share in Kierkegaard's aversion to the higher-critical modernistic approach to the Scriptures which looks "*at the mirror*" rather than looking "*in the mirror*" to "*see yourself.*" Kierkegaard, *For Self-Examination*, 25. Thus "Kierkegaard does not so much talk *about* the Bible as kaleidoscopically *use* it." Polk, *The Biblical Kierkegaard*, 17. But

Introduction

those who represent the gospel of faith and thereby further contribute to the gospel being "in the dock."

Jonah: The Prophet of God and "the Gospel in the Dock"

The prophet Jonah, who personifies the evangelizers of the gospel for us, is an example of one who "lovingly hated" God. Jonah is well-known for being told by God to go and preach to the great and bloodthirsty city of Nineveh, but instead boarded a ship heading in the opposite direction (Jonah 1:1–3). If Jonah had been "employed" by any human boss, he certainly would have received a memo saying, 'You're fired!" But God's memo was a storm at sea which contained a great fish to swallow him and submarine him to Nineveh, much to Jonah's dismay. For Jonah had a love/hate relationship with God. More accurately, he loved God—or at least thought he did—but *hated the gospel*. Thus, as already mentioned, one major purpose of this book is to demonstrate that the gospel was good for Jonah, and is good for the church, though the church often believes otherwise. Of course, if the church has the gospel in the dock, that produces a ripple effect circling outward into the wider culture, contributing to the culture's own further relegation of the gospel to the dock.

The notion that one can "love God" and presumably not place him in the dock, and yet have the gospel in the dock—raises questions regarding what C. S. Lewis meant in his essay "*God* in the Dock." In his essay Lewis explained that,

> The ancient man approached God (or even the gods) as the accused person approaches the judge. For the modern man the roles are reversed. He is the judge: God is in the dock."[29]

To Lewis there was a substantial division between two eras of humanity which he called the Great Divide, and which signified a great cultural change in the modern West:

> But roughly speaking we may say, that while all history was for our ancestors divided into two periods, the pre-Christian and the Christian, for us it falls into three, the

---

"Kierkegaard's concern was not that one should exegete scripture in a certain way, rather that Scripture should be allowed to exegete life." Rosas, *Scripture*, 46.

29. Lewis, *God in the Dock*, 244.

pre-Christian, the Christian, and what may reasonably be called the post-Christian.[30]

Surprisingly, this Great Divide was not between the pre-Christian and Christian eras, as one might expect him to say, but between the Christian and post-Christian eras. He further explains,

> I'm thinking of them simply as cultural changes. And when I do that, it seems to me that the un-christening is an even more radical change than the christening. Christians and pagans had much more in common with each other than either has with the post-Christian. The gap between those who worshipped different gods is not so wide as that between those who worship and those who don't.[31]

To Lewis the ancient Pagans and the Christians who succeeded them were alike in their general approach to God as those "accused" *before* God. But the modern man this side of the divide differs from both of these groups, approaching God as though "*God* is in the dock."

Intriguingly, Lewis's view of ancient man presented in that essay seems contrary to his view in "Till We Have Faces," which we saw in the fourth "incident" above, with its story of the placement of "the god of the Grey Mountain" *in the dock* by Queen Orual. For she was an ancient person of a Pagan culture before the time of Christ. Her "God in the dock" attitude is made more explicit in this passage at the beginning of the lengthy novel which mostly consists of her letter of "complaint" against this god:

> I am old now and have not much to fear from the anger of the gods. I have no husband nor child, nor hardly a friend, through whom they can hurt me. My body, this lean carrion that still has to be washed and fed and have clothes hung about it daily with so many changes, they may kill as soon as they please. The succession is provided for. My crown passes to my nephew. Being for all these reasons, free from fear, I will write in this book what no one who has happiness would dare to write. I will accuse the gods, especially the god of the Grey Mountain. That is, I will tell all he has done to me from the very beginning, as if I were making my complaint of him before a judge.[32]

---

30. Lewis, *The Great Divide*, para. 3.
31. Lewis, *The Great Divide*, para. 4.
32. Lewis, *Till We Have Faces*, 3. (Hereafter TWHF.)

Introduction

What can we make of this tale by Lewis which seems to contradict his notion of the Great Divide? It seems evident that in TWHF Lewis was simply telling our modern story for modern readers through the lens of an ancient myth. Thus, Queen Orual is the voice of modern man. Her younger sister is the voice of faith. The controversy between them is between reason and faith, or more accurately perhaps, between *sight* and faith as was evident in the "incident" we saw earlier. This means that the appearance of an ancient Queen who places this "god" *in the dock* was not an instance of Lewis contradicting himself, and more importantly he was not contradicting the divide that he saw between ancient and modern man.

But with this understanding of TWHF we can proceed to temporarily further complicate things in order to ultimately clarify the view of Lewis in relation to our "riffing" off of his title for the Gospel in the Dock. Our "complication" is this: Though ancient and Christian man came to God as the accused before whom *they* were in the dock, the all too often hidden truth was that they had nevertheless placed *the way of faith,* and therefore had placed *the gospel* in the dock. This complication does not contradict Lewis, but actually compliments his view. This can be demonstrated by the following two steps:

First, an example from the NT exhibits that two of the closest disciples of Jesus, "ancient men" to be sure, fell to loving God, but hating the gospel.

> And it came to pass, when the time was come that he should be received up, he steadfastly set his face to go to Jerusalem, and sent messengers before his face: and they went, and entered into a village of the Samaritans, to make ready for him. And they did not receive him, because his face was as though he would go to Jerusalem. And when his disciples James and John saw this, they said, Lord, wilt thou that we command fire to come down from heaven, and consume them, even as Elias did? But he turned, and rebuked them, and said, Ye know not what manner of spirit ye are of. For the Son of man is not come to destroy men's lives, but to save them. And they went to another village (Luke 9:51–56, KJV).

James and John certainly did not believe that they had placed *God* in the dock before them. In fact, their request is evidence of the opposite. Nevertheless, *the gospel* of Jesus to save rather than destroy lives *was* in the dock before them. Looking more closely at this incident shows that the "spirit that they were of" was not the spirit of the gospel, of the way of faith. Instead, it was "the spirit of the way of the will to power," the way of sight that wished to *see* enemies destroyed by *force* to establish the kingdom of God. They didn't know or trust *the wisdom* of God's way to bring the kingdom *apart from* force and the will to power, through the *weakness of the cross*. It seems that sin against the way of faith was crouching at their door (Gen 4:7). They were being tempted to the will to power of the way of Cain who killed Abel.

Second, we can simply posit, without the need to produce evidence, that what was true of James and John was true of the lives of Pagans and Christians before the Great Divide. As Lewis said, they did not hold God to be in the dock before them. But history demonstrates in most cases that their lives were contrary to the "gospel" way of faith. By applying this to Pagans who had never heard of Christ we mean that they "naturally" lived their lives by attempting to procure "good" providences through their will to power, whether by war, or through the religious use of "magic" to manipulate "God(s)" and "providence" for their livelihood.[33] Much of the OT narrates how the Israelites were often tempted, and often succumbed to that way of magic.[34] That way of "magic" was the essence of pagan "religion," because it was the "technology" of the day. Today, our technology is more sophisticated and based in science, but the idolatry remains.

Of course, at this point in history, most of us in the culture of the West not only have placed the gospel's way of faith "in the dock," but God also. Today, the gospel and God, being "in the dock," is simply contained in the "package deal" that modern culture invariably delivers "through our mother's milk" to everyone this side of the Great Divide.[35] The philosopher Charles Taylor asks the question that reveals our systemic modern unbelief that "automatically" relegates God to the dock:

> Why was it virtually impossible not to believe in God in, say, 1500 in our Western society, while in 2000 many of us find this not only easy, but even inescapable?[36]

Taylor asks why it is now "inescapable," *to not believe in God*. Of course, his answer to that required a doorstop of a book, of careful historical, philosophical, and cultural reasoning.

---

33. Westphal, *God, Guilt, and Death*, 107.
34. On Israel's relation to magic see: Oswalt, *Golden Calves*, 10–17.
35. Tyson, *Returning to Reality*, 19.
36. As cited in Smith, *How (Not) to be Secular*, 19.

For our part, we will return from our side of the Great Divide to ancient Jonah who certainly wouldn't have considered himself to have placed God in the dock, we propose that he certainly *had* placed the gospel in the dock. This is because Jonah, like James and John after him, would much rather have *seen* God's judgment poured upon the enemies of Israel and all humanity, than to *trust* that God's way of faith in "gospel" compassion and mercy could solve the problem of Nineveh, "the City of Blood." Jonah, the religious insider, would have preferred that God *meet force* and the will to power of the Assyrian Empire with an answering *overpowering force* and will to power.[37] But if God did that, what would that really mean concerning God? Would that truly be the victory over evil God intends? What happens when *God* (Yahweh) succumbs to what Walter Brueggemann called the "animal yearning for destructiveness that will destroy both the victim and the perpetrator?"[38] Was a derailing of Jesus's fulfilling God's mission to "overcome the world" through the "weakness" of the cross what the Devil was after when he tempted Jesus to "worship" him (Matt 4:8–9)? Will God's destructive "final judgment" at the end signal God's eventual capitulation to the way of sheer force?[39] These questions serve to introduce the gravity of the situation in regard to whether the stewards of the gospel, or even Jesus and God, follow the way of force or faith. In other words, whether the church is following a God of force or faith is inestimably important as to whether they are following the true God of the gospel of peace.

Thus, we need to explore one of the major concerns of this book, whether or not the gospel is "good for the church!" For the church all too often does not view the gospel's way of faith as good, in regard to its self-concerns or even what it thinks are God's concerns. The church often prefers the means of power rather than the means of faith, to achieve its "gospel" ends. Of course, that is glaringly contradictory. Therefore, many Jonahs in history and at the present will be considered in this book as

37 "Our author wants to stimulate a new way of thinking. He wants to provide an *internal self-correction* within Judaism . . . The story of Jonah is the story of the religious "insider"—in post exilic Israel, at the time of Jesus, and today in the Synagogue as well as in the Church." Golka, *Divine Repentance*, 125, 132.

38. "Sin is an aggressive force ready to ambush Cain. Sin is larger than Cain and takes on a life of its own (see Rom 7:17). Sin is lethal . . . Sin has a desire for Cain. Sin lusts after Cain with an animal hunger . . . In the world of Cain and Yahweh, there is an animal yearning for destructiveness that will destroy both the victim and the perpetrator." Brueggemann, *Genesis*, 57–58, loc. 384.

39. See our excursus following this introduction on the relation of God to force.

to whether they are "in the faith" of the gospel (2 Cor 13:5). That is the question God always asks his gospel stewards.

Humankind: Its Hopes and Prospects with Its Only True Gospel "in the Dock"

It is hoped that what will be presented may help each reader more clearly discern the difference between the two ways of force and faith in relation to Christ who became the incarnate "tree of life" for all humanity. For all may be encouraged as Cain was meant to be encouraged when God said to him *"timshel."*[40] For God's *gospel* word, "thou mayest rule over it"—the overbearing force that lay crouching at Cain's door, is "invitation, challenge, promise."[41]

And that threefold gospel-word pertains to the quality of life of all communities within their particular worlds. Otherwise, there is only the alternative of the anti-gospel for human communities. For Cain first killed Abel, and then went on to build the first city, dedicating it to force.[42] Cainite builders went on to build the tower of Babel, the greatest monument to the "city of man" that humankind, relocating to the "east of Eden," builds. Shoemaker, graphically interprets Brueghel's painting of Babel's tower, and ends posing several questions that echo Orual's questions to Psyche, but instead places the city of man "in the dock:"

> In Pieter Brueghel's sixteenth-century painting of the tower of Babel the project of building the tower has completely dominated every aspect of the city's life, its size completely dwarfs the

---

40. The final spoken words of "East of Eden," John Steinbeck's masterful reimagining of the oft-repeated story of Cain and Abel. Steinbeck, *East of Eden*, 601.

41. Brueggemann, *Genesis*, 59, Loc. 1360. Brueggemann presents an interesting discussion of Steinbeck's *East of Eden*, and *timshel*. See also Steinbeck, *Journal*, 107–9, 122, 129, for Steinbeck's questions and inquiries regarding the word. Note that the invitation to "rule over it" is not through the will to power, but through Christ who enables us to "participate" in his victory over sin through faith.

42. "Cain take destiny on his shoulders, refusing the hand of God in his life. And if someone thinks I am drawing unwarranted conclusions, let him remember that the city is called Enoch . . . "*Enoch*" means "initiation" or "dedication" (*chanakh*: to dedicate, inaugurate, initiate). Cain dedicates a new world." Ellul, *Meaning*, 5–6. Of course, Cain's city was "away from the presence of the LORD . . . east of Eden." See Gen 4:16. Lopez notes that "Romulus kills Remus and builds 'Creation'"—showing that Cain's way disclosed in Genesis became the way of Rome and is undoubtedly the way humanity generally proceeds to build "civilization." Lopez, *Apostle of the Conquered*, 63.

city and casts a shadow over the whole town. The tower looks like a concentration camp. Pride and anxiety have issued into a totalitarian project. If you look carefully at the picture, you see almost everyone conscripted into work: only three are not working. Where is God's *shabbat*? Where is God?[43]

God always intended and still intends for humankind to become truly *humane* in a community of faith. If there is no way other than the will to power, then the word humane has no *significant* meaning and is but an empty hope, a cloud without water. But Irenaeus was following the gospel trajectory by claiming that the Church, of the way of faith, had been planted as a paradisus in this world. It was planted by the master-gardener of Eden as the visible beginning of a *new creation*, a truly humane community in the world. It was not created by the descendants of Cain or the human will to power, although that alternate "gospel" has been continually followed from the time of Eden until the present day. For any such "paradise" of the will to power will be found to have been built through its commerce in "slaves, that is human souls . . . the blood of prophets and saints, and of all those who have been slain on the earth" (Rev 19:13, 24). Those excluded from such "utopias" will include the crazy Jonahs of God, upon whom *the lot* of guilt falls, the sign of *the scapegoat*, leading to their being cast overboard to "save" the ship of humankind (Jonah 1:7–16). For the builders of the city of man see nothing but the threatening storm before them, no "paradise" planted on the shore of the earth. There is no "palace" *not* in *some* Jonah's "fancy," no mysterious God who comes in "the holy darkness," and before whom the sea ceases "from its raging."

Nevertheless, as we proceed, we endeavor to show that the gospel's way of faith, the way of the Abels of whom the world of force was not worthy, is the true and only hope of the world. But how so? For faithful Abel—true to his name, *vapor*, was killed. Jonah was cast overboard as hopeless, to certain death. Jesus was crucified as an insignificant nobody before the vast empire of self-evident force. Therefore, we will need to consider the sign of the prophet Jonah—cast alive into the storm to certain death—three days "buried" in the belly of the beast but vomited forth on dry land, miraculously alive to then proclaim the gospel to the enemies of God and humanity. For Jonah is the only sign given to humanity, and given to the church, of the better way of faith against force, the sign in which God still

---

43. Shoemaker, *GodStories*, 34.

declares to all, "*timshel—thou mayest rule over it.*" Indeed, through Christ it may be so. Humanity and the world have nothing to lose, except perhaps the "warre, as is of every man, against every man."[44]

"The 'Gospel' You Have Heard and Seen Is Not the Gospel of Christ"

The good news of God for humanity being "in the dock" before it, does not bode well for humanity's response to, and enjoyment of, its reconciliation in Christ. This is the reason that the gospel needs "rehabilitation." But what shape will that rehabilitation take? Most generally, the rehabilitation this book offers are various ways to demonstrate that "the gospel" that has been heard and seen by humanity is not the gospel of Christ. I believe that this "method" mirrors that of the NT itself.

If we were to travel back to the time of the earliest church communities that Paul wrote to, and imaging what "gospel" those outside them might have heard and seen, we can understand this method. For an observer of the "saints" in Corinth or Philippi may well have said that the gospel heard from them and seen in their lives did not appear to be good news. And Paul may well have replied that "the gospel you have heard and seen is not the gospel." For many of Paul's letters exhibit that one of his main purposes for writing was to tell the early church communities that what they proclaimed by their words and with their lives was not the gospel. For instance, Paul wrote to the Corinthians,

> When you come together, it is not the Lord's supper that you eat. 21For in eating, each one goes ahead with his own meal. One goes hungry, another gets drunk. 22What! Do you not have houses to eat and drink in? Or do you despise the church of God and humiliate those who have nothing? What shall I say to you? Shall I commend you in this? No, I will not (1 Cor 11:20–22).

If one wanted to hear and see the gospel proclaimed by the Corinthians, it would not be seen in the practice of their communal gatherings. But Paul's purpose was not merely to point out their failure, but to positively

---

44. Hobbes, *Leviathan*, 77. Only a more *positive* force, faith, and that being *of* Christ and God, can disarm the animality of the way of nature because it is the force of God, who is love (1 John 4:8). "I am crucified with Christ: nevertheless, I live; yet not I, but Christ liveth in me: and the life which I now live in the flesh *I live by the faith of the Son of God*, who loved me, and gave himself for me (Gal 2:20, KJV emphasis mine). On "faith of the Son of God" see Torrance, *Incarnation*, 28, 114–16.

Introduction

encourage them in the way of the gospel. Thus, to the Philippians he wrote of how their words and lives should be shaped by the gospel of Christ:

> So if there is any encouragement in Christ, any comfort from love, any participation in the Spirit, any affection and sympathy, complete my joy by being of the same mind, having the same love, being in full accord and of one mind. Do nothing from selfish ambition or conceit, but in humility count others more significant than yourselves. Let each of you look not only to his own interests, but also to the interests of others. Have this mind among yourselves, which is yours in Christ Jesus, who, though he was in the form of God, did not count equality with God a thing to be grasped, but emptied himself, by taking the form of a servant, being born in the likeness of men. And being found in human form, he humbled himself by becoming obedient to the point of death, even death on a cross. (Phil 2:1–8).

Thus, the rehabilitory method of this book will mirror this method of Paul, showing what the gospel, its evangelism, and its evangelizers are by showing how those are not mirrored in the words and lives of the stewards of the gospel.[45]

The main place where this method will *not* be followed is in Chapters 1 and 2, where we follow a different NT method that was necessary from the beginning because of the very nature of the gospel itself. For much of the NT in regard to the gospel proper, consists in a rehabilitation of the gospel that was needed because the gospel itself was *not* self-evident. This will be explicitly discussed as we proceed. If I were to name this rehabilitory method, it would be "the method of understanding the sign of the prophet Jonah" which we will seek to thoroughly explain beginning in Chapter 1 and especially in Chapter 2. This means that my "rehabilitation" of the gospel follows that of the NT.

On Seeing the "Familiar" Gospel Anew, or for the First Time

The overall aim of this book is to allow the reader to gain a new view of the gospel, or perhaps even a first real view. Most in our culture probably

---

45. A more detailed treatment of the entire "rehabilitory" method of the NT is seen in Hays who writes: The church must be a *community* living in conformity to the paradigm of the *cross* and thereby standing as a sign of the *new creation* promised by God. Hays, *Moral Vision*, 469, Loc. 12988.

have some familiarity with the gospel. But familiarity is usually the bane of existence, shrinking our original wonder-filled views of life, just as a "first love," in time becomes familiar, taken for granted, and tragically discounted. G. K. Chesterton, the "defiantly joyful" Englishman born in 1874, claimed that he "discovered England," and practiced a method of overcoming the falsehood of over-familiarity by replacing it with the newness of discovery:

> There are two ways of getting home; and one of them is to stay there. The other is to walk around the whole world till we come back to the same place.[46]

The view of approach on the return, seeing "as for the first time" from the completely other side, what had become overly familiar, rekindles the original, good familiarity of home, no longer taken for granted. Rowan Williams similarly discusses the purpose of "Narnia" in the quite adult "children's books" of C. S. Lewis:

> The point of Narnia is to help us rinse out what is stale in our thinking about Christianity—which is almost everything.[47]

Thus, Lewis brought his enraptured readers into an *alternate* world of mythical significance and epic encounter, filled with life's first joys and elemental horrors, hard-won redemptions and terrible damnations, to enable the view of approach on the return journey to *our* real world of all the same profundity, but which had become reduced to a monotonous level plane, void of meaning, where it is "always winter, but it never gets to Christmas."[48]

I cannot re-present the gospel with the sheer intellectual wit, or the genuine spiritual winsomeness of a Chesterton or Lewis. But I nevertheless hope that the many and various "rehabilitations" presented in this book will help rinse out the staleness of the "familiar" gospel and provide a new view on the return approach to "the gospel in the dock." And perhaps, for those gaining their first meaningful encounter, theirs will be a sight that views the gospel for what it is, *good news* for the church, humanity, and the world.

---

46. See Chesterton, *The Everlasting Man*, 9; Chesterton, *Orthodoxy*, 171; Belmonte, *Defiant Joy*.

47. Williams, *The Lion's World*, 28.

48. C. S. Lewis, *The Lion*, 40.

Excursus

God and the Way of Force

GIVEN THE SCOPE OF this book, we can only offer the following brief sketches on questions relating to God's use of "the way of force" in the various main categories of his actions in providence, creation, and even in redemption.

God Providence and Human Violence

The story of the "mark" that God put on Cain, in answer to his pathetic plea for protection as he nevertheless "went away from the presence of the Lord," reveals the way that God providentially enacts a form of justice without himself participating in violence. The mark "promised" "sevenfold" *vengeance* on any who would kill Cain to avenge his killing of Abel (Gen 4:15). The text does not specify that God himself will carry out this vengeance but seems to rather say that it "shall" be inevitable. This mark on Cain seems to signify God's introduction of a crude form of natural *justice* set in the providential inevitability that vengeance always begets vengeance in an exponentially increasing way. Strictly speaking, this was God's *gracious* warning against an escalation of vengeance that would follow this course of action, just as was the warning given to Adam and Even against partaking of the fruit that would invariably lead to their death and the escalation of death to all humankind.

It must be noted that the text in Genesis almost immediately further develops God's "institution" of the mark of warning against humans taking revenge on the first murder. For as the primeval couple "mocked" God's warning to them, so Cain's descendant Lamech mocks God's warning in his prideful boast of killing a man. For his boast "predicted" that the "sevenfold" vengeance on anyone killing Cain would be exponentially increased "seventy-sevenfold" on anyone that might dare killing him (Gen 4:24). Lamech falls into the pattern of humans who think they can ignore or manipulate God's decrees to their advantage, and for that reason fall into a snare they set for themselves, as Psalm 7:12–16 shows. For that snare *exists* because God has instituted this crude form of natural providential justice, which is self-perpetuated by those pursuing evil.

> If a man does not repent, God will whet his sword; he has bent and readied his bow; he has prepared for him his deadly weapons, making his arrows fiery shafts. Behold, the wicked man conceives evil and is pregnant with mischief and gives birth to lies. He makes a pit, digging it out, and falls into the hole that he has made. His mischief returns upon his own head, and on his own skull his violence descends.

One could summarize by saying that in this form of justice, God simply provides the rope by which evil individuals, tribes, nations, and empires, eventually hang themselves.

The mocking prophecy of Lamech was the means by which God revealed humankind's further resolve to follow the way of force and the will to power. Through Lamech's boast, God also revealed the ignorant and foolish self-justification of evil as though God's mark was a license to kill.[1] Lamech's boast was amplified by his *implied threat* of a seventy-sevenfold vengeance of his death, by the power of his kin, as though that would secure his protection against falling into the trap. But there is no avoiding this self-set trap. The next, even more boastful Lamech, will slay Lamech, ad infinitum. For Lamech reveals the law of the land, east of Eden, pictured for many as "The Wild West," with its cities named Tombstone, and desolate wildernesses called the Badlands. Of course, the Wild West symbolizes the whole land "east of Eden" where Lamech's prophecy has come true in the ever-escalating cycles of war and vengeance.

Jesus seemed to affirm the same "law" when he said to Peter, brandishing a sword, "Put up again thy sword into his place: for all they that take the sword shall perish with the sword" (Mt 25:52, KJV). Jesus's warning was in fact a prophecy, of the "investment return" Israel would gain from her impending war against Rome, that would bring Rome's wrath on that generation of Israel (Mt 22:1–7; 23:37—24:2). Jesus's prescription

---

1. "Violence is glorified, and the mark of Cain no longer stands as a stigma of exile but as a badge of honor that brings protection equivalent to invulnerability." Walton, *Genesis*, 278.

of "seventy times seven" forgiveness is likely meant as antidote for Lamech's deadly justification of revenge (Mt 18:21–22).

These biblical factors altogether demonstrate that God's "mark" of providential justice signifies that following the way of vengeance is inherently self-destructive, and that God is not the immediate executor of such destruction and is therefore not himself engaging in the way of violent force. Rather, God permits the "way of nature" to have "independent" existence in the lives of humans, when they, given the gift of choice, "travel" away from God's good land and "settle" in the way of Cain and Lamech, East of Eden.

God's Final Judgment

Curiously, we find a similar scene in the final chapter of Revelation where "murderers" and other sinners have settled "outside" the new city of God that contains the tree of life (Rev 22:14–15). Both scenes portray "settled" human existence away from the presence of the Lord and within the way of force in the will to power. But note that one scene is of "life" *before* God's final judgment, and one of "life" *afterwards*. This presents intriguing questions regarding the nature of human existence following God's "final judgment," and even of the nature of that judgment in relation to God's use of violence. (See Gen 4:13–16; Rev 22:1–5, 14.) We note that G. K. Beale is content to write,

> "This "outside" location is "the lake of fire," since essentially the godless people listed in 21:8 are consigned to "the lake of fire." The punishment of being cast outside the garden, which began in Gen. 3:23–24, continues for the reprobate into eternity, on an escalated scale."[2]

The point is that God's final judgement does not seem in any way to consist of God's direct, active punishment of those that appear to be finally unrepentant. It rather seems that God's "punishment" is like that of Cain's, the allowance of a voluntary departure from the presence of God, accompanied with the preservation of life, through the resurrection of the just and the unjust (Matt 25:41, 46; John 5:28–29; Acts 24:14–15). As with Eden, those outside cannot partake of the tree of life inside. As those outside Eden were unable to save their fallen life against the Cherubim's "flaming sword" guarding the way back to Eden's tree of life, so those

2. Beale, *Revelation*, 1142.

outside the new Eden/City are unwilling to "wash their robes so they may have the right to the tree of life and that they may enter the city" (Gen 3:24; Rev 22:14).

This all seems similar to the view of C. S. Lewis that "Hell" consists in a composite "punishment" of" torment, destruction, and privation," based in Christ's words in the Gospels. This also does not seem to require God's "forceful" activity but may well consist in the punishment of the resurrected unjust becoming "banished from humanity . . . *remains* . . . an ex-man or 'damned ghost.'" Lewis notes that it is "impossible to imagine what the consciousness of such a creature . . . would be like" just as it is impossible to imagine the existence of those the Revelation depicts as outside the city.[3] Lewis held that all that God could do for these in final judgment has been done, and that God's "miracle" of creating creatures such as humans are, capable of becoming "successful rebels to the end," where "the doors of hell are locked on the *inside*," results from "the horrible freedom they have demanded, and are therefore self-enslaved just as the blessed, forever submitting to obedience, become through all eternity more and more free."[4]

So, to summarize regarding our question regarding God's actions of final judgment, all that can be said is that God: created them with free volition; became incarnate for them in Christ; provided atonement for them in Christ; sought to reach them in their lives by the Spirit and the gospel; and resurrected their bodily existence after their death. It may be noted that in all those things God provided, his actions required self-violence *against* himself, *for* the good of those who choose to depart from God's presence. Whether such a departure is possible in every sense is another question, and it may be that it is not possible. In that case, the wholly benevolent presence of God would itself seem to be a "punishment," just as being in the presence of a "holy" or "saintly" person will "naturally" be unpleasant to an unholy person, and a reactive hatred, "crouching at their door," potentially escalates (Gen 4:7). In eternity that continual escalation would seem to characterize a damned soul.[5]

---

3. Lewis, *Problem of Pain*, 112. See Bauckham and Hart, *Hope Against Hope*, 145–47, on the challenge of reading the varied biblical imagery in a responsible way that does not "sap the seriousness" from God's final judgment, but is also not "inconsistent with what we know of God and God's purposes in Christ."

4. Lewis, *Problem of Pain*, 113–14.

5. C. S. Lewis chillingly explored this reality in Lewis, *The Great Divorce*.

Excursus

God's Providence and Nature

In relation to God's providential control over the "forces of nature," we run into the age-old question of humankind, whether in the face of nature's "evils" there can be a "good" God. Being the question of the ages, we can only briefly answer. Therefore, we will merely present several thoughts based in the thorough study of G. C. Berkouwer on this question of "theodicy." He points out two possible ways to follow in the face of this inscrutable problem. The first is in what some think an "oversimplification," of "the Church's confession of God's Providence over all things." The second is "other more rational ways . . . to square God with this actual world."[6] Berkouwer's view is that *all* the rational attempts fall short and invariably leave,

> . . . a feeling of uncertainty, a suspicion withal that the bruising reality of life cannot thus be justified . . . Does not an honest conscience, if not reason, forbid the preaching of an all-embracing harmony, which takes black and evil within itself and displays it as white?"[7]

Therefore, Berkouwer finds the only possible refuge in the church's confession. He holds that such a confession is based on the following. First, a rational theodicy assumes that nature speaks meaningfully, but the truth is that only God can reveal what it "says."

> They have abstracted thought from God's revelation. It has been assumed that the world and its events, apart from revelation, speak their own language and their speech can be understood and translated by our natural reason. God and His righteousness take place, not at the *beginning*, but at the *end* of this process of thought . . . The Light that illuminates the world is found only in faith. Reality, isolated from this light, remains, in the end, enshrouded in darkness. This is why all theodicy is principally unacceptable . . . The illusion has arisen that the world can be understood in its deepest meaning and that reality is correctly defined by such concepts as fate, grief, "existence unto death," dread, guilt, doom, and death. But the reality thus pessimistically construed is not the reality of God . . . This is not to deny the possibility of a believing apologetic. But an apologetic will have to begin with faith, not with uncertainty and doubt, if it is

---

6. Berkouwer, *Providence of God*, 245.
7. Berkouwer, *Providence of God*, 245–46.

to be fruitful and a blessing to anyone ... Must we then, it may be asked, in the absence of a theodicy flee into the irrationality of a hidden God?[8]

Berkouwer shows why rational theology falls short in dealing with reality in relation to God, and why the church's confession is the only alternative. But by turning the corner from theodicy to confession he asks whether this is a flight to the irrationality of a "hidden God." In answer to this we need to remember seeing in our introduction that God's *mystery* is the reason for God's *revelation*, and that faith in God's sovereignty is not directed to God as an abstract being of bare power but as the living God. Thus, "theodicy" is more accurately the flight to imagining God abstractly, as what Berkouwer calls "a super power." And the confession of faith is more accurately the rational, reasonable response to God's mysterious, living and active goodness. Thus also, God's "incomprehensibility is apprehended only through revelation", and God's "incomprehensibility" is "wholly other than irrationality."[9] God's "unsearchableness" is not "in the same category as the enigmas of fate or fortune ... happily, all concepts of fate are poles removed from faith in the God and Father of our Lord Jesus Christ ... He who has understood the statement: 'He who hath seen Me, hath seen the Father,' possesses the sufficient knowledge that this sight gives."[10]

In sum, God has revealed his relation to the "the force of nature" by historically demonstrating what we will see in the first two chapters, that in Christ's incarnation, death, and resurrection, and apart from mere "super power," God overcame the "evils" of nature through his active, living, goodness.[11]

God's Original Creation

The even more basic question of the relation of God to force arising from the question of God as the Creator is equally beyond the scope of this book. But we will offer the following few thoughts.

---

8. Berkouwer, *Providence of God*, 247–48, 249, 252–53.
9. Berkouwer, *Providence of God*, 255.
10. Berkouwer, *Providence of God*, 255–56.
11. Several other treatments of "theodicy" include Lewis, *Problem of Pain*; and Dembski, *End of Christianity*.

Some read into the biblical accounts of creation the violence that is inherent in the creation myths of other ancient cosmologies. This can lead to the view that the very God of violence is whose image humankind is made in, which would thereby legitimate human violence.

In other ancient cosmologies, the pre-existent matters that are re-formed to achieve the present creation, are invariably deified as "gods," so that creation essentially entails violent conflicts between these deified aspects of creation. But the Genesis account removes any hint of violence from God's work of creation. Several summarize this saying,

> The biblical accounts resoundingly dismiss the concept of deified elements of creation by treating all of creation as devoid of personality and totally subservient to the spoken will of God.[12]

Tremper Longman and Daniel Reid concur, and write that "Genesis 1 and 2, if anything, distance themselves from any suggestion of creation by conquest."[13]

J. Richard Middleton sees in the creation account many aspects of God's relation to power that stand in dramatic contrast to other ancient cosmologies. Sacrifices to God are not required to provide for God's sustenance; God does not require sacrifices to be made willing to provide for humankind's needs; God shares power with humankind at large, both male and female; God's overall purpose of creation is to provide "shalom."[14] Middleton summarizes that "Gen 1 signals the Creator's original intent for shalom and blessing at the outset of human history, prior to the rise of human (or divine) violence."[15]

In sum, God's works in the original creation portray a non-violent process, in contrast to other "gods," and also portray God as relinquishing power in relation to humankind.

God's New Creation in Christ

The trajectory of the Bible's progressive revelation necessitates giving due weight to the revelation of God *in Christ*, as disclosed in the NT. Of course, this is the main subject matter in this entire book on the gospel

---

12. Miller and Soden, *In the Beginning*, 144.
13. Longman and Reid, *God*, 77.
14. Middleton, *A New Heaven*, 51–52.
15. Middleton, "Created," 355. See Middleton, *A New Heaven*, 50–53.

of Christ which therefore will present many arguments that support the gospel as God's way of peace. So, at this point we will only present an approach to Paul, the major NT exegete of the Christ event, which for our present purpose most accurately emphasizes the nature of the gospel as inherently against conquest by force.

In "The Apostle to the Conquered," Davina Lopez presents the well supported view that Paul envisioned his apostolic mission to the Gentiles as extending God's gospel of liberation from the world's way of achieving "civilization" through conquest and slavery.[16] Lopez understands Paul's allegory of Sarah and Hagar as being about the opposition "between the covenant of Caesar (leading to slavery) and the covenant of God (leading to freedom)."[17] Lopez shows that Paul's conversion meant that "Paul's perception changes in a dramatic way when he realizes that his 'earlier life in Judaism' (Gal 1:13), which in all essentials was in accordance with Roman imperial ideology, is not in accordance with the true mission of Israel. In order to become an apostle to the nations, *Paul must adopt the subordinate position among the other defeated nations,* which means taking on another identity . . . establishing a sense of solidarity between the Jews and the nations."[18] This means that Paul's gospel was against the conquering ways of Rome which his earlier Judaism had participated in violently against those Jews who had followed Christ. This also clarifies that Paul was an enemy "not of the local synagogue, but of the worldwide drive toward civilization/slavery."[19] Lopez thus summarizes Paul's apostleship:

> His integration program, or alternative destiny, for the nations is relief under the umbrella of the father of the promised land, not of the father of the fatherland. And the terms of integration, according to Paul's Galatian formulation, are not conquest and slavery but interconnectivity and freedom.[20]

Lopez shows that Christ's gospel of the kingdom, *in mission,* liberates humanity in ways diametrically opposite to the nations' ways of force. Of course, the gospel is that God was *on mission* in the atonement of Christ. Badcock, citing Balthasar narrates this saying,

---

16. Lopez, *Apostle to the Conquered.*
17. Zetterholm, *Approaches to Paul,* 222. (See Gal 4:21–31.)
18. Zetterholm, *Approaches to Paul,* 221–22.
19. Lopez, *Apostle to the Conquered,* 167.
20. Lopez, *Apostle to the Conquered,* 167.

According to Balthasar, this is . . . the expression of a divine love, which must "annihilate, cauterize, and excise (Heb 4:12) all that is not love." In the cross, we see "God himself being seared, even out of the very hellfire of sinful non-love itself, by the fire of divine love."[21]

Therefore the "force" that makes the new creation is the self-sacrificial mission of the God who is love, in contradistinction to the conquering way of violent force. (1 John 4:8).

Summary

This brief consideration of God's relation to the world regarding the use of force, evidences that the Scriptures on the whole do not present God under the "traditional scheme of power and omnipotence," but rather as exhibiting "a kind of power of powerlessness . . . something unconditional but outside the parameters of power and force."[22] For as Paul wrote, "the weakness of God is stronger than men" (1Cor 1:25). The Lord, who "by wisdom founded the earth" and says, "do not envy a man of violence, and do not choose any of his ways," does not seem capable of being a God who violates the ways of peace.[23]

---

21. Badcock, *The Way of Life*, 115–16.
22. The quoted words are from Caputo, "Beyond Sovereignty," 21.
23. See Prov 3:19, 31.

1

Evangel
The Primal Gospel

> For I knew that you are a gracious God and merciful, slow to anger and relenting from disaster.
>
> —JONAH 4:2

The Challenge of Understanding the Gospel of Jesus Christ

IN THIS BOOK WE consider the gospel of Jesus Christ as the *primal* gospel since the gospel—the *evangel*—originates in God alone.[1] We see in the text above that the prophet Jonah knew the very character of God to be "gospel" even toward Nineveh—the capital of the Assyrian Empire and then current great and terrible enemy of Israel. Jonah found this goodness of God to be unreasonable, and therefore to Jonah, God's goodness was in the dock as though it was *non-goodness*.

God's goodness is always linked to his ability to create, and his intent was creating Nineveh anew. The two most significant "gospels" are the original creation of "the heavens and the earth," and the new creation in Christ. The words that begin the book of Genesis—"*In the beginning*"—are the same words that begin the Gospel of John where they

---

1. "Gospel," is an English translation, and "evangel," an English transliteration, of the Greek word *euanggelion*—which means "good tidings."

present "Jesus as God's Genesis Word continuing to speak creation into existence."[2] In what was probably the first Gospel narrative to be written, the Gospel of Mark, we see another allusion to creation: "The *beginning* of the gospel of Jesus Christ, the Son of God."[3] The original creation of Genesis and the new creation in Christ both exhibit the inherent goodness of God's two primal creative acts.

But there are a number of "gospel" events besides these two. Walter Brueggemann very broadly writes of four gospel events of God's creative overcoming of evils:

- good vs. evil
- life vs. death
- Yahweh vs. Pharaoh
- Jesus vs. Satan, sin and death."[4]

He then lists even more specific gospel events:

- *Cosmic Encounter*—Yahweh vs. the Gods (Ps. 96:4–6)
- *The Exodus*—Yahweh vs. Pharaoh (Exod. 1–15)
- *The Homecoming*—Yahweh vs. Babylon (Isa. 46–47)
- *Christmas*—Yahweh vs. the empire (Luke 2, Matt. 2:13–18)
- *Jesus' Ministry*—Yahweh vs. Blindness (Mark 10:46–52)
- *Easter*—Yahweh vs. death (1 Cor. 15:54–55)
- *Paul*—Yahweh vs. Satan, sin, and death (Rom. 5–8)."[5]

This demonstrates that "gospel" as "good news" is always based on God's saving *events* throughout history and can be understood as a category of events. But all the differing events find their ultimate coherence in the character of God, as we saw above. For God orchestrated all these gospel events to be derived from, centered upon, and fulfilled in Jesus Christ. That the events occurred in different times does not prevent the fact that events "before" Christ are grounded in Christ the center (Acts

---

2. Peterson, *Christ Plays*, 87. Peterson dedicates nearly a half-dozen pages explaining how the Gospel of John is a *"rewriting"* of Genesis 1–2; cf. John 1:1–5.

3. See Garland, *Theology*, 101; Myers, *Binding the Strong Man*, 122.

4. Brueggemann, *Biblical Perspectives*, 19.

5. Brueggemann, *Biblical Perspectives*, 39; emphasis and punctuation added.

15:18). Therefore, the task for this book about the gospel is first of all to seek to understand specifically what this gospel of Jesus Christ is.

What Is the Gospel of Jesus Christ and How Is It Interpreted?

The question "what is the gospel of Jesus Christ" is of course the subject of entire books. This is because there is no short and simple answer. The gospel can be briefly summarized, as Paul does in 1 Cor 15:1–4, but that doesn't mean that the gospel is simple or simply understood.[6] Paul's brief summary can be compared to his longer expositions of the gospel, such as his lengthy "Letter to the Romans." There are also the four relatively lengthy documents in the NT known as Matthew, Mark, Luke, and John, each of which call themselves "Gospels"—showing that communicating the gospel even scripturally can require an entire short book.

To adequately understand what the gospel is, one must also consider how it relates to virtually everything else of importance, because it makes certain universal truth claims.[7] In light of these initial observations, the answers in this book are admittedly partial and presented only for the sake of the topics of this particularly focused book. So for our purposes we will start rather broadly and then narrow the focus with an eye to developing our main concerns regarding the gospel.

The Gospel of the Scriptural Narrative

We begin with what we call the "gospel of the scriptural narrative." Narrative is probably the overarching literary genre of the whole Bible because an overall story runs throughout all its pages. Christopher J. H. Wright has presented a massive "Unlocking of the Bible's Grand Narrative" in his book "*The Mission of God.*"[8] Wright sees the basic story progression of the Bible as fivefold with, five "agents" all with a mission: *God, Humanity, Israel, Jesus,* and *the Church.*[9] These five elements were all included in

---

6. As Timothy Keller writes "The Gospel Is Not A Simple Thing." Keller, *Center Church*, 39–45.

7. As Timothy Keller writes "The Gospel Affects Everything." Keller, *Center Church*, 46–52.

8. Wright, *Mission of God*.

9. Wright, *Mission of God*, 61–68

the gospel events listed by Brueggemann and they follow the same basic chronological narrative.

The unitive trajectory of the agents Wright has identified root all human missional tasks in God's gospel mission. The *"Bible's Grand Narrative"* thus reveals the *origination* of all God's missional agents in God's creative and redemptive purposes. Thus, Wright scripturally demonstrates that "human" activities such as *evangelism* are integrally related to God's own mission, since God is the primary agent "on mission" for the sake of the world. This means that the Church was "made . . . for God's mission."[10]

It may be helpful to clarify the significance of Jesus as *one* of the agents with a mission" in Wright's outline. Otherwise, it could seem that Jesus was simply another step on the same level of other human agents in God's mission in the world. Brueggemann's categories could also give that impression. But as we noted above the significance of Jesus is that in God's overarching mission, he is *the very center*. What is important to note at this point is that in contrast to the other human agents only Jesus completely fulfilled that mission: by having no agenda of his own, by only doing what he saw his Father doing, and by not failing to be faithful even to the death on the cross (John 5:19). This was the way that "in Christ God was reconciling the world to himself" (2 Cor 5:19). We also point out that Jesus always followed the way of faith rather than the way of the will to power.

The Gospel of the Scriptural Focus

On that note we now follow the Scripture's own centering method of coming to understand what the gospel is by considering "the gospel of the scriptural focus." As we have just been considering, the overarching narrative narrows down to focus upon Jesus. C. S. Lewis wondrously captures the scriptural narrowing of the entire OT narrative to the point where the incarnation of Christ begins.

> Then another thing. We, with our modern democratic and arithmetical presuppositions would so have liked and expected all men to start equal in their search for God. One has the picture of great centripetal roads coming from all directions, with well-disposed people, all meaning the same thing, and getting

---

10. Wright, *Mission of God*, 62. Wright clarifies that "God has a church for his mission"

closer and closer together. How shockingly opposite to that is the Christian story! One people picked out of the whole earth; that people purged and proved again and again. Some are lost in the desert before they reach Palestine; some stay in Babylon; some becoming indifferent. The whole thing narrows and narrows, until at last it comes down to a little point, small as the point of a spear—a Jewish girl at her prayers. That is what the whole of human nature has narrowed down to before the Incarnation takes place.[11]

Paul also "observed" this quantitative narrowing process of Israel to Christ and wrote of how it *began* even further back in a qualitative narrowing or "humbling" of *God's own self* entering into human life, even to the lowest point of dying on a cross:

> (Christ Jesus,) who, though he was in the form of God, did not count equality with God a thing to be grasped, but emptied himself, by taking the form of a servant, being born in the likeness of men. And being found in human form, he humbled himself by becoming obedient to the point of death, even death on a cross. Therefore, God has highly exalted him and bestowed on him the name that is above every name, so that at the name of Jesus every knee should bow, in heaven and on earth and under the earth, and every tongue confess that Jesus Christ is Lord, to the glory of God the Father (Philippians 2:6–11).

Paul begins with the pre-incarnate Christ, *the Word which became flesh* according to John 1:1–14. The pre-incarnate Christ "took the form of a servant" by becoming "human." As a human he was "obedient" even to the lowest form of execution known at that time in the ancient Middle East. That form of death was meant to completely de-humanize the one executed.[12] That the death of Christ, and *that death* in particular, is part and parcel of the "good news," is what creates the need for *lots of explaining*, to put it colloquially. That it originally needed much explanation leads us to have to pause before proceeding further with an inestimably important question which is easily overlooked in our now post-Christian culture. For from the viewpoint now, the Messiah and his death on a cross are seen as compatible things, rather than as wholly incompatible.

---

11. Lewis, *God in the Dock*, 84. In those words Lewis is touching on aspects of what is known as the "scandal of particularity" which we will discuss to some depth in chapter 4.

12. See Rutledge, *The Crucifixion*, 72–104.

At the time of Christ, the possibility that God's anointed Messiah would be crucified was not assumed by *anyone*.

Before considering that question more fully, we simply note that in the narrowing, harrowing processes, by which salvation was provided, God did not in the least follow the way of force in the will to power. God followed the exact opposite way of a self-emptying negation of power to the point of death. It is easy to overlook the fact that the gospel is only the gospel *because* God and Christ fully followed the way of faith rather than the way of the will to power.

The Gospel in the Dock, Where It Began

Since Christ died on a cross, the gospel actually *began* "in the dock" since the very idea of a crucified Messiah was the most scandalous idea imaginable to those waiting for God's deliverer. Therefore, why the gospel began "in the dock" is what we need to more fully explain, by looking to the OT to understand the background for the Messianic hope of a divine deliverer of the people of God.

Many of the Scriptures of the Bible exhibit imagery from the Exodus demonstrating that the release/departure of the enslaved Israelite people from the empire of Egypt is the major Biblical paradigm of salvation.[13] The Exodus of the Israelites from slavery by the Egyptians is thus also paradigmatic of the gospel of Jesus Christ and is exhibited in many ways in the New Testament. One of the most explicit usages of the pattern, albeit an easily missed allusion, is found in the Gospel of Luke in a statement that brings together the OT Exodus and the soon approaching death of Christ.[14]

> Now about eight days after these sayings he took with him Peter and John and James and went up on the mountain to pray. And as he was praying, the appearance of his face was altered, and his clothing became dazzling white. And behold, two men were talking with him, Moses and Elijah, who appeared in glory and spoke of his departure, [*exodus*] which he was about to accomplish at Jerusalem (Luke 9:28–31).

The reason we have brought up the exodus paradigm is to show that although the NT explicitly draws the parallel, the empirical fact of the

---

13. See Fretheim, *Exodus*, 18–20; Middleton, *A New Heaven*, 77–93.
14. See: Beale and Carson, *Commentary,* 311–12; Bock, *Luke,* 173.

matter of an analogous "exodus" of God's people that somehow took place *in the death of Jesus on a Roman cross* was anything but obvious. The disciples that are present at this "transfiguration" of Jesus where he met with Moses and Elijah do not understand the connection of his coming death with the Exodus. This is because the original paradigmatic Exodus in itself clearly portrayed its meaning. Slaves literally and physically left their bondage in Egypt to head towards new lives in God's "promised land." But that Jesus was executed as no-one of *any* importance to *anyone* would only *obviously* mean that he had been cursed by God (Deut 21:22–23; Gal 13:13). This is why the "good news" *in* the death of Christ was *anything but* self-evident. It was why the hope of the disciples that Jesus was the Messiah were completely dashed when he died (Luke 24:19–21). It certainly did not appear to be "good news" for Jesus, or any saving "kingdom" he claimed to be bringing. It certainly was not obvious to Israel or the citizens (and actual slaves) of the Roman Empire that this was the primal evangel, the salvific *exodus-type* event of all human history.

Paul openly acknowledged that this had been his own conclusion before the risen Christ appeared to him. He called it a knowledge of Christ "according to the flesh," i.e., *who he appeared to* be according to the then normal Jewish criteria and expectations (2 Cor 5:16).[15] Simply put, the Crucifixion of Jesus was "a stumbling block to Jews" and "foolishness to Greeks" wherein Jews and Greeks signified two different but "normal" ways of viewing Christ at that time. Paul knew that the gospel he came to know as *"Christ the power of God and the wisdom of God"* did not *appear* to be either "power" or "wisdom," let alone "the good news" of the redemption of Israel and the entire world (1 Cor 1:23–24). Thus, the task in Paul's day was for the apostles such as he to "bring out" the goodness of the gospel from what appeared to be its apparent "badness." In Paul's time his project was to rehabilitate the death of Christ the Messiah of Israel, so that it could be conceived of as good news. Likewise, in today's post-Christian West, the *good-news-ness* of the gospel is anything but self-evident, though for many other additional reasons.

This means that, once again, the gospel needs to be "rehabilitated." To many today, Jesus may at best seem to have been a well-intentioned but misunderstood revolutionary hero being put to death by the powers that be. There is much difference between the task of the early church to rehabilitate a supposedly "risen" Messiah who had died before Israel and

---

15. See Wright, *Paul for Everyone*, 64.

under Rome, and today's task of rehabilitating before the post-Christian West a *once accepted but now again rejected* Messiah. Nevertheless, in both cases the need for rehabilitation leads to the basic project of examining the data related to Christ's life, death, and resurrection, to see how the NT itself originally rehabilitated the gospel of this Christ. One could also posit the basic idea that the reason the news about Christ was good then might have some bearing on whether it could still be good news very nearly two millennia later.

The Rehabilitation of the Gospel, Then and Now

In both historical horizons, the evangelical task was and is to communicate that the gospel is true and good. The special emphasis of the first horizon was probably on the truth of the gospel, whether or not Jesus was Israel's Messiah. That the Messiah would be good—at least for God's chosen people Israel—was taken for granted. But in our historical horizon the emphasis probably needs to be on the goodness of the gospel, since the major obstacle to accepting truth in our postmodernism era, is the suspicion of all "truth claims" as thinly disguised power plays. Therefore, openness to the truth of the gospel today may only follow if and when the gospel's *goodness* seems plausible to a suspicious generation. Given the complexities and perplexities of the human condition, we may only be able to see the gospel as true when we see it as desirable. This may seem to the skeptic to be an admission that the gospel only works through Freudian "wish-fulfillment."[16] But we see that condition as valid due to the subjectivity of lives that are mostly lived in the domain of desire, weak as those desires are, by those who mistakenly consider themselves to be wholly objective thinkers. In other words, if the gospel can be seen as desirable, because it is *good*—or would be if it were true—it may more easily convince those who are not nearly as objective as they suppose.

Thus, we will turn in the next chapter to the matter at hand, the audacious attempt to rehabilitate the gospel of God. Of course, much of that process will be to attempt to re-narrate the NT's own rehabilitation of the gospel. But it is an audacious task because, properly speaking, why should the gospel of God need rehabilitation? I think it was the famous

16. To which Lewis replies, "If Freud is right about the Oedipus complex, the universal pressure of the wish that God should not exist must be enormous, and atheism must be an admirable gratification to one of our strongest suppressed impulses." Lewis, *World's Last Night*, 19.

preacher Charles Spurgeon who spoke of the folly of a person defending a lion, and the gospel is certainly the lion of God in the sense of not needing human defense. But practically speaking, because of the placement of the gospel in the dock by humanity at large, it needs rehabilitation. But also, in the course of inquiry, I trust that simple exposure to the gospel will loose the lion.

Of course, many do not wish to meet that lion, because he is quite interruptive and requires us to wrestle with him to the point of virtual death. It is in one sense, much easier and more comfortable to guard against these things. David Benjamin Blower discusses "interruption" throughout his short but wonderfully, powerfully disruptive book called "Sympathy for Jonah." Blower sees *interruption* as an integral category of *gospel* that even the prophet Jonah needed:

> But we may at least start with the fact that this is, after all, a book about a man who runs from his issues and ends up confronting them on his knees in the warm, wet hell of the monster's belly. He undergoes a night sea journey, a dark night of the soul. And it is thought by some that all of us must either embark on such a journey and be changed by it, or else barricade our entire lives against its cruel interruption. [17]

Jonah was resisting the call of the gospel's interruption. Jonah had placed the gospel in the dock, by placing himself in the ship heading the other way. But God's storm, followed by his pet sea monster quite interrupted him, and brought him face to face with the gospel's claim on him that he so desperately wanted to avoid (Rom 11:29). He actually preferred death, and in a sense desired it quite heroically. We will more fully consider his conflicted self as we proceed.

But like Jonah, most of us seek to safely quarantine ourselves away from the gospel with all its disruptive and inconvenient "interruptions." For Spurgeon's interrupting lion or Jonah's whale may also be encountered through the Scriptures. That is why, if one happens to have a Bible, it is generally quite dusty if kept in our living space, quite musty if kept in our storage space, or simply forgotten or lost. Annie Dillard speaks powerfully to the subtlety of our ways of avoidance when she relates a story of the adults in her childhood. They seem to have fairly well inhabited a cultural view of God, for they would have certainly sworn on the Bible that their God was not "in the dock." But she was all the while recognizing, as

---

17. Blower, *Sympathy for Jonah*, 4.

the obviously precocious child she was, that the gospel was safely placed in their dock so that they could be safe from its subversive interruption that could accost them through this unsuitable book:

> The adult members of society adverted to the Bible unreasonably often. What Arcana! Why did they spread this scandalous document before our eyes! If they had read it, I thought they would have hid it. They didn't recognize the vivid danger that we would, through repeated exposure, catch a case of its wild opposition to their world. Instead, they bade us study great chunks of it, and think about those chunks, commit them to memory, and ignore them. By dipping us children in the Bible so often, they hoped, I think, to give our lives a serious tint, and to provide us with quaintly magnificent snatches of prayer to produce as charms while, say, being mugged for our cash or jewels.[18]

Alas, God's interruption had gone unnoticed, hidden to the "worldly" wise but revealed to the perceptively simple! This demonstrates the sign of the prophet Jonah—the center of all gospel in the Bible—always concealed in Jonah yet therein also revealed!

> At that time Jesus declared, "I thank you, Father, Lord of heaven and earth, that you have hidden these things from the wise and understanding and revealed them to little children; yes, Father, for such was your gracious will (Matt 11:25–26).

Therefore, we must soon turn our attention, in the following chapter, to more fully consider the gospel of Jesus Christ and its signification in the very unusual story of the prophet Jonah. Our purpose will not be to attempt to go beyond the "simple" way of faith to the "wise" crutches of sight. For running wildly with restored legs and spit aided vision is more expedient in God's mysterious world than hobbling about shakily on man-made appendages in the reality-construct we create and think we see with our reality-detecting eyeglasses (John 5:8–9; Mark 8:23–25).

---

18. Dillard, *American Childhood*, 134. Soren Kierkegaard powerfully reveals the cultural "power" of Christianity to insulate us from interruption in an article he published roughly a century earlier in Denmark: "Verily there is that which is more contrary to Christianity, to the very nature of Christianity, than any heresy, any schism, more contrary than all heresies and all schisms combined, and that is, to *play* Christianity. But precisely in the very same sense that the child plays soldier, it is playing Christianity to take away the danger (Christianly, 'witness' and 'danger' correspond), and in place of this to introduce power (to be a danger for others), worldly goods, advantages, luxurious enjoyment of the most exquisite refinements . . .". Kierkegaard, *Attack on Christendom*, 8.

Of course, our purposeful denigration of sight and reason here is for the purpose of showing that they are but inferior forms of understanding existence because their trust is in the power of self rather than in the power of God.[19] But our overall purpose of seeking to understand this gospel that subverts sight through faith, is to admit that the way of faith may seem like death, but it gives life for it is the way of life. The "sight" of the will to power gives death for it is the way of death though it aims to save its life.[20] As Jesus said,

> Whosoever shall seek to save his life shall lose it; and whosoever shall lose his life shall preserve it (Luke 17:33, KJV).

But we must add that looking at the gospel in this way, apart from "seeing" Christ living it all out before us in his life and death, leaves us merely "interrupted" and ready to regain the composure of being left alone.[21] So the eternally ironic story of Jonah, which we will yet fully explore, is that he, the one who sought to avoid God's interruption, came to personify it, by embodying beforehand the interruption that Jesus embodied, as none else ever have, or ever could. This relation of Jonah to Jesus, and vice-versa, is a twisty "Back to the Future" type of scenario. The point at this juncture is that the gospel calls all to welcome its interruption, but we can only do so because the gospel is this: Jesus was voluntarily interrupted by all the powers of the world—God, the Devil, the dregs and dictators, oppressed and oppressors, of humankind—and transformed that interruption into good news for all of us, so that through Christ interrupting us, we may live by, and follow in, Christ's gospel way.

Christ's interruption that is the gospel will be more fully considered in the following chapter, where we will see all the various powers of the world that God says were orchestrated together in a gospel-storm, to create a new world, because in that storm, Christ overcame the self-destructive and world-destructive ways of the will to power. Following

---

19. Terry Eagleton writes, "An enlightened trust in the sovereignty of human reason can be every bit as magical as the exploits of Merlin, and a faith in our capacity for limitless self-improvement just as much a wide-eyed superstition as a faith in leprechauns." As cited in Harvey, *Taking Hold*, 58, loc. 1692.

20. "This, as the Bible understands it, is the fundamental conflict within the human condition: the struggle between the *will to power* and *the will to life*." Sacks, *Not in God's Name*, 255.

21. Lewis speaks for all of us: "Remember, I had always wanted, above all things, not to be 'interfered with.' I had wanted (mad wish) 'to call my soul my own.'" Lewis, *Surprised by Joy*, 228.

the will to power appears to be the self-evident way to secure and prosper life, because by doing so one thinks they see what one is getting. But what it gets is the loss of what humans really need, for the gain is what doesn't fulfill life as God created it to be. But through faith, the goodness of the primal gospel of God becomes "visible" to the eyes of faith, as what endures unto the life of the ages through the mysteries of life and death (Heb 12:22–24, 27–28).

On the Necessity of "Wrestling" with God, Faith, and the Will to Power

"Wrestling" is perhaps the commonly unnamed but most important responsive "activity" for humankind in relation to our "interruptive" God, which is the reason for the renaming of Jacob by God to be *Israel*—meaning "He strives with God"—because Jacob "wrestled with God and with men and prevailed" (Gen 32:28). We touch on this essential activity in relation to God in a few places in the book and have already been doing so just above, when discussing "interruption" which is certainly a form of wrestling. Diogenes Allen, writing of the poet George Herbert, says something that aptly relates to the admittedly "torturous" process of this book which we hope yields its "hard to get" blessing to those striving in one way or another with the very idea, or actual reality, of the gospel in the dock, and with the God of the gospel. Allen writes,

> George Herbert did not simply repeat his own religion in a conventional way. The arrogant protection of Christianity from all questions is too easy and often degenerates into self-righteousness. Instead, Herbert squeezes and tortures the Christian vision and allows it to squeeze and torture him until it yields to him its profound truth and spirit, and then he yields himself to that truth. Such wrestling is not particularly noticeable in American popular religion nor in the academic circles in which I move.[22]

We therefore hope to promote some necessary wrestling through the match portrayed in these pages, in which we are all in some manner squared off against the gospel and God. As with Jacob, this includes the odd fact of wrestling with God as we encounter and wrestle with him while wrestling with others. God and man are not as easily separated as we moderns suppose. Only wrestlers prevail in life, in the holy darkness

22. Allen, *Steps Along the Way*, 38.

of the night "against" their mysterious adversary whom they cannot defeat, nor let go, till the desired blessing is surrendered. That we will subsequently "leave" the match with a life-long limp is the small cost to pay for the enduring reminder that our will to power was not what prevailed, but our faith—provoked by our terrible and loving adversary who would not let us go without a necessary and gracious severe touch upon our vital parts. Karl Barth talks of how God thus makes the creature *holy*:

> To *call a person holy* is to say that God eternally disturbs him and fills him with a joy, that God has laid his hands upon the creature. The creature is attacked and wounded where he is most vital, in his subjectivity, his existence. Existentially, he is no longer his own. He himself no longer lives. He resembles an off-centered wheel, which no longer revolves around its own center.[23]

Jacob painfully but joyfully wobbled away from his dark night of wrestling, carrying in himself the wound of blessing and thereby signifying the promise of all human wrestlings with God and man to become God's wounded *Israel*, the promise of a new humanity. Our serious, life and death wrestling with God is the way that God re-frames our dust, fallen in the death of self-love and the will to power with Adam, breathing and birthing it to be a true Christian *humanity*.[24]

Our life-long wrestling is an internal struggle in relation to our external circumstances, which of course is implied in all that has been said of this wrestling. But we need to make explicit that in this we continually wrestle with the temptation to follow the serpent/dragon of Eden's will to power, to struggle past "him" by choosing to follow the way of faith.

> The dragon is at the side of the road watching those who pass. Take care lest he devour you! You are going to the Father of Souls, but it is necessary to pass by the dragon.[25]

But Christ has already slain the ancient dragon of Eden, as will be seen as we consider the primal gospel.

We can further clarify the existential complex of wrestling with God, faith, and the will to power, by drawing together Jacob the striver with the vaporous Abel. They both epitomize the way of faith and wrestling

---

23. Barth, *The Epistle to the Ephesians*, 66.
24. "Jacob wrestled to be in *submission* to God." Jordan, *Primeval Saints*, 113.
25. Cyril of Jerusalem, as cited in O'Connor, *Collected Works*, 979.

with God and man, though Abel "lost," while Jacob "won" their respective "matches." But Abel's loss signifies no helpless martyrdom, but rather also, as with Jacob, the victory of faith. Thus, Abel and Jacob demonstrate that the way of faith is neither of "the Tolstoyan pacifist" nor "a Nietzschean worshipper of brute resolve and relentless drive."[26] Thus we can clarify a middle way between the sheer way of the will to power, and an overly quietist way of faith, that would only make a caricature of God's righteous Abels. Abel's wrestling is thus perhaps even seen post-mortem, in "the voice of his blood crying to God from the ground" that would altogether overcome Cain except for a measure of God's mysterious mercy given even to him (Gen 4:10–15.)

On the Language of "Rehabilitation"

Before moving into our "rehabilitation" proper in the next chapter. the language of "rehabilitation" perhaps needs to be clarified as not indicating that the NT presents a rationally crafted and/or manipulatively motivated "revisionist history" of the life and death of Christ. Barnett writes,

> On historical grounds I will argue that the early Christians were neither mistaken nor willful, but that the preresurrection Jesus believed he was the "One who was to come," and that his disciples also came to hold that conviction.[27]

What this means is that the NT "wasn't written to outsiders. It was written by people of faith to people of faith, an act of personal communication . . . From beginning to end they are telling what they see; they don't see facts and *then* put an interpretation on it."[28] And what they saw was Jesus, who as it turned out after all, was the Messiah of Israel and Savior of the world, despite the "hour of darkness" when their hopes were dashed, and they fell into deep despair (Luke 22:53; 24:20–21). Thus, from the beginning, the fellowship of eyewitnesses of the resurrection proclaimed what they had seen, and the NT inscripturated that living testimony. Therefore the "rehabilitation" of the death of Christ the NT preserved was no revisionist history, and the rehabilitory language is

---

26. Wood, *Chesterton*, 144.
27. Barnett, *Finding the Historical Christ*, viii.
28. Springsted, *The Act of Faith*, 70.

merely an accommodation for the sake of those of the past and present to whom Jesus was or is "in the dock" because of his death.

A revisionist history of early Christianity *was* historically presented by the heterodox Gnostics, who denied that Jesus was fully human, was resurrected, or accomplished anything having to do with the redemption of creation and the *bodily* life of humankind. The Gnostic *revisionist* history was true to color by being self-serving, whereas the orthodox early Christians suffered greatly for their storied history that brought suffering.[29] Given the reality of the first three centuries of the early Christians, if the NT was "revisionist history," all that it provided its "writers" was several centuries of self-disregarding self-sacrifice in relation to the Roman Empire and society. In other words, the NT narrates the lives of people living in the difficult countercultural way of faith for the sake of others, not the easy road of the compromising way of the will to power buttressed by a revisionist history which the Gnostics promoted.

---

29. See N. T. Wright, *Judas and the Gospel of Jesus*.

2

Rehabilitating the Gospel

> So they picked up Jonah and hurled him into the
> sea, and the sea ceased from its raging.
>
> —JONAH 1:15

> An evil and adulterous generation seeks for a sign, but no sign
> will be given to it except the sign of the prophet Jonah.
>
> —MATTHEW 12:39

On "Getting" the Sign That We Wanted

WE HAVE JUST CONSIDERED in the last chapter the fact that the gospel was, and in a sense, still ought to be anything but self-evident. This "lack" therefore calls for a "rehabilitation" of the gospel which was summarily given by Jesus in reference to a "mere" sign, although I hope to show that this sign was anything but "mere." The two texts above, demonstrate that seeing the good result of the gospel is not usually as evident as it was when Jonah was cast into the sea. When the sea ceased from its raging after Jonah was thrown into it, it was obvious to those sailors that they had just witnessed a "gospel" event. So also, Jesus said that the good of the gospel event in him would become "seen" by comparing his life, death and resurrection to "the sign of the prophet Jonah." But Jesus also says that this was the *only* sign that would be given *because* the people sought for a sign and would not accept Jesus for what he did and taught—which *ought* to have been signs enough. And so, a sign they wanted, and a sign they were given! Of course, Jesus is saying this because the gospel in him will *not* be evident, apart from a "baptism"—an *immersion* into the biblical imagery and meaning embedded in this old and strange story of the prophet Jonah, wherein *life came out of death*. Jesus was admitting that only by the light of *that* sign could the inconceivable truth of his impending execution be seen. The sign, like the reality it pointed to, was subversive of their expectations, but it was also fully perspicuous as to its meaning, after Christ had been resurrected like Jonah was.

But it is a sign that speaks in many ways, one being that it is a sign of the gospel's way of faith. Thus, it is a sign that tested the faith of Israel by calling them to be willing to have their very lives baptized into the same sign as followers of God's anointed Christ, to thereby be shaped into the cruciform pattern of death and life. For that is the only way to become the truly human image of God which was lost to "adam" and all his kin but gained by Christ for all of his.[1] Essentially, biblical signs do not merely challenge the intellect. They interrupt life itself with what appears to be death.

For God's signs call us to a new life that is only understandable through a new worldview. The "sign of Jonah" was perhaps the primary parable of Jesus. Jesus often used parabolic stories to provoke and propagate the new worldview in which "the only sign" could make sense. The parabolic method challenges its hearer by bringing them "virtually" into a scene where they temporarily "inhabit" an alternative world, to help them see the truth of God's real world—in this world. Of course, there are always points of reference to the "old world" as we conceive it, as the taking off point. But the parables of Jesus typically present quite shocking turns in relation to the traditional social mores, expectations, and understandings. This creates tensions and begins deconstructing the social "geography" of the old world, to clear the way for paths to be made straight, and new seeds to be sown, germinate, grow, and bear fruit in new conceptions of life (Luke 3:4–6; 8:4–8). In fact, Jesus drew many metaphors from the agricultural world of his hearers, which served as organic "seed truths" of his kingdom.

---

1. See Mark 10:39 for Christ's assurance that all his followers will be shaped by the cross of suffering, but that way is the way to life as shown in Mark 8:34–37. Also see 1 Cor 15:22 for 'adam' and Christ.

We believe that the biblical use of signs and parables may demonstrate the way to proceed for understanding the gospel and its goodness. Therefore, our exposition of "the sign of the prophet Jonah" will seek to discover *the* "alternate world" in which the gospel of Jesus was arriving. For our use we will borrow and build upon a parabolic metaphor of a "perfect storm," developed by the master storyteller, historian, and theologian N. T. Wright. We hope to show that "the perfect storm" helps us understand the "perfect sign" of the prophet Jonah, which was designated by Jesus as the master sign of his gospel and was therefore fittingly an organizing theme in the written Gospels of both Mark and Matthew.[2]

"The Perfect Storm"

N. T. Wright obviously loves to use metaphors in his writing, teaching, and preaching, and uses his own "really good" ones repeatedly, following the lead of the master storyteller Jesus who reused "ideas and scenes in his kaleidoscopic display of parables."[3] "The Perfect Storm" illustration appears to be one of Wright's favorite metaphors. Indeed, he uses it sequentially as a master illustration in Chapters 3, 4 and 5 of his book "Simply Jesus" to reveal and analyze the modern theological "storm" of today's world and the first century religiopolitical "storm" into which Jesus came. Of course, the "Perfect Storm" name originates from the meteorological event in late October 1991, five-hundred miles off the coast of Gloucester, Massachusetts which was memorialized in the movie of the same name. This modern storm consisted of three main elements described by Wright as: a steadily gale force western wind; an overheated, turbulent and complex high-pressure system; and a tropical hurricane nor-easter. The three first-century realities the perfect storm illustrates through these elements are, respectively: the Roman "storm" as the world superpower; Israel as a "storm" itself in its ongoing story-drama; and, the massive "hurricane" which *signifies* God. Wright calls the third element, the hurricane, "*the strange, unpredictable, and highly dangerous divine element . . . the wind of God.*"[4] And Wright shows how the gospel is the news that God through Christ entered into the cataclysm of these three realities to inaugurate a new reality called the kingdom of God.

2. See Anderson, "Jonah," 172–86.
3. Wright, *Simply Jesus*, 27, loc. 536.
4. N. T. Wright, *Simply Jesus*, 38; Loc. 715.

Wright's metaphor helps us to remember the strangeness of the creative power of God, who is able to bring to birth *a new creation* from the earth which was, as far as seeming to have any potential, "without form and void" as described in Genesis 1:2. Out of a "perfect storm" that seemed to promise only *perfect destruction* came God's *new creation* in Christ, because the "hurricane that is God" was "*reconciling the world to himself in Christ.*" The realist-fiction writer Flannery O'Connor would simply call this unexpected return for violence "grace," while the imaginative high-fantasy writer J.R.R. Tolkien would, true to character, linguistically embellish that "sudden and miraculous grace" as a "euchatastrophe," compellingly combining the blessed word "eucharist" (to give thanks) with the cursed word "catastrophe."[5]

We find another helpful metaphor by borrowing from the title of a book called "Improbable Planet—How Earth Became Humanity's Home."[6] Ross demonstrates that the "so called natural evils" are "inherently beneficial to human existence," and that "dreaded dangers" such as earthquakes are necessary and enable life to persist. He also writes that "this universe serves as a launchpad for the new creation to come," which parallels the "perfect storm" as the launchpad for the new creation in Christ.[7] If we followed Ross's creational metaphor, we might thereby call the result of God's perfect storm the *"improbable gospel."*

The gospel was, and always remains to our sight, "un-obvious" and "improbable" but nevertheless is "good news" of the "euchatastrophe" of God. Therefore Tolkien, summarizing the story of Christ writes,

> The Resurrection is the euchatastrophe of the story of the incarnation.[8]

Just as the forces of destruction Ross mentioned prove to be ultimately beneficial and, in some way, related to the beginning of a second and more glorious creation to come, so also the first-century *perfect storm* proved to bring the euchatastrophe of *atonement*, because working therein was "the hurricane of divine love." And the news thereof proves to be *good news*, something that calls forth *eucharist, thanksgiving*. Improbable

---

5. Sandner, "Between Euchatastrophe," 171. See Tolkien, *Tolkien Reader*, 85–90; Morrow, *Seeking the Lord*, 15–16, 31–32, 100, 125.

6. Ross, *Improbable Planet*.

7. See Ross, *Improbable Planet*, 224; 111; 13.

8. Tolkien, *Tolkien Reader*, 88. (To paraphrase, the apparent catastrophe of the incarnation led to the euchatastrophe of the resurrection.)

gospel *indeed*, but with God—*all things are possible*. This first-century perfect storm was the historic setting for the *Genesis* of God's new creation which will in the end completely fill the entire cosmos as the hurricane of divine love continues to build "a place" for the flourishing of humankind and all of creation.⁹

Our next step in this process of "rehabilitating the gospel" from a strange un-obvious sign to the gospel worthy of thanks is to try to further build the picture of the "alternate world" within the sign of Jonah in which something called "atonement" was achieved. We therefore need to "gather" many other "weather elements" that contributed to the perfect storm that God molded into atonement.

Collecting Storm Data

Given our perfect storm metaphor, in many ways understanding how *atonement* works will be similar to understanding the weather. There are various weather factors which interact with one another to create the weather that happens. To understand the *atonement storm*, we must try to identify the various factors that work together, or better, were *worked together* by God, to result in *atonement*. We already saw Wright's identification of the major factors: The Roman Empire, Israel, Jesus, and God. In his own book Wright fills in those basic factors with the details required for understanding the historical situation that culminated in the death and resurrection of Christ along with their significance as "the gospel." We will need to follow that basic method to some extent also, in our own way.

Starting with Wright's four basic factors, the Roman Empire, Israel, Jesus and God, the simplest observation is merely that the human, divine, and demonic factors are the primary "players" in the atonement story. We could say that this presents the problem that atonement solves, namely that in their relations to each other, humans and God need "at-one-ment" and the Devil wishes to thwart that. But we first need to better understand what that solution means.

The visible division of the word *atonement* into three parts shows that the word is a metaphor derived from life. Similarly, *reconciliation* speaks of a tangible process understood to mean that disparate things become reconciled, whether bank account records, or people. Ted Peters

---

9. Ross, *Improbable Planet*, 230. For a similar view from modern astronomy see Gonzalez, "Eschatology," 51–65.

narrates the origin of the English word, derived from "Anglo-French usage by the Normans after the conquest of the Anglo-Saxons in 1066 with the phrase *ere a un,* meaning 'to agree.'"[10] Subsequently, Anglican Bibles of the sixteenth and seventeenth centuries began using "atonement" to translate the Hebrew term for *expiation* and the Greek term for *reconciliation*.[11] Thus the term indicates the "*at-one-ment*" of God and humans, achieved through the person and work of Christ. This gives us a clearer definition of what atonement is abstractly. But unless we consider the storm data that "resulted" in "the perfect storm" of atonement, our conception of the whole will be like seeing the end of movie without first witnessing the events that gave meaning to its climax.

We will therefore consider several fuller narrations of the story given by Paul and other NT writers to: first, gather a pool of "storm data;" second, identify "weather patterns;" and third, see how God worked them together in the perfect storm of atonement. Of course, the data we will see is drawn from the "rehabilitory" project of the NT itself that exposited the death of Jesus that fulfilled the sign of the prophet Jonah and reconciled humanity.

2 Corinthians 5:10–19

> For we must all appear before the judgment seat of Christ, so that each one may receive what is due for what he has done in the body, whether good or evil. Therefore, knowing the fear of the Lord, we persuade others. But what we are is known to God, and I hope it is known also to your conscience. We are not commending ourselves to you again but giving you cause to boast about us, so that you may be able to answer those who boast about outward appearance and not about what is in the heart. For if we are beside ourselves, it is for God; if we are in our right mind, it is for you. For the love of Christ controls us, because we have concluded this: that one has died for all, therefore all have died; and he died for all, that those who live might no longer live for themselves but for him who for their sake died and was

---

10. See Peters, *God,* 203.

11. The Greek word *katallasso* "originates from the social-societal sphere (cf. 1 Cor. 7:11) and speaks in general of the restoration of the right relationship between two parties. In the pronouncements of Paul, it is often placed over against "enmity," "alienation". . . just as in a positive sense it has the meaning of "peace." Ridderbos, *Paul,* 182.

> raised. From now on, therefore, we regard no one according to the flesh. Even though we once regarded Christ according to the flesh, we regard him thus no longer. Therefore, if anyone is in Christ, he is a new creation. [creature] The old has passed away; behold, the new has come. All this is from God, who through Christ reconciled us to himself and gave us the ministry of reconciliation; that is, in Christ God was reconciling [Or God was in Christ, reconciling] the world to himself, not counting their trespasses against them, and entrusting to us the message of reconciliation.

Although Paul mentions the reconciliation the gospel brings at the end of this excerpt, it is the basis for everything he writes. This is because Paul consciously wrote as one who rightly saw the essence of his life and all human lives caught up in and forever changed in *some* manner by the storm of atonement that God has already accomplished in Christ.[12] This "good news" was therefore about receiving the salvation accomplished in Christ, understanding God's new creation in Christ, and being increasingly transformed by living accordingly (Rom 12:1–2). In sum, the gospel was the means by which God's love accomplished a change in the nature and character of human existence in *all* its relationships, and which therefore calls for all to respond to God's *objective* reconciliation of them—"not counting their sins against them"—by themselves "being reconciled to God." Therefore, reconciliation originates from God and is *primarily objective*—but secondarily *calls* for and enables a *subjective response* by each person. The essential goodness of the gospel that Paul "brings out" was admitted by him to be hidden to the view of "normal" human "fleshly" estimates of Christ and his cross. Paul called for all to instead view Christ according to God's declaration, made *through the resurrection,* that Christ's death was the very means of God's reconciliation of the world to begin a new creation (Rom 1:4–5). Paul thus declares the way of faith instead of the old way of sight, and the cross as God's own "death" to the "will to power" which is to also be the way for all through death to the will to power into new life in the faith of Christ. For God the Father "gave his only Son" relinquishing power, and Christ the Son gave up power by "becoming obedient to . . . death on the cross" (John 3:16, Phil 2:8).

12. Emphasizing the gospel as "news" N. T. Wright says, "The four Gospels in the Bible, Matthew, Mark, Luke, and John, were originally written precisely to say, "This is what just happened, and everything is forever different as a result." Wright, *Simply Good News,* 65.

Hebrews 2:14–16

> Since therefore the children share in flesh and blood, he himself likewise partook of the same things, that through death he might destroy the one who has the power of death, that is, the devil, and deliver all those who through fear of death were subject to lifelong slavery. For surely it is not angels that he helps, but he helps the offspring of Abraham.

This text shows that the incarnate Christ was fully human, and necessarily so in order to help humanity, which had fallen to the overpowering powers of the Devil who holds us in bondage through our fear. This shows that the Devil's way is the coercive way of force. The fallen powers that infiltrated God's creation and the human condition have placed humanity in "lifelong slavery." The text has "the children" and "the offspring of Abraham" in mind, but other texts show that Christ became human not only for Israel or the Church but for the whole world, being "the propitiation . . . for the sins of the whole world" (1 John 2:2). The word propitiation signifies *appeasement,* that God appeased God's own self, through the sacrifice of Christ.[13] It is worth noting that the Devil was "destroyed" not though overpowering force but through the paradoxical overwhelming weakness of Christ's death. Christ's "partaking" in human nature in relation to the will to power and its negative effects of sin, fear and death was a voluntary "sharing," not a necessary *sinful* suffering. In other words, as the letter of Hebrews also says, Christ was fully like us with the same human nature and the same experience of human life but was without sin in his sameness.[14]

Colossians 1:15–23

> He is the image of the invisible God, the firstborn of all creation. For by [that is, by means of; or in] him all things were created, in heaven and on earth, visible and invisible, whether thrones or dominions or rulers or authorities—all things were created through him and for him. And he is before all things, and in him all things hold together. And he is the head of the body, the church. He is the beginning, the firstborn from the dead, that in

---

13. See Torrance, *Atonement,* 68–69.
14. See Heb 4:15. See also Torrance, *Atonement,* 82–83, 150, 212.

> everything he might be preeminent. For in him all the fullness of God was pleased to dwell, and through him to reconcile to himself all things, whether on earth or in heaven, making peace by the blood of his cross. And you, who once were alienated and hostile in mind, doing evil deeds, he has now reconciled in his body of flesh by his death, in order to present you holy and blameless and above reproach before him, if indeed you continue in the faith, stable and steadfast, not shifting from the hope of the gospel that you heard, which has been proclaimed in all creation [or to every creature] under heaven, and of which I, Paul, became a minister.

In his letter proclaiming the gospel to the church in Colossae, Paul both narrows the focus down to the inner transformation brought to individuals while also broadening the scope out to survey the far-reaching effects of the atonement in the entire cosmos. Thus, Christ's atoning work is integrally related to his becoming human and restoring the image of God in humanity to achieve a new creation, with Christ himself being the preeminent "firstborn," with the new image of God, which overcomes the old order of creation. *Therefore,* Christ has a new creational form of power and authority over all other "old" powers and authorities of earth or heaven. This means that all the fulness of God and all that implies dwells in Christ who is "Lord"—but not after the manner of the old ways of human "lordship." The atoning work of Christ is described as God making peace through Christ's death by reconciling humans to God in holiness and blamelessness, whereas they were previously alienated from and hostile toward God, and therefore, practitioners of evil. The truth of this reconciliation needs to be held on to by its hearers through faith and hope so that they can continue to live according to the new reality of Christ. Paul's statement about the proclamation of the gospel is probably meant to indicate that this glorious "cosmic" gospel of peace and reconciliation is meant to benefit all of humankind. Of course, it does so when those hearing the gospel of peace continue in its way of faith which was demonstrated by Christ's "making peace through the cross."

1 Corinthians 15:1–6

> Now I would remind you, brothers, of the gospel I preached to you, which you received, in which you stand, and by which you are being saved, if you hold fast to the word I preached to

you—unless you believed in vain. For I delivered to you as of first importance what I also received: that Christ died for our sins in accordance with the Scriptures, that he was buried, that he was raised on the third day in accordance with the Scriptures, and that he appeared to Cephas, then to the twelve. Then he appeared to more than five hundred brothers at one time, most of whom are still alive, though some have fallen asleep.

This exhortation of Paul provides some necessary grounding which will become helpful in our next step. Several fairly obvious observations are that the gospel is of primary importance and is something capable of being proclaimed, and that it is the means of salvation to those believing and holding to it. Paul then provides a short summary of the content of the gospel, saying that it includes the facts that Christ ("the anointed one") died for "our sins" and was also "raised," and that this was "according to the (OT) Scriptures."[15] This means that the Old Testament provides the basic framework necessary for understanding the gospel. Paul narrates some historical evidences of the Resurrection in eyewitness accounts of both individuals and of five hundred at one time. Paul also mentions an early Christian euphemism which reveals that Christ's gospel has changed the significance of physical death for Christians so that their bodies are considered to be merely "asleep" and awaiting their physical resurrection. This text highlights the Resurrection of Jesus which vindicated his way of faith that as we saw in previous texts resulted in his death. Ultimately, as with Cain, the way of force seeks to overcome the way of faith, but as with Abel, the way of faith is vindicated by God and so counterintuitively overcomes through a wholly different sort of power.

Matthew 20:25–28

But Jesus called them to him and said, "You know that the rulers of the Gentiles lord it over them, and their great ones exercise authority over them. It shall not be so among you. But whoever would be great among you must be your servant, and whoever would be first among you must be your slave, even as the Son of Man came not to be served but to serve, and to give his life as a ransom for many."

---

15. Christ is "Literally, 'the anointed one,' the title designating Jesus as the Messiah." Erickson, *Concise Dictionary*, 29.

Matthew 26:17–19

> Now on the first day of Unleavened Bread the disciples came to Jesus, saying, "Where will you have us prepare for you to eat the Passover?" He said, "Go into the city to a certain man and say to him, 'The Teacher says, My time is at hand. I will keep the Passover at your house with my disciples.'" And the disciples did as Jesus had directed them, and they prepared the Passover.

Matthew 26:26–29

> Now as they were eating, Jesus took bread, and after blessing it broke it and gave it to the disciples, and said, "Take, eat; this is my body." And he took a cup, and when he had given thanks he gave it to them, saying, "Drink of it, all of you, for this is my blood of the covenant, which is poured out for many for the forgiveness of sins. I tell you I will not drink again of this fruit of the vine until that day when I drink it new with you in my Father's kingdom."

Our first observation is that the atoning person and work of Christ exhibit a different type and place (or distribution) of authority than what was known in "Gentile" kingdoms. This is because the person and work of Christ is characterized by his being a "servant," which is a term "loaded" with OT significance. To Jesus, being this "servant" meant first and foremost the giving of one's life as a "ransom for many" so that others could be reconciled to God and to the "servant mission" in the world. The significance of this "ransom" is partly found in its being linked to the "Passover" recorded in the book of Exodus and the manner in which it was memorialized as an annual sacramental meal. Jesus claimed to be the fulfillment of this meal so that the body and blood of Jesus that he "gives" for others represents God's "New covenant . . . for the forgiveness of sins." This means that the Exodus event that liberated Israel from Egypt's "will to power" over them, was not achieved by *their* "revolutionary" revolt, but by their participation in the way of faith that was based in the subversive power of the lamb sacrificed before God. The ultimate fulfillment of that symbolic lamb's death was the "exodus" in Christ's atoning death on the cross and its integral relation to the "kingdom" of God (Luke 9:28–31). The *death* of the messiah would certainly *not* have been seen by *any* in

Israel as the means by which God's Kingdom would arrive, although their sacrificial lambs and the "sacrificed" Jonah had "predicted" it.

Acts 3:22–36

"Men of Israel, hear these words: Jesus of Nazareth, a man attested to you by God with mighty works and wonders and signs that God did through him in your midst, as you yourselves know—this Jesus, delivered up according to the definite plan and foreknowledge of God, you crucified and killed by the hands of lawless men. God raised him up, loosing the pangs of death, because it was not possible for him to be held by it. For David says concerning him,

"'I saw the Lord always before me,
for he is at my right hand that I may not be shaken;
therefore my heart was glad, and my tongue rejoiced;
my flesh also will dwell in hope.
For you will not abandon my soul to Hades,
or let your Holy One see corruption.
You have made known to me the paths of life;
you will make me full of gladness with your presence.'

"Brothers, I may say to you with confidence about the patriarch David that he both died and was buried, and his tomb is with us to this day. Being therefore a prophet, and knowing that God had sworn with an oath to him that he would set one of his descendants on his throne, he foresaw and spoke about the resurrection of the Christ, that he was not abandoned to Hades, nor did his flesh see corruption. This Jesus God raised up, and of that we all are witnesses. Being therefore exalted at the right hand of God, and having received from the Father the promise of the Holy Spirit, he has poured out this that you yourselves are seeing and hearing. For David did not ascend into the heavens, but he himself says,

"'The Lord said to my Lord,
"Sit at my right hand,
until I make your enemies your footstool."'

> Let all the house of Israel therefore know for certain that God has made him both Lord and Christ, this Jesus whom you crucified."

Jesus of Nazareth was visibly attested to Israel by God through mighty works, wonders and signs, and in the definite plan and foreknowledge of God was delivered to death by the hands of lawless men, delivered to be the victim of their "force" against him. But God raised *faithful* Jesus from death because it had no capability of holding him. The *paradox* that makes the gospel hidden to us is *explained* by God's subversion of what is thought, esteemed, and embraced by humans as power. As we saw above in Paul's summary of the gospel in 1 Cor 15, the OT Scriptures prophetically foretold of the death and resurrection of Christ, so that Peter beforehand had similarly appealed to OT texts in his sermon to "the house of Israel" at Pentecost. Peter's "punch line" to "all the house of Israel" was that through the Crucifixion of Jesus by Rome, that the Israelite leaders had instigated, God had made *this Jesus* both Lord and Christ by his resurrection and ascension to God's "right hand" of authority. It was "euchatastrophe."

1 Corinthians 2:1–10

> And I, when I came to you, brothers, did not come proclaiming to you the testimony of God with lofty speech or wisdom. For I decided to know nothing among you except Jesus Christ and him crucified. And I was with you in weakness and in fear and much trembling, and my speech and my message were not in plausible words of wisdom, but in demonstration of the Spirit and of power, so that your faith might not rest in the wisdom of men but in the power of God. Yet among the mature we do impart wisdom, although it is not a wisdom of this age or of the rulers of this age, who are doomed to pass away. But we impart a secret and hidden wisdom of God, which God decreed before the ages for our glory. None of the rulers of this age understood this, for if they had, they would not have crucified the Lord of glory. But, as it is written,
>
> "What no eye has seen, nor ear heard,
> nor the heart of man imagined,
> what God has prepared for those who love him"—

We *saw* above that Paul said that the gospel could be proclaimed, since it is "good news." Here Paul explains that his apostolic proclamation of the gospel was not done with high rhetorical speech or philosophical wisdom. This means that the simple *form* of "news" about Jesus Christ crucified therefore *in itself demonstrates* the Spirit and power of God. "Preaching" therefore coheres with the "method" of the cross as the subversive power of God and does not (or should not) operate according to the false method of the "gospel of force" that uses worldly power or rhetoric. In other words "powerful preaching" is not confirmed as such according to the worldly standard of power. So also, the unbelieving rulers of the age are doomed to pass away because they fell (and still fall) in relation to God's true power through their reliance on "worldly" forms of power. But believing people become mature through faith that receives the secret, hidden *wisdom* of God that was decreed before the ages, and which we saw in our introduction was the wisdom of God that in Eden renounced the way of the will to power. Paul says that no rulers or authorities of this age had understood this hidden power of God and seems to say that if they had known they wouldn't have "played into God's hands" by crucifying the Lord of glory. By their reliance on force, they destroyed themselves instead of him. We also saw earlier that if Jesus had bowed to the Devil's temptation to power, *he* would have played into the Devil's hands. In his letter to the Colossians Paul writes that God *revealed* the shameful truth of the way of unjust force against the innocent Jesus: "He disarmed the rulers and authorities and put them to open shame, by triumphing over them in him" (Col 2:15). In short, the gospel way of faith, reveals and disarms the way of force.

These texts especially demonstrate the problem of trying to understand the gospel according to merely human notions of power. This shows that any "gospel" understanding *of* the gospel must accept what is revealed therein regarding God's ways and power, being willing to undergo a changed *way of thinking* about everything. That "repentance" or *change of mind* is to be in regard to the life, death, and resurrection of Christ, and the nature, way, and wisdom of the "kingdom" of God. For it is a kingdom unlike any normal human kingdom in its manner of authority and glory. The glory of human kingdoms is to fight for them, but in glorious contrast the glory of God is to die for his enemies and

Rehabilitating the Gospel

become the servant of all.[16] God's way is the wiser way of "overcoming" evil through good as Paul wrote in Rom 12:21.

We now turn to the step of seeking to recognize the various "weather patterns" that are present in all this collected "storm data." We will see that a few of the "weather patterns" may not seem to be that *weather-like.* But they are weather-related, being like things that materialize from the ominous fog on a "dark and stormy night" in a horror film.

Identifying Storm Patterns

The God-Storm Pattern

The first pattern that comes forth out of the storm matrix is the breath that created life, the wind/storm who is God. We had seen at the beginning of this exposition of "the perfect storm" that N. T. Wright considered God to be the massive hurricane—*the strange, unpredictable, and highly dangerous divine element . . . The wind of God.*"[17] Some may wonder whether admitting that Yahweh, who is Richard Dawkins's most unfavorite character "of all fiction," is *the God-Storm,* is to give up the possibility of the rehabilitation of the gospel of such a "highly dangerous" God of violent force.[18] But we will see that this "Storm" is *strange,* like no others, and *as ultimate force* acts according to a wholly different and self-defining dynamic than is known by any and all other instances of force (Isa 28:21). It seems that Richard Dawkins merely projects the normal dynamics of human force upon God. But Soren Kierkegaard and Karl Barth didn't call the God who has revealed God's self "the wholly other" for nothing, and most certainly not because God is like *us* or *any* force we know of.[19] For the God-Storm

> risks failure in seeking the love of the creature, who is truly free
> to respond otherwise . . . Yet humankind is nonetheless created

---

16. See Caws, *Causes of Quarrel,* Ch. 7–9 for "Glory" as a common cause of conflict.

17. Wright, *Simply Jesus,* 38, loc. 715.

18. "The God of the Old Testament is arguably the most unpleasant character in all of fiction: jealous and proud of it; a petty, unjust, unforgiving control-freak; a vindictive, bloodthirsty ethnic cleanser; a misogynistic, homophobic racist, infanticidal, genocidal, filicidal, pestilential, megalomaniacal, sadomasochistic, capriciously malevolent bully." Dawkins, *God Delusion,* 31.

19. See Sponheim, *Existing Before God,* 95.

good, for the path to full imaging of the divine commitment in love is nothing less than a path can be. Indeed, God in Christ can tread that path as the "prototype," "*ahead* beckoning." A path can be made available, but love cannot be coerced to walk that path. [20]

This non-coercive God-Storm is the ultimate author of the perfect storm of atonement, bringing about a new creation from its midst—reconciling the world to himself in Christ. We will call this God the *God-Storm pattern*, first tangibly revealed "in the beginning" of the book of Genesis as the "spirit"—or more literally—the breath or wind of God "hovering over the face of the waters" before the acts of creation. Then, in the creation of humankind "LORD God formed the man of the dust of the ground and *breathed* into his nostrils the *breath* of life, and the man became a living creature" (Gen 1:2; 2:7). Scripture also shows that God as spirit/wind/breath is also the God of the storm:

> He lays the beams of his chambers on the waters; he makes the clouds his chariot; he rides on the wings of the wind; he makes his messengers winds, his ministers a flaming fire (Psalm 104:3–4).

The first recorded *appearance* of God to the primeval pair of humanity in Eden is found in Gen 3:8–10 and it is possible that God appears there *in* or *as* the "wind of the day."

> And they heard the sound of the Lord God walking in the garden in the cool [Hebrew: wind] of the day, and the man and his wife hid themselves from the presence of the Lord God among the trees of the garden. But the Lord God called to the man and said to him, "Where are you?" And he said, "I heard the sound of you in the garden, and I was afraid, because I was naked, and I hid myself" (Gen 3:8–10).

The translation "the sound of the Lord God walking in the *cool* of the day" in many of the English versions seems likely to be a mistranslation, as the ESV notes by providing the literal Hebrew word as actually *ruah*—"wind" in a parenthesis. John Walton says that "cool of the day" is "certainly interpretive" and provides some tantalizing evidence that the Hebrew text could be translated "They heard the roar of the LORD moving about in the garden in the wind of the storm."[21] The specific word combination in the

---

20. Sponheim, *Love's Availing Power*, 19.
21. Walton, *Genesis*, 223–24, loc. 224. See also Sailhamer, *Genesis*, 52–53, who

Hebrew text is the only place of that occurrence in the entire OT, so despite comparison with near parallels in the OT and extra-biblical Akkadian terminology that supports Walton's alternative translation, that rendering can only be held tentatively.[22] For our own purposes of seeking ways to illustrate God's storm complex of atonement we see no reason that God's first scriptural appearance *as* possibly "breath/wind" in Genesis should not inform God's characterization in this "atonement storm." That God appears fearfully as the God-Storm in the atonement storm is partly because like Adam and Eve, we have followed the *alien* voice of the serpent's temptation to disobey God's warning against eating from the forbidden tree, and have fallen into the fears of sin, death, shame and alienation—becoming *homo incurvatus in se*—"turned in on oneself."[23] Of course God, in a sense always appears fearful, as the wholly other, the "*mysterium tremendum et fascinans.*"[24] But faith was meant, and is still meant, to allow us to live in vital relation to our God who is love, and to having our fear "cast out" through Christ's perfect love (1 John 4:8, 18–19).

Nevertheless, implicit in the perfect storm matrix is the righteous wrath of the God-Storm, who *because* of his love is angered by the self-inflicted tragedy humans anxiously *leaped* into.[25] But God's thwarted intent does not mean that the fall to sin caught God by surprise. This is because God had planned, before the creation of humanity and the ages of history began, for the incarnate work of Jesus Christ to be the

---

provides other evidence that God was appearing as a storm theophany of great and powerful wind "coming in judgment and power."

22. See Walton, *Genesis,* 223–24, loc. 224.

23. Janz, *Westminster Handbook to Luther,* 127. Obviously, the nature of that transformation which was "alien" to human nature as it was intended provides a hint that atonement has to do with the work of God in turning humankind *from* that deadly inward turning. The incarnation of Christ shows that redemption is not essentially alien to human being. "The whole thrust of the saving act of God in the incarnation . . . is toward the humanizing and personalizing of human beings 'in Christ.' They have come to have a share in the mission of Christ *itself,* rather than in something secondary to it, or even something apparently 'alien' to it." Badcock, *The Way of Life,* 115.

24. Westphal writes ". . . mysterium tremendum et fascinans, the awful and fascinating mystery. The holy is a mystery, not because it is a puzzle to be solved, but because it is something out of the ordinary. Thus, it is in Otto's oft quoted phrase, 'wholly other.'" Westphal, *God, Guilt, and Death,* 38.

25. Soren Kierkegaard, known for his "leap of faith," held that the choice of sin also entails a "leap." In both cases a "leap" is involved because of human finitude and uncertainty. See Kierkegaard, *Concept of Anxiety,* 32. Also see, Evans, *Kierkegaard's Christian Psychology,* 57–65.

primordial center of atonement, and the giving of the Spirit to breathe a new creation humanity.

As we continue to find other storm patterns, we will see how they relate to the God-Storm who works "the good" of atonement in Christ in relation to these other patterns. In order to try to do justice to the historical realities of humanity implied in our storm data texts we have found that we need to recognize that there is not one, but several "different" narratives of humanity which emerge as "storm patterns."

The Fallen-Breath Wind Pattern

We will call the first humanity storm pattern the fallen-breath wind pattern. This pattern reveals the most basic need of atonement as the presupposed contextual OT background of the gospel which we noted in some of the storm data. Just above we saw in Genesis 3 how "the man and his wife" had hidden from God in the garden, withering in shame before the approach of the God-Storm. What we must now consider is how this presents a first and most basic pattern of humanity in the atonement storm matrix. Genesis 1 shows that God's breath/word spoke everything into its own "independent" existence. This reveals that God's acts of creation created "force" as it is "expressed" in all that was created. The human's own creation to become living creatures was an even more intimate creative process, with God's very breath of life "breathed" *into* them and giving them a more self-conscious use of "force" than other breathing creatures were given. Simone Weil wrote that,

> Men have received the power to do good or harm not only to the body but to the souls of their fellows . . . men who are not animated by pure charity are merely wheels in the mechanism of the order of the world.[26]

God's breath given to them was to enable their "pure" charitable stewardship of the breath of God for the sake of the rest of creation.

It is therefore interesting to consider what humankind literally does with its borrowed breath. The most glorious thing humanity could do is *participate* in the goodness and glory of *God's* breath by breathing forth and living in God's Spirit/Breath from which theirs came. The force of their *breath* would then be expended in the service of: God's name being

---

26. Weil, *Waiting for God*, 98.

hallowed; God's kingdom filling the earth; God's creation being tended; God's garden/temple being ex-tended to fill the entire earth with God's breath, will, and glory. And this would be their "daily bread."[27] But the breath of humankind has become fallen and is instead *breathed out* in various manifestations of force as the will to power whether in self-flattery and selfish concern, or by untamable "tongues set on fire by hell," and "breathing threats and murders" against others (James 2:6, Acts 9:1). The *fallen*-breath wind pattern first "appears" in complete *silence* before God with the human pair quietly hiding from God—as if to demonstrate the "loss" of truly *useful breath* and the "gain" of *useless shame*—before the mighty God-Storm's creative and wholly *positive* life-giving wind/breath. Of course, shame has a use for fallen creatures just as pain does, just as the proper use of breath is not strictly utilitarian on God's part but is rather a shared blessedness. But the degradation of our borrowed breath speaks to the height of the fall of humankind.

This first pattern of humanity represents a base-line pattern of fallen human existence. This is in itself a very *pessimistic* picture of the human condition. It is undoubtedly a primary reason that non-Christians who know something of the faith, do not look farther into it. What has been known as "miserable sinner Christianity" is thought by many to be downright harmful, something to be avoided and categorically denied. "We cannot be *that* bad, and with that *negative* thinking it is no wonder so many are not good," is, or *was* the basic reaction, since for the most part our post-Christian society has rejected the very idea of sin, unless it is committed against us of course. But to somewhat moderate this "pessimism," it is true that there is indeed a spectrum of behavior in the continuum of human sinfulness. But the bottom line is that all of humankind needs to be reconciled to God because all share in a "common core" of "sin." On the other hand, we must bear in mind that other "patterns of humanity" are exhibited in the Scriptures, and all people are not as *accomplished* in sin as some are, as we will see in a moment. Therefore, positing a baseline pattern is also *optimistic* by not placing everyone "in the same boat" regarding the *practice* of sin, while nevertheless placing everyone in the same *predicament* of sin and in need of atonement. This also means that some are "closer to the kingdom of God" than others, and

---

27. See Beale, *The Temple*, for a tracing of the "expanding garden/temple motif" throughout the Scriptures; Also see Middleton, *A New Heaven*, 46–49, 163–65, 168–72. For an interesting episode of Jesus modeling an *expending* of breath as a *receiving* of "bread," see John 4:31–34.

gospel evangelists should follow the lead of Jesus who spoke to people in terms of their nearness, to encourage their seeking (Mark 12:34).

We now will consider another pattern of humanity that is integrally related to the storm of atonement. Our consideration of this pattern will demonstrate why a practical theology will follow the Bible's recognition that in the stream of humankind, there are differences between those swimming there.

The Poor and Oppressed Wind-Blown Pattern

This pattern stands in contrast to the baseline pattern and another one that increases from the baseline in an increased practice of evil. The *poor and oppressed wind-blown* pattern by contrast increases in its possibility of implicit or explicit receptivity to God. Human life is "known by bondages to false *lesser-than-God* powers including sin, self, others, society at large, the Devil, and death. While this is true of all, *how* humans live in relation to these bondages can and does differ. One way to demonstrate this is to simply observe "the crowds" in the gospel of Mark portrayed as *poor and oppressed* and *therefore* calling upon Jesus for help, healing, and deliverance from the humanity pattern and "principalities and powers" which oppress them.[28] In other words, the poor and oppressed are that because they are "wind-blown" by the overtly *oppressive* pattern of humanity and a diabolical storm pattern we will see.[29] In the Scriptures, oppression vs. having compassion and care for others, is shown as the litmus test that indicates whether people are following the reconciling gospel. Thus, reconciled Israel was commanded to receive and not oppress the displaced "strangers" of other nations, because they were once so themselves. Jesus's parable of the "good Samaritan," through both the Samaritan and the one he helped, were meant to show the leaders of Israel their failure in this regard.

The crowds of people that NT Scripture depicts as following Jesus are not only present in the time of Christ, but throughout the Scriptures of Israel. The prophets especially express God's concern for the poor and oppressed. In Mark's gospel all are sinners, but some become overt oppressors of others, while others do not. In Luke 4:18–19 Jesus presents

---

28. Myers, *Binding the Strong Man*, 156.

29. There is certainly a form of being "poor and oppressed" by the hands of nature, and salvation from that is part of the overall atonement storm and its euchatastrophe.

himself as come to liberate the *"poor and oppressed wind-blown pattern"* of humanity:

> "The Spirit of the Lord is upon me, because he has anointed me to proclaim good news to the poor. He has sent me to proclaim liberty to the captives and recovering of sight to the blind, to set at liberty those who are oppressed, to proclaim the year of the Lord's favor."

This is an important difference that has often been overlooked when considering the entire scope of humanity "on the ground" in relation to God and others, rather than an abstract humanity "understood" only through theological categories. Certainly, the latter has its use, but in real-life proclamations and promulgations of the gospel and its proper "social justice" concerns, the former must be considered, especially if we "follow the lead" of Jesus, John the Baptist, and other biblical figures who made distinctions in their audiences.[30] Simply put, the poor and oppressed wind-blown pattern of humanity depict the potentially willing recipients of the atonement the storm will bring.

When the gospel stewards fail to distinguish between patterns of humanity, in relation to "receptivity" to the gospel, they fall to pessimism as though none are ready to receive the gospel's liberation not only from oppressive others but also from their own sins. The early proclamations of the gospel in Luke clearly imply the ready welcome of the good news by the poor and oppressed wind-blown people, as shown in Mary's "Magnificat, in 1:46–55, and Zechariah's prophecy in 1:68–78. "The desire of nations" has come, though not the desire of the humanity pattern that God "shakes up," and which we will consider next (Hag 2:7, cf. Heb 12:26–28). For in those same texts of salvation in Luke, they are the "mighty" ones "brought down," and the "rich" ones "sent away empty." For they are the "enemies" the poor and oppressed are "delivered from."

In sum, the poor and oppressed wind-blown pattern, commonly depicted in the Scriptures, shows people existing between the way of faith and the way of force. They are the victims of oppressive force while not yet fully justified in, liberated for, or resolved in following the way of faith. For they are also tempted towards becoming oppressors themselves,

---

30. "It is not that God is prejudiced in some way, still less that the poor are more deserving because of their poverty. Rather, because he is a God of justice, God opposes those who perpetrate injustice, and he sides with the victims of oppression." Chester, *Good News*, 21.

given the opportunity. We will now consider that oppressive pattern, a third pattern of humanity involved in the atonement storm.

The Raging Sea-Wind Pattern

The third humanity storm pattern is the fallen rulers and their allegiant peoples who in relation to God and others are as a raging sea-wind. This pattern has bought into the false "gospel" of the way of force. Psalm 65:5–7 portrays them in relation to God whose saving justice supports the confidence of the oppressed:

> By terrible things in righteousness wilt thou answer us, O God of our salvation; who art the confidence of all the ends of the earth, and of them that are afar off upon the sea: Which by his strength setteth fast the mountains; being girded with power: Which stilleth the noise of the seas, the noise of their waves, and the tumult of the people (KJV).

In the OT the heathen nations are commonly thought of under the symbolism of the noise of the seas and waves, a "tumult" of people in hostility against God, creation, and Israel. The Genesis account of God's wind/breath/spirit "hovering over the face of the formless waters" provides the pictorial backdrop for this Psalm where the tumultuous nations signify a destructive power of de-creation in relation to Israel and other peoples ("the ends of the earth"). As God's breath/word spoke creation from the formless void, so now God's power stills the raging forces bent on de-creation.[31] Isaiah 17:12–14 is similar in its symbolism:

> Woe to the multitude of many people, which make a noise like the noise of the seas; and to the rushing of nations, that make a rushing like the rushing of mighty waters! The nations shall rush like the rushing of many waters: but God shall rebuke them, and they shall flee far off, and shall be chased as the chaff of the mountains before the wind, and like a rolling thing before the whirlwind. And behold at eveningtide trouble; and before the morning he is not. This is the portion of them that spoil us, and the lot of them that rob us. (KJV)

---

31. Middleton sees Genesis 1 as portraying God's "normative" way of *non-combative* creation in contrast to other scriptural passages which *depict* God's creative power as combative, such as in Psalm 65. Middleton, *Created*, 346. See our excursus following the introduction.

Isaiah 8:7–10 portrays the Assyrian threat under dual images of mighty raging floodwaters and a "huge bird of prey" overshadowing "the whole land, ready to pounce" against Israel and Israel's God, in a venture that will prove to be an ironic unintended *self-destruction*:[32]

> Now therefore, behold, the Lord bringeth up upon them the waters of the river, strong and many, even the king of Assyria, and all his glory: and he shall come up over all his channels, and go over all his banks: And he shall pass through Judah; he shall overflow and go over, he shall reach even to the neck; and the stretching out of his wings shall fill the breadth of thy land, O Immanuel. Associate yourselves, O ye people, and ye shall be broken in pieces; and give ear, all ye of far countries: gird yourselves, and ye shall be broken in pieces; gird yourselves, and ye shall be broken in pieces. Take counsel together, and it shall come to nought; speak the word, and it shall not stand: for God is with us. (KJV)

Psalm 2:1–3 is another instance depicting the raging sea-wind pattern:

> Why do the nations rage [*nations noisily assemble*] and the peoples plot in vain? The kings of the earth set themselves, and the rulers take counsel together, against the Lord and against his Anointed, saying, "Let us burst their bonds apart and cast away their cords from us."

Altogether these texts and others like them form the basic backdrop of the faith and experience of Israel expressed in her Scriptures, so that Israel was well acquainted with what we will call the "raging sea-wind pattern" of humanity—or perhaps better—*inhumanity*. This pattern is the sea-wind which rages against God, God's purposes for Israel and other "poor and oppressed wind-blown" nations and even against creation itself.[33]

This pattern of humanity claims a societal advance upwards through the worldly gains of power and glory—but in truth it exhibits a grave societal downturn—even from the "baseline" shown in the first humanity pattern. The text above is from the second Psalm, drawn from the historic

---

32. Motyer, *Isaiah*, 92.

33. Isaiah depicts a hyperbolic yet nonetheless devastating de-creation scene of the entire world in Isaiah 24. Motyer comments on verses 1–3 saying that "It is intrinsic to the doctrine of creation that human beings in sin are the supreme environmental threat." Motyer, *Isaiah*, 197–98.

rule of the house of King David. It portrays subjected Gentile nations restlessly "raging" to throw off the "bonds" of Israel's God mediated in the rule of his "Son," King David. The Psalm, along with others, became endued with messianic hopes the Christians believed to be fulfilled in Christ. They were claimed as scriptural support that the resurrected Jesus was God's anointed one, "the Christ," by the early church. The seemingly "historical" narrative portrayed in this Psalm is thought to be an "ideal" picture of Israel's dynasty based in "the Jerusalem ideology and its assumptions of divine authorization to power by Yahweh," to which the reality never rose.[34] Regardless of the exact historical basis, these Scriptures portray the potentiality and probable eventuality of nations and their rulers in a posture *"agitated like the waves of the sea"* against any mediated rule of Yahweh over them.[35] And because of that posture, the early churches saw the Psalm as fulfilled by the raging sea-wind's posture against Jesus and them, in relation to the storm we have been considering. The raging sea-wind of the Psalm was declared by the apostles Peter and John to have been active in recent history:

> When they were released, they went to their friends and reported what the chief priests and the elders had said to them. And when they heard it, they lifted their voices together to God and said, "Sovereign Lord, who made the heaven and the earth and the sea and everything in them, who through the mouth of our father David, your servant, [or child] said by the Holy Spirit, "'Why did the Gentiles rage, and the peoples plot in vain? The kings of the earth set themselves, and the rulers were gathered together, against the Lord and against his Anointed'[or Christ]—for truly in this city there were gathered together against your holy servant Jesus, whom you anointed, both Herod and Pontius Pilate, along with the Gentiles and the peoples of Israel, to do whatever your hand and your plan had predestined to take place (Acts 4:23–28).

In the Gospel of Mark, the crowds were often used as a foil against which to show the rulers raging and plotting against Jesus from the beginning. Several authors have presented discussions of the "Authorities" depicted in Mark under the following headings:

> Without true authority from God; No love for God or neighbor; Blind and deaf; Willful blindness; The authorities save

---

34. Wilson, *Psalms*, loc. 2327. See also VanGemeren, *Psalms*, 64–67.
35. VanGemeren, *Psalms*, 66–67.

themselves; Fear is at the root of their actions; The authorities lord over people.³⁶

With such "qualifications" they oppressed, manipulated, and incited the crowd, turning those who had welcomed Jesus into a mob demanding his crucifixion.

This oppressive pattern was a major target of the OT prophets who were therefore also oppressed, persecuted, and killed by them. Matthew 23 records Jesus's prophetic "Jeremiad" against them, just before his entrance to Jerusalem and his final showdown with that particular raging sea-wind. His Jeremiad reveals these ruler's social and economic oppressions of the poor that "enraged" Jesus, and further enraged them against him to result in their plotting his execution.

Before considering a fourth humanity pattern, we need to consider a not-so human one secretly at work inspiring the ages-long conflict of humanity just mentioned by tempting the raging sea-wind patterns by the allure of the will to power.

The Leviathan Sea-Monster Pattern

Beneath the raging sea-wind and the wind-blown crowds of humanity lies in wait the engulfing jaws of Leviathan, the sea monster of the deep abyss, associated with the Devil. In our illustrative purposes for this "weather pattern" we are following the lead of Revelation 12:17—13:1 where the dragon (Satan) "standing on the sand of the sea" (before the raging sea-wind pattern) summons a Leviathan "beast" from its deep to fulfill his earthly purposes against God's "anointed" and God's "anointed" people. This shows that the Devil inspires human principalities, the rulers and governments meant to be earthly servants of God and the common good, to become the "raging sea-wind pattern," for his purposes of thwarting God.³⁷ We had just seen the result of Satan's efforts above where Acts 4:27 says

---

36. Roades, *Mark as Story*, 117–23.

37. Two classic texts, alternatively showing the "normal" relative "office" of a principality and power and the "abnormal" absolutizing (and therefore) fallen one, are respectively Rom 13:1–7 and Rev 13:1–10. Of the latter text, Hanns Lilje, writing while imprisoned by the Nazis during WW II says "it means the imperial world power as a perverted political institution, the cunning ruthless greed of the empire, which absorbs everything it meets. The 'perversion' consists in the fact that the imperial power adorns itself with a religious halo, and in so doing claims an absoluteness to which it

> . . . in this city there were gathered together against your holy servant Jesus, whom you anointed, both Herod and Pontius Pilate, along with the Gentiles and the peoples of Israel, to do whatever your hand and your plan had predestined to take place.

The Devil had a huge stake in attempting to overcome God's "holy servant Jesus," and needed to be overcome for God to deliver oppressed humanity and restore creation. We saw in our data collecting step the *violently non-violent* purpose and method of Christ to overcoming the Devil through *his own* death, "*. . . that through death he might destroy the one who has the power of death, that is, the devil, and deliver all those who through fear of death were subject to lifelong slavery.*"[38] Again, to engage in a war against God and his anointed is to engage in self-destruction. We will see more regarding God's *abnormal* manner of conquering as we consider the death of Christ and how *by his death,* he defeated the Devil and the raging sea-wind he instigates. This leads us to the necessity of considering a fourth humanity storm pattern.

The Jonah Cast-Into-the-Storm Pattern

A fourth humanity storm pattern comes forth from the dark mystery hidden from the foundation of the world in the secret wisdom of God. Its OT sign was the prodigal prophet "Jonah" thrown into the raging storm-whipped sea of force, swallowed whole and descending into Leviathan's Sheol-like belly, only to be ejected and still alive three days later. A "second Jonah" followed the pattern of the first, but actually died, was then resurrected to life. But viewed from God's plan from eternity, the OT prophet, the *historically first* Jonah *followed* the second Jonah. For this second Jonah was the *primal Jonah,* dying and "being swallowed by death." He couldn't be held by that power and on the third day was spat out upon dry land *resurrected.* He faithfully lived as God's *Israel servant* and *died—cursed—*on the cross as God's *blind servant* (Isa 42:19).

In light of who Jesus claimed to be, his death made him the ultimate victim of force, so that his executors tauntingly placed the placard on his cross signifying that this crucified one was the "king of the Jews" (Luke 23:38). But this *Jonah,* cast-into-the-sea, was *the holy servant of God*

---

has no right." Lilje, *Last Book,* 189.

38. See Hebrews 2:15. This also touches on the subject of the excursus following the introduction.

who was faithful to the uttermost. In his death he *became* the prodigal prophet/nation of Israel which held the gospel in the dock. Thus, Jesus in his death bore the covenantal curses *servant Israel* deserved. God raised him as faithful *servant Israel,* as the new locus of all humankind, both Jew *and* Gentile, the *one* new humanity that Israel was meant to be *midwife* for. We will need to fill in more detail of this dark mystery, to see how God worked *atonement* in this perfect storm. For now, we begin with a brief recap with some additional new insights, of the six storm patterns that came together in that perfect storm of atonement.

The Perfect Storm of Atonement

1. *The God-Storm pattern,* whose *violent* love subverts the *violence* of force: *planned* the perfect storm of atonement from before the beginning; *entered* into it through the incarnate Son; and *orchestrated* all things together for the ultimate *good* of the reconciliation of God and humanity, the news of which is the gospel.

2. *The fallen-breath wind pattern* of humanity, that was created through the breath/wind of God but *failed to live* by a faith relation to God and so became the *fallen-breath* of God. It descended into the alienation of sin and death, which permeated every relation of life: the relations to God, self, the neighbor, society at large, and the "natural" creation itself.

3. *The poor and oppressed wind-blown pattern* of humanity exemplifies the portion of humanity that to some extent recognizes and mourns its own fallenness and that of the powers that oppress it. For the most part it silently cries, for lack of visible and viable hope of liberation from its oppressors both human and demonic. This pattern is in this sense ready and waiting for the gospel of reconciliation which will "set the world to rights."[39] On the other hand, this pattern, given opportunity, may easily be tempted to rage against its oppressors, or to itself rage as oppressors, to follow the ways of force and "the will to power."

4. *The raging sea-wind pattern* of humanity progresses further than the fallen-breath baseline pattern in its alienation and hostility to God

---

39. A seemingly favorite term of theologian N. T. Wright that seems to appear regularly in his talks written or otherwise.

and others, and in its false gospel of the will to power hopes to *win* a Hobbesian "war of every man against every man." It becomes a useful tool for the Devil's own raging war against God and humanity. Because of God's enemy-love this pattern is also reconciled to God in Christ along with the poor and oppressed wind-blown pattern, but apart from accepting that reconciliation, remains on a collision course with the various forms of self-destruction.

5. *The Leviathan sea-monster pattern* of the Devil harnesses the demonic forces and demonized hostiles of humanity in its war against God and God's agents. It seeks to deceive, oppress, and destroy humanity, even those who participate in *the raging sea-wind pattern*. Its destruction is achieved through engulfing everything it can into its way of force and the will to power. It also, is inherently self-destructive.

6. *The Jonah cast-into-the-storm pattern* of Jesus has merely been introduced and will now be developed further.

The key to understanding this pattern is that Jesus himself pointed to the historic prophet Jonah as in a some sense the "only sign given" to that generation of Israel and the Roman Empire. The historical "recipients" of that sign signify for Paul the "old categories" of humanity as either, "Jews and Greeks"—the religious and the philosophers—so that by implication Jonah is the only sign given to "old" humanity at large, humanity of all times and places. Jesus announced the sign to answer the request for a sign.

> Then some of the scribes and Pharisees answered him, saying, "Teacher, we wish to see a sign from you." But he answered them, "An evil and adulterous generation seeks for a sign, but no sign will be given to it except the sign of the prophet Jonah. For just as Jonah was three days and three nights in the belly of the great fish, so will the Son of Man be three days and three nights in the heart of the earth (Matt 16:38–40).

Matthew shows the conflict between Jesus and the *raging sea-wind* pattern that from the beginning opposed Jesus and only grew in their opposition. That is why, in light of the multitude of *rejected* signs previously given by Jesus to that generation, the sign of Jonah became *the definitive sign* and thus was and remains the *only* sign given. A sign they wanted, and so a sign to end all signs they were given.

Of course, as we have seen this was always God's plan (Matt 11:25–30). For the sign of Jonah pictured the shape the gospel must take in the death and resurrection of Christ. To further elaborate on this, we will need to show more precisely how Jesus fulfills the *Jonah cast-into-the-storm pattern*. So naturally we must begin to consider the narrative of Jonah's sign/mission. (*I recommend that the reader pause at this point to read the entire short book of Jonah.*)

We will now consider more fully how the *prodigal* Jonah story is paradigmatic of the *faithful* Jesus story. Jonah, being one of Yahweh's Israelite prophets, was meant to be an agent of God's redemptive mission for humanity as was discussed in Chapter 1. Jonah's disobedience to God's calling reveals the basic historical pattern of Israel as in the end failing to fulfill the mission for which God had originally "created" Israel. For Israel was to be blessed of God, while also becoming the means of God's blessing of all nations. This was the purview of the covenant God made with Abraham as recorded in Genesis 12:3, that through Abraham all the families of the earth would be blessed. Abraham's grandson Jacob famously "wrestled with God" and for that grueling match under the dark of night was given the name "Israel" which means "*He strives with God*" (Genesis 32:28). Thus, Abraham's descendants *became Israel,* wrestling with God and gaining admittance to the dark and difficult mission of God for the nations.

But for the most part, Israel's subsequent history records her failure to be that *means* whereby God's blessing would flow to the world. This all provides the background for Jonah to "signify" the prodigality of Israel regarding God's universal "gospel" purposes for her. The book of the prophet Isaiah includes a series of oracles known as the "servant songs" that depict Israel as the servant of God who fulfills God's purposes. In one of those oracles God laments the prodigality of his servant and juxtaposes prophetic portraits of a *faithful* servant with those of a *blind and deaf* servant, in Isaiah 42:1–7; 18–25. (*I recommend pausing at this point to read those passages.*)

The first picture shows God's *faithful* servant, given as a covenant for the people and light for the nations, pictured as blind and deaf prisoners in need of deliverance, just as Israel herself had been delivered from captivity in the Exodus from Egypt. The second picture shows God's *blind and deaf servant*, in captivity again, signifying being under God's judgment for prodigality toward covenantal faithfulness for delivering others. One might summarize Israel's fall as a fall from the way of faith to the way of the will to power, a fall that as far as being a means for "gospel" purposes was a fall from Israel's covenantal reason for existing.

Isaiah's pictorial history of the positive mission and prodigal failure of God's Israel gives us the necessary "backstory" to revisit Jonah. In Jonah's story we see how he broadly patterns Israel's story. He is called to participate in Israel's servant mission to the nations. He flees from God's gospel mission on a seafaring ship away from the "mission field." Jonah can well be considered as "blind and deaf" in regard to the mission—shown by his being "asleep" in relation to it. Therefore, Jonah comes under God's judgment/storm at sea while he slept—*under* the deck in a heathen vessel—*under* the heathen sea in his prodigality from the election of Israel to be *Israel*. It is as if Jonah/Israel has become submerged again in heathendom, reverting to a pre-Abrahamic status, seemingly even fallen below the "fear of God" that was evident in the heathen crew. We will consider Jonah's motivations more as we proceed. In the meantime, we next see the mariners casting lots and determining that Jonah is the cosmic catalyst of indigestion inflaming the storm. Jonah simply affirms this and says that sacrificing him to the storm will calm the sea. After valiantly trying to avoid that terrible measure without success, and left with no other way to survive, the mariners throw Jonah into the sea to *propitiate* its "god" through Jonah's *certain* death. In a drastic turn of events, undoubtedly *hidden* in the depths and *unknown* to the sailors, God mercifully "appointed" a great fish to swallow Jonah, and thus save him, and then *vomit* him alive from the depths of the fish onto the land of the living, after three days and nights in the Sheol-like "grave" of its stomach.

At this point we need to explicitly draw together the pattern of Jonah and Jesus, to see the "the sign of Jonah" that prefigured *Jesus* being cast into God's "perfect storm of atonement." I will try to do this by producing a chart picturing the multifaceted sign of the prophet Jonah, tracing the sign chronologically as much as is possible in regard to the story of Jonah and the life, death, resurrection and post-resurrection ministry of Jesus. I don't claim that this is an exhaustive list by any means and am sure to have missed some parallels. Some of the signs are summaries that are not easily connected chronologically so they are merely plugged in where they seemed to fit. These items will not all be considered in detail afterwards although some of them will be. Many of them "correspond with Jonah" while others exhibit "contrast to Jonah." In some instances, both comparisons are evident. These comparisons are presented here to demonstrate the scope of correlation in this multivalent sign, and also to begin to reveal the extent of *sig*nificance which exhibits the cohesion of the "obedient" way of faith to the "dynamic" way of God—just as a tree's fruit is intimately connected to the root from which it organically grows.

Table 1: The Sign of the Prophet Jonah

Jonah	Jesus
Was firstly human, the image of God	Was fully human, the full image of God
Was God's chosen agent to reach the nations	Was God's chosen agent to reach the nations
Flees from that election in God's sight	Appears to flee from that election in Israel's sight
Is an apostate to God's gospel	In the estimation of Israel was an apostate
Fails his election by being faithful to Israel	Fulfills his election, contrary to Israel's opinion
Followed the way of force	Followed the way of faith
God sent a raging sea-wind storm of nature	God sent a "raging sea-wind" storm of humans
Was the voluntary propitiation to calm the storm	Was the voluntary propitiation to calm the storm
Empties himself of the will to power for "Israel's will to power" and became the victim of force	Empties himself of the will to power for "Israel's faith" and became the victim of force
Was in Israelite conflict with Pagan Assyria	Was in conflict with "Pagan" Israel and Pagan Rome
Was willing to die for tribalism	Died to overcome tribalism
Appeared to die because of his election	Actually died because of his election

Jonah	Jesus
Was of the poor and oppressed wind-blown pattern of humanity	Was of the poor and oppressed wind-blown pattern of humanity
Descended into "the grave of Sheol"	Descended into "the grave of Sheol"
Was swallowed by "Leviathan" (see Isa 27:1, and Ellison, *Jonah*, 374–75; Parry, *Biblical Cosmos*, 68–70)	Was swallowed by the Dragon (see Rev 12:4, and Beale, *Revelation*, 637)
Was vomited from the belly of "death"	Death could not hold him down (Acts 2:24)
Was "resurrected" to the land to proclaim the gospel	Was resurrected to the world to proclaim the gospel
Was sinful and saved by God while unfaithful	Was sinless and saved by God for being faithful
Was saved from the "Sheol" of Leviathan	Was saved from the "Sheol" of the Dragon/Devil (Heb 2:14)
"Leviathan" was the means of Jonah's and Nineveh's salvation	The Devil contributed to the salvation of the world
Feared and resisted the salvation of *a* nation	Loved and fulfilled the salvation of *all* nations
Was unconcerned for the stewardship of cattle and creation (see Jonah 4:5–11)	Was concerned with the restoration of the stewardship of creation
Remained "unconverted" after his "resurrection"	Israel remains largely unconverted after Christ's resurrection (see Matt 24:39; Rom 11:25–26)
God orchestrated Jonah's mission of salvation	God orchestrated "the perfect storm" of atonement

Thus, in this multifaceted sign of the prophet Jonah we see prefigured the incarnate person and atoning work of Christ, in whom "*God was reconciling the world to himself.*" This complex sign resists simple summation. Perhaps the best summation was given by Paul—that "Christ died for our sins, according to the Scriptures." We will, however, try to add a few summary thoughts pertaining to how this perfect storm of atonement related in specific definite results for each of our six "storm patterns."[40] There is of course "overlap" of results in the patterns, but the focus will be on results that specifically relate to their particular character.

1. *The God-Storm pattern* orchestrated everything to become "the perfect storm" of atonement "by working all things together for good" (Rom 8:28). This orchestration was not merely an *ad hoc* reaction to the various other patterns but was God's plan from the foundation of the world (1 Pet 1:19–20; Rev 13:8; Eph 1:4).

2. *The fallen-breath wind pattern* was reconciled by God because Jesus was fully human and therefore was able to fully pay the penalty for failing to be the image of God and to fully live and fulfill the image God intended and thereby restored it for all humanity. Therefore, by faith we can now participate in the good use of our *given breath* and *creative force* in the task of expanding the garden-temple of God to fill the entire earth for the good of all humanity and creation itself.

3. *The poor and oppressed wind-blown pattern was* reconciled in the atonement of all humanity. This reconciliation includes their liberation from the oppressive human and demonic patterns which at times successfully tempted them to collusion against Christ and their very salvation. Therefore, their reconciliation and salvation need to be worked out historically as the kingdom of God grows in the world, with God's will being done on "earth as it is in heaven" (Matt 4:10). This liberation is part of the reason for the urgency of the call of evangelism so that the nations are discipled in the peaceful and universally beneficial ways of the gospel. Their liberation also promises to ultimately free them from the bondage that all of creation groans under, along with the liberation of nature itself (Rom 8:18–25).

4. The *raging sea-wind pattern* was the primary active human agent in the evil use of force in the perfect storm. But God's enemy-love in Christ turned their evil but ignorant intent in the execution of God's anointed Christ into the good of at-one-ment, including their own (Luke 23:34). The death of Jesus was also effectually the decisive

---

40. These are merely summary thoughts, drawing on some of the scriptural data we saw earlier and adding some new data, since each "pattern" could be developed and discussed much more thoroughly.

battle in God's war on demonic oppression and death itself, forever subverting and sublating them as means of power over the various patterns of humanity.

5. *The Leviathan sea-monster pattern* was the behind-the-scenes evil conspirator and deceitful conductor of the symphonic atonement storm—but God proved to be the more ultimate good composer and true conductor who orchestrated even the Devil's treason against God, and his anointed Christ, and humanity at large, into the perfect storm of atonement for humankind. For through the atoning death and victorious resurrection of Jesus, God achieved the reconciliation of the entire cosmos in Christ. This victory of God over death and sin in principle defeated the one who held the power of death—the Devil—since Christ died for all and will therefore raise all humanity in the resurrection of the just and the unjust.

6. *The Jonah cast-into-the-storm pattern* was of course Jesus, "the man attested by God" to be the active and passive agent of God's reconciliation of the world through his own relinquishment of the ways of force and the will to power. The prophet Jonah was and remains "the only sign given" of this perfect storm of atonement. Otherwise, it just looks like perfect "evil" in a storm that was only destructive. This "sign" had evidentiary significance to Israel, who expected their anointed one, but what sort of a sign was it? We need to look a bit closer.

> Then some of the scribes and Pharisees answered him, saying, "Teacher, we wish to see a sign from you." But he answered them, "An evil and adulterous generation seeks for a sign, but no sign will be given to it except the sign of the prophet Jonah. For just as Jonah was three days and three nights in the belly of the great fish, so will the Son of Man be three days and three nights in the heart of the earth (Matthew 12: 38–40).

It seems fairly plain now, this side of the resurrection and the subsequent prominent acceptance of Jesus as the Savior of Israel and the world, that the summary of the sign of Jonah was of "death" and "resurrection." This "sign" then had no immediate "significance" to them, and only could have any *after* the death and resurrection of Jesus. Those were soon coming, and the ones requesting the sign would carry out the first part. But the very idea that Israel's God-Anointed Messiah would die was, as we saw in Chapter 1, an offense to them. But the Resurrection of Jesus ought to have been alarming enough to provoke a "second look." Of course, many took that second look, believed and followed the risen Christ.

But what is there that might prevent that? The answer is the deeper aspect of offense as an affront to one's independence. The offense of "the only sign given" is that it is not merely an offense to the reason, but an offense to the manner of life. The gospel is a strange and pungent medicine provided by God to cure the ills of humanity that began because of the desire for independence that was buttressed by the "reason" of finite creatures, mere babes in a nursery, so to speak. Humanity has always, and to this day still desires "to come of age" apart from God.[41]

The sign of the prophet Jonah is merely the discovery that one has encountered what theologian Karl Barth called the "Strange New World within the Bible"—a world completely foreign to us who are fallen from God's way of faith.[42] An interesting text is from the book of Nahum, a prophetic diatribe of the "good" God himself against the brutal Assyrian empire and it's capital city Nineveh—"the City of Blood." Nahum describes God as completely overcoming his enemies by pursuing them "into darkness."

> The Lord is good, a stronghold in the day of trouble; he knows those who take refuge in him. But with an overflowing flood he will make a complete end of the adversaries, and will pursue his enemies into darkness.[43]

This pictures the descent of Jonah/Christ into all the various dark and deathly facets of the "storm" and "belly of the beast" that we have considered, only to in that place overcome the powers of sin, death, and the Devil plaguing all of creation. C. S. Lewis poignantly described this in his address called "The Grand Miracle" saying,

> Or else one has the picture of a diver, stripping off garment after garment, making himself naked, then flashing for a moment in

---

41. Bonhoeffer seems to express the irony of the prodigal son parable, saying of his "coming of age" that, "The human being is thrown back on his own resources. He has learned to cope with everything except himself." Bonhoeffer, *Letters and Papers*, 500., cf. 425–31.

42. Peterson, *Eat This Book*, 6.

43. Nah 1:7–8. Note that the Assyrians were God's enemy *because* they were the enemy of "all humanity" so that we also read "for upon whom has not come your unceasing evil" (Nah 3:19). Nahum shows that God's judgement of the enemies of humanity is part of the "good news" that is seen coming "upon the mountains" (1:15).

the air, and then down through the green and warm and sunlit water into the pitch black, cold, freezing water, down into the mud and slime, then up again, his lungs almost bursting, back again to the green and warm and sunlit water, and then at last out into the sunshine, holding in his hand the dripping thing he went down to get. This thing is human nature; but associated with it, all nature, the new universe.[44]

It is hoped that the limited encounter with that strange world of the Bible we have here pursued with its perfect storm of atonement and the sign of the prophet Jonah have helped to convey the magnitude of God's pursuit into darkness of all of his enemies—including each of us—to fulfill the "multi-variegated wisdom of God" in the complex and mysterious process of reconciliation (Eph 3:10).[45] The final step is to look for what makes this gospel storm and its sign "good news"—finding the rehabilitation that we set out to find at the start of the chapter.

"The Perfect Sign"—Finding the Goodness in the Storm

The goodness of the storm is simply in the fact that God turned what seemed only bad into something only good. Allen writes,

> The crucifixion of Jesus was not meant to be a sacrifice as far as human beings were concerned. It was a rejection. God's love turned it into a sacrifice; God's love made it something holy . . . God lets us see the effects of our malice and indifference by letting us injure not only others and ourselves, but also himself. God, the maker of heaven and earth, allows us to reject him and, to win our hearts, shows us only his love. This love is what the crucifixion reveals and turns it from being our rejection only and into a sacrifice, a holy action.[46]

It is completely accurate to say that the goodness found in the storm is in the fact that coming out of it—as Jonah came forth from the destroying storm and its Sheol-fish on dry land—was Jesus rose from the grave in a garden as the earth's new gardener/steward to begin the new creation, as Lewis hinted at toward the end of the excerpt above.[47] It would

---

44. Lewis, *God in the Dock*, 82.
45. Ephesians 3:10; See Morris, *Expository Reflections*, 95–96.
46. Allen, *Steps Along the Way*, 42,
47. That he was mistaken as the gardener may allude to Christ as the first human

be wonderful if this new creation in the cross-resurrection events was now as self-evident as it one day will be. But the dynamic engine of reconciliation and new creation lies hidden from human eyes beneath the surface of this storm complex, just as *the good* of Jonah's being swallowed and delivered by the great fish from the deep was hidden from the eyes of the sailors. We must remember that we are dealing with *signs* which have been given to us, and the fact that signs are *necessary* points to the character of human life in agonistic relation to God. And this agonistic character generally resists God's signs apart from the mediation of suffering. Yet we ironically wonder why there is suffering and think it precludes there being a good God or a gospel. Thus "God's megaphone to rouse a deaf world" needs to sound, as Lewis declared.[48] Because, suffering *can* help us to not settle for an unreconciled life.

Part of the hiddenness and offensiveness of the gospel is certainly due to the violence of the "perfect storm" which on the face of it presents an obstacle to finding the possibility of goodness accomplished in and through such means. The Southern Catholic fiction writer Flannery O'Connor has extensively explored the relation of violence to grace, and titled her second novel "The Violent Bear it Away."[49] In the majority of her writings some form of violence is counterintuitively shown to be revelatory through the amplification of human character, and when tied to God's redemptive "methods" can become a vehicle of grace, or "a severe mercy" as Sheldon Vanauken put it.[50] So also the violence that "intrudes death into the Godhead," in the Father's sorrowful abandonment of the Son to the suffering unto death, became the "means of grace" for the

---

restored to the proper stewardship of the earth-garden in the dawn of the first day of the new creation. See John 20:1, 11–16. Also see Zahnd, "Mistaken as the Gardener."

48. Lewis, *Problem of Pain*, 83.

49. "From the days of John the Baptist until now the kingdom of heaven has suffered violence, and the violent take it by force." Matt 11:12. *Douay-Rheims 1899 American Edition*. Bruner writes of O'Connor's method: "By subverting conventional notions of beauty, goodness and truth, O'Connor is not extolling their opposite—ugliness, evil, and dissemblance. It isn't as if what is ugly is actually beautiful, or what is true suddenly appears as a lie, or what is evil is actually divine goodness. She is instead suggesting, by creative implication through her fiction, that our conventional categories be baptized, as it were, to include their divine extensions, so that what is beautiful is also sometimes terrible, and what is true is also sometimes foolish, and what is good is also sometimes violent." Bruner, *A Subversive Gospel*, 2.

50. Vanauken, *A Severe Mercy*.

redemption of all of humanity.[51] The cross of Christ was in one sense, exclusive to him—in atoning for all of humanity. But in another sense "the cross" lies at the core of all human life and is thus inclusive for all—living "in territory held largely by the devil" as Flannery O'Connor also wrote.[52] Thus as the kingdom of God advances into that territory, "violent actions might be the only means possible to redemption" as "heaven can be taken through violence, as though won in some kind of war for the soul" so that the redeemed invariably must bear their own cross and participate in some manner in Christ's own suffering of violence.[53]

What is perhaps most interesting is to consider that God and Christ together "embraced" violence, by their suffering the violence of the perfect storm. In a sense, it was the violent God taking the kingdom of God by force, such that the non-violent God pursued violence against God's self, to subvert violence. As Michel Henry wrote, "without doubt, he had no other recourse than to proceed forcefully," to subvert the will to power.[54] Indeed, "the violent bear it away."

The means of violence used toward God's good ends of atonement present an immediate obstacle, but the Scriptures plainly claim that "gospel" was the result. To try to bring this into clearer focus we will conclude this chapter by considering a final storm pattern of atonement which has previously been mentioned as to its fact, but not explicitly named as a pattern, or emphasized as it now needs to be. It is perhaps interesting, although only the accident of our organization of biblical material, that this final pattern is the seventh pattern, and we probably all have heard that according to the seventh day pattern of God's work, "God rested from all his work that he had done in creation" (Gen 2:3).

---

51 See Lewis, *Between Cross & Resurrection*, 224–25.

52. Cited in Kirk, *Critical Companion*, 135.

53. Kirk, *Critical Companion*, 135. Ralph Wood writes that "Grace does not complete and perfect nature in a smooth and seamless way, as Aquinas is sometimes wrongly interpreted; the image of God in man must be wrenched from its unnatural thralldom to false lords in both the church and the world. Vocation, the summons to live out the privileges and requirements of the Christian faith, is the point of this most radical wrenching." Wood, *Flannery O'Connor*, 219.

54. Henry, *Words of Christ*, 123.

The Calm After the Storm Pattern

This pattern is named from the immediate consequence of Jonah being tossed overboard in the storm at sea.

> So they picked up Jonah and hurled him into the sea, and the sea ceased from its raging (Jonah 1:15).

The calming of the storm portrays the *goodness* that came of the storm. Previously, to the mariners in the storm, to Jonah in the great fish, and to Jesus on the cross in his ultimate cry of derelicition, all had seemed lost (Mark 15:34). The calm for the sailors pictures a restored creation, saved from the threat of primordial chaos. But beneath the calm Jonah was descending deeper into the formless void of Sheol's dark waters seemingly shut off from the hope of rising again to the promised land. But Jonah says, "I called out to the Lord, out of my distress . . . out of the belly of Sheol I cried, and you heard my voice" (Jonah 2:2). The Leviathan sea-monster of *Sheol* could not hold its prey in death, and Jonah was "spat" forth on dry land. So also, Jesus, "cursed by God" on the cross prayed, "Father, into your hands I commit my spirit! And having said this he breathed his last" (Luke 23:46). But in Acts 2:24–28, Peter quoting Psalm 16:8–11 narrates that,

> God raised him up, loosing the pangs of death, because it was not possible for him to be held by it. For David says concerning him, "I saw the Lord always before me, for he is at my right hand that I may not be shaken; therefore my heart was glad, and my tongue rejoiced; my flesh also will dwell in hope. For you will not abandon my soul to Hades, or let your Holy One see corruption. You have made known to me the paths of life; you will make me full of gladness with your presence."

The parallels are undeniable, the "sign of the prophet Jonah" *was* "the only sign given" of the reality and goodness of Jesus as *the Christ*. On the face of it this new reality of God would seem to be undeniably *good*, since according to Christ and his eyewitnesses his "death and resurrection" were for all humanity and signify the beginning of a new creation. Who could deny that the "victorious" calm after a violent storm that seemed to threaten every aspect of life in the "hour, and the power of darkness" is good (Luke 22:52–53). For Jesus, *this primal Jonah*, his existence seemingly nullified, engulfed whole into the dark abyss of Sheol by the jaws of the murderous Leviathan, became the expulsive pill that enacted the exodus of all and effectually destroyed the ravenous consumer that could not hold Christ and ransomed humanity in its diabolical belly.[55] Christ's cry of dereliction—"my God, my God, why have you forsaken me?"—became a war cry of victory because he *"tasted death"* for all to lead his children to glory (Hebrews 2:9–14). *This* death calmed *the storm* that God orchestrated *to be perfect* for achieving the *"at-one-ment"* that God had originally intended for humankind and the world. For Christ is the restored image of God, the preeminent firstborn of the restored gardeners of the new Eden. Thus, from the perfect storm that brought death to Christ, God worked the calm after the storm, the new life from the dead, Tolkien's blessed *euchatastrophe*, even now spreading to fill the entire cosmos.[56] Following are some new creation realities that portray the significance and goodness of the gospel:

- The rescue from the false gospel of the way of force in the will to power.
- The restoration of the image/breath of God as stewards of God's creation.
- The reconciliation of God and humans, humans and humans, and humans and creation.
- The repair of humanity broken in relations to self, others, the world, and God.
- The redemption of humanity from bondage to fallen principalities and powers.
- The reception of the very breath of God to fulfill human be-ing, receiving Spirit in flesh.
- The reconfiguration of creation itself wherein now "all things are become new."
- The recalibration of humanity in relation to force to achieve "timshel."[57]

---

55. I see Jesus as the primal Jonah because Jesus was the Lamb foreknown before the foundation of the world, so that in God's plan, Jonah *follows* the pattern of Jesus. See 1 Peter 1:19–20. (See Davids, *First Epistle of Peter*, 73–75.)

56. C. S. Lewis, said "Thus the filth that our poor, muddled, sincere, resentful enemies fling at the Holy One, either does not stick, or, sticking, turns to glory." Lewis, *God in the Dock*, 32.

57. *Timshel*—"Thou mayest rule over it" as was discussed in the introduction.

To summarize we might simply ask if the things we have just listed as aspects of the goodness of the gospel were actually true, could any reasonable person think they weren't good? If humankind did what it was created to do, living in a universally harmonious and beneficial way before and in relation to God, reconciled with all others, the earth and all its fellow creatures, and even with oneself, who would rightly cry foul? Paul and a Psalmist summarize what could be the only response to these results of the gospel:

> Oh, the depth of the riches and wisdom and knowledge of God! How unsearchable are his judgments and how inscrutable his ways! (Rom 11:33). But, as it is written, "What no eye has seen, nor ear heard, nor the heart of man imagined, what God has prepared for those who love him" (1 Cor 2:9; Ps 94:1).

Of course, we don't see those things lived before us. For we have in a sense only glimpsed God's reconciliation of the books, the rehabilitation of the death of Christ the NT presents. So, looking at the world today, "the perfect storm" still seems to be raging. Is it possible that the rehabilitation of evangelism and the evangelizers will help further rehabilitate the gospel of Jesus Christ? Maybe, because the rehabilitation of the gospel we have seen in this chapter is God's *word* on the reconciliation. But, *according* to God's word, more is needed than even God's word. For Jesus himself said that the victory that would be accomplished by his "being lifted up" in death to draw all people to him, *that very way* would need to be *shared in* by his followers. That manner of life would need to be *lived out* by them to *complete* the witness to the world as Jesus declared:

> Now is the judgment of this world; now will the ruler of this world be cast out. And I, when I am lifted up from the earth, will draw all people to myself." He said this to show by what kind of death he was going to die . . . If the world hates you, know that it has hated me first . . . As you sent me into the world, so I have sent them into the world. And for their sake I consecrate myself, that they also may be sanctified in truth. "I do not ask for these only, but also for those who will believe in me through their word, that they may all be one, just as you, Father, are in me, and I in you, that they also may be in us, so that the world may believe that you have sent me (John 12:31–32; 15:18; 17:18–21).

We have hopefully seen the significance of "the sign of the prophet Jonah" as "rehabilitated" by the Word of God. But according to Jesus we must also see the sign of Jonah as rehabilitated in regard to the prophet Jonah. In short, Jonah, now signified by the Church, needs to be rehabilitated, because he is who the world sees. Jonah's rehabilitation is dependent on his dual calling: the fact and quality of his bringing the gospel where it is to be proclaimed, and the fact and quality of Jonah's gospel-shaped life. The gospel way of faith must be faithfully declared by, and seen in, the followers of Jesus. They must essentially enflesh the gospel's words, for the gospel of Christ was not mere words, for *the word become flesh* and dwelt among us (John 1:14). It seems that perhaps God's mercy and grace has indeed stooped to our level to provide us the way of sight we desire. But will God's Jonahs allow themselves to be that sight?

Of course, *this* way of sight cannot be provided in the abstract, in a book such as this or any book at all. Therefore, the ultimate rehabilitation of the gospel is the responsibility of the stewards to live the gospel in their flesh, touching the unclean lepers and healing the sick, that "the life may be seen with our eyes, looked upon and touched with our hands, the life, made manifest" (1 John 1:1–2, very loosely paraphrased). But the patterns of humanity we have seen in this chapter are *our* patterns, so that at first, we see only a troublesome Jonah, or a too radical Jesus, either cast overboard or lifted from the earth. And so, they remain, and again become the only sign given to this generation of the way of faith that overcomes the way of force in the will to power.

3

Evangelism

The Stewardship of the Gospel

> Arise, go to Nineveh, that great city, and call out
> against it the message that I tell you.
>
> —JONAH 3:2

IN THE PREVIOUS CHAPTER we began to "rehabilitate" the gospel of Christ that in the words of Paul appears to be "foolishness" under the "normal" criterion of humankind by seeking to uncover its hidden goodness. We now turn to our second main topic, evangelism which is also "in the dock" with the gospel. Our overall aim is to try to similarly rehabilitate the evangelism of God's Jonahs as we sought to do for the gospel in the sign of Jonah.

What is Evangelism?

We begin by asking what evangelism is. Biblically speaking the answer is very simple. This is because the gospel means "good news" and news, especially if it is good, deserves to be spread wherever it would matter. Since the gospel is supposed to be good news about God bringing about the reconciliation of the entire world in Christ, then it naturally follows that such news ought to be published to the whole world for as long as the present form of the world lasts. And this simple definition exactly portrays the "logic" of evangelism that is found in the gospels:

> And Jesus came and said to them, "All authority in heaven and on earth has been given to me. Go therefore and make disciples of all nations, baptizing them in the name of the Father and of the Son and of the Holy Spirit, teaching them to observe all that I have commanded you. And behold, I am with you always, to the end of the age" (Matthew 28:18–20).

That definition will make many wonder about the sociopolitical world(s) that the gospel is therefore to be proclaimed in. Evangelism is not political in the sense in which most people understand politics, but it is *overtly* political in a broader sense of the term. The difference is that politics is commonly understood to be one sphere of human life lived in relation to others. But politics derives from the word "polis"—*city*—and indicates the totality of the common life-together of a people. This means that since evangelism is related to the formation of a new sort of community of people, evangelism is always inherently political.[1] And that can seem problematic, and often is, just as Jesus was quite problematic. But this does not mean that evangelism inherently represents a "power move" of "the gospel of force" meant to dominate and use other peoples for purposes of utility and glory. It *can* become dangerously intertwined with such false gospels when the church overly equates the gospel with a partisan politics of a nation or culture. True evangelism instead enables the partisan-transcending transformation inherent in the gospel to bring "life more abundantly" to any and all peoples of the world, liberating them *from* the will to power sought in their native partisanship. Jesus said that one must be "born again" to see and enter the kingdom of God to signify that in a most basic sense following Christ's gospel means that one is literally reborn into a new kingdom with new and universal allegiances which greatly relativizes previous ones. This relativizing was the division and "sword" that Jesus brought to free people from the tribalistic false gospels of the will to power (Matt 10:34–39). Political colonialism and its fraternal twin religious nationalism bring subservience to their "subjects" in the name of liberation. True evangelism is of the gospel that declares its recipients "the heirs of all things." But the heirs are nevertheless to

---

1. "Because the church is the presence of God's city, His theopolis, the church is inherently *political*. It's inherently like a city, a civic reality. The New Testament makes this clear in the terminology it uses to describe the church, nearly all of which comes from ancient political theory." Leithart, *Theopolitan Vision*, 14.

"be subject" to the relative authority of rulers when they remain "the servants" of God *for* humankind rather than become the "beast" *over* humankind (Rom 8:17; 13:1–7; Rev 13:1–10). This makes evangelism good in itself when consistent with the way of faith rather than of force. Carl Raschke rightfully claims against "politically correct thinking" that evangelism is not the remnant of "some lingering imperial drive of one civilization to dominate the other or even of one religion to dominate over all the others."[2]

In Matthew's account cited above, Jesus is risen and speaking to his disciples as the Lord of all with liberating "authority" over the entire cosmos. The things that he tells the disciples to do are simply to follow the community-forming practices that are consistent with and should increasingly characterize the lives of those living in allegiance to Christ as the people of the new creation begun in him. The prominent twentieth-century British evangelist John Stott put it very simply saying,

> We must be global Christians with a global vision because our God is a global God.[3]

Thus evangelism, when true to the liberating gospel, creates local expressions of a global community of peoples united in Christ as one body, the multi-faceted tribal-transcending family of God.

When I write "when true to the liberating gospel," I imply the question we will be getting to in the following chapter. What *true* evangelism is will therefore be further seen throughout this chapter and the next, although there will certainly be some overlap that touches back upon the *evangel* of the first two chapters and forward to the *evangelizers* of the final two chapters. But evangelism proper is an action, a task done by some agent or agents. Our emphasis on this point will be on the task orientation of evangelism, focusing upon several different factors related to that task. We call the task of evangelism "the stewardship of the gospel."

What is the Stewardship of the Gospel?

Stewardship is a term used in the NT that pertains to what a steward does. A steward is a person that manages a household or an estate. The term denotes the responsibility to care for the "concerns" of what is

2. Raschke, *GloboChrist*, 47.
3. As cited by Raschke, *GloboChrist*, 15.

managed. In Matthew's gospel, "steward" is the term used by the owner of a vineyard when he speaks to his manager. (Mt. 20:8) The apostle Paul speaks of himself as a steward of God's mysteries, adding that stewards must be "trustworthy."

> Think of us in this way, as servants of Christ and stewards of God's mysteries. Moreover, it is required of stewards that they be found trustworthy" (1 Cor 4:1–2, NRSV).

Paul's understanding of stewardship then would include a delegated *authority*. Also, implied in being trustworthy is a *responsibility* regarding what is entrusted to the steward's care, and most essentially some *capacity* of "working knowledge" regarding what is entrusted. That this implies a stewardship of the gospel to Paul can be seen by considering what he meant by "God's mysteries." Earlier in this letter to the Corinthian church Paul had spoken of his apostolic ministry as imparting "a secret and hidden wisdom of God" which the Spirit revealed to him by the means of "spiritual truths," that were "hidden" *in* the OT Scriptures that the gospel was "according to" (1 Cor 2:6–13; 15:1–4). It also seems proper to combine Paul's conception of his apostolic stewardship of the gospel with the teaching of Jesus we saw above in Matthew 28:18–20 that makes the gospel the basis for all practice and teaching. So, evangelism—the stewardship of the gospel—is the broad category under which everything else falls for followers of Jesus. For those that may struggle with the cultural baggage of the term *evangelism*, it is important to note that it simply means that *everything* the followers of Christ were taught *to do* is to become the *teaching content* of the gospel. In other words, it is teaching about life that is to be lived and taught in a way that is true to the fact that life and doctrine are not mutually exclusive but mutually inclusive.

In addition to this general description, there are additional specific factors that must be considered regarding *what* gospel stewardship entails. The other factors can be revealed by the simple method of asking of evangelism not only *what*, but also *when, where, why, who, and how*. Utilizing these interrogatives will greatly enhance the picture of what the stewardship of the gospel is. We will also see that asking these questions of what seems to be a simple task will reveal the depth of responsibility that is included in the "sacred trust" that God places in his stewards regarding the most important thing beside the world-changing reconciliation itself, the *faithful* proclamation of that event. We will see that "faithful" doesn't merely pertain to the bare fact of "proclaiming," but is implied as necessary in each of the interrogatives.

So, at this point we provide the following table to provide the basic outline of "The Gospel in the Dock's" submitting evangelism and evangelizers to the questioning of the "examining prosecutors:" *when, where, why, what, who, and how,* in the remaining chapters of this "trial".

Table 2: A Basic Overview of "the Prosecution of Evangelism" in Chapters 3–6

"Examining Prosecutors"	Gospel Factor "in the Dock"	Segment of "Trial"
When, Where, Why	Evangelism as a needed task	Chapter 3
What	The evangelism of the stewards	Chapter 4
Who, How	The lives of the evangelizers	Chapters 5 & 6

Therefore, faithfulness in relation to the interrogatives "when," "where," and "why" will be considered now as we proceed in this chapter. These three interrogatives reveal a question that to many presents a problem, or in fact, a scandal.

The Gospel and the Modernist "Scandal of Particularity"

As just noted above, in this first step we will mainly subject the stewardship of the gospel to the interrogatives "when," "where," and "why." We will be dealing with these three together, and very broadly, as we consider how the stewardship of the gospel relates to them. This step is literally about the basic space/time task of evangelism. Therefore, the interrogating witnesses ask; *when,* temporally, and *where,* geographically, the gospel is to be evangelized. The "why" therefore literally signifies the question *why* the gospel needs evangelism. In other words, these three interrogatives ask why some agent(s) must carry out the task of evangelism, in regard to the universal gospel, in the terrestrial world of time and space. The rehabilitory aspect of this step is therefore to try to answer the supposed scandal of a "universal" gospel being literally "grounded" by the particularities of time and space.

The scandal of particularity as it is generally known is the proposition that it is *scandalous* and offensive that God achieves his universal purpose for humanity by the means of one "line" of historical *particulars*: the one people of Israel, of all the peoples of the world; the one religious leader, Jesus of Nazareth, of all the religious leaders of the world; and, the one Christian religion, of all the many different religions of the world.[4] The scandal is that this one line of historical particularity is claimed to be the means of mediating the *universal* God to all. This is seen as a scandal because it does two things. It elevates this one particular line in history "above" every other line in regard to its relation to the God who is supposedly universal. It also relativizes, degrades, and judges all other historical lines including all peoples other than Israel, all religions other than Christianity, and all saviors other than Jesus. The problems with seeing the scandal of particularity as a *valid* scandal are several.

First, this one elevated line, understood biblically, is only elevated to a vocation, and was neither chosen because of, or to result in, any inherent superiority. Human solidarity in sin is the real basis and operative term in the redemptive process of biblical particularity.

Second, this one elevated line was therefore only elevated to its vocation in order to become the means by which all other lines may be brought to salvation. The image from C. S. Lewis we saw in Chapter 2, of Christ as the one particular "diver" raising up all of humanity is the biblical paradigm for all God's "particular" agents as means toward universal redemption.

Third, this one elevated line is therefore good in itself as the means of salvation for the world. If one medical scientist or one team of scientists discovered the one true cure for cancer, that "scandal of particularity" would soon prove itself to not be a scandal, but the one salvation from cancer for all humanity. The gospel of Jesus Christ claims to be the one true cure for the universal problem of sin and death. Thus, the only true "scandal" would be to restrict a cure for cancer, or the cure for sin and death, from their promise of universal efficacy.

Fourth, the scandal of particularity is integrally connected to the exclusivism of the one true cure of humanity's ills, the gospel of Jesus Christ. But does the claim that the gospel is the only true cure require that apart from conscious knowledge and application of it, there is absolutely no hope for any and all segments of humanity which for particular reasons of time and space which are beyond their control—and are actually

---

4. See Weston, *Lesslie Newbigin*, 48–53.

supposed to be in God's control—never encounter the gospel that is only *explicitly* found in this one "line" of time and space? The word "explicitly" may make all the difference in that scenario. Because the gospel that was historically revealed in this one line may possibly exist implicitly in other lines. The questions raised in this point are fairly extensively discussed in our rather lengthy "postscript" since this is perhaps the core of the "scandal of particularity."

Fifth, the possibility that the exclusive gospel of the one line of particularity may possibly work implicitly within all other lines would certainly rehabilitate the "scandal" of particularity by demonstrating what may more accurately be "the secret of particularity"—revealing that the "mystery" of the gospel contains God's "hidden" goodness for all people of all times and places. This "secret" working, by and large remains secret, since it does not explicitly participate in the historical outworking of the explicit gospel of God's kingdom. For the visible kingdom of God challenges and re-forms the very nature and character of the life-existence of all sociopolitical cultures.

Sixth, the particularity of the gospel of Christ properly fits and coheres to his ultimate purposes for humanity and is therefore another reason why its particularity is good. In other words, God's use of particular means requires those encountering and responding to it to immediately encounter *the way* of the gospel, not merely the *what* of the gospel. This is an evidence that we should not cry "scandal" because of the gospel but rather see good grounds for the legitimization of its particular human agents as receivers and stewards of the gospel, and of the goods that result from this "election" of some to bear such "goods" to others. For this "arrangement" of God presses a *responsibility for others* onto his "particular" gospel stewards while also pressing a mutual *dependence of others* on these stewards for receiving the gospel.

God's plan to involve particular agents in the spreading of the gospel requires "other-centeredness" on every hand. Just as *the gospel event* required God's self-giving to be answered by self-indebtedness on the part of others, so also *the evangelism events* catch all up together in the others-centered gospel dynamic of self-giving and self-indebtedness. Humans are necessarily caught up in the others-centered life that characterizes the God who is love. God's gospel was to bring about "at-one-ment" between God and all of humanity, and also to bring about at-one-ment between all human beings. Thus, true evangelism invariably brings a veritable foretaste of participation in the end-goal of the gospel in the very process of its proclamation and reception. The gospel's means and ends are wholly one.

The at-one-ment of humanity and God was already accomplished in Christ in the center of our time and space cosmos. It is something that remains unknown to those not yet consciously participating in that reconciliation of God. Evangelism, done by "others" for the sake of "others," in itself witnesses to the at-one-ment between "others" and promises the reality of their "life-together" in Christ. The complete fellowship of all in God will not be fully known until the Kingdom community of God is consummated in its fulness. Nevertheless, even the beginnings of participation in Christ with others is *sign*ificant as the firstfruits of the at-one-ment at the center of the new community of humanity.

This reveals the goodness of the stewardship of the gospel that is dramatically in contrast to the will to power. Self-giving and self-indebtedness are opposite the will to power, and in fact graphically define *hospitality*. The gospel of Christ is revealed to be the ultimate remedy bringing what God from the first intended for humankind (Matt 22:36–40). And so, God's creation of human community begins in the very way that the gospel of Christ inhabits true evangelism in the so-called "scandal of particularity." The missionary-theologian Lesslie Newbigin explains this powerfully, saying,

> Are you asking for a relationship with God which is in principle accessible to everyone individually apart from any relationship with his neighbor? That is in fact what the unredeemed ego in each of us really wants. At the most secret and central place of our being, do we not constantly want to be in the position where we do not have to be debter to any other man? . . . His purpose is precisely to break open that shell of egotism in which you are imprisoned since Adam first fell and to give you back the new nature which is content to owe the debt of love to all men . . . God's plan for the salvation of the world is a consistent whole, the means congruent with the end. The end is the healing of all things in Christ, and the means therefore must involve each of us from the very beginning inescapably in a relationship with our neighbor. Salvation comes to each of us not, so to say, straight down from heaven through the skylight, but through a door that is opened by our neighbor. We cannot be saved except through and with one another, for salvation means making whole.[5]

---

5. Weston, *Lesslie Newbigin*, 50.

The scandal of particularity is *not* scandalous and is simply the way that the gospel of God's kingdom begins, moves and grows in the space-time existence within which we live and move and have our being. Evangelism presses the way of faith in relation to others upon those bringing the gospel and those receiving it. Those bringing it need compassion and those receiving it need humility, and that relational pattern was the same for the evangelizers who beforehand passed through the same Red Sea of passage to life. The way of the will to power, such as has been exhibited in "evangelical" colonialisms in the past, simply does not cohere with true evangelism. For true evangelism, done in congruence with the gospel, for all those involved necessarily promotes participation in the ways of the gospel. And the gospel itself is simply the good news of God's non-scandalous redemptive action in space and time. Torrance summarizes:

> The Christian faith is not simply composed of a body of timeless truth which is always in the end simply abstract idea, but we are concerned primarily with a Person, with God himself acting in relation in his creatures who live in time and history. Christianity is concerned, yes actually concerned, with God-in-Time, with God-in-Action in relation to men. Apart from that historical act of God with historical people, there is for us no knowledge of God, no living experience of Divine help or redemption.[6]

The Gospel and the Postmodernist Scandal of the Knowledge of God

Another "problem" relating to evangelism is not so much related to the question of *why* the universal gospel needs evangelism as to the challenge of universal knowledge itself. This is a more basic and preliminary, presuppositional "what," than will be considered in the next chapter. It will be considered here, because like the "when, where and why" it is basically part of a prolegomena to the *what* proper. For this *what* is whether there is such a thing as *revelation* in the form of cognitive content from God? If so, how can we finite humans share that "gospel," which by definition is good *news* that presupposes something capable of being known by human beings and communicated to others?

Obviously, we can only skim a rock over this huge subject, but hopefully that can provide some clarity to the present situation and perhaps

---

6. Torrance, *The Doctrine of Jesus*, 4.

create some hope that God's "gospel" can become to readers more than a mere momentary and insignificant splash upon the dark waters of modern skepticism and postmodern nihilism. The modern and postmodern projects were both, partly and in different ways, philosophical reactions that eventually became widespread cultural reactions against the Christian claims to a revealed knowledge that buttressed Christianity and Christendom in the West. Of course there's the rub, in the fact that the "Christianity" and "Christendom" had become "suspect" for reasons both good and bad in the complex of theology, philosophy, and science as they related to the problems of the source of human knowledge especially as that was entering the fray of shaping the very approach to the embattled questions of God and man, or church and state, as nation-states arose from and against the medieval synthesis of Christian humanism based in Christian Platonism.[7] The result was that Modernism largely unraveled the threads "connecting" creation to a transcendent God and thus a reality which reflected upon its Creator, while Postmodernism has for the most part followed-up to effectively cast doubt upon the possible reweaving of any sacramental tapestry of reality that might point again toward the plausibility of a transcendent Creator in connection to a creation where God "speaks" to humankind intelligibly.[8] To be more precise, this problem is actually "the scandal of knowledge," which is the distinctly "postmodernist" response to objective knowledge. This "scandal" is in contrast to "the scandal of particularity" which was a distinctly "modernist" response to the gospel. Modernism, through its notion of pure "objectivity," eventually presumed it had effectually dethroned God and brought about "the death of God." Strangely, Postmodernism objects to any and all notions of pure objectivity in the knowledge of reality but nevertheless generally accepts modernism's funeral for God. Also, postmodernism's project, although not a monolithic one, seems to be generally posed to prevent any "resurrection" of "God," or at least of the "God" that modernism deposed.

Our very brief response is threefold. It is to first agree with postmodernism's view that "pure objectivity" is a hubristic fiction of modernism. But secondly, it is to disagree with postmodernism's belief that it is

---

7. See Zimmermann, *Incarnational Humanism*, 52–162.

8. I am alluding to Hans Boersma's book that narrates this unraveling and then "rehabilitates" the sacramental tapestry: Boersma, *Heavenly Participation*. For an excellent introduction to the subject God and creation see, Gunton, *Doctrine of Creation*, 141–57.

impossible for humans to gain any "objective" knowledge of God and the gospel. The third part is to simply recognize the door these first two responses open to what Soren Kierkegaard called "possibility."

The initial agreement with postmodernism may be opposed by Christians, thinking that a denial of "pure objectivity" is to abandon the entire hope of true cognitive contact with God. But without that step, Christian faith that brings *real contact* with the *real transcendent God* will fall along with modernism to the main true insight of postmodernism. What is that main insight of Postmodernism? It is the dethroning of philosophical "foundationalism" or said positively, the positing of an "antifoundationalism."[9] What then is "foundationalism"? It is the view perhaps most associated with Rene Descartes who "thought" to build the foundation of all certain knowledge upon human rational thought. In foundationalism, philosophy came to be regarded "as the necessary prolegomena to theology; the findings of theology had to be validated by philosophy."[10] This is why much of what is thought to be "Christian theology" falls with postmodern antifoundationalism. A more precise definition of foundationalism is given by Alister McGrath:

> "That there are foundational or basic beliefs which guarantee their own truth, which are accessible to any rational person, irrespective of their historical or cultural context."[11]

The last few words of McGrath's definition provide the entrance point of postmodernism, because modernism held to the notion of universal objective knowledge of truth regardless of "historical or cultural context." In other words, modernism denied the "community, contingency, and creaturehood" of the knower of knowledge.[12] Thus modernism's denial of creaturehood, and Christian theology which "bought into" the modernist project, were both denials of the biblical view of humans as finite knowers. That is why we can accept the contingencies of creaturehood along with a host of Christian thinkers that in many ways began explicitly with Soren Kierkegaard but was followed by "Abraham Kuyper, William Alston and Nicholas Wolterstorff and, for that matter in anticipatory fashion by Augustine, Aquinas, Calvin, and Edwards."[13] James

---

9. See McGrath, *Scientific Theology*, 20–35. See also Leithart, *Solomon*, 59–102.
10. See Newbigin, *Proper Confidence*, 18.
11. McGrath, *Scientific Theology*, 21.
12. See Smith, *Who's Afraid of Relativism*.
13. Smith, *Who's Afraid of Relativism*, 27.

K. A. Smith provides a biblical critique of skeptical modernism and by extension its cousin of "Christian foundationalism" for their supposed "God-like" objectivity saying,

> to know God is God (and we are *not*) is to own up to the tenuous fragility of our existence. This is to recognize that *everything* depends—not just our life and breath, but also truth and knowledge, even our epistemology and metaphysics. But all too often we construct accounts of knowledge and truth that effectively deny our dependence, that efface our vulnerability and try to 'secure' us from the relativity of being a (rational, knowing) creature . . . The picture of knowledge bequeathed to us by the Enlightenment is a forthright denial of our dependence, and it yields a God-like picture of human reason.[14]

A little imagination can show that Smith is retelling the story of the fall of humans from dependent creaturehood in Eden to the way of sight (or reason) and the will to power. This is why Kierkegaard said, "truth is subjectivity"—because he sought to realign us to our embodied creaturehood in relation to God who alone is purely objective and who alone can fully know reality as "a system."[15] Paul Tyson writes that the true Christian "communal, contingent and creaturely" knowledge of God means that,

> God, the transcendent source of the qualitative richness of the reality we inhabit, is beyond rational capture. This means that all human attempts to understand God and to build a human world that has some analogical relation to reality, are situated in their own particular contexts, can never attain perfection, are always richly laced with historically specific and explicitly human creative motifs, and cannot be the same. To seek to live faithfully to reality now will not be a copy of previous attempts to do that by patristic and medieval thinkers and communities. There is something fundamentally new about each generation's attempt to live in reality and for this reason the human worlds constructed within history are always moving feasts.[16]

But they are feast's, because there is contact with the reality of God lived in and known, albeit not fully, through Christ. Smith summarize the

---

14. Smith, *Who's Afraid of Relativism*, 35.
15. See Kierkegaard, *Concluding Unscientific Postscript*, 119.
16. Tyson, *Returning to Reality*, 6.

postmodern lack that has already become evident in our consideration of *the blessings* of "community, contingency and creaturehood," saying,

> the Christian claim about contingency is not that *everything* is contingent but rather that everything *created* is contingent. Everything depends upon the triune Creator who, alone, is necessary. And that makes all the difference, Hauerwas points out, because it means that the Christian understanding of contingency is itself dependent. "The liberal nihilists are, of course, right that our lives are contingent," he says, 'but their account of contingency is unintelligible. Contingent to what? . . . Christians know their contingency is a correlative to their status as creatures. To be contingent is to recognize that our lives are intelligible only to the extent that we did not discover we are characters in a narrative we did not create." And that very discovery, I would add, depends upon our being "in Christ."[17]

It is hoped that *possibility*, our third response to modernist skepticism and postmodernist nihilism has to some extent already surfaced in this discussion of the supposed "scandal" of the knowledge of God, reality, and the gospel. But let's briefly consider where possibility may further lead, beginning with what Kierkegaard said.

> At this point, then, salvation is, humanly speaking, utterly impossible; but for God everything is possible! This is the battle of *faith*, battling madly, if you will, for possibility, because possibility is the only salvation. When someone faints, we call for water, eau de Cologne, smelling salts; but when someone wants to despair, then the word is: Get possibility, get possibility, possibility is the only salvation.[18]

In Chapter 1 we mentioned that in our postmodern times the regaining of the *possibility* of the goodness of the Gospel may be the necessary first step to a second one, the capacity for accepting it as true. A major and often overlooked obstacle to both its goodness and truth is our preexisting enthrallment to the elephant in the room—the false "gospel" of the way of sight (or reason) in modernism, and the way of the impossibility of sight in postmodernism. The latter enthralls us by granting us no accountability to anything objective, at least anything we can know of, such as God. So, in both modernism and postmodernism, it seems that

---

17. Smith, *Who's Afraid of Relativism*, 36. The portion of the quote is from: Hauerwas, "Preaching," 9.

18. Kierkegaard, *Sickness unto Death*, 38–39.

both inhabit the will to power, since they seem to deliver what we want—which is to *not* want God (or the gospel). But do they really deliver what we want? For the question is, what do we really *desire*?[19]

From the time of early childhood C. S. Lewis was driven by his insatiable quest for what he called "joy." Louis Markos writes that,

> All people, if they are honest, will recognize times in their life, especially when they are younger, when they have felt an overwhelming desire for something beyond our physical, natural, material world. That yearning, which Lewis variously refers to by the German word *sehnsucht* or the English word *joy*, can be set off by almost anything: a landscape, a tune, a line of poetry. But whatever the trigger, the quality that makes the joy unique is that it points us toward a something that is beyond nature.[20]

So, when we speak of desire, we mean a deep and even painful longing which many or most of us tend to quench superficially through what Blaise Pascal called "diversion." This means that our enthrallment is itself superficial, even though our habit of diversion has strengthened it so that it tends to hold us, rather than we, it. Our methods for coping tend to become our addictions. But most of us would probably reluctantly admit that the dominant cultural "gospels" of narcissistic consumerism are enslaving emperors that have no clothes. Nevertheless, we bow down to our propped-up deity, and our soulless, and actually largely mindless culturally driven *preoccupation in diversion*—certainly a misnomer that speaks of our inverted psyche—and sadly prevents the gospel from being *immediately* compelling to our perverted desires. We won't continue to pursue this depressing line of thought, for we had merely wanted to introduce possibility in a world where it seems that humankind has sabotaged itself through following the "reasonable" way of the will to power. Hopefully throughout these pages the encounter with the gospel will continue to present possibility as the redemptive good that we all need as individuals, communities, and as a global community. For the gospel redeems our

---

19. "*In faith there is an implicit element of desire* . . . Desire transcending lack and need—but still rooted in our own lives—is what we have to understand as implied in faith." Henriksen, *Desire*, 28, 29.

20. Markos, *Atheism on Trial*, 114. The fullest non-fictional treatment of the subject by Lewis that we know of is contained in "Preface to Third Edition," in Lewis, *The Pilgrim's Regress*, 5–14. Of course, that entire fictional work deals with the subject, as does his autobiography *Surprised by Joy*.

contingency, community and creaturehood as the original blessings of our Creator.

As modernists we have foolishly thrown the blessings of creaturehood away for the sake of what seemed to be the promise of deifying "reason." Indeed, Adam and Eve became the first modernists by seeking their self-deification. As postmodernists with our reason now dethroned, we find our seeking brought radical skepticism, as far as any sufficient knowledge of reality itself goes. Indeed, Adam and Eve became the first postmodernists, their deifying quest reaping shame and self-doubt. But we can see, in that bent worm hole of existence where ancient and postmodern humans cross over, that we are Edenic postmoderns, Annie Dillard's Heideggerian-like bewildered infant, looking about and wondering into what place he's been *thrown*.[21] But the gospel says we don't need to fake it as toddler-modernists knowing all, or flounder as infant-postmodernists knowing nothing. The gospel frees us to live in God's original creational blessings of finite creaturehood, exploring the neighborhood, through the way of faith. For Christ's gospel has provided "contact with reality" for all.

The universal experience of human longing for the transcendent demonstrates that none of us fully escape the magnetic pull of our kinship in the breath of God. That pull signifies our *longing* for complete reconciliation—*in which* "we live and move and have our being." And lo and behold, reconciliation has been provided. We thirst because there is such a thing as water.[22] We long for reconciliation in the midst of our thrown-ness, because there is such a thing as at-one-ment. Yet the gospel and its evangelism that tell us what our desire means, remain for many or most in our culture, in the dock. Therefore, we will conclude this chapter by returning to the matter at hand regarding evangelism itself and further considering the question of its being "in the dock."

Evangelism in the Dock

Like the gospel itself, evangelism also *began* in the dock, for the same reason of the gospel's sheer hiddenness that we explored in Chapters 1 and 2.

21. "For Heidegger, the state of being 'thrown' into the world, without a concept or word to explain it manifests itself in moods. In boredom and angst we feel the nothingness of our existence." McGrath, *Heidegger*, 7.

22. "Creatures are not born with desires unless satisfaction for those desires exists." Lewis, *Mere Christianity*, 106.

But now it is also in the dock for being in a sense too well known. But we must ask whether what is known is the gospel. For many in the world see Jonah the prophet of God on the run from the gospel. They see the gospel co-opted by false gospels of the way of force and the will to power. Therefore, we need to remember the New Testament's rehabilitative method of the stewardship of the gospel that we discussed in the introduction where the Scriptures repeatedly call attention to the shortcomings of its stewards. Similarly, in the next chapter we will witness a veritable parade of false gospels and in Chapter 6 will see some tragic caricatures of true gospel stewards. But as we discussed in the introduction, the backwardness of evangelism and its stewards can serve to highlight the primal gospel and in fact demonstrate that it originates not in the corrupt constructs of "gospel stewards" who in many ways view the gospel as *not good* for them, but in the creative and redemptive love of the triune God.

Therefore, evangelism must be rehabilitated from the dock where it has been placed not only by the world, or on account of the gospel evangelizers' sub-gospel proclamations, but by the Gospel stewards' lives which variously capitulate and cater to the ways of force and the will to power. In the next chapter we will concentrate on "what" has often been promoted and also often accepted as "gospel" by both the world and the gospel stewards, leading to the placement of the gospel, evangelism, and the evangelizers "in the dock." But all the while, in the midst of this confusing gospel corruption, God is sending the true proclamation:

> Arise, go to Nineveh, that great city, (or any city) and call out against it the message that I tell you.[23]

---

23. Jonah 3:2. The gospel in that text is admittedly hidden beneath the fact that any message from God to the Assyrians, even a message of coming judgment, *always* implies the opportunity to repent because of God's loving intent to redeem all, even those who are the enemies of all. (See Jer 18:7–10 and Jonah 3:3–10.) We add the parenthetical words "or any city" because the gospel is to be proclaimed universally. (See Matt 28:19; Luke 24:45–48; Acts 1:8.)

4

Rehabilitating the Stewardship of the Gospel

> And should not I pity Nineveh, that great city, in which
> there are more than 120,000 persons who do not know their
> right hand from their left, and also much cattle?
>
> —JONAH 4:11

The Gospel and Purity

THE ABOVE TEXT SHOWS that God's sending Jonah to Nineveh with the message "repent!" was the equivalent of having compassion on Nineveh. In other words, God's pitying and Jonah's sending are two actions flowing from the same thing, the compassion of God. This reveals that the question of the purity of the gospel is in essence only the question of the correlation between the message delivered and the intent of the one who sends it. Strictly speaking, the gospel messengers simply need to preserve the gospel by delivering it intact to its destination.

But since evangelism is in the dock, we need to examine whether the gospel message delivered is the same one God sent. Of course, if the message proclaimed *is true to the gospel*, that would not necessarily mean that the gospel would *not* be in the dock, since as Paul summarized "the gospel is "a stumbling block to Jews and folly to Gentiles."[1] In both cul-

---

1. "What we have to do is overcome the wrong stumbling block in order to bring

tural offenses to the gospel, "the will to power" lies at the bottom. For the "Jews" desired an obviously *significant* (powerful) Christ to *establish* the city of *Israel* at the head of the nations; and the "Gentiles" (Greco-Romans) obviously most desired to retain the power they already had, so that their "seeking after wisdom" became increasingly hubristic and overshadowed by their "vested interests" of power and the *establishment* of *their* Cainite cities. For both groups, their reaction to any perceived threat to the power they either desired or already enjoyed gave the lie to the purity of their pursuit of "wisdom."

The "interrogative" method we began in the last chapter we now continue with the step of subjecting evangelism "in the dock" to the court prosecutor named "what." This *what* is for the purpose of testing the trustworthiness of the stewardship. It is to ask whether the stewards have been good caretakers of the gospel's content, or whether the gospel has become "damaged" in transit. The gospel was given to the stewards in the manner of a sacred trust, and we intend to consider whether that stewardship has resulted in the *pure* evangel being proclaimed accordingly. If the gospel does not retain its purity in the proclamation, retaining its "goods," so to speak, people will mistake what was delivered for the gospel itself. Of course, this is all but a manner of speaking, for the gospel cannot be intrinsically damaged. But it can be proclaimed in ways that make it seem so, and its goodness largely unknown or worse yet, known as evil.

The big question of the relation between "the primal gospel" and the proclaimed gospel is what practical method should be used to determine the resulting "purity." What are the criteria for testing purity? We have decided to use the two main "ordinances" or "sacraments" as they are variously called by the different Christian communities. These are "baptism" and "the Lord's Supper." The reason we think them suited to be criteria is because together they encapsulate the core message of the gospel and its way of faith. In fact, that "the faith" was so "signified" in these two practices is because they were "given" to the church partly for the purpose of summarizing what following Christ meant. Therefore, a comparison with the way of faith as encapsulated in these practices will reveal when the gospel has been coopted by the ways of sight, force, and the will to power. Hopefully this will become evident as we proceed.

---

people face to face with the right stumbling block and enable them to make a genuine decision. Will the Christian churches be able to remove the wrong stumbling blocks in their attempts to communicate the gospel?" Tillich, *Theology of Culture*, 213.

Therefore, we begin with basic, non-exhaustive definitions of both practices as they relate to the gospel.

Baptism is the initial rite and sign of entry to Christ's community. It signifies allegiance to Christ's person and work in the way of faith as the basis of that new life. It signifies solidarity with Christ's death at the hands of the powers-that-be and thus proclaims each person's "death" to the old life in former allegiances. Therefore, baptism signifies death to the old ways of force, sight, and the will to power, being united in the death, burial and resurrection of Christ to participate in the kingdom's way of faith lived in the new creation of the new human community. To summarize, baptism is a "pledge of allegiance to the lamb" which is both an "eschatological and political act."[2]

The Lord's Supper is the ongoing rite that signifies fellowship in Christ's community. It signifies allegiance to the "table fellowship" of God's kingdom which unites all "tribes" in one "body of Christ." The community of Christ continually lives in the way of faith on the basis of the death of Christ signified by his "being" the broken body/bread and poured out blood/wine (Mt 26:26–28). The very form of this "supper" of the early Christians was in itself a "subversive meal" because it broke custom with the way of force that was ideologically promoted in the "Roman banquet protocols that were instituted to uphold the socioeconomic and political platforms of the empire."[3] Thus the "Lord's Supper" serves to maintain the new community in allegiance to Christ and his kingdom. Like baptism, it is also an inherently eschatological and political act.

Baptism and the Lord's supper both provide a sort of life narration in the way of faith lived in the gospel, in dramatic contrast to the false gospel lived in the way of self-love and the will to power. At this point perhaps another category of life will help demonstrate these two opposing gospels, namely the question of justice.

The Gospel Way of Justice

Nearly half a millennia before Christ came, Plato exploded the conventional notions of justice. Louis Markos explains that,

2. See Streett, *Heaven on Earth*, 225–38.

3. See Streett, *Subversive Meals*, 234. Streett adds that "Rather than embracing a patron/client model of feasting, based on a rigid caste system, the followers of Jesus strove to practice classless fellowship that included slaves reclining side by side with elites, women taking leadership roles, and everyone ministering to each other."

> The *Republic* begins with Socrates tearing apart two conventional definitions of justice: that it means doing good to friends and bad to enemies, and that it is nothing more than the will of the stronger.[4]

This recognition seems to call into question the relatively simple notion of justification that many or most Christians hold to by showing that such a view would merely be based on God acting according to the way of force and the will to power against all His enemies (all of humankind) who are annihilated "in Christ" through God's wrath on Christ. Before commenting on this we will consider another statement from Markos who adds,

> Justice is not something that man makes up, but that he recognizes and participates with. When a man gives in to injustice, he does more than play around with words: he literally "starve[s] the human being within him to the point where he can be dragged wherever the other parts of his soul want to go" (589a). When, for example, he steals gold, he does more than break a manmade law; he "enslave[s] the most divine part of himself to what is most unclean and shameful" (589e). The absolute tyrant turns out, in the end, to be the most abject of slaves, for his embrace of injustice enthralls him, literally, to the appetitive parts of his soul. The just man, on the other hand, even if he is condemned, is free, for all the parts of his soul exist in proper harmony.[5]

We cannot much enter into comparing Plato to the revelation of the gospel of Christ, but we do need to make several important points.[6] Plato's recognition of justice has obvious ramifications not merely in regard to those subjected to one's justice, but more importantly for our use, to one's own inner orientation toward the reality of justice. But at the undoubted certainty of oversimplification, we only say that the "problem" with God following such a picture of justice is that it can easily overlook what was undoubtedly revealed in the gospel, namely that God's "wrath" was ultimately motivated by God's love and compassion for the guilty. Overlooking God's declared motivation (John 3:16) seems to very

---

4. Markos, *Atheism on Trial*, 126.

5. Markos, *Atheism on Trial*, 128. The parenthetical numbers refer to Plato's *Republic*.

6. "Plato certainly had in mind Socrates himself, who was condemned and executed by the citizens of Athens in 399 BC, and yet the description uncannily reads like a pagan prophecy of Christ." Markos, *Atheism on Trial*, 126–27.

Rehabilitating the Stewardship of the Gospel

nearly posit that God's embrace of justice "enthralls him, literally, to the appetitive parts of his soul." This tendency is evident in that "evangelical" preaching of the gospel's "penal substitution" all too often leaves God's love out of the transaction.

How this all fully relates to aspects of "the mechanics" of atonement that we considered in Chapter 2 is beyond the scope of this book. But we point out that the gospel demonstrates the way of God's own self, who rejected the will to power and the way of force to accomplish through the way of *loving* justice, *redemptive* justification. We also see that God's way of justice *required* that in Christ, *God* submitted to a death carried out by the principalities and powers wielding unjust force. And what this means in relation to the stewardship of the gospel *in purity* is simply that it must always be proclaimed as being the gospel *because God followed* the way of faith, the way of God's loving justice, the way of God *surrendering* power.[7] We will hopefully see more of the significance of this as we proceed to consider several impure "gospels" that God's stewards and humans in general have "proclaimed" by their words and lives. The names of these false gospels are presented in the singular case, but the intent is not that there is one monolithically known "gospel" of each named type, but that there are several permutations of each that surface in different historical contexts.

The Gospel of War

The proclamation of this gospel would be, "The gospel of war follows self-love, and the will to power against others, as the best way to achieve salvation." The gospel of war began implicitly with Adam and Eve against God. That immediately brought conflict into their relationship (Gen 3:16), and then war became explicit in their children when Cain killed Abel (Gen 4:8). Through Cain, Genesis showed the inward force of sin and desire first wars within the person, as the NT also recognizes (James 4:1–2; 1 John 2:7–11, 15–16). Yet God promises that through "grace" they may overcome the "solution" of war "crouching at the door" within (Gen 4:6–7; 1 John 2:17). Humankind is thus engaged both inwardly and outwardly in the war between two gospels, and that the wrong way is so often chosen may be the most common reason for the gospel being in the dock.

---

7. "At the center of the whole picture we do not find a wrathful God bent on killing someone, demanding blood. Instead, we find the image—I use the word advisedly—of the covenant-keeping God who takes the full force of sin onto himself." Wright, *The Day*, 185., cf. 289.

Humankind seems to "naturally" fall to force as the best way to obtain what is wanted. Of course, force is necessary if what is wanted is not one's to take. Thus, the inner struggle is with self-denial, and the battle lost when self-love prevails in the desire and "war" for immediate satisfaction. The way of faith does not promise an immediate solution. It provides no imaginary foretaste to set the mouth to watering for the satisfying fruit, at least not for those enthralled to the appetitive parts of the soul.

Humankind also falls in the desire for "justice," as conceived of by the wronged, by conveniently providing the appetizing imagination that well-nigh guarantees glorious vengeance. The choice between the gospel of peace and the gospel of war is in many ways a war of the imagination. But since the "fall of man," humankind is generally not proficient at imagining and doing the good, much to the lament of the Creator (Gen 1:3; 6:5–6).

We often opt for war of some sort to provide security against the anxiety of uncertainty, not knowing that faith brings the peace that passes understanding to us finite creatures (Phil 4:7). When it's up to us, we will need to worry about our future. When it's up to God we are freed from worry for tomorrow. Jesus said that the lilies and the birds teach us such plain truths.[8]

Needless to say, the gospel of war, apart from when it is merited as "just" which is probably a much rarer occasion than is claimed, is the perennial temptation and entrapment of humankind and of God's gospel stewards. The fallen-breath wind pattern of humanity is tempted to become the raging sea-wind pattern, especially when it has become the poor and oppressed wind-blown pattern, using our earlier categories. Jesus himself dealt with this temptation throughout his ministry, as when Peter, aiming to protect Jesus from unjust arrest, sought to "live by the sword" (Matt 26:52). Jesus was tempted to gain all the kingdoms of the world illicitly by "bowing" to Satan, presumably implying following some coercive *means* of force and conquest to gain the *end* of the kingdom which were only to be gained by the way of the cross (Matt 4:8–9; 28:18).[9] Thus the baptism of Jesus as the agent of God's alternative way was immediately tested in the wilderness and in his subsequent ministry just as it is continually tested in all the followers of Christ who are all

---

8. See Matthew 6:25–34. Also see Kierkegaard, *Spiritual Writings*, 85–224.
9. See Wolf, "The Continuing Temptation," 288–301.

Rehabilitating the Stewardship of the Gospel

baptized into the way of the cross (Matt 28:19). David Benjamin Blower explains the essential freedom of God's gospel stewards even though that is often tested:

> Baptism is a political act in which we become free from our obligations to the politics of the old order with its borders, boundaries and its imperatives of competition, expansion, security, survival, and conquest.[10]

Baptism is the NT universalizing sign of the OT sign of circumcision, which for Israel was not the creation of a "God approved" tribe of "the will to power" but was in reality God's creation of "a parody-tribe."[11] Thus baptism does not signify the creation of a warring tribe of holy warriors, at least not ones with fleshly weapons of warfare. Paul, living in the gospel way of faith as its ambassador *in chains*, taught the churches that the battle was not "against flesh and blood but against principalities and powers" (1 Cor 10:3–4; Eph 6:10–20). God's community is indeed a "warring" community, but its weapons, warfare, and power are of a wholly different order than the will to power. In relation to the "elemental powers of the world" they are opposite and subversive. But the stewards of God seem to easily succumb to the worldly ways of warring, all too often saying "let us become like the nations," and thereby becoming "caught up in the powers and principalities of the age" to their own harm, and the effectual loss of the gospel.[12] Barry Harvey summarizes that,

> The good news of God's apocalyptic intrusion into the world in Christ and his church is that we are free from the presumption that war is necessary. In the offering of our Passover lamb, sacrifice comes to its proper end, its proper purpose; for in this, the offering of God to God, God refuses to let the never-ending slaughter-bench determine the course of human history.[13]

The desire for war and a warring King only "pays" in what Samuel foretold for Israel: heavy taxation of our livelihood to support the war-machine, and the heavy "taxation" of our lifeblood in our just-grown

---

10. Blower, *Sympathy for Jonah*, 28.
11. Leithart, *Delivered from the Elements*, 89.
12. See 1 Samuel 8:1–20 for Israel's fall to this temptation which God was against but permitted. See also Harvey, *Can These Bones Live*, 93–127 for his chapter that is titled and subtitled with the words quoted above, on this perennial and dangerous temptation for God's peoples of all ages, including ours.
13. Barry Harvey *Can These Bones Live*, 272.

children.[14] And then there is also the "payback" of the perpetuation of the endless cycle of war:

> As John of Patmos saw it, there is the conqueror who rides from the West on a white horse, wearing a crown of legitimacy and sovereignty and bringing its imperial peace through violently righteous conquest. And on the other hand, there is the barbaric warlord who rides from the East on a red horse bringing a sword of war and chaos against the conqueror's power. There's the empire you live under and the counter empire that rages against it."[15]

The victory of any conquering empire sows the seed of the counter empire. When will the nations cease to learn war? (Isa 2:1–5). Certainly not when the very stewards of the gospel of peace fall prey to the temptations and entrapments of the "gospel" of war.

The ongoing "culture war" is the war of choice now for many Christians. It is important to note that this warring is easily excused and not even seen *as* warring, but simply as "survival." It seems a necessary reaction to the steward's context of "tribulation" within the world's "increase of lawlessness," its warlike and sinful ways, and its persecution of the "hated" disciples (Matt 24:6–10). After all, when the Cainite city of man seeks to war against God's "Abels," what is first seen by them are enemies *as enemies*. But the gospel is not a call to normal life, but a call into a difficult baptism like Christ's (Mark 10:32–40). Jesus said that the "natural" response to these tribulations falls short of the gospel because it signifies "the love of many growing cold" (Matt 24:12). For the steward's task is not war but enduring in the "proclamation of the gospel" until the end (Matt 24:13–14). The culture war and the better way will be a recurring theme as we proceed. So, at this point we simply summarize that the gospel of war is a false gospel, especially for the gospel stewards who should "know better." Preston Sprinkle presents a historically aware view from a Christian perspective when he summarizes that,

> We live in a strange scene of redemptive history when opposition to war, violence, and militarism is deemed unchristian.[16]

---

14. See 1 Samuel 8:10–22. Kenneth Waltz writes, "Perhaps . . . from the perspective of mankind, war has never 'paid.' Yet war recurs. The beast in man may glory in the carnage; the reason in man rebels." Waltz, *Man, The State and War*, 224.

15. Blower, *Sympathy for Jonah*, 33. See also Beale, *Revelation*, 375–79.

16. Sprinkle, *Fight*, 16.

The Gospel of "Christianity and"

The proclamation of this gospel would be, "The gospel of 'Christianity and' supplies its followers with a multitude of ways to bring the gospel of Christ into subservience to the form of salvation they most value." C. S. Lewis introduces "Christianity And" through a fictitious demonic "member" of the Satanic bureaucracy over world affairs. "Uncle Screwtape" is the trainer of his "nephew" in the diabolical arts to tempt Christians away from the simplicity of being "merely" gospel centered Christians. Behind this diabolic strategy is the Trojan Horse strategy in which the hidden content of this new construction of Christianity will to some measure harm the gospel and destroy those receiving its gift. Of course, this reveals another tact of the "Leviathan" pattern arrayed against God. "Uncle Screwtape" writes,

> The real trouble about the set your patient is living in is that it is *merely* Christian. They all have individual interests, of course, but the bond remains mere Christianity. What we want, if men become Christians at all, is to keep them in the state of mind I call "Christianity And." You know—Christianity and the Crisis, Christianity and the New Psychology, Christianity and the New Order, Christianity and Faith Healing, Christianity and Psychical Research, Christianity and Vegetarianism, Christianity and Spelling Reform. If they must be Christians, let them at least be Christians with a difference. Substitute for the faith itself some Fashion with a Christian coloring. Work on their horror of the Same Old Thing.[17]

The tactic brings the gospel into subservience to current, cultural and "fashionable" concerns. This divides Christians into issue-centered factions and also brings the gospel under question through too close an identification with truly controversial and divisive theological, political and social issues. To supplement the mid-twentieth-century list Lewis gave, we might now add things like Christianity and: six-day young-Earth creation, social-justice, identity-politics, climate-change, end-times prophecy, Christian-America, and last but not least the culture-war. Some of the titles Lewis gave were probably meant to be humorous, to illustrate the danger of all distortion, division, and distraction from the central focus of the gospel.

---

17. See Lewis, *Screwtape Letters*, 147.

Recognizing the dangers of "Christianity And" does not require Christians to ignore important issues they should be vitally concerned with. What it means is to recognize the danger of subtly changing the gospel to serve our parochial or tribal interests and becoming warlike in support of those. Sadly, the temptation to the way of force always crouches near the door of religious conviction as Blaise Pascal noted: "Men never do evil so completely and cheerfully as when they do it from religious conviction."[18]

Lesslie Newbigin wisely noted that though Christ was the servant of all, he didn't allow himself to simply be "at the disposal of others," and therefore resisted the "temptations to do what people wanted the Messiah to do."[19] Screwtape presents this common human desire as the grounds for another nuance of the "Christianity And" tactic, writing,

> Certainly we do not want men to allow their Christianity to flow over into their political life, for the establishment of anything like a really just society would be a major disaster. On the other hand we do want, and want very much, to treat Christianity as a means; preferably, of course, as a means to their own advancement, but, failing that, as a means to anything—even to social justice as a thing which the Enemy demands, and then to work him on to the stage at which he values Christianity because it may produce social justice. For the Enemy will not be used as a convenience. Men or nations who think they can revive the Faith in order to make a good society might just as well think they can use the stairs of heaven as a short cut to the nearest chemist's shop. Fortunately it is quite easy to coax humans round this little corner[20.]

"Screwtape" calls this "addition" to the gospel a mere turn "round this little corner." But the *ease* of coaxing humans around it shows that Lewis thought it *a very common* corner. Karl Barth also spoke to this danger and possibly did so a bit earlier than Lewis did. Speaking of Barth's views, Ralph Wood writes,

> Karl Barth spent his entire career reiterating the basic truth that all attempts to identify the Gospel with this or that worldly enterprise, no matter how worthy, end in the worst of all idolatries.

18. Pascal. *Pensees*, #894.
19. Newbigin, *The Gospel*, loc. 4184.
20. Lewis, *Screwtape Letters*, 139–40. Note that a "Chemist's shop" is "a drugstore or pharmacy."

> They make Christ the servant of such endeavors, when he is meant to be their Lord . . . Barth knew that an acculturated Christian existence can offer no prophetic critique, even against a culture as palpably evil as Nazi Germany . . . For Barth there is no such thing as a Christian politics or Christian culture, a Christian music or Christian philosophy . . . He was extraordinarily chary about using the word "Christian" as an adjective of any kind . . . In one of his wittiest sayings, hidden amidst the eye-straining small print of the Church Dogmatics, Barth declared that God's greatest enemy is the fatal little word "and."[21]

The scope of possible "ands" is as wide as are Christian's concerns that seem integral to Christianity. Therefore, to prevent the proliferation of such hybrids is a recognition of the universal aspects of the gospel that prevent it from being hijacked by parochial and partisan interests. Counterintuitively, a focus on the universal interests leads back to the simplicity of the gospel. Carson presents a sort of blueprint for this saying:

> Their allegiance . . . set above all national, cultural, linguistic, and racial allegiances . . . Their commitment . . . is to the church everywhere . . . and not only to its manifestation on home turf . . . They see themselves . . . citizens of the heavenly kingdom and therefore consider all other citizenship a secondary matter . . . As a result they are single-minded and sacrificial when it comes to the paramount mandate to evangelize and make disciples.[22]

Carson's last statement shows that the necessary single-mindedness requires a "sacrificial" posture in relation to all "special interests." What these criteria signify is a conformity to Christ who lay down any and all self-interests for his Father's redemptive kingdom.

But we must also note that when the stewards engage in their particular culture as "world Christians," this has the potential of being extremely unpopular in relation to the norms of *their* culture's "national, cultural, linguistic, and racial allegiances." This was what brought the early Christians under the scorn of *their* culture as the enemies of humanity and as "atheists" who forsook the Roman "Gods" that preserved the Empire. This only demonstrates that a faithful proclamation of the gospel will bring offense. Thus, offense is necessary, though it is not sought for

---

21. Wood, *Contending for the Faith*, 9.
22. Carson, *The Cross and Christian Ministry*, 116–17.

or a matter of rejoicing. Kierkegaard held that being that offense causes Christ immeasurable suffering.²³

We can summarize by relating this false gospel to baptism and the Lord's Supper. For the stewards are baptized into Christ's universal redemption, which brings the cup of baptismal suffering given by the cultures of the world that are threatened by the single-minded universal interests of the kingdom of God. The practice of the Lord's Supper signifies the universal table of fellowship, which also subverts cultural ways and allegiances that are fallen to self-interests and the will to power. Of course, the stewards often fall from the gospel, to their overly special interests that become nearly all, through the word "and."

The Gospel of "Cheap Grace"

The proclamation of this gospel would be, "The gospel of 'cheap grace' promises all of the benefits of salvation, as they are conceived of by its practitioners, without all the negatives of 'costly grace.'" The gospel of "cheap grace" mistakenly believes that it does *not* have God in the dock when all the while *living* with the gospel securely and safely *in the dock*. The term "cheap grace" was popularized by Dietrich Bonhoeffer in his classic book, *Discipleship*, which begins with the bold statement,

> Cheap grace is the mortal element of our church. Our struggle today is for costly grace.²⁴

That the book became a classic testifies to the fact that the stewards of God do not intend to follow the false gospels we are reviewing, though each represents "temptations common to man" (1 Corinthians 10:13) that must be revealed, resisted, and overcome through adherence to the true gospel. Although Bonhoeffer coined the term and popularized its significance, he derived it from the writings of Soren Kierkegaard from nearly a century earlier. Bonhoeffer's struggles against the Third Reich drew from and built upon Kierkegaard's gospel imperatives embodied in his own "attacks" on the State Church in Denmark. Kirkpatrick shows the "Genesis" of the term in Kierkegaard:

---

23. "The mystery of suffering, as no human being can comprehend it or them: to be oneself the sign of offense in order to be the object of faith!" Soren Kierkegaard, *Practice in Christianity*, 99.

24. Bonhoeffer, *Discipleship*, 43.

"Especially in Protestantism, especially in Denmark," everyone is assumed to be a Christian. It is not surprising that here we find one of Kierkegaard's first descriptions of cheap grace as . . . "a *wohlfeil* (cheap) edition of a Christian." In the face of the absolute paradox and its offensiveness, of the extreme rigorousness of imitation, the secular world has converted Christianity into the palatable affirmation of life in all its peace, comfort, and security . . . Danish society does not want to eliminate Christianity because the issue of eternal happiness remains crucial to the individual's security . . . Such people desire the benefits of spirituality, religion, and its promise of eternal happiness, with the joys and security of this world.[25]

The life and works of both Kierkegaard and Bonhoeffer were in the context of their respective Lutheran state churches in Denmark and Germany. Thus the "Christianity And" of "civil-religion," is often the breeding ground of cheap grace. This "cheapness" results when Christians do not follow the earthly pattern of the life of Christ.[26] The gospel of "cheap grace" is simply a failure in discipleship, which of course was the subject of Bonhoeffer's book.

Cheap grace is essentially a "Christianity and hedonism," because of the hedonism that it allows in "discipleship." This "Christianity" admits much of the common hedonism of the national culture. The gospel becomes *mere* doctrine, while the life is freed for *mere* hedonism. Of course, the admitted hedonism will be what the culture deems acceptable. But compared to the ethics of God's kingdom, a culture's acceptable morality is in reality a *cultured* hedonism that masks the will to power. Thus, Kierkegaard considered the Christians in Denmark to be "Heathens."[27] Thus a commentator on Kierkegaard writes,

> Paganism in Christendom consists in combining the outward marks of Christianity with a dominant mode of being-in-the-world that has given itself over to the values of a materialist, consumerist society. In the process God is pushed to the periphery insofar as God claims to be the absolute source of meaning and normativity over against which society's ethos is only

---

25. Kirkpatrick, *Attacks on Christendom*, 153–54. See also Law, "Cheap Grace," 111–42.

26. See Kierkegaard, *Practice in Christianity*, 238–43.

27. Kierkegaard wrote a series of sermons for his fellow Danes, called "The Anxieties of the Heathen." Kierkegaard, *Christian Discourses*, 5–93.

relative. But the god who plays second fiddle to the social mores of any society is no God at all but an idol.[28]

In Western Christendom, a descending stairway appears evident in this pagan hedonism. First, self-serving faith and politics is the basis of "civil religion." Second, the fall from that civil-religion manifests itself as a more fully-realized secular form of civil-religion that inverts the "morals" of the first level, and supports the new quasi-religious totalitarian state.[29]

Cheap grace in civil-religious establishments entice their religious citizens, whether the old guard conservatives or the new woke liberals, to think that the gospel is somehow "in the driver's seat." But the gospel is barely even, a "back-seat driver"—but is fabricated and propped up to distract from the real driver, the will to power.[30] The church communities become places the Lord despises for their empty rituals and social injustice (Amos 5:21–24). In short, all gospels of cheap grace dangle a carrot of *some* religious establishment, while denying the true gospel of following Christ. But that false gospel is based in a hedonistic self-serving will to power, and is an idol slated for destruction (Isa 10:10–11). For only the gospel of "costly grace," of the God who has nothing to do with idols, is good for the church (Hos 14:8).

The Gospel of Reaction

The proclamation of this gospel would be, "The gospel of reaction allows its followers to reformulate the gospel according to their conception of salvation that is opposite to the false gospel they most vehemently oppose." This "gospel" describes a common error in methodology, rather than any particular error of gospel content. That means that it is a generic "false" method that enables constructions of false gospels more than itself being one per se. Thus, it signifies the birth of a new "gospel" formed by reaction to something other than the gospel itself—perhaps even in reaction to a false gospel. This is the danger of being moved from the ground of the gospel proper while trying to preserve the gospel. Such gospel

---

28. Westphal, "Paganism in Christendom," 30.

29. Called "moral inversion" by Michael Polanyi who saw it as the dynamic beneath totalitarian post-Christian states. Polanyi, *Personal Knowledge*, 231–35.

30. The "back seat driver" indicates the historical reality of the influence of the gospel on "Renaissance Humanism." See Zimmermann, *Incarnational Humanism*, 131–62.

"reformulations" are reactions to historical developments rather than the positive proclamation of the gospel. This reactionary gospel occurred following "Luther's reformation" in Lutheran Denmark, as discussed by a commentator on Kierkegaard:

> Danish Christianity is just as much a perversion of the Gospel as medieval Catholicism was. The lamentable result of Luther's reformation of the inadequate works-based Christianity of his day is that the pendulum has swung too far in the other direction. Kierkegaard quotes a comment from Luther to this effect: The world is like a drunken peasant; if you help him up on one side of the horse, he falls off on the other side" (FSE, 24). Luther's critique and correction of medieval Catholicism was valid and needed to be made, but his successors have taken Luther's critique to such an extreme that the gospel is again in danger of being lost. The problem is that the secular mentality has exploited Luther's emphasis on justification by grace through faith as a means of *avoiding* the gospel (FSE, 16) . . . to reduce Christianity to an either/or of faith and works, where in reality Christianity is a both/and.[31]

Thus, the gospel of "cheap grace" developed out of Luther's own prior over-reaction to the "new law" of medieval Christianity and its unbearable burden of "meritoriousness and works-righteousness."[32]

Another example of a gospel of reaction is seen in two antithetic reactions that squared off in another false dichotomy based in the different presuppositions underlying "personal salvation" and "the social gospel." Today, the latter is seen in the Christian wing of "the social justice movement" which is still in many ways a reaction to the "personal salvation" gospel. These two mutually reactionary *either/or* "gospels" were seemingly concerned with *either* heaven *or* earth and largely developed in relation to the widely divergent sociological/theological constructs of the gospel of the "liberal" and "fundamentalist" sides of the church in the modern West. The former sought to follow Christ's teachings regarding social needs but largely did so apart from belief in the supernatural elements of the faith—thereby itself being a *reaction* to the "higher criticism" of the Bible and the rise of the theory of evolution. Ironically the fundamentalist churches had been more socially activist previously, showing that

---

31. Law. "Cheap Grace," 113–14. "FSE" signifies Kierkegaard's book "For Self-Examination."

32. Law, "Cheap Grace," 112.

their reaction to the liberal practice changed their own former beliefs and practices. This dramatic change became known as "the great reversal."[33]

Carl Henry's now famous book "The Uneasy Conscience of Modern Fundamentalism" was itself a reaction to both of those in a worthy attempt to re-conjoin the personal, social, and supernatural (or metaphysical) elements of the gospel, signaling the birth of what became known as "Evangelicalism" in the mid 1900s.[34] But much of the church continues to hold to these reactionary false dichotomies in theory or practice, or both, to the present day.

The gospel of reaction in one sense only demonstrates that the gospel necessarily collides with historical developments. The danger is when the gospel itself becomes reformulated in the process and in a sense is brought to wrongly "collude" with what it collides with. The gospel needs to be contextualized, or in other words—meet the new cultural context in a meaningful and intelligible way, as it "travels" to the ends of the earth. But contextualization needs to transpire in such a way that the primal gospel is not lost or diminished. Reactions, in relation to the gospel, are always taking place. What is important is that the gospel does not become a different "gospel" *formed by reaction*, but remains the primal gospel, albeit contextualized in a new culture. The gospel itself is in some sense ever-being revealed, due to the fact of God's "use" of the historical process in tandem with the finitude of the gospel stewards (John 16:12–15). In other words, there is a dialectical complexity involved here which we cannot in this book enter into any further than this mention.

The danger in this challenge between proper contextualization and wrong reaction, is that the gospel itself may be become corrupted rather than further elucidated, and that the resulting reactions can become the occasion of the problems connected to "Christian" divisiveness. Again, the truth and practice of baptism and the Lord's Supper ought to be preventative measures against the dangers.

The Gospel of Escapism

The proclamation of this gospel would be, "The gospel of escapism promises the rewards of heaven without sharing in the tribulation of Christ for the sake of the world." This gospel is a gospel of "cheap grace" because

---

33. See Catherwood, *The Evangelicals*, 123.
34. See Henry, *Uneasy Conscience*.

it denies the "costly grace" that calls the Church to the baptismal life of suffering with Christ for the sake of the world. Instead, it claims God's ultimate call to the church is to be "ready" to vacate the earthly premises slated for impending demolition. This denies not only the calling of gospel stewards to their broader stewarding service in the world, but also denies that the gospel intends to redeem creation.

This gospel is almost wholly born of the gospel of reaction.[35] Its historical "Genesis" can be traced and is well known. Unfortunately, it is not well known by those following it who seem to think that it originated in God's "dispensational plan" that ensued when Jesus's "gospel of the kingdom" was rejected by the nation of Israel. For those small details it is wholly based upon, only emerged in the 1800's in England and migrated to America in pietist/revivalist Christian fundamentalism. The dispensational details were seminally developed by John Nelson Darby, codified in Cyrus I. Scofield's widely distributed "reference Bible," and disseminated in many "end times" oriented books, Bible conferences, colleges and seminaries, and fully erupted in modern America in the mini-series of books by Hal Lindsay in the 1970s, followed by the "multi-series" of books by Tim LaHaye and Jerry Jenkins from 1995 to 2007.

One could in a general sense attribute its ready welcome to the "age of anxiety" and disillusion that was arriving in the post-Reformation religious uncertainty, secular modernism's failed vision of unlimited progress of man's kingdom, and Christian postmillennialism's religious version of the same as regards God's kingdom. These things altogether served as psychological/sociological "steroids" for this heightened gospel of reaction. Viewed more specifically and doctrinally, it was formed in reaction to the historical developments of doctrinal liberalism in the church that we saw earlier under the "gospel of reaction." Thus, its reaction consisted of two main developments: 1) Eschatological views of the "end-times" including: worldwide apostasy from God; the "rapture' of the true church to heaven before the coming of God's wrath in "the great tribulation; and God's reinstatement of national Israel to fulfill his original "kingdom" plan; 2) Separatism of the true church from the "apostate" dead bodies of Christendom, which in effect brought a hyper-denominationalism. The belief that God's "dispensational plan of salvation" required the *removal of the true church* to heaven from the earthly situation itself, signifies the most perspicuous escapist aspect, although the implied change in the

---

35. For a brief overview of the escapist gospel see Jewett, *Mission and Menace*, 165–67.

temporal mission of the church, "the great reversal," also signified the gospel of escapism. The vocabulary of "escape" is not "officially" used, but that ethos greatly inhabits this gospel, at least in the multitudes who follow it. The leaders certainly had more righteous motives for their teaching, though that does not make the eschatology biblical.

But as the movement progressed, especially into the media age where "the medium is the message," it seemed to shift towards a more base and naturally human motivation. Thus "escape" became part and parcel of the vocabulary, as seen even in the emotionally sensationalistic titles of Lindsay's and LaHaye's books. They spoke of "the late" planet earth and the church's escape from the world's "great tribulation" which would bring great sufferings of God's wrath to those "left behind." Of course, these views are supported with a patchwork of "plain" and "literal" interpretations of scriptures which, generally speaking, misinterpret the biblical symbolism and historical context of the original books. Ironically, for all the desire to be biblically sound the fundamentalists holding to this view come very near to falling to the heretical Gnostic thought which is condemned in the NT in 1 John 4:1–6. The main commonality with Gnostic thought is that present existence is seen more as a preparation for salvific escape away from the "fleshly" existence of the earth, than a call to perseverance in God's redemptive movements toward earth.[36] Thus they do not see themselves so much as "sent" to the world God reconciled in Christ, but more as destined to be removed from it, in violation of the express prayer of Christ that they be left in the world, rather than taken out (John 17:14–15). That hope seems but a "cheap grace," desirous of escaping tribulation, but still reaping the reward that is only *in* Christ's victory over the world. In short, this discipleship bypasses the need to participate in the cross of Christ by which he overcame the world, though Christ clearly delineated that path (Matt 24:9–14).[37]

I have presented this "gospel" starkly according to its doctrine and "logical" practice, knowing that many holding to the doctrine do not follow its "spirit" though fully adhering to its "truth," in a case of fortuitous

---

36. For a lively scholarly yet accessible treatment of both the early and latter day "Gnosticism" see Wright, *Judas and the Gospel of Jesus*.

37. The construction of John 17:15 is the closest parallel to the text of Revelation 3:10 which is foundational for this gospel of escape: "Because you have kept my word about patient endurance, I will keep you from the hour of trial that is coming on the whole world, to try those who dwell on the earth." See Easley, *Revelation*, 57–58; and especially Beale, *Revelation*, 289–92 for an extensive discussion.

inconsistency. After all they do need to evangelize the entire world before the "end period" so that more can also *escape* "the tribulation." Thus, they inhabit and proclaim a gospel of escape. In regard to its *present posture* to the world, this "gospel" turns the outward looking and living "community of God" into a "fortress church" that follows the self-security way of Cain's fortress city.[38] In regard to its *future hope* for the world the escapist gospel denies the gospel's hope in its flight from the world, rejecting the basic trajectory of the mission of God towards the world (John 3:16). It mirror's Jonah boarding the ship and taking the gospel with him in the opposite direction from Nineveh.

In relation to the criteria of the church's ordinances, it rejects the meaning of baptism wherein Christ's disciples follow him into "great tribulation," which requires a willingness to die to their natural worldly concerns.[39] In Christ the gospel stewards are not only buried in baptism to their old desires but risen to life on the shore of evil "Nineveh" to bring the good news to them, their real enemies and the enemies of God, but also "120,000 persons, who do not know their right hand from their left, and also much cattle" (Jonah 4:11). It fails the meaning of the Lord's Supper because it doesn't seek the worldly hope of God's coming banquet/kingdom for all the nations that the supper signifies in microcosm (Isa 25:6). Its antagonism perpetuates the old ways of humanity divided into us and them. But of "us and them" the true gospel says "there is no them; there is only us" since all were included in Christ's reconciliation.[40]

This "gospel's" exclusivism renders it warlike because it essentially divides humans into heavenly and earthly tribes as the by-product of "proper" interpretation.[41] This gospel inhabits a cheap grace without works (James 2:14–26) by half-heartedly throwing a bone to social works for the sake of soul-evangelism, reducing salvation to the way to heaven.[42] We saw in our brief introductory history that it was originally based

---

38. Scotty Smith uses the term "fortress church" as he discusses the church "placed in a strategic location in a pagan culture" for "opportunity and ministry" rather than "build Camp God and be a community of ingrown navel-gazers merely holding on 'till the rapture." Smith and Card, *Unveiled Hope*, 56.

39. See Romans 6:3, Acts 14:22, Revelation 1:9; 12:10–11.

40. Zahnd, *A Farewell to Mars*, loc. 2047.

41. See Poythress, *Understanding Dispensationalism*, 9.

42. For critiques of the escapist gospel and positive expositions of the eschatological hope of this world see: Hoekema, *The Bible and the Future*, 194–222; Poythress, *Understanding Dispensationalists*; Wright, *Surprised by Hope*; and Middleton, *A New Heaven*.

in a complete denial of the this-worldly "gospel of the kingdom" that Jesus preached, seeing such "worldly" concerns as "postponed" until the coming "millennial kingdom." Thus, the escapist gospel is perhaps the ironic epitome of the modernist theologian's lament that "Jesus came proclaiming a kingdom and what arrived was the church."[43] For the gospel of escape creates "gospel stewards" who are "descended" from Jonah, sitting outside *their* Nineveh, eagerly waiting for its judgment rather than hoping for its salvation. This puts the modern-day Jonah quite at odds with the gospel he was called to proclaim, and thereby puts the gospel "in the dock." It should also be mentioned that the concentration of the escapist gospel on God's wrath certainly communicates that God's "end game" seemed more about destruction than redemption (John 3:16). Accordingly, the gospel proclaimed is not easily read by the world as containing good for humanity and the world. Furthermore, this gospel is only good for the church as a means of escape from humanity and the world.

Again, I emphasize that I emphatically paint this gospel quite starkly, in order to point out its sub-gospel tendencies, all the while knowing that many Christians following these very "gospels" do much for God's kingdom, because their partially gospel-shaped lives are better than their gospel-eschatology. The greatest problem of this escapist gospel is a sin of omission, the not seeking to be formed into the "good-works" community of God which is, the "salt of the earth, city on a hill, and lamp on a stand for all in the house" that is not slated for destruction but for salvation (Matt 5:13–16).

The Gospel of Correct Doctrine/Correct Practice

The proclamation of this gospel would be, "The gospel of correct doctrine or correct practice provides its followers with the assurance of salvation that is signified by their allegiance to their Church community." This gospel basically holds that salvation is dependent on a person believing the correct doctrinal or practical formulas for a particular Christian denomination or community. These lead to a legalistic view of salvation, and an "us and them" divisive way of viewing the body of Christ. The minutia of details in the formulas is what gives them traction in the sociological formation of the community.

---

43. The saying that Alfred Loisy is most known for. See Wikpiedia, "Alfred Loisy."

In traditionally fundamentalistic/evangelical "tribes" the minutia may include particular views of scriptural inerrancy, views on baptism and the Lord's Supper, the literal creation of the universe in six days, the existence of hell, views of the "end times," or the fate of the unevangelized. In a liberal/progressive "tribe" the opposite is the case, namely those tenets have the reverse significance so that their *denial* is a sign of salvation. A more positive view of the "progressive" minutia would include particular practices such as spiritual disciplines, social justice, or activism.

What is interesting is that those two titles can serve as a diagnostic Rorschach self-test. Each side will view the other's framing of the faith as ridiculous and "legalistic" in opposite senses. The true gospel does in fact call for belief and practice, but neither of those "saves," while it is also certain that a faith that "works" is the better sign than mere "belief" (Jas 1:14–26). But in both cases, "the teeth" of such gospels is in their psychological and sociological pressure that derives from the "power" of inclusion or exclusion. The nature of "salvation," and exclusion or inclusion, may be quite differently conceived on each side, with a spectrum of variation lying between them.

The dangers of this "gospel" are twofold. First is the danger of an "us and them" attitude that grows from the manner with which these views are held, in relation to other Christian denominations/communities with different views, more than from the specific doctrines or practices. Second is the danger of this "method" replacing the atonement in Christ which alone is "saving," and is the foundation upon which the community of Christ can truly be "formed." And in all of this generalizing language, the truth is that the dangers in this false gospel are wholly based in the emphasis given to doctrine and practice, and the tendencies to elevate those to near-salvific significance regarding inclusion and exclusion from the respective communities and from "salvation" however that is conceived. For we must speak very generally to speak broadly. Perhaps the best way to conceive of the danger is to consider this the false gospel of religion in contrast to the gospel of reconciliation in Christ alone.

Bonhoeffer held that this false gospel is another form of cheap grace, saying "Cheap grace means grace as doctrine, as principle, as system."[44] In short, this false gospel mistakes adherence to its *conception* of "Christianity," and its religious response, as the gospel. But strictly speaking, one is saved by Christ alone. Jesus said something to the religious leaders

---

44. Bonhoeffer, *Discipleship*, 43.

of Israel that shockingly reveals another name for this "gospel." For Jesus warned against a "gospel of *the Scriptures*," saying:

> You search the Scriptures because you think that in them you have eternal life; and it is they that bear witness about me, yet you refuse to come to me that you may have life (John 5:39–40).[45]

Jesus reveals two indivisible truths regarding Scripture. The first is the *necessity* of the Scriptures, because they *do* "bear witness" to Christ. The second is that they *only* "bear witness" because *they* are not Christ. The gospel was achieved in the person and work of Christ. Salvation through the Scriptures themselves, as more than pointers to Christ, would turn the gospel into a system of knowledge and works. The gospel of correct doctrine elevates one's knowledge of Christ, and a gospel of correct practice elevates ones following of Christ. Both subtly devalue Christ's person and work. It is a subtle but dangerous shift of emphasis. In a discussion of Paul's statement that "the letter killeth, but the spirit giveth life" (2 Cor 3:5–6), Wilson summarizes this as a mistake of *staring at* the means God has provided for faith rather than *looking through* them.[46] And faith, properly speaking, is itself based in loving rather than in knowing God.[47]

Thus, the proponents of various gospels of correct doctrine or practice (that there are many versions reveals their falsity) need to consider whether they subtly shift the ground of salvation from Christ onto a body of knowledge or practice and the individual's subjective response. This leads to collaterally damage a true gospel-shaped discipleship by producing struggles with perfectionism, legalism, intellectualism, sectarianism, and separatism. These also damage the wider fellowship in Christ's one "community of faith" through tribe-centered hostilities of pride, comparison, competition, and slander. Thus this "gospel" is not only destructive

---

45. "Their tragic failure to grasp God's truth was nowhere more clearly manifest than in their approach to the Scriptures. It was not that they were negligent of this magnificent deposit . . . But Jesus points out that their primary motivation in such diligent study was the hope of final acceptance by God: you think that by them you possess eternal life . . . Jesus insists that there is nothing intrinsically life-giving about studying the Scriptures, if one fails to discern their true content and purpose. These are the Scriptures, Jesus says, that testify about me." Carson, *Gospel According to John*, 264–65.

46. "We make the same mistake with ritual, with doctrine, and with sacraments. We stare *at* instead of looking *through*." Wilson, *Against the Church*, 65.

47. "One needs to recall here that the first and greatest commandment is to love God, not to know him." Badcock, *Light of Truth*, 5.

of the gospel itself, but of the one body of Christ. For the unity of the church is not based in systematic doctrine or practical permutations, but in the nature of the church as already made one "in Christ."[48]

This may all seem to be the straining at a gnat Jesus spoke of, but we reiterate the two main dangers. This "gospel" subtly shifts the focus from Christ as the basis of salvation and as the basis of church knowledge and practice. And that subtlety can also result in the replacement of Christ, as the true gospel-dynamic of the creation and living of the church community, with doctrine or practice as the means of "creation" and "living." This gospel's error seems to be ultimately based in a mistake regarding the objectivity of the person and work of Christ, and the subjectivity of the human appropriation, wherein "salvation" is based in the subjective response rather than in the objective Christ. Baptism and the Lord's Supper show the Christ-centered objectivity of the creation and living of each and every church community, which are ironically also often used overly subjectively to the point of countering the gospel in Christ. Church members should *reflect* that reality, as they participate in the doctrine and practice of Christ, but they do not *determine* their participation therein. Again, these are subtle yet important distinctions that separate between "pure religion" and the "form" thereof (James 1:27; 2 Tim 3:5).

This "gospel" is in many senses based in a subtle shift from the gospel's home ground. But in the next "gospel" we will explore, the very working of the gospel is seen to be wholly based in the *opportunity* for subjective response rather than on the *good news* of God's objective reconciliation.

The Gospel of Conditionality

The proclamation of this gospel would be, "The gospel of conditionality promises that if anyone turns from their sins and believes in Jesus, then God will provide atonement for their sins and reconciliation with God." This false gospel is a matter of serious important theological doctrinal difference, but those holding to it and those opposing it will both proclaim that humans need to "repent and believe in the gospel" (Mark 1:15). The difference between those viewing it *as* the gospel and those viewing it as

---

48. "The foundation of unity is the nature of the church itself. Nothing else than one flock and one shepherd (John 10:16) is conceivable." Berkouwer, *The Church*, 50.

not the gospel, is in whether or not the gospel is the announcement of God's good news of the accomplished reconciliation of the entire world in Christ, or whether the gospel is the announcement of God's good news of the opportunity for individuals to become reconciled in Christ. Strictly speaking, according to Paul, the gospel presupposes the first, and *on that gospel basis,* proposes the second:

> In Christ God was reconciling the world to himself, not counting their trespasses against them, and entrusting to us the message of reconciliation. Therefore, we are ambassadors for Christ, God making his appeal through us. We implore you on behalf of Christ, be reconciled to God (2 Cor 5:19–20).

Therefore, the difference is that Paul held to an unconditional objective gospel which is to be subjectively responded to, while those holding to this false gospel see the gospel itself as conditional. Wilson summarizes "Paul's" unconditional gospel by saying,

> The ministry of reconciliation is based on the fact of the cosmic reconciliation. People reconciling with God does not create the ministry of reconciliation. The ministry of reconciliation brings the fact to those who have already been reconciled and yet still need to be reconciled . . . You have been reconciled; therefore, be reconciled.[49]

Those holding to the conditional gospel may think they hold to Paul's balance, but as we proceed, we hope to show that they do not, but subtly subtract the very unconditionality of the gospel that makes it "the good news" to be proclaimed.

The harm that this gospel presents is in the fact that if the gospel is unconditionally "good news," then the "conditional gospel" that has instead been almost universally proclaimed in Christianity is not the proclamation of the gospel *as* good news. This would also mean that the conditional "gospel" that has been proclaimed, and which is "in the dock," is *not* the gospel. Furthermore, as to the steward's gospel responsibility, they will first and foremost find themselves "in the dock" *before God*, and quite possibly before humanity, for their tragic failure.

The conditional gospel is based in a generally unquestioned philosophical "common sense" understanding of the atonement and how it relates to "final salvation." It is therefore integrally related to the very nature of the gospel. These are deep theological waters to tread, and it

---

49. Wilson, *Against the Church*, 111.

is extremely challenging to accurately write about what is revealed, although we will try. In the final analysis, those reading this presentation will probably need to dig deeper on their own in relation to these two complex areas of theology: the nature of the atonement, and the nature of human response to God. The following table lays out the basic differences our presentation will explore.

Table 3: Is the Gospel Conditional or Unconditional?

Conditional	Unconditional
Possible	Accomplished
Places salvation in the response to gospel	Places salvation in the gospel event
The gospel is the announcement of present opportunity	The gospel is the announcement of past event
Salvation is ultimately based on the individual's existential decision	Salvation is only based on Christ's finished work
Views Scripture through the lens of a modern philosophical view of the self and faith	Views Scripture through the lens of a pre-modern theological view of the self and faith
Is less willing to accept scriptural paradox	Is more willing to accept scriptural paradox
Is more prone to explain causality	Is less prone to explain divine causality

Therefore this "gospel" is about the efficacy of the gospel event. The question is whether the gospel is the announcement of what God has already accomplished for all people regardless of their response, or whether it is the announcement of an opportunity for something that can now be accomplished if people respond to that opportunity? This may seem to be a splitting of theological hairs, but many will already recognize that there is a rather dramatic difference, and many will suspect the unconditional gospel as the false one. For as we proceed, we will see that the answer does change the very nature of the gospel and the character of faith, demonstrating that this is no small side issue. For the true unconditionality of the gospel reveals that a conditional gospel that *merely* announces a new opportunity quite simply denies the gospel as the announcement of "the finished work of Christ" (John 19:30).

In order to more clearly examine the specific scriptural question of conditionality vs. unconditionality it seems that there are three main "procedures" that need to be followed. These are:

- *First*, the need to keep separate: 1) the saving event itself, and 2) the announcement of that event, and 3) the response to the event, as three distinct factors.
- *Second*, the need to proclaim these three factors in ways that preserve the integrity of each, even though there may remain certain "logical" or "paradoxical" tensions necessitated by the Scriptures.
- *Third*, to recognize that the attempt at complete understanding may simply reveal the limitations of human reason (Deut 29:29). After all, this is not only the "strange new world" of the Bible, but the strange God whose ways cannot be fully comprehended, even, or perhaps especially, by modern man's truncated views of God and reality.

Walter Brueggemann sees evangelism as the narration of a drama with three scenes of beginning, middle, and end.[50] He also notes that throughout the Scriptures there runs a recurring pattern of narrated three-scene dramas at important pivotal points of redemptive history, and the descriptions of these scenes provide what he calls "A Taxonomy of Evangelism" (37–43).

The Gospel Event

The first scene that Brueggemann sees is "*The Hidden Victory*" (39) where "there is combat, struggle, and conflict between powerful forces who battle for control of the turf, control of the payoffs, control of the future" all taking place in "a *theological conflict* hidden from our eyes" (17, 19).

One might ask whether in this drama enacted in the life, death and resurrection of Jesus, it is proper to call this a "hidden victory." We need to remember that our study of the gospel in Chapters 1 and 2 demonstrated that its victory was not *obvious*, because what was seen did not *appear* to be a victory. The death of Jesus *appeared* to be the exact opposite, dashing

---

50. Brueggemann, *Biblical Perspectives*, 16. In the rest of this section we cite the page references in the main text above.

the hopes of the followers of Jesus who *"had hoped that he was the one to redeem Israel"* (Luke 24:21). Nevertheless, the Apostle Paul's exposition of the gospel reveals that all of humanity was already *redeemed* in the reconciling person and work of Christ. Thomas F. Torrance explains that,

> It must be pointed out that justification is essentially a *corporate* act. 'In that Christ died, all died' (2 Cor. 5:14). The modern world with its renaissance view of man completely misunderstands the biblical teaching of justification and sanctification when it shuts its eyes to the essentially corporate nature of the deed of atonement and justification and sanctification. The individual is not left out of sight in the New Testament, but the emphasis is on the corporate union in Christ, and justification is expounded only within that corporate emphasis. In the widest sense and in a very profound sense, Christ's death for all mankind means that all men and women are already involved in God's act of justification—Christ died for them when they were yet sinners (Rom 5:8), and in that he died, all died, all were condemned, and all came under his substitutionary atonement—anything else completely disintegrates substitutionary atonement and breaks up the wholeness of justification and destroys it.[51]

Herman Ridderbos further explains that the corporate nature of atonement is also seen in Paul's view of the corporate nature of human life in sin. In writing of the corporate nature of Christ's atoning work Ridderbos says,

> All this does not speak in the first place of personal, individual regeneration, the individual past and the personal renewal. It is a matter here of redemptive-historical categories of old and new. Undoubtedly this does not mean a de-personalization of salvation. The new man, as we shall see still further, is not merely a collective or supra-individual quantity. But as in the doctrine of sin, where the individual's inclusion in the great corporate relationship of solidarity in sin was the dominating point of view, so also in the doctrine of renewal, what predominates is the inclusion and participation in the new creation that has taken effect with Christ and is represented by him.[52]

---

51. Torrance, *Atonement*, 128–29. For a thorough examination of the theology of Thomas F. Torrance see, Radcliff, *Claim of Humanity in Christ*.

52. Ridderbos, *Paul—An Outline of His Theology*, 206.

The Gospel Announcement

The second scene that Brueggemann sees is "*The Announcement*" (39) by "an additional character not present in the first scene . . . the announcer, the proclaimer, *the witness who gives testimony and tells the whole outcome he has watched*" (17).

Brueggemann adds an important clarification of evangelism. He writes, that "evangelism is a *three-scene drama* in which each scene must be kept distinct from the others. Our propensity is to collapse everything about evangelism into the second scene of announcement." (37) D. A. Carson also emphasizes the need for distinction and avoiding this collapse by emphasizing "the heart of the gospel." His also shows that the response to the gospel must be kept distinct.

> The heart of the gospel is what God has done in Jesus, supremely in his death and resurrection. Period . . . Repentance, faith, and obedience are of course essential, and must be rightly related in the light of Scripture, but they are not the good news. The gospel is the good news about what *God* has done. Because of what God has done in Christ Jesus, the gospel necessarily includes the good that has been secured by Christ and his cross work. Thus, it has a present and an eschatological dimension. We announce the gospel.[53]

As we proceed, we will indeed see the propensity to collapse all of the gospel into the announcement so that it, rather than the gospel event, becomes the scene where the gospel's victory occurs, in the experience of the hearers rather than in the historical event of the victory of Christ.

The Gospel Appropriation

The third scene that Brueggemann sees is "*The Lived Appropriation*" (39) which implies the question "'What shall we do?' (Luke 3:10, 12, 14). It is the question of appropriation of the news" (34). Carson added to his clarification of the gospel as what God has done—and the need to keep what has been done distinctly separate in its telling—the following caveat:

> Yet we must be careful not to make the lines too crisp . . . the "good news" is not like the news that says there has been an accident on the Dan Ryan Expressway. That sort of news does not

---

53. Carson, "What is the Gospel?" 162.

intrinsically demand anything of us (unless we happen to know the victims). By contrast, the gospel, the good news has an *intrinsic* demand to it, such that our rearticulation of the demand for repentance, faith, and obedience cannot be divorced from the gospel itself. Of course, the demand for repentance, faith, and obedience *divorced from Christ and his cross work* is no more the gospel than hope for a consummation divorced from Christ and his cross work is the gospel. But I do not see how one can be said to be truly preaching the gospel without spelling out the demands that the gospel makes.[54]

In Carson's words, one cannot "be truly preaching the gospel without spelling out the demands that the gospel makes." But we need to consider what would constitute a *divorce from Christ* in relation to these demands. It seems that what he is saying is that the response to the gospel cannot leave the responder "on their own." For if they are left on their own, then their response is from the place of "divorce" and their "lived appropriation" is essentially what saves them rather than the gospel event. A "divorced response" is to proclaim a conditional salvation.

Historically, the majority of evangelicals in Western Christianity, have posited a conditional salvation. This is because they view *the pivot point* between universal atonement and *actual salvation* as dependent on the temporal *existential decision* of each individual. But the *basis* for that temporal decision is the already accomplished atonement of Christ for them. That atonement basis thus serves as the "marriage" to Christ's cross work. But in the conditional gospel their actual salvation is *conditioned* on their temporal *existential decision* in response to an *external* Christ leaving them "on their own." This separation at the pivot point therefore constitutes not a marriage but a "*divorce from Christ.*" This means that the "accomplished atonement" of Christ for them, because of this conditionality, throws them back on their existential decision, their independent divorced response. Thus, it seems that a conditioning based on the existential decision essentially amounts to a divorce from Christ at the crucial pivot point.

A different view that seems to overcome this problem of divorce from Christ at the pivot point of decision is perhaps best represented by T. F. Torrance. In his view *the pivot point* between universal atonement and actual salvation is the already accomplished "existential decision" for God *already made by Christ for all humanity* during his life and even

54. Carson, "What is the Gospel?" 162–63.

on the cross. The following table further compares and clarifies the substance of the two views.

Table 4: The Place of Decision in Conditional and Unconditional Salvation

Conditional Salvation	Unconditional Salvation
In conditional salvation the pivot point between universal atonement and final salvation depends on the temporal existential decision of each individual in response to the already accomplished atoning work of Christ for them.	In unconditional salvation the pivot point between universal atonement and final salvation depends on the temporal existential decision of Christ for God as part of the already accomplished atoning work of Christ for them.
There is an "existential divorce" or separation from Christ at the pivot point.	There is a "marriage" or union with Christ at the pivot point.
Salvation is conditioned on the autonomous response to God of each individual.	Salvation is unconditioned and is based on participation in the response of Christ to God.
All individuals are viewed as objectively in Adam in the old creation and decision signifies the way of becoming part of the new creation.	All individuals are viewed as objectively in Christ in the new creation and decision signifies willing participation in the new creation.
Ultimately "throws man back upon himself" at the point of decision.	Ultimately "throws man upon Christ" at the point of decision.
The human decision initiates God's new creation.	God's new creation initiates the human decision.

In the unconditioned view, the *basis* for the "lived appropriation" necessary for each and every individual is therefore also already provided in Christ.[55] This does not deny that there is a further necessary, subjective, and personal aspect of "lived appropriation." But it also does not deny that God is intimately involved *in that appropriation* through the incarnate life of Christ. There is no *divorce from Christ* in this view

---

55. "Christ is so one with God that what he did God did, and so one with us that what he did we did." Torrance, *Atonement*, 152, cf. 158–66. Also see Torrance, *Incarnation*, 25–27. It is interesting that French phenomenologist Michel Henry says much the same. See Henry, *The Words of Christ*, 123.

because the individual's existential decision is a *participation* in Christ's existential decision that was part of the atonement he provided for all in his incarnate life and vicarious death. In this view the lived appropriation by the individual is not *divorced from Christ* but is a *participation* in an already accomplished at-one-ment. In the proclamation of the gospel individuals are not thrown back upon themselves at the pivotal point to depend on their own autonomous response. Thus, there is no "failure" in the atonement due to a tension between a universal atonement and its lived appropriation because the atonement itself provides the means. If it is objected to on the grounds that it still leaves actual salvation up to the existential decision of each individual, the truth is that the individual's failure is not due to some incomplete atonement, or even some insufficient grace, but rather simply and mysteriously on the mystery of human agency that still chooses to say "no" to God's unconditionally sufficient "yes" to them. The unconditional view accepts as a given that the atonement was universal, which traditional Calvinists will probably reject. But T. F. Torrance represents what is now called an "Evangelical Calvinism" that sees a complete efficacy in the atonement, but an efficacy for all of humanity rather than only for "the elect" as a limited group.[56]

It is admitted that there are Scriptures which on the face of it appear to emphasize the individual's decision as what includes them in the atoning work of Christ, but ultimately the unconditional gospel view is based on texts that indicate that believers and all their "works" are "created" by God as his "workmanship," and do not *become* created by God in response to their decision (Eph 2:8–10).

In the end, the answers depend on what is considered to be most true to Scripture regarding what is objective and unconditional in the gospel itself. And all seem to see some basic objectivity and unconditionality in the gospel event itself, and that those are the reasons it is unbelievable, important, and world-changing good news. Our human limitations in the face of God's own inscrutable God-ness, and the lack of a complete understanding of "The Strange New World in the Bible," call us to not ultimately rely on accepting only what seems rational to us. Remember Adam and Eve? Rather the call to the steward of the gospel is first and foremost to preserve each factor of evangelism in their separate integrities. An incomplete understanding need not prevent the proclamation of God's new wine that always pressures the old wineskins with which

---

56. See Torrance, *Incarnation*, 52, 177–80; Torrance, Atonement, 183–84.

we seek to understand it.[57] We feel it is safe to summarize by saying that the gospel is wholly unconditional. The only question is of exactly how the unconditional gospel relates to its "lived appropriation." Some reject its unconditionality outright, supposing that an unconditional gospel requires a complete universalism which would deny the reality of any individuals falling short of ultimate appropriated salvation. We have relied quite a bit on the views of T. F. Torrance in this section and he emphatically denied that he was a universalist or that there was no such thing as a "hell," while also rejecting resorting to man-made understandings when faced with divine paradox.[58] In regard to the rationalism of universalism and limited atonement Torrance writes,

> Here we see that man's proud reason insists on pushing through its own partial insight into the death of the cross to its logical conclusion, and so the great mystery of the atonement is subjected to the rationalism of human thought.[59]

This defense we have made of the gospel as unconditional, against the conditional gospel which seems to reign in Evangelical theology and proclamation, will still seem to fall short to many who think that they *are* following the Scriptures *apart from rationalism*, only in a better way even than Torrance. Therefore, we need to consider the broader picture within which we invariably theologize and philosophize.

---

57. "Think once more of the instance of Jesus's healing of the paralytic man as recorded in Mark, where he said to the man, 'My son, your sins are forgiven', and then also 'Rise, take up your pallet and walk'. There we have forgiveness breaking in as a creative act and evidencing itself by its own actuality in healing. So in the cross of Christ and in the Resurrection, justification is proclaimed and it comes breaking in upon us as the creative act of God acting upon us radically. It is that creative element that baffles our understanding, as indeed all creation does." Torrance, *Atonement*, 129.

58. Walker explains, "If we cannot understand how Scripture holds together certain things which we find difficult (such as the unconditional love and forgiveness of God for all, the finished work of Christ, the gospel imperative to repent and believe, and the fact that some refuse and are judged by the very gospel that offers them life) then it is not open to us to resolve the tension through a man-made logical schema which emphasizes some elements at the expense of others. We need to be crucified with Christ in our natural reason and through the transforming of our mind begin to penetrate into 'the interior logic of Scripture' so that we may learn to think as Scripture thinks and hold together what it holds together. Both universalism and limited atonement for Torrance fail to do that." Torrance, *Atonement*, 188, n. 70.

59. Torrance, *Atonement*, 187.

Rehabilitating the Stewardship of the Gospel

On the Objective Gospel and Subjective Salvation

Many following the gospel of conditionality will undoubtedly have the greatest objections because of their concern with subjective salvation, which we called "final salvation" above in Table 4. For in a sense there is an objective "salvation" which we showed in Table 3. But these are not to be equated. Just above we noted that the unconditional gospel does not posit a universal final salvation. So, the problem and solution are to preserve the objective gospel and the subjective lived appropriation, or "final salvation," in their own integrities, as was mentioned earlier. The gospel of conditionality collapses the objective saving gospel event and the subjective lived appropriation of the gospel into one "salvation." Of course, that raises paradoxical space/time problems that are probably greater than those of the unconditional view. (The root problem of all paradox in both views is in the relation to the past saving event and the present existential response.)

Our central concern has been with the objective gospel and how it ought to be proclaimed in its *past* universal efficacy. Strictly speaking, *present* subjective salvation is another matter. Because of the sinful will, the gospel posits that appropriation can only be based on the objective person and work of Christ, but the objective gospel does not automatically provide subjective salvation. This opens a door we cannot here enter, regarding the fate of the pre-evangelized, unevangelized, and what I call the over-evangelized, who have "rejected" a "gospel" that was not the true gospel. We have dealt with this a bit in our "excursus," and to some extent in our "postscript" although in neither place was this exact question our subject. In passing we note that C. S. Lewis is the author we know of who has seriously engaged the subject in several of his books, although he did so mostly through fiction.[60] Lewis imaginatively portrays people *objectively* in heaven, but *subjectively* in hell. This is certainly a paradox, but it seems required by the objectivity of the gospel, the bodily resurrection of "the just and the unjust" from the dead, and some form of hell, as the scriptures posit (Acts 24:15; Rev 22:14–15).

In passing it is interesting to note that before the rise of rationalism's "difficulties" with accepting scriptural paradox, much of the early church held that God's universal atonement requires viewing all as *saved* unless the Bible shows otherwise, rather than viewing all as *lost* unless the Bible

---

60. See Lewis, *The Great Divorce*; Lewis, *The Last Battle*, 171–86, (chapter 13); and Lewis, *The Pilgrims Regress*, 177–82.

shows otherwise.[61] This shifts the "burden of proof" toward the efficacy of the objective gospel, but also shows that the "grey areas" ought not be filled in merely for the sake of "rational theology." Therefore, we must conclude this section with some consideration of that subject.

On Unconditional Salvation, Biblical Faith, and Modern Philosophy

The main obstacle that modern "Bible believers" face, in regard to being able to accept an unconditional gospel, is that they have been born on this side of "The Great Divide" of the "Age of Enlightenment." T. F. Torrance sought to expound the gospel that originated from the far side of this great divide. He held that *"the modern world with its renaissance view of man . . . completely misunderstands the biblical teaching of justification and sanctification."*[62] Torrance brought to the exegetical table his awareness of the modern challenge of reading the Scriptures without undue influence from the current philosophical worldview. This is simply to posit a philosophical self-consciousness which tries to be aware of our modern understandings that filter and color our interpretations. Apart from self-consciousness of our prejudicial position in history, we default to seeing through the lenses of modernistic spectacles. This hinders *a responsive participation* in the revealed mind of Christ with a dangerous undetected substitute: *a creative prescribing* of Christ's mind which is co-opted according to its Lockean "common sense" understanding.[63] Wilson describes this just as philosophically, but reveals the oft-present reason for it, saying,

> Something is given that is wild and heavenly, and we expend all our energies to make it domesticated and earthly.[64]

---

61. See Punt, *A Theology of Inclusivism*, 8–11, 60–61.

62. Torrance, *Atonement*, 128.

63. Bradley Green writes that "The more conservative streams of Christianity generally bought into the basic premises of the Enlightenment—the quest/need for certainty, autonomous individualism, the centrality of reason—and from that vantage point tried to articulate a Christian response to the Enlightenment. This effort was doomed to fail, for these Christians naively assumed the very presuppositions and worldview to which they should have been offering a constructive and biblical alternative. Thus, as some see it, this more conservative stream of Christianity did not really respond to the Enlightenment but was already co-opted by Enlightenment thinking. Green, *Gospel and Mind*, 57. See also Marsden, *Fundamentalism*, 14–21.

64. Wilson, *Against the Church*, 113.

Thus, the reason self-awareness is needed is simply because we think as historically embedded creatures of space and time and imbibe the ethos of our culture.[65] Persons living in different eras simply think differently, apart from any conscious choice of their worldview.[66] And the important difference in this debate on the gospel is that the earlier situation before "the Great Divide" more fully inhabited the way of faith, as the gospel's revelation was diffused into human reality. The latter situation, though born from the earlier era, resulted in wholly different assumptions regarding faith, self, God, and even life and reality.[67]

A single text, John 3:21, can serve to challenge our modernistic assumptions and provide a bridge to a more gospel-based way of approaching the difficulties of the unconditional gospel.

> But whoever does what is true comes to the light, so that it may be clearly seen that his works have been carried out in God.

This text can be considered as a summary of the totality of human response to God's revelation. Borchert says that it shows that believing "is not merely a matter of mental affirmation but of life commitment."[68] Carson says "This strange expression makes it clear that the lover of light is not some intrinsically superior person. If he or she enjoys the light, it is because all that has been performed, for which there is no shame or conviction, has been done 'through God.'"[69]

---

65. Westphal writes, "Our inextricable embeddedness within history and its traditions means that our interpretations arise from particular locations. We are always somewhere (in semantic and cognitive space) and never achieve what has been called 'the view from nowhere.' Just as in ordinary vision, where we stand determines what we can see and what we cannot see of the object at which we are looking. This embeddedness means that understanding is necessarily plural, partial and perspectival." Westphal, "The Philosophical/Theological View," 74. Also see Peters, *Logic of the Heart*, 36–42.

66. Mark Twain's "Connecticut Yankee in King Arthur's Court" well pictures the cognitive dissonance that would result if time travel were possible, since the journey would be to a place of wholly different embedded human existence. The point is that the "natives" to each time and place suffer *no* cognitive dissonance in comparison to what displaced persons would suffer when viewing the *same* realities.

67. See Tyson, *Returning to Reality*, 189–205. Regarding a main view of reality delivered in modernism, Tyson writes, "after the long cultural evolution of Western modernity—the separation of subjective belief from objective knowledge is in our mother's milk" (19).

68. Borchert, *John*, 186.

69. Carson, *John*, 208.

Now at this point we need to refrain from repeating the pat theological answers that we think explain what this "strange expression" means. If we don't refrain, it may signify that our mind has been colonized by modern philosophy that thinks it can adequately explain the relationship between human freedom and divine sovereignty. The better way, in light of the text's mystery is to recognize that it aims to brings us into the theological terrain of the God of the Bible, rather than leaving us in the philosophical gymnasium of modern reason. Pascal perhaps put it best in his "Memorial" to God—who he called "FIRE"—a far cry from the god of the philosophers:

> FIRE. God of Abraham, God of Isaac, God of Jacob, not of the philosophers and scholars.[70]

Modern Protestant theologians such as Calvin, Edwards, and others, in the cusp of this great divide, sought to retain a foothold while the earth's metaphysical foundations shook and eventually cleaved. It seems that their footing "held" by trying to occupy the space opening in emerging reformulations of the human self and faith to posit fairly rationalistic deterministic notions of the nature of the undisclosed nexus, the causal gap that John 3:21 revealed but did not "rationally" bridge.

Thus, modern man attempts to philosophize what lies behind the veil of mystery, engaging in theological casuistry. But this "understanding" sidesteps the unity of the divine/human interaction that can only be "understood" *in* faith.

> To recognize the unity is then to recognize that the question of faith in God stays put within the context of *faith* and not outside it. As Newman put it in describing the project in *The Grammar of Assent*: "I am not to draw out a proof of the being of God, but the mode in which practically an individual believes it" (GA, 139). Faith is the mode of believing in God. Anything else is at best dealing with the god of the philosophers.[71]

Faith is therefore not about a response to God akin to the "Lockean view" of response to the news we read in the daily paper, which then requires philosophical gymnastics articulating "grammatical rules" about

---

70. A cited in Wells, *Pascal's Recovery*, 92.

71. Springsted, *The Act of Faith*, 244. Note that GA abbreviates "Grammar of Assent."

"how *faith* interacts with God" in regard to the causal reasons why some respond one way and some another.[72] Springsted clarifies all this, saying,

> To talk about interaction with God is not to talk about how faith is possible, or to uncover the "causal joint" where God acts or where we act in faith. To talk about God is to talk about *faith* in the first instance . . . To know God, to think about God with assent, is not first to know *about* God and then to assent to it, as Locke suggested. In the case of a revealed, and personal religion, it is to take God at his word and to live within the covenanted conventions God has revealed . . . What we think is the good that we will. This goes to the heart of moral self-identity; our selves are linked to the good we will and to which we aspire. This is not to deny that our knowledge of God is intellectual, but it is artificial to separate it from the God to which we assent. In Samuel Johnson's phrase: "We are perpetually moralists, but we are geometricians only by chance."[73]

Springsted's clarification demonstrates that his understanding of faith inhabits the view of self and faith exhibited in John 3:21, rather than the modern views of both. The person "doing the truth" and "coming to the light" does so "within the covenanted relations God has revealed," which is the unconditional New Covenant in Christ's person and work, in which our causal explanations dissolve as abstractions. Torrance held that there could be no divide between the love-motivated election of God and the love-in-action work of Christ.

> Whatever we do, we cannot speak of an election or a predestination behind the back of Jesus Christ, and so divide God's saving action in two, into election and into the work of Christ on the cross. God's eternal election is nothing else than God's eternal love incarnate in his beloved Son, so that in him we have election incarnate. God's eternal decree is nothing other than God's eternal Word so that in Christ we have the eternal decree or Word of God made flesh. Election is identical with the life and existence and work of Jesus Christ, and *what he does is election going into action.*[74]

---

72. Springsted, *The Act of Faith*, 69, 245.

73. Springsted, *The Act of Faith*, 245, 251. Quoting Robert W. Jenson, Green writes, "in that the gospel comes to speak of God, it affirmatively interprets all aspiration for truth's unity: if there is a God, all knowledge must finally be knowledge of him or his gifts." Green, *Gospel and Mind*, 172.

74. T. F. Torrance, *Atonement*, 183. Berkouwer writes, "It is not true that there is

This is simply the scriptural answer, content to rest in what remains mystery in John 3:21 which matter-of-factly pictures the human morally accountable self responding to the unconditional gospel. For this moral self signifies the repentant believing self which by "invitation" of incarnate atonement "participates" in Christ's covenantal relation with all humanity. This invitation was signified in Christ's own baptism by John, in solidarity with sinful humanity. Springsted goes on to present an interesting, simplified reformulation of the complex interaction between God and all people that the gospel invites and provides, viewed through the lens of God, the "Good Samaritan" to all of us as, "the wounded man by the side of the road."

> We are on the receiving end of care, for we need to be healed, to be reminded of the good that claims us. Faith accepts and sees the space opened to us, and the gift of new life . . . It is to give attention to the one who gave attention to us. We live humanly in human space as room given to us, not as created by us. We cannot live well in that space without having recognized and assented to our being the recipients of such a gift, and the objects of the compassion of a giver. We fully occupy such a space only in recognition of the Giver.[75]

The views of Springsted and Torrance which we have been considering greatly challenge all of us, living on the "enlightened" side of "the great divide," and which invariably lands God and the gospel "in the dock" before enlightenment "reason." We have seen that part of the rehabilitation of the gospel is the recovery of biblical understandings of faith and self and how both relate to our response to the gospel.

It is beyond doubt that this book contains instances of this writer's "Renaissance" thinking, since the author is at best a recovering modernist. But in the course of writing, whenever some topic was related to the unconditional gospel, a tension arose to elicit a more careful presentation that acknowledged the accomplishment of the gospel. This conscious effort undoubtedly influenced much of the "flavor" of the book by trying to consistently present the unconditional gospel un-hemmed by modern over-determinative views of faith and salvation. This is mentioned only to point out that the unconditional gospel is perhaps the most potent

---

some mysterious background of election which creates a message of bad news next to the message of good news . . . The doctrine of election is in essence the announcement of a Yes and not of a No." Berkouwer, *The Triumph of Grace*, 91.

75. Springsted, *The Act of Faith*, 251–52.

factor against modern reason which would "overcome" the gospel of the transcendent God (John 1:5).

Can the gospel of conditionality fall into some of the shortcomings of the other "gospels" we have considered? It seems that it can in several ways. A conditional gospel is the ultimate ground for a tribalistic exclusivity because it separates out from the universal atonement those persons who were either "chosen," or of themselves "willing." But because of the universal atonement in Christ, we "from now on regard no one according to the flesh" which leads to the old ways of tribalism and war (2 Cor. 5:16). Wilson says that apart from Paul's unconditional gospel the stewards can only see Ezekiel's vast valley of dry bones that cannot hear and become living flesh.[76] We could add that when the stewards have sometimes only seen the old fleshly distinctions, they have sometimes turned living flesh into valleys of dry bones in fallen carnal tribalistic warfare for "the kingdom of God" (1 Cor 3:3; Eph 6:12).

It is tragic and ironic that racism has plagued the church in America and America itself, thought to be one of the most "Christian" nations of history.[77] It is fact that many church congregations in America, because of racism, denied the meanings of baptism and the Lord's Supper, both of which signify crucifixion to the separatist elements of the world and a new life oriented by the essential equality of all peoples in Christ. The most powerful aspect of the unconditional gospel is that it requires all of humankind to be viewed as the same, not because they have the opportunity to be united to the new humanity in Christ, but because all already are. In relation to the gospel, the old "liberal" belief in "the fatherhood of God and the brotherhood of man" is not so liberal after all. In relation to the church and subjective salvation, that is a more fully realized "brotherhood," but it is only born because of the unconditional gospel and there is no essential, *objective* difference between the humans of each, and that objectivity is the basis of all *gospel* faith and practice toward those "outside" the church.

There is one additional "false gospel" that we have already glimpsed, but which needs to be considered more fully. For this false gospel is a hidden cause of all false gospels as the gospel-shipwrecking icebergs which continually "support" the surface gospels from beneath. These are

---

76. Wilson, *Against the Church*, 110–11.

77. For recent studies of racism in relation to Christian "mission" that was insufficiently based in Col 1:15–20, see Harvey, *Taking Hold*, 178–206, and Smith, *Awaiting the King*, 170–79.

the unseen *pre-existing gospels* over which all steward ships journey with their precious cargo of good news. At the outset of this exploration of false gospels we noted the gospel of war was perhaps *the* foundational false gospel. At this point we will seek to understand how *that* foundation has a symbiotic relationship with the gospel of culture and how both "battle" against the gospel of Christ.

The Gospel of Culture

The proclamation of this gospel would be, "The gospel of culture only requires following the tested and true laws and customs of one's people."[78] The reason that the gospel of Christ often appears to be of little or no good and therefore "in the dock" is due to the pervasive success of the pre-existing *gospel of culture* that invariably precedes it. In fact, this actually means that the gospel itself is the counter-gospel, since the primal gospel was rejected in Eden in exchange for the gospel of the will to power. The gospel of culture is not one huge monolith appearing everywhere, but rather manifests itself according to the specifics of each particular historical context. In essence each particular cultural gospel functions as the sacred core, the *mythos,* for the culture.[79] One could look at humanity in light of the Scriptures and easily posit a common baseline culture of sin *as* the culture's *religion,* as unpleasant as that notion is.[80] One could even posit that humanity's cultural engine that motors it on its way as it inhabits and expresses its self-love and the will to power, is "the world, the flesh, and the Devil." Of course, the "cultured" don't posit such barbarisms.[81] Nevertheless the triune engine just mentioned is revealed in a slightly different order in the Scriptures, in which we will italicize the three:

---

78. Wherein the norms of the culture represent the highest ethic, which as Kierkegaard showed in his book "Fear and Trembling" in relation to Abraham's call to sacrifice Isaac, is to be "suspended" by the higher call of God. See Westphal, *Kierkegaard's Concept of Faith,* 49–51, 54, 94. Kierkegaard, *Fear and Trembling,* 54–67.

79. "Viewed historically, most of man's worlds have been sacred worlds." Berger, *The Sacred Canopy,* 27, loc. 447. "Mythos is more basic than logos as far as human culture (the interpretive lens of all truth discourse) goes." Tyson, *Returning to Reality,* 76.

80. C. S. Lewis paints a dismal picture of a culture where *sin* is obviously its very religion, albeit unrecognized by *all* its inhabitants. See Lewis, *The Great Divorce.*

81. "'We call it hell.' . . . 'There is no need to be profane, my dear boy.'" Lewis, *Great Divorce,* 39.

And you were dead in the trespasses and sins in which you once walked, following *the course of this world*, following *the prince of the power of the air*, the spirit that is now at work in the sons of disobedience—among whom we all once lived in *the passions of our flesh*, carrying out the desires of the body and the mind, and were by nature children of wrath, like the rest of mankind (Ephesians 2:1–3).

Since all human cultures exhibit the life of fallen humanity in sin they share in that common cultural heritage. But that does not reveal the specific "hook" that exists as *gospel* in a culture.[82] For as we have already insinuated, the cultures of humanity do not generally advertise their "good news" as the wonderful salvation provided by "sin," or "the will to power," or "the world, the flesh, and the Devil," or "how to go to hell." This is because from the time of Cain's first city, cultures evaded their essential nature in relation to God and so dedicated more positive unitive objects to embellish their gospels. Seemingly, "*the city*" itself *was* the first explicit "hook" of a gospel *outside* Eden.[83] And as the cities like Cain's spread, so also did the false gospels of culture.

N. T. Wright provides a telling description of the nature of the preexisting gospel of the "cultured" cities of the Roman Empire in which any counter-narrative *gospel* arrived as the upstart and challenger, the "new kid on the block" which would be summarily put in its place.

> The early Christians very quickly gave Jesus's cross meanings that were deep, rich, and revolutionary, but this was done in the teeth of the meanings that the cross already possessed. It already had a *social* meaning: "We are superior, and you are vastly inferior." It had a *political* meaning: "We're in charge here and you and your nation count for nothing." It therefore had a *theological* or *religious* meaning: the goddess Roma and Caesar, the son of a god, were superior to any and all local gods. As Jesus of Nazareth hung dying that Friday afternoon, all those meanings would have been deeply intuited and understood not only by

---

82. Nor does it reveal that cultures are wholly sinful, or that any culture is based wholly on a hidden (or not so hidden) gospel within it. On the many facets of the relation of culture and the gospel see: Keller, *City Church,* 181–247.

83. Inside Eden it seems their "gospel" was objectified in the "wisdom" of the fruit from the tree of the knowledge of good and evil. Of course, self-achieved "wisdom" was also the goal of Cain's city.

the Roman soldiers, but by the weeping women at the foot of the cross and the disgraced disciples behind their locked doors.[84]

Wright goes on to show that the gospel of Christ as a counter-narrative encapsulated in Jesus's cross "demands the rethinking of categories." Willie James Jennings points out that the Roman Empire's "gospel" was essentially the "citification" of the world, and in light of what we saw earlier of Cain's "will to power" project of "the city," we can see that the empire fully inhabited Cain's anti-gospel way.[85] Truly, the gospel faced an unbelievable challenge, but also a remarkable promise, as it "arrived" on the scene in the flesh of Jesus and his early followers. For the promise in David Dark's statement concerning the gospel's inherently "alien" and "dangerous" nature must not be overlooked:

> Properly understood, the gospel of Jesus is a rogue element within history, a demythologizing virus that will undermine the false gods of any culture that would presume to contain it.[86]

Nevertheless, the people of a culture generally, at the first, continue with "business as usual" because their cultural conditioning and inhabitation pre-exists and prevents the "would-be gospel" from gaining traction. Their "gospel" automatically has the advantage of supporting the entire preexisting established order. Though the gospel of culture generally operates "below the surface" of consciousness, when challenged, the subjects of the order can produce some "goods" of their "gospel" with its particular "hooks" of good-news propaganda that prevent any new gospel-challenger from gaining a foothold (or more properly, an imagination-hold).

The pre-existing gospels will thus contain various appealing ingredients that prevent reception of the gospel of Christ. If and when Christ's gospel "gains ground," the pre-existing cultural gospel will generally remain to become the hidden iceberg-like foundation for "new" false gospel constructs that "surface" from below. One example is the gospel of conditionality just considered above. It is a "gospel" philosophically influenced by "the modern world with its renaissance view of man," and thus a syncretistic cultural gospel.[87] Several others would be the culture/

---

84. Wright, *The Day*, 60.
85. Jennings, *Acts*, 5.
86. Dark, *The Gospel*, 8.
87. Torrance, *Atonement*, 128.

gospel hybrids that Paul revealed to the churches in Corinth and Philippi, that we saw in the introduction.

Another example is provided by Walter Brueggemann who has presented a masterful "naming" of a predominant pre-existing gospel of our culture today as *"therapeutic, technological, consumer militarism"* by revealing its "script." He presents a nineteen-point expose of that script under the title "Some Theses on the Bible in the Church." We will only need to consider his third thesis:

> The dominant scripting of both selves and communities in our society, for both liberals and conservatives, is the script of therapeutic, technological, consumer militarism that permeates every dimension of our common life . . . *therapeutic* . . . the common assumption that there is a product or a treatment or a process to counteract every ache and pain and discomfort and trouble, so that life may be lived without any inconvenience . . . *technological* . . . the assumption that everything can be fixed and made right according to human ingenuity . . . *consumerist* . . . the whole world and all of its resources are available to us without regard to the neighbor . . . *militarism* . . . that pervades our society serves to protect and maintain a monopoly that can deliver and guarantee all that is needed for therapeutic technological consumerism.[88]

Brueggemann's presentation and application of this "dominant script" to the church is a very serious call to recognize its seductiveness and pervasiveness.

> It is important in my judgment that the script be named; it is equally important to recognize that all of us, across the spectrum, are powerfully inducted into it; none of us a priori can claim high moral ground.[89]

Brueggemann's expose and application reveals much of the content of one of our main cultural gospels today in America and elsewhere. It is important to think through that brief description and consider its subtly seductive warlike ways against the nature of created life itself, against its Creator, and against our neighbors. But this militarism is fairly well hidden to those enjoying its tempting fruit in the center of the empire.

---

88. Brueggemann, *Mandate to Difference*, 192–93.
89. Brueggemann, *Mandate to Difference*, 192.

But Brueggemann's expose is also now several decades old and since that time it appears as though *that* cultural gospel has become the backdrop for the emergence of a more blatantly visible *warlike* gospel which inhabits "social justice" and "identity politics." This new gospel is rooted in a phenomenon called "Cultural Marxism," a term more descriptive than precise, by those who recognize *some* ideological descent from Marx.[90] The roots of this unfortunately *quite real* cultural gospel were exposed in the middle of the twentieth century by the Hungarian scientist turned philosopher Michael Polanyi.[91] He proposed that the engine driving "social justice" that had been at work in the "revolutionary" Marxist influenced totalitarianisms was what he called "moral inversion." In his magnum opus called "Personal Knowledge" he wrote that,

> *Man masked as a beast turns into a Minotaur.*[92]

The genealogy of his definition is that "man" (as moral from Christendom) "masked as a beast" (through Enlightenment skepticism) "turns into a Minotaur" (of moral fury in fanatical perfectionistic social justice). Obviously, this is a culture/gospel hybrid. Mark T. Mitchell further clarifies that the morality inherited from Christendom yields a new form of puritanism, wherein that moral impetus is transformed into Polanyi's "Minotaur" through the "will to power" that prevailed following the cultural "death of God" in the modern period of the Enlightenment.[93] Mitchell writes,

> When social justice warriors demand equality or justice, they are invoking the Puritan myth, which they explicitly deny but upon which they necessarily depend. When they demand liberation of the oppressed, they are echoing the Old Testament prophets, mediated through Christianity, without which liberation gains little purchase. At the same time . . . Nietzsche's atheistic myth has made substantial, if only partial, inroads into our

---

90. This "tag team" arose because of the success of previous "gospels" of skepticism, nihilism, materialism, consumerism, and ironically because of the moral influence of Christianity. For exposes see Murray, *Madness of Crowds*; Mitchell, *Power and Purity*.

91. See Mendenhall, "Cultural Marxism is Real."

92. Polanyi, *Personal Knowledge*, 231–35.

93. See Mitchell, *Michael Polanyi*, 52–58, 147–50. Polanyi's "Minotaur" reveals the fact that all cultural gospels this side of Christendom are in some way grown from "Christianity" because of their cultural genealogy. This is why many historically aware atheists are of late self-identifying as "Christian atheists."

consciousness. Social justice warriors embrace the tactics and rhetoric of the will to power.[94]

The warlike quality of this gospel in the "tactics and rhetoric" mentioned by Mitchell seem to be the necessary result of a nihilistic cultural fall from grace which nevertheless pursues "social justice."[95] One doubts whether its militant puritanical proponents "self-righteously" employing the Nietzschean "will to power" can to any extent *truly* promote justice and equality or whether it in reality only aims to achieve Brueggemann's dominant script for themselves when they hold the militaristic power against those they envy. For as Polanyi's Minotaur, they resemble C. S. Lewis's "men without chests" who as the skeptical enlightenment culture's modernistic nihilistic geldings *cannot* be morally reproductive.[96]

This fall to the will to power and warring indicates a substantial fall from implicit gospel ways such as has been tragically repeated countless times in human history since 'adam' and Cain and is even more significantly a fall from *the explicit gospel* in the post-Christian West.[97] This all leads theologian Peter Leithart to designate our age as not merely one of secularization but also as a fall to "Galatianism" in "the Galatian Age."[98] That fall partly indicates a fall from *some* practice of forgiveness as a societal principle of necessity. Max Scheler was probably right in his view that Nietzsche's "ressentiment" that animates today's cultural gospel was not, as he supposed, caused *by* the gospel, but rather by the fall *from* it.[99]

---

94. Mitchell, *Power and Purity*, 135.

95. Alister McGrath provides a short expose of the warlike religious zeal secular idealists often adopt as they pursue "social justice." McGrath, *Why God Won't Go Away*, 77–80.

96. "We make men without chests and expect of them virtue and enterprise. We laugh at honour and are shocked to find traitors in our midst. We castrate and bid the geldings be fruitful." Lewis, *The Abolition of Man*, 35.

97. For instance, Brian Zahnd narrates Rome's "rehabilitation" of the Greek god of war "Ares" to be renamed "Mars . . . reborn with a positive public image. If Ares was feared and held in contempt, Mars was believed and celebrated. A farewell to Ares and a welcome to Mars." Zahnd, *A Farewell to Mars,* loc. 1792. Similarly, Simone Weil held that Hitler was "an inevitable product of the cult of grandeur that was part and parcel of the West's glorification of the Roman Empire." Chenavier, "Simone Weil," 69.

98. See Leithart, *Delivered from The Elements*, 258–81. Leithart's terms are from Paul's letter to the Galatians: "I am astonished that you are so quickly deserting him who called you in the grace Christ and are turning to a different gospel—not that there is another one . . ." (Gal 1:6–7). For a specific account of America's fall from earlier (albeit imperfect) gospel ways, see Leithart, *Between Babel and Beast*.

99. See Max Scheler, *Ressentiment*, 34.

Forgiveness though is not meant for, and cannot become the basis for the excuse and enablement of evil practice in a license to sin so that "grace may abound" to those continually wielding the way of force in the will to power. But a truly just society would nevertheless need to be ultimately founded on some orientation to the reality of forgiveness since it is an integral aspect of the reconciliation of the sinful world, in Christ.[100] It is probable that the West's fall from the gospel has exacerbated the hostility of many toward the sociopolitical merits of "mercy in judgment." Though the gospel cannot be conceived of as having become substantially embodied in the culture of Christendom, "mercy in judgment was nevertheless to some extent present because of the gospel. Identity politics, "Cultural Marxism," and militant tribalism/nationalism of the right, all seem to simply have no place for even a shred of mercy and therefore manifest the hostility of a judgment oriented societal fall from grace in a Galatian age.[101]

It seems that the "natural" propensity toward "war" in the culture demonstrates that it is largely *unconsciously* and *schizophrenically* "fought" on the left and the right which have both been commonly shaped by two foundational historical developments. The first development is the lapsed Christian/modernistic "moral" perfectionism that motivates the "pseudo-religious crusade." The second development is the post-modernistic relativistic moralism in regard to transcendent virtues that shapes "the means of war." Thus Polanyi's "moral inversion" synthesis of perfectionism/skepticism drives the resulting tendency toward a violently utilitarian and outwardly focused "immanentization of the eschaton," as Voegelin called it.

---

100. Smith addresses the issue of "mercy in judgment" in relation to government that dovetails with Leithart's tracings of the Reformed/Roman-Catholic Galatianist battles with each other, by showing that "one of the gospel's craters in the Western political landscape is the *limiting* of judgment (and government) and the incorporation of mercy *in* judgment." Smith, *Awaiting the King*, 102–12. In light of Leithart's historical analysis and Smith's thought informed by Oliver O'Donovan, it seems to me that the latest surge of "judgment" we are discussing above signifies a further fall to Galatianism from the West's political liberalism that included an "evangelical" gospel effect that survived the Reformation conflicts. The main point is that one could say "one step forward, two steps back" in regard to gospel-influenced "mercy in judgment," as we see a more merciless ethos emerging in the left and right socio/politics today.

101. "The eyes of Jesus did not view the evil, the immoral, and the despised in terms of the popular stereotype and distinctions of superiority and inferiority of the day; the eyes of Jesus always saw others, regardless of their shortcomings, as human beings, fellow children of adam, and loved by God." Baggett, *Seeing*, 136–37.

We cannot enter more fully into an expose of this "gospel" other than by simply summarizing that through it the "gospel of war" has found new purchase in the common "strife-together" of us as not-so liberated moderns and postmoderns. For moderns, the warlike tones of its cultural gospel were previously fairly well hidden under the patriotism that could support the expansionist empire that used force against exploited non-citizens elsewhere in the world to promote Brueggemann's *therapeutic, technological, consumer militarism.* The new cultural gospel of postmoderns allows us to more conspicuously participate in interpersonal warfare against other citizens as *the rightful means* of liberation.[102] "Freedom of expression" *cultivates* "shouting down" and "cancelling" every suspected opponent of "political correctness" and "wokeness." Western liberalism's prized virtue of "tolerance" *cultivates* the ugly tyranny of intolerance because of its "horror of honest argument," its will to power preference to relegate any opinion other than of the established authority to the private sphere.[103] The reactionary recoil of "freedom of religion" through self-interest *cultivates* the exclusion of people of other faiths from citizenship. Thus this "holy war" of the left finds a willing sparring partner in those on the right who fight "the culture war" tooth and claw as the means of *the will to power* for their own cultural gospel, what is "politically correct" to them. But for warfare to become the gospel of the common life of a culture is antithetical to communities in need of reconciliation. Such warlike "means" manifest the divisiveness and hostility of a Hobbesian "warre of every man, against every man" waged on home turf. How easily we fall to the gospels of war and culture.

When we introduced the gospel of war, we said that it may be the most pervasive gospel in some way always lying beneath all the others. But the gospel of culture is perhaps simply the positive face of the good cop/bad cop symbiotic relation in a unified gospel of culture/war. And this gospel is democratically available to all, right or left, following the will to power no matter a self-conception otherwise. In either case, one aspect is the "war" that we like to conceal, the other the "culture" that we deem fit to reveal. Of course, this two-sided coin is for the most part

---

102. There is amazing irony in the fact that father postmodernism's quest, as "vapor's revenge" upon modernism's "pervasive power," has increased power's practical use for postmodernism's children's quest for "liberating knowledge." See Leithart, *Solomon*, 137–50. I partly basing this statement on what I can understand of Leithart's quite packed expose and partly on my own understanding of his subtitles.

103. See Wood, *Chesterton*, 132–39.

lying in the unconscious recesses of our culture/war gospel will to power as the unexamined "given" of today's common ethos. But as said before, if for some reason we need to justify our way, we can generally conceive of self-evident reasons why our "gospel" is necessary and good. All culture/war gospels say it protects the *home front*, but as in all war—even a cold one—it is a *front*, nonetheless. But it increasingly seems that the cold war of a "balanced" culture/war gospel seems only a thing of the past, as the bad cop seems to be overcoming the good cop in all "interrogations" of domestic threats.

But God in Christ has launched what C. S. Lewis called the "good infection."[104] Perhaps that's not a winsome illustration in light of 2020–21 and Covid-19. But the truth is that the gospels of war and culture were themselves infections that were caught in Eden's maternity ward for "humanity" and are perennially and particularly contagious to humans in all times and places. But we have grown accustomed and adjusted to post-infection life because of its supposed benefits. Or have we? For when we fail to keep up the disciplines of our diversions, as Pascal noted, we tend to remember the basic dis-ease of our Freudian "Civilization and its Discontents" and notice our longing for healing from the self-propagated plague we have democratically oppressed ourselves and others with.[105]

Perhaps a community living by the strange signs of baptism and the Lords Supper, signs of *death together* toward the old ways and *life together* in a new way, could demonstrate that the gospel of Jesus Christ is good for the church, humanity and the world. But when the stewards of God's *true gospel/culture* have themselves proclaimed and lived "gospels" that are contrary, they tragically, though only temporarily, "poison the well" of God's water of life for humanity. For their succumbing to the false and empty glories of war and culture, and their susceptibility to the infections of sin and forms of death, would indeed poison the well if their failures were not already overcome by Christ. But Christ's unconditional gospel was already accomplished, and still remains, through veiled by the darkness of the steward's "jars of clay." For God still says, "let light shine out of darkness" (2 Cor 4:6–7). Our book's methodology exposes the sins of the stewards, and we have already seen them under some magnification. But Paul Tyson says of the situation,

---

104. C. S. Lewis, *Mere Christianity*, Book IV:4
105. See Pascal, *Pensées*, #131.

> The community of those who seek to live in the life of God is located within the larger world of idolatry, as a site of redemption for the world. This is true even though the church is a community of sinners where the psychic illness that characterizes the world is found in abundance within the church. The crucial difference between the church and the world is that the church exists to *treat,* rather than to admire, the illness of sin.[106]

The steward community's struggle against its "psychic illness" signals a rumor of a true glory, flowing from the wounds of Christ's stewards, wounded for the sake of the world, as was he.[107]

The Gospel of "The Kingdom of God"

The proclamation of this gospel would be, "The gospel of the kingdom of God is that through the incarnate life, death, and resurrection of Jesus God began a new creation of humanity. It is a veritable new Genesis, with Christ as the firstborn of a new humanity reconciled to God and their image of God bearing task in the world."

The presence of this gospel at the end of this list of false gospels presents a sort of a Rorschach test. How it "worked" will be left for the reader to ponder. For this gospel *is* the gospel. We thus conclude the list partly to "clear the air" and also to give the gospel more precise definition by way of contrast with these false gospels.

The earliest designation of the gospel is "the kingdom of God" as seen in the words of Jesus in Mark 1:15. It calls on people who hear it to "repent and believe in the gospel." The gospel of the kingdom flows from God's own pre-existent trinitarian "culture" of love to become the new Edenic garden/city made fully alive through and with its gospel-culture (Rev 21:9—22:4).

We will try to very briefly imagine different nuances of meaning revealed when the gospel of the kingdom "meets" each of the false gospels.

The gospel of war, for the gospel stewards especially, inhabits their remaining Cainite desire to "be like all the nations" with "our king" to "go out before us, and fight our battles" (1 Sam 8:20, KJV). In contrast, the gospel of the kingdom creates a people of all nations to be "one *holy*

---

106. Tyson, *Kierkegaard's Theological Sociology,* 45.

107. Recognition of good speaks of a fundamental goodness created by God. And deep longing for healing *at-one-ment* speaks of a remedy we were created to receive. See Lewis, *Mere Christianity,* Book 3:6.

nation" *set apart* from the merely human nations and existing not *against* the worldly nations but *for* them, having their feet "shod with the gospel of peace" (1 Pet 2:9; Eph 6:15). The warfare of the kingdom of God is "not against flesh and blood, but against principalities, against powers, against the rulers of the darkness of this world, against spiritual wickedness in high places" (Eph 6:12). The gospel of war follows the way of sight and force to overcome its enemies. The gospel of the kingdom follows the way of faith, love, and hope, and the warrior-king of the kingdom of God lays down his life to liberate all, including his enemies.

The gospels of "Christianity And," and "cheap grace," forget that the the kingdom of God is *God's* kingdom, *not theirs*. God's kingdom is not their church, church-state, civil-religion, or even their particular gospel-culture. The gospel of the kingdom is not their formula for church growth, pet peeve of doctrine or practice, social justice cause, or a means to their ends. The gospel of the kingdom is not about their baptized desires but their desire's baptism into the death and life of Christ to be raised to the larger hope of God's universal reign in the new humankind being formed in Christ.

The gospel of reaction mistakes the concern of the hour for the universal mission of the eternal God. It starts its gospel race three-quarters of the way down the world's track in relation to the latest scientific, philosophical, or social development and submerges the gospel beneath that present concern. It is formulated in reaction and warfare with the winds and waves of man rather than by participation in the emerging way of God that meets the present concerns with the eternal gospel that overcomes evil with good (Rom 12:21). The gospel of reaction is distracted by the skirmish of the day and forgets the gospel-war of the ages.

The gospel of correct doctrine or practice replaces the gospel of the kingdom of God with its human understandings thereof. It trusts its comprehension instead of participating in God's inscrutable and ever-new redemptive acts flowing from the event of Christ. It subsumes the kingdom of God under its principles and practices. It think that the process of gospel-reality can be presented and understood as is a mathematical theorem written on the page. Simply put, it domesticates God to its finite understanding. The gospel of the kingdom calls for ever-expansive doxologies of glory (Rom 12:33–36).

The gospel of escapism replaces the invasive this-worldly coming of the gospel of the kingdom with a desired flight to the heavenly harps, away from the fray of *the* kingdom that *necessitates* "worldly" tribulation for its citizens (Rev 1:9). Its "Gnosticism" effectually denies God's self-giving missional movement toward the world in incarnation, redemption, and transformation. It replaces those with the selfish Jonah-like desire for retreat and security. It seeks to save its life and thereby loses it, rather than gaining it by losing it for the gospel. The gospel of the kingdom brings God's will, "on earth as in heaven" (Matt 6:10).

The gospel of conditionality replaces the accomplishment of the already accomplished good news of the kingdom with news of an if/then opportunity it holds over the heads of humanity, controlling, domesticating, and reducing the universally efficacious reconciliation Christ won to mere potentiality. It essentially replaces good news with "good advice," negating the appeal and power of the gospel, and throwing humans back upon themselves and their dis-ability to respond, accompanied by the anxiety of worrying whether their response is sufficient. The gospel of the kingdom proclaims that they have *no* capacity for response and must rely on and participate in Christ's incarnate response to God.

The gospel of culture looms beneath all preexisting "gospels," but the gospel of the kingdom has already overcome them all, albeit without overt "culture warfare" but with the cross of weakness that subverts its Cainite ways of self-love and the will to power. The gospel of culture justifies and baptizes the desires of fallen Adam and all his descendants, but the gospel of the kingdom justifies and baptizes fallen humankind in Christ the second Adam, and all his descendants (Rom 5:18–19; 1 Cor 15:45–49).

As can be seen, the false gospels are like the layers of an onion, and not a particularly sweet one for that matter. Their unravelling can bring tears to the eyes of the strongest. Even Pontius Pilate seemed to tear up at the diabolical onion layers he saw Jesus peel away before him as he made "the good confession" of the gospel way of faith (1 Tim 6:13). For his kingdom was "not of the world" though it is fully birthed in the world through much tribulation to liberate its captives (Col 1:24; Rev 1:9). The gospel is therefore of a wholly different kingdom, a king like no other, and a participation of all its citizens in the weakness of the cross of reconciliation.

The Gospel and Human Agency

We move now from the interrogative witness "what" to the step in which we will subject the stewardship of the gospel to "who" and "how." We considered the *fact* of agency with "when, where and why" and the *message* of agency with "what." Now we need to consider the *agents themselves* simply *as* agents, and also their *personal manner* by bringing them before "who and how."

We have already seen that the "stewardship of the gospel" necessarily involves the lives of the stewards. Obviously the "who" exactly pertains to them but the "how" also does. And the fact of the matter is that *how* the stewards conduct themselves is of paramount importance in the stewardship of the gospel. And so, to consider how they carry themselves and handle their responsibility is to narrow down the focus of the stewardship of the gospel to the aspect of its *agency*.

The stewardship of the gospel necessarily involves stewards. But beyond that bare fact the truth is that they need to be caught up into the dynamic of the gospel, *the manner of the gospel* so to speak. In the nature of the case, we should expect this given that they carry life-changing news. To think that such news would not change them in some manner would seem to give the lie to their claim to be God's messengers and God's claim that they are so. We might liken the stewardship of the gospel to the task of carrying fire. In God's intention, when one carries the gospel fire, one is called to become engulfed by it. In fact, without such a result, the fire, which is to be revealed, is not revealed *as fire*. Christ spoke of the difficult baptism that his disciples would undergo, and this baptismal fire was their induction into the fellowship of the sufferings of Christ (Luke 12:49–50; Matt 20:22–23a). But as we have seen, the stewards participate in the strange reality of God who consumes evil by being burned but not consumed in that encounter, becoming the "burning bush" that Moses saw on the mountain of God:

> And the Lord appeared to him in a flame of fire out of the midst of a bush: and he saw that the bush was on fire and was not burnt (Exod 3:2, Douay-Rheims 1899 American Edition).

The gospel stewards participate in the suffering sign of the burning bush in Egypt, and in the sinful sign of Jonah in the belly of the beast. In both cases it seems they ought to be consumed in their tribulation in the world. For in the eyes of the world they are seen as without rights, and as good as dead, as far as serving any redemptive purpose. They are merely Israelite slaves for the welfare of the established order, or the Israelite scapegoat for its salvation. But the paradox is that those "benefits" signify Israel-steward's election in the elect Christ, who became sin to suffer for the life of the world (1 Pet 2:6; 2 Cor 5:21). Thus, the oppressions and sins of Israel prophetically signify the dark calling of their election for the ultimate good of humanity and the world. Their lives in sin and death are sacrificed for the world, thus signifying the rehabilitation of their oppression by the Devil/Pharaoh, and their sinful "death" in the Leviathan/Sea-monster.

5

Evangelizers

The Stewards of the Gospel

> Now the word of the Lord came to Jonah the son of Amittai, saying, "Arise, go to Nineveh, that great city, and call out against it, for their evil has come up before me." But Jonah rose to flee to Tarshish from the presence of the Lord. He went down to Joppa and found a ship going to Tarshish.
>
> —JONAH 1:1–2

Evangelizers in the Dock

WE HAVE SEEN THE primal gospel, considered its necessary stewardship in evangelism, and hopefully provided some contribution to their rehabilitation before the judgment of our culture. We now come to what is perhaps the most difficult subject. This is because the stewards are the most visible part of the "evangel" trilogy and therefore the necessary rehabilitation is of lives, not messages. Not to say that the gospel is not, in essence, the life that is the message as 1 John 1:1–3 declares.

The verb *"evangelize"* is used 54 times in the New Testament and is generally translated as "preach the gospel." This signifies that those doing so can be rightly called *evangelizers* and that this can be a term derived from the Scriptures that describes the activity of any or all followers of

Christ who are witnesses of "the good news of the kingdom of God" Jesus told them to declare.[1]

In the text from Jonah above, we see that Jonah was sent to be one such evangelizer, but that Jonah's fleeing to Tarshish signifies that he instead put the gospel "in the dock." And we saw earlier that Jonah stands for more than this one solitary person. Part of the "sign of the prophet Jonah" is that he is a prophetic sign of all God's stewards of the gospel when they "flee" from God's call for them to bring the gospel to their enemies and would instead prefer to see God destroy their enemies. Stated so starkly it seems horrific to any with moral sense. But Jonah signifies a very natural and wholly understandable reaction, which we will consider as we proceed. Nevertheless, such Jonahs represent an obvious scandal to the gospel inasmuch as their call is to proclaim it to all, including their enemies, but instead cater to their own self-interests. Such Jonahs seem to give the lie to the gospel, so to speak. And this is a huge problem to a humanity already skeptical of any God that any such Jonahs claim to be related to. For their skepticism finds a ready visible target in the evangelizers. For, regardless of the reality of their God and gospel, these "Jonahs" are unfortunately but undeniably *present* within the "immanent frame" of the metaphysically shrunken era in which any reality of God other than the evangelizers seems conspicuously *absent*. And as we have already seen, the gospel event is something that occurred *beyond* the realm of normal sight. People *saw Christ crucified*, but no one actually *saw the Devil being defeated*. Nevertheless, these gospel stewards are stubbornly visible. And for that reason, they can be more easily inspected, rejected, or neglected as simply irrelevant to "real life." For these reasons they are the gospel "particularity" most annoyingly capable of *being the scandal*, bringing the offense by *being* the offense. We don't intend to merely "paint it black" as though in relation to the stewards there is only a complete void of "good" even though some indeed paint them so. But since our purpose is mainly to rehabilitate them and their presumed "non-goodness" we simply follow that presumption and view them as safely moored "in the dock" before our culture.

---

1. See Morris, *Expository Reflections,* 126. The noun form translated as "evangelist" is only used three times in the New Testament for those who "evangelize," but its usage always signifies persons with a particular gifting of evangelism. I therefore will use "evangelizers" to differentiate between the NT's "evangelists" and each member of God's people who can rightly "proclaim the gospel" in ways that would not fall under what most would consider to be "the work of an evangelist." (See 2 Timothy 4:5.)

But looking at part of the multifaceted sign in the *prophet* Jonah in the text above, we *see prophesied* the hidden victory of the gospel already *present* in the God of all. For God in compassion, wills to act in response to the knowledge rising *in his own empathetic pathos,* of the evil "coming up before me"—evil from the "City of Blood"—evil quite painfully known *by all* the peoples of that day and region around Nineveh the capital of the world-oppressing Assyrian empire. In short, the gospel in God's compassion was already moving to do something about the Nazi's of that day.

But we also *see visibly* God's steward of the gospel fleeing from the presence of the Lord, fleeing from the compassion of gospel, fleeing from the possibility of salvation for Nineveh. God suffers *in* his compassion, but Jonah suffers *lack* of compassion, for his gospel is "in the dock." This is part of the sign of the prophet Jonah, given to reveal the hearts of all, whether of the stewards, or the oppressors, or of those somewhere in-between.

Evangelizers of Disorientation and Shalom

God's stewards are sent to a culture foreign to them, for they are the representatives of God's gospel culture which is alien to humankind which perennially participates in the fall from God's culture. J. Richard Middleton has thus proposed that the garden God planted in Eden signifies "a cultural project," saying,

> Indeed, since God planted the garden (Gen. 2:8), this means that God initiated the first cultural project, which humans—in the divine image—are to continue.[2]

This fills in the picture we saw earlier where Cain's "city" was the first false cultural "gospel" to provide security after the humans were banished from God's original cultural project of Eden. Humankind was meant to extend God's culture throughout the earth but having fallen from the faith relation to God we became incapable of participating in and extending *God's culture* to the ends of the earth for the benefit of all humanity and the world. The situation of the stewards of the gospel parallels God's original cultural mandate. It requires participation in God's new creation culture and extending it outward "to all nations . . . to the end of the age" (Matt 28:18–20). The question therefore is always whether the stewards

---

2. Middleton, "Reading Genesis 3," 76, loc. 1942.

can remain true to their "home" culture of the new creation as they extend it into the alien culture(s) of humankind.

Therefore, looked at from the viewpoint of the merely human cultures under the immanent frame, God's stewards appear to be utterly alien—as well they should inasmuch as they represent God's new culture. But we must remember that this means that their alien nature is due to the fact that what they represent remains unperceived by the culture, just as a bona-fide alien from someplace other than the third rock from the sun will provide no concept of where "it" is from or what its native cultural life is like. The now famous image of a Kierkegaardian "solitary individual" standing in Tiananmen Square before the massive tank representing China's power witnesses to what we speak of. This solitary individual, seemingly alone and utterly vulnerable like Jesus before Pilate, stood silent, unrepentant, and resolute, before the threatening immanent frame of the crushing totalitarian power, as the witness to the coming apocalypse of the greater transcendent force of God. The "alien" gospel stewards thus challenge the established order merely by standing apart in a different alignment, according to a different dimensional physics of power.³ And the power of the gospel is *in* the positive alignment to the transcendent kingdom of God, *not* in a mere reactionary misalignment to the kingdom of the world. For in misalignment, one's definition is derived from and thus controlled by what is perceived as the "greater power." But an immanent Jesus, defined by the transcendent God alone, always threatens cultures whose defensive reaction proves their accountability, as they become defined through God's witness. All authority in heaven and on earth has been given to Christ, and the gospel stewards are sent *to* the world, and set *in* the world *in* that transcendent *become immanent* authority (Matt 28:18–20).

The stewards are "ambassadors" of God's transcendent kingdom and therefore bring cultural cognitive dissonance to the world's cultures when aligned to their "home" culture (2 Cor 5:20–21). But dissonance is uncomfortable for the stewards and those they "interrupt" with the good

---

3. C. S. Lewis provides his imaginary description of an angelic being: "It was not at right angles to the floor. But as soon as I have said this, I hasten to add that this way of putting it is a later reconstruction, what one actually felt at the time was that the column of light was vertical, but the floor was not horizontal—the whole room seemed to have heeled over as if it were on board ship. The impression, however produced, was that this creature had reference to some horizontal, to some whole system of directions, based outside the Earth, and that its mere presence imposed that alien system on me and abolished the terrestrial horizontal." Lewis, *Perelandra*, 16–17.

news of a better way in alignment with the greater kingdom. Most of us have to admit that when going about our business we do not normally appreciate interruptions. But God's interruptions always matter, and intend the better, as did the hungry fish to the "good as dead" Jonah, or the "risen" Jonah to the people of Nineveh, or Jesus to the moneychangers in the temple. So also, faithful evangelizers appearing *in our way* always matter for the better, as would a messenger with good news that one's unpayable debts have been cancelled (2 Cor 5:19).

Therefore, God's stewards are not meant to be ultimately dissonant, and their very humanity provides the bridge of word become flesh by which they are enabled to communicate the goodness of their alien gospel to humanity. Jesus was in one sense "wholly other" than humanity, but in another sense, he was "wholly one" with humanity. The transcendently *distant* God became immanently *close* in him. This dialectic of dissimilarity and similarity holds true for the "embodied" task of the evangelizers of the gospel as the transcendent gospel "takes on flesh" in them. We hope to show that they are meant to fully represent an alternate city to Cain's fortress cities—by being the new-creation community of shalom and welcome—participating in God's new garden/city descending from heaven in the midst of the cultures of the world.[4] But this alien city seeks *the peace* of the city, in their exile away from home, breathing something of the peace of the city of God into Babylon itself, so that the peace of the gospel can become the shalom of the city of man (Jer 29:4–7).[5] Barry Harvey sums up much of what we have been trying to portray, saying that,

> Christianity entered history as a new social order, or rather a new social dimension. From the very beginning Christianity was not primarily a "doctrine," but exactly a "community." There was not only a "Message" to be proclaimed and delivered, and "Good News" to be declared. There was precisely a New Community, distinct and peculiar, in the process of growth and formation, to which members were called and recruited, Indeed, "fellowship: (*koinonia*) was the basic category of Christian existence. Primitive Christians felt themselves to be closely knit and bound together in a unity which radically transcended all

---

4. See Revelation 21:1—22:5. This is a future hope, but there is an aspect of "already" to its "not yet." See Matthew 5:14–16; Hebrews 12:18–29.

5. Thus, we more positively see that the true gospel is the *anti-escapist gospel* that nevertheless looks to the heavenly city to come that cannot be shaken (Heb 12:22–29).

human boundaries—of race, of culture, of social rank, and indeed the whole dimension of "this world."[6]

Evangelizers Always Evangelize

The final chapter will consider various evils and cultural challenges that God's stewards have too often met with compromise to their gospel. It is hoped that in the process of considering those challenges, the stewards of the gospel can be rehabilitated. For in their rehabilitation lies not only the witness of the gospel itself, but the manifest hope of the world. We will begin by again asking *who* these stewards are, and whether they can really be *that* important without in the process betraying themselves and their gospel by becoming pridefully self-important. Are they those who can be seen as having "beautiful feet" for *being* stewards and sentinels of Christ sent to and set in the world as was he—to suffer selflessly in a new way of human being—with and for the sake and good of all of oppressed humanity? Can and do they demonstrate a different way in the world than the way of the will to power acting by the means of force and war? These questions represent some of the current challenges God's stewards must face in their need for rehabilitation from being "in the dock" before the culture(s) of the world.

Our use of the term "evangelizers" is meant to indicate that God's stewards of the gospel can be found in any and every "denomination" of Christians. Evangelizers must also be considered as those who no matter what they are doing, are always invariably "doing" evangelism. In other words, God's stewards of the gospel are its evangelizers, even when—like Jonah—they are running in some way, shape or form in the other direction *from* evangelism and thereby placing the gospel in the dock. That is why they are a main part of the "scandal of particularity." Dietrich Bonhoeffer wrote of the challenge of being a person who has *become* part of God's "particular"—that *personhood-in-community*—in every circumstance they inhabit:

> A truth, a doctrine, or a religion needs no space of its own. Such entities are bodyless. They do not go beyond being heard, learned, and understood. But the incarnate Son of God needs not only ears or even hearts; he needs actual, living human beings who follow him. That is why he called his disciples to follow

6. Harvey, *Another City*, 21–22.

him bodily. His community with him was something everyone could see. It was founded and held together by none other than Jesus Christ, the incarnate one himself. It was the Word made flesh who had called them, who had created the visible, bodily community. Those who had been called could no longer remain hidden; they were the light which has to shine, the city on a hill which is bound to be seen.[7]

Thus, all evangelizers *continuously* "speak" of the gospel for good or for bad. Since evangelizers are always witnesses to the gospel they cannot *not* represent it faithfully or badly. Any non-goodness in their lives can easily cause those in our post-Christian culture to see their failings as the capstone of the mounting evidence of the absence of God, and the void of any true gospel in the world "under the sun" (Eccl 1:3).

> [Vapor] of [vapors] says the Preacher, [Vapor] of [vapors]! All is [vapor].[8]

The stakes could not be higher, regarding the situation and outcome of the stewards in the dock.

On an inestimably large side note, it would be a great oversight to not call attention to what else is implied in the statement "evangelizers always evangelize." For this implies that all humans invariably evangelize *some* "gospel." Thus, almost every post on Facebook, tweet on Twitter, implicitly lived or explicitly stated message about life, is evangelizing *some* gospel. And of course, this also means that if there is any valid defense or critique of any of these "gospels," then there must be some true gospel. Thus, all human "evangelical" life is always lived, and always "judged," in relation to the true gospel which humans have themselves judged and placed in the dock by their words and actions.

> Vanity of vanities, saith the Preacher, vanity of vanities; all is vanity.[9]

---

7. Bonhoeffer, *Discipleship*, 226.
8. Ecclesiastes 1:2, as translated in Meyers, *Table in the Mist*, 41.
9. Ecclesiastes 1:2, KJV. This more well-known translation makes a moral judgment on the multitude of the vaporous acts of humankind, which is fittingly summarized at the conclusion: "Let us hear the conclusion of the whole matter: Fear God, and keep his commandments: for this is the whole duty of man. For God shall bring every work into judgment, with every secret thing, whether it be good, or whether it be evil Eccl 12:13–14, (KJV).

The irony could not be greater, nor the stakes higher, regarding the situation of the gospel in the dock.

Jurors in the Dock?

To conclude this chapter and lead up to the final chapter dealing with the rehabilitation of the gospel stewards proper, we will follow the way of God's rejection of the will to power in response to that ironic injustice, and instead will present a bit of a plea for mercy on behalf of the stewards in the dock. So, I would ask the reader to consider the difficulty of rightly judging God's stewards. For as we have discussed just a bit earlier, even when they are faithful, the alien quality of the steward's lives presents an obstacle to an unbiased judgment. Perhaps another look at the excerpt from C. S. Lewis that we placed at the beginning of our introduction may set a sober tone for our consideration of the gospel infractions of the stewards.

> "Have done with it, Psyche," I said sharply. "Where is this god? Where the palace is? Nowhere—in your fancy. Where is he? Show him to me? What is he like? She looked a little aside and spoke, lower than ever but very clear, and as if all that had yet passed between us were of no account beside the gravity of what she was now saying. "Oh, Orual," she said, "not even I have seen him—yet. He comes to me only in the holy darkness."[10]

Lewis's pre-Christian historically pagan scene of Psyche, her husband "god" and his palace—"in the dock"—before her sister Queen Orual may yield us some valuable sympathy toward God's stewards. Orual is quite conflicted, without knowing it herself consciously, over the claims of her younger sister. For to all reasonable appearance her sister Psyche is in the grip of either a powerful self-delusion or a perverted crafty deceiver. She is living in *the wilderness* alone and nearly in rags yet believes that she dwells in *the palace* of her husband, the god of the holy mountain. Orual is thus, to her own thinking, selflessly seeking the welfare of Psyche because of her faithful and undying love for her. But Orual's perception of her conflict is her own construct placed over her self-centered "cares" for Psyche. So Orual "lovingly" interrogates her deceived sister regarding her palace and the god, asking for a shred of evidence that they exist anywhere other than in her imagination. Psyche then gravely admits what

10. Lewis, *Till We Have Faces*, 122–23.

seems the most telling detail of her present life, that she has never yet *seen* her husband god, for he only comes to her "in the holy darkness." This is telling in more ways than one. It speaks to the reality of her life, although no-one other than she can know this truth. It also speaks to the fact that the intimate human/god relationship Lewis write of partakes in the truth the apostle Paul freely confessed, that in the present life the lover and follower of Christ only sees God "darkly."

> For now we see through a glass, darkly; but then face to face: now I know in part; but then shall I know even as also I am known (1 Cor 13:12, KJV).

This scene Lewis provides reveals several things that may help the "jurors" interested in the sustained courtroom scene that is this book. For it reveals the conflicted interests of the great inquisitor, Orual. She at the least thinks herself to be dutifully and lovingly seeking the welfare of her wayward younger sister. In another work, the *ex-atheist* Lewis said,

> Here is a door, behind which, according to some people, the secret of the universe is waiting for you. Either that's true, or it isn't. And if it isn't, then what the door really conceals is simply the greatest fraud, the most colossal "sell" on record. Isn't it obviously the job of every man (that is a man and not a rabbit) to try to find out which, and then to devote his full energies either to serving this tremendous secret or to exposing and destroying this gigantic humbug?[11]

But one may ask how many today seek the truth or falsehood of the gospel for the welfare of others. Or is there some agenda hidden even to themselves of basic self-preservation (the old self-love and will to power). Of course, the divisive and "I'm correct" knowledge-based nature of our culture (again, the old will to power) has trained many or most of us to want simply be on the winning side of arguments, rather than on the side of those willing to grow through correction, or even be compassionate to those who are self-harming. Hopefully, more sincere reasons are motivating most readers here such as a genuine interest in the gospel and the question of *what is good* for themselves, the rest of humanity, and the world. But we point out these possibilities merely to clear the cultural clutter that tends to prevent open-ended seeking of the very mysteries of human existence. Perhaps a discovery of self and God through the gospel may take place.

11. Lewis, *God in the Dock*, 111–12.

The scene also reveals the difficulty of the accused Psyche who in the nature of the case has an intimate relationship with some *one* who largely remains hidden in darkness and mystery, invisible to the rest and thus in the most tangible ways invisible to herself, and especially in this case to her own sister who she genuinely and selflessly loves. Psyche is "called" upon by her sister to demonstrate the reality of the one that she herself only knows in darkness. But the reality of Orual's true self (or psyche) is revealed through the primitivity of the scene with the manifold primal forces swirling both within her and without. The "god of the grey mountain" has been the means of at least two revelations: the lack of at-one-ment between the sisters; and the true nature of the loves of each of the sisters. Psyche *loves* her unseen husband god *and* Orual, while Orual loves *the notion* of her love for Psyche, who she no longer really sees and perhaps never did. The conflict of reality is calling both unto the holy god's dark and dangerous interruption, his ways of terror and fascination, and ultimately to *holy* love where the love between humans must be mediated and consummated in the God who is love, or forever subverted under self-love that would consume all, even the "loved" other, in its own shrunken, demonic ends. May this mode of mystery and mood of awe—at the holy drama that ought to terrify *and* attract—permeate and even *interrupt* the dark courtroom drama that follows. For the stakes are grave in any case, with the *purported good gospel* of "the god of the holy mountain"—"in the dock" along with his steward bride Psyche, and now also, along with the *purported loves* of the reader. In sum, we hope for God's *interruption*.

Therefore, with all of these serious and dark, but hopefully somewhat provocative or even promising thoughts in mind, we move in our next and final chapter to explore several of the serious offenses of God's stewards that have especially reflected negatively back upon "their" gospel and the "god" of their "fancy." Our concern with their sin will aim to focus on their sins as "stewards" rather than as "regular" people, since sin in general is the *universal* scandal of all, but also a greater scandal for the stewards claiming to have sin's "cure." But we will mostly concentrate on the sins of the stewards that are explicitly against the gospel, as their own *particular* scandal.[12] We will therefore place the immediately fol-

---

12. One of the reasons that God's stewards are placed "in the dock" *as stewards* is because if their particular "sins" can somehow discredit the truths of the gospel and God, then humanity at large is removed from "the dock" of sin, since there would then be no such thing as sin for people to worry about.

lowing "court" proceeding into a "confessional booth" context, to depict a sober-minded narration of at least several steps necessary for our "wayward" Jonah-steward's rehabilitation, through the very gospel they have in their *unholy* darkness so often transgressed. We do so for the sake of the knowledge of their *holy* God of the darkness and God's gospel, and the goodness of both for humanity and the world.

6

Rehabilitating the Stewards of the Gospel

> And the LORD spoke to the fish, and it vomited Jonah out upon dry land.
> —JONAH 2:10

The Stewards and Repentance

APART FROM FAITH, REPENTANCE is perhaps the main message of the Bible, in regard to what humans are called to do in relation to God and the gospel. It is everywhere, whether explicitly narrated or simply implied. It is thus in Cain's wrestling with God's "timshel," Jonah's wrestling outside of Nineveh, Judas's betrayal of Jesus, and even in the fish's vomitous repentance of Jonah, symbolizing death's vomitous expulsion of Jesus.

Therefore, the main order of business for the rehabilitation of the stewards in light of everything we have already considered in this book is *repentance*. And this is not first and foremost repentance before the culture, but before God. Repentance will be the underlying theme of this entire lengthy chapter as we present a complex of repentance including six aspects: *sin, repentance, confession, faith, peace, and beauty.*

In general, then, we need to remember "Jonah" as Israel, and also as the church, fleeing from God's purpose, resistant to the saving mission of God for their enemies because of care for "their" communities. Using Jonah as a paradigm for the stewards of the gospel, given the radical nature of the call to go to Israel's worst enemy of the day, sets the gospel hurdle rather high. But we do so to shatter the validity of a supposed difference between a greater or lesser call. For if the "extreme" gospel call is to dangerously love the worst enemy, so also does every "lesser" gospel call to love any "other" require the self-sacrificial way of faith. For the truth is that bearing the cross is the *entry* requirement for any and all self-less gospel tasks to others no matter the danger or *safety*. Ultimately the sacrifice of bearing the cross is required because of two responsibilities: *the gospel need* of all those who are "others" to the stewards, *and the gospel reality* that requires participation in its cruciform significance—in contrast to the intellectual assent that is thought to be sufficient to faith. Jonah's "extreme call" was therefore meant to bring him to question the reality of his having truly answered the call. This truth of the *revelatory* call of God is what lies behind Jesus's statements regarding loving only those who love us or loving our enemies (Matt 5:43–48). So, while there is no difference in "calls," there is difference in how various calls *reveal* our faith, and *repentance* regarding "self." Self *too easily* "loves" those who love it, which is why God even "tests" loves, to bring *real* love, made possible by the gospel. With this in mind we return to our consideration of Jonah's call. David Benjamin Blower writes,

> To see the cross as only an inward process is to enter into the belly of the whale without ever going to Nineveh. To see it only as a done deal is to never leave home at all. It must ultimately be embraced as a path to trod through the world, for the sake of the world. "If anyone would come after me," says Jesus, "let him deny himself and take up his cross and follow me." It is to continuing works of interruption that Jesus calls his disciples: to radical acts of enemy love, to radical declarations of grace and forgiveness, to radical transgressions of social boundaries and radical compassion for total monsters. And it was into this purpose that they were called to baptize others.[1]

But wayward Jonah nevertheless "fulfills" God's purpose by drawing back from participation in the gospel's danger to himself and his home people to be cast into the storm—ironically *swallowed* into the *deathly mission* by the Leviathan beast which vomitously *delivered* him onto dry land—to finally participate in the baptized-into-death gospel-mission

---

1. Blower, *Sympathy for Jonah*, 53–54. Blower notes that Assyria was indeed "baptized" into this *salvific* bearing of the cross for enemies as he discusses how Assyrians were among the first peoples to embrace Christianity, and that in the last two centuries have become the victims of some "total monsters" of today's world. He says, "it is none other than Jonah's Assyrians—the Christians of the Mosul on the Nineveh Plains—who are being brutalized by Islamic state Militants." (35–36)

that saved the enemies of God, all of humanity, and the stewards themselves. The stewards can get there by their way, or by God's way. But taking the long route to "Nineveh" by God's way is indeed a "dark role" for God's "good" stewards, albeit merely a "human all too human" role. This charts the long running historical course of *sign*ificant "Jonah," wherein the repentance of God's "Jonahs" in the belly of whatever their respective beasts may be, precedes the salvation of the nations. Judgment begins in the house of God (1 Pet 4:17) for it is God's judgment of the *Jonah church* which has fled from God's gospel, slept "safely" out of the kingdom's tribulation (Rev 1:9), been cast out as worthless salt to be trampled upon by men (Matt 5:13), become swallowed by the worldly powers, and therein descended into a Hades of fruitless non-existence. Ched Myers calibrates all of this to the Jonah church of today, saying,

> Like that beleaguered prophet, we have been, most of us, in full flight from our vocation to 'cry against the great city' (Jon 1:1). It is only when we have abandoned—or are thrown overboard from—the metropolitan "ship-of-state," so to speak, that we are able to awaken to imperial reality in the "belly of the beast." Only there do Christians realize that "those who pay allegiance to vain idols forsake their true loyalty" (Jon 2:8). Our task, in the well-known words of the nineteenth-century Cuban anti-imperialist writer Jose Marti, is to live "inside the monster and know its entrails."[2]

Thus, the judgment signifies being cast into the raging sea and consumed within Leviathan seemingly unable to fulfill the mission from that grave-like Sheol. But God's election of Jonah for the world still stands as God's plan. Jonah's life was brought up from the pit for the proclamation, bringing salvation to "Nineveh, that great city," that God's great love pitied. And therefore, God's mission required that Jonah physically go to Nineveh, and if he wouldn't go of his own accord, the whale would interrupt him through seeming *death* and become the means of transport (and transformation). In a chapter called "*The Five Deaths of the Faith*," G. K. Chesterton writes,

> Christendom has had a series of revolutions and in each one of them Christianity has died. Christianity has died many times and risen again; for it had a God who knew the way out of the grave.[3]

2. Myers, *Binding the Strong Man*, 454.
3. Chesterton, *The Everlasting Man*, 250.

Therefore, we must seek to see how our modern-day Jonah stewards can in a sense rise again from the grave, becoming released from their false gospels and sub-gospel ways. For the repentance of the stewards is generally speaking, a release from their "Babylonian captivity" where they have found themselves in judgment as the blind and deaf servant, the wayward Jonah, the steward who buried the gospel treasure in the ground for "safe keeping" (Matt 25:25–30). But God's treasure can never be preserved in the ways that come natural to the stewards. Of course, God created us to be *true* humans and came in the incarnate man Jesus so that through him we could "think about God as humans should think about God."[4] We add that through Jesus we can also see how we ought to think about sin, in relation to God. Therefore, we will focus more specifically on sin as the first of the six elements of the gospel steward's repentance unto their rehabilitation.

Sin

An expose of the sins of the stewards could be very difficult to present briefly because there is so much that could be presented. Indeed, much has already been seen in our considerations of their false gospels. But the examples we will consider will be augmented by the fact that sin will "haunt" the majority of this chapter, including our positive picture of what the gospel stewards should look like. We won't always call attention to the ghost, but it will always be there in the background.

We begin with a clarification of what sin is, given that most consider it the opposite of doing good. We instead assume Soren Kierkegaard's view that the opposite of sin is not goodness but *faith*.[5] This is because for Kierkegaard the criterion of sin is the person of God, not abstract "moral" principles of goodness which contribute to the "pagan" view of a merely "human criterion."[6] This means that the definition of sin we are concerned with is that "sin is a *theological* position, it is a statement primarily about one's relation to God rather than an assessment of one's goodness or badness."[7] The major contention of this book is that one's actual relation to God is revealed by the relation to the gospel's way of faith.

---

4. Westphal, *Overcoming Onto-Theology*, 80.
5. See Walsh, *Living Christianly*, 19.
6. Kierkegaard, *Sickness unto Death*, 82.
7. Tietjen, *Kierkegaard*, 92.

This means that our criterion for the sins of the stewards of the gospel will be the gospel. The gospel shortcomings we will be considering will not be those of simple human immorality, but rather of their "virtues" in some way explicitly relating to their stewardship. But their apparent "virtues," considered under the criterion of the gospel, in various ways undermine either its way of faith, or its content, or both. Of course, many or most people who view the stewards as "in the dock" for their "common" sins of the flesh will probably not be looking from that biblical viewpoint, even though their recognition of vices is ironically largely based in the culturally pervasive influence of Christianity. Post-Christian nations are full of lapsed "Christians" and "Christian" atheists.

So, to more accurately consider the sins of God's gospel stewards we need to look at a deeper, more insidious, more indicting, and more revealing category of sins, namely, the sins that are related to their "virtues" related to the stewardship of the gospel. What then are these sins of virtue? The stewards themselves have long recognized this danger. An Archbishop, John Chrysostom, who lived from 349–407 wrote that,

> Where virtue is, there are many snares.[8]

Methodist Pastor Todd Outcalt notes that "The Scriptures are replete with the same observation" and that Jesus "even experienced these temptations himself."[9] In his expose of "The Seven Deadly Virtues" Outcalt demonstrates how the virtues of *faith, love, family, power, success, good, and generosity* are all susceptible to becoming "vices" and "our virtues can even be in opposition to the gospel."[10] This subtle but dangerous shift is for the most part caused when faith in God and the gospel stewardship become corrupted by the steward's will to power that is manifested in varieties of "Christianity And," as was discussed in Chapter 4. The prominent sociologist Peter Berger saw this as occurring on a large scale when social groups such as churches, states, or church/states, use "religion" for the "world-construction" of what he calls a "Sacred Canopy." This "canopy" serves as a unifying umbrella for the "world" they build, and which is then preserved by their diligent "world-maintenance."[11] Theologian Merold Westphal recognizes this tendency and temptation

---

8. As cited in Outcalt, *Seven Deadly Virtues*, 15.
9. Outcalt, *Seven Deadly Virtues*, 15, 23.
10. Outcalt, *Seven Deadly Virtues*, 12.
11. Berger, *The Sacred Canopy*, vi, loc. 31.

as what supported the Danish Christendom in "Golden Age Denmark" that Kierkegaard "attacked" as he sought to "reintroduce Christianity into Christendom."[12] Westphal writes,

> Without any help from Marx, Nietzsche, Durkheim, Weber, or Scheler (but with a lot from Hegel), Kierkegaard is sensitive to the sociology of knowledge. He knows that social groups make themselves legitimate through the propagation of belief systems in which the established order is justified. He also knows that religions are usually the most effective institutions in the practice of this "world-building" and "world-maintaining" function.[13]

Of course, such world-building is not something peculiar to the stewards of the gospel since all societies build such "worlds," which is the main point of Berger's "Sacred Canopy." But the stewards ought to more explicitly "know better" than to so use the gospel than their secular world-building counterparts who commonly use "religion" for their ends. We thus hint at the sin in this "virtue" of the stewards but need to more explicitly draw out its essence. Merold Westphal writes of the great "master of suspicion" Nietzsche's critique of the Christian world-builder's "virtues" saying,

> Nietzsche's response is that the virtues of the Christians are splendid vices. They are splendid because they represent no small spiritual achievement; but they are doubly vices, first, because they mask a self-centered will to power that by their own criteria is the essence of immorality, and second, because in hiding this fact from themselves and from others, the votaries of these "virtues" engage in systematic self-deception and hypocrisy.[14]

The point is that the deeper and most telling sins of the *gospel* stewards are those that are born through their so-called *gospel* virtues, when those are shifted to the religious establishment they either seek or already preside over. This changes them from *gospel* stewards to "Lords" of their own project with the result being a self-serving "faith." Thus, was the zeal of Jesus's pharisees, Paul's Judaizers, and of many of the "gospel stewards"

---

12. Tietjen, *Kierkegaard*, 42.
13. Westphal, *Kierkegaard's Critique*, 22–23.
14. Westphal, *Suspicion & Faith*, 246.

up to the present day. In that process *faith* is generally replaced with *belief*, and belief does not necessarily produce virtue.[15] Outcalt writes,

> In essence, faith as *belief* can be a problem, and Jesus warned his disciples to beware of faith's dark side: the allure of self-righteousness, the adherence to unyielding rules, demonstrations of hatred in the name of witness, and the subtle self-serving ends faith can lead to. In fact, Jesus warned us about *ourselves* and what we might build in the name of faith . . . Wesley noted that the faith of many was no longer a life-giving grace but a deadly virtue. Faith had become belief rather than the love of Christ moved to action. Many of the clergy of Wesley's time wouldn't allow him to preach from their pulpits. At times church mobs—intending to protect their turf and honor the traditions of the Church of England—became loud and boisterous, sometimes driving away those who had come "in the name of the Lord" to speak good news to the poor, the outcast, the disenfranchised.[16]

Outcalt's example of the transformation of virtues to become "deadly" at the time of Wesley can certainly find comparable examples throughout church history up to the present. Such "virtuous" sins against the gospel and its intended good for others reveals the depths of the need and scope of repentance. Therefore, we now turn to repentance proper as the second ingredient in the complex of repentance.

Repentance

Metanoia, the Greek word translated as "repent" in the New Testament means literally "change of mind," and signifies turning from the old life with its old thinking toward the life of God's kingdom. Through the atonement of Christ, it is made possible, and through providence it is made desirable to the stewards.[17]

---

15. "Faith is a virtue. Believing is not. To believe is not in itself virtuous." Smith, *Faith and Belief,* 142. See also, of course, James 2:19–26.

16. Outcalt, *Seven Deadly Virtues,* 19, 22.

17. The "possibility" of repentance was fully provided for in the unconditional gospel in which Christ repented, having assumed the full human nature of sinful humans, so that we can participate in his, as we saw in our consideration of "the gospel of conditionality." See Torrance, *Atonement,* 3–4, 76; Torrance, *Incarnation,* 61–65. By "desirability" we simply mean the outward aspects of life that God uses to incite the stewards to change their minds to a fuller gospel conformity. In answer to several objections to the general idea of "participation" see Radcliff, *Claim of Humanity in Christ,* 136–41.

For example, to many Christians in America, everything that is happening appears to be the death of the old life in "Christian America." But it is in fact a death calling for repentance. Thus, these stewards may be like Israel was when its hopes were devastated by God's judgment that sent her to captivity in heathen Babylon.[18] Many Christians in America think that their only hope for the future is the recovery of "Christian America," which oddly coexists with "the gospel of escape" we saw in Chapter 4. This hope is in many respects for the recovery of *their* sacred canopy, while God's kingdom is not about building or preserving any such sacred canopies which can never approximate God's kingdom.[19] In fact, God is always the ultimate iconoclast intent on destroying all idols which is why the gospel stewards require an ongoing renewal of the mind (Rom 12:1–2).[20]

Repentance therefore must embrace the death God's providence inevitably brings against any anti-gospel and sub-gospel establishments. Chesterton spoke correctly when he said that Christianity has died many times, but when it is raised from the grave it is never the same Christianity. God's judgments bring apocalypse, an end that is followed by a new beginning. The stewards are responsible to "come to birth" in the way God's kingdom is *now* unfolding and not foolishly resist God's *gracious* temporal judgment and come to death, as "Ephraim" had done.[21]

An illustration from the NT of this responsibility of God's stewards is seen in Jerusalem's religious leaders who would not "come to birth" in what Christ was bringing. They foolishly held on to the false hope of "establishing" Israel through a holy war against Rome. Jesus lamented that the peace he would bring was "hidden from their eyes," and their

---

18. The entire book of Lamentations serves of an example of God's judgment of his stewards to incite a changed mind toward their past "stewardship" and God's present and future covenantal "gospel" purposes. See Robin A. Parry, *Lamentations*, 28–34.

19. See Grindheim, *Living*, 43–49.

20. The life-long renewal of the mind is the "refashioning" of what Calvin called "a perpetual factory of idols," located in each steward's "heart," by a "rewiring" of the "plasticity" of their thinking apparatus. Rob Moll calls this mind-change renewal *neuro-transformation*. See Moll, *What Your Body Knows*, 155–70. See Calvin, *Institutes*, 107–8.

21. "The iniquity of Ephraim is bound up; his sin is kept in store. The pangs of childbirth come for him, but he is an unwise son, for at the right time he does not present himself at the opening of the womb." Hosea 13:12–13. See Beeby, *Hosea*, 169–70.

willful blindness would bring Rome's terrible destruction on Jerusalem and Herod's temple from 66–70 AD.[22]

> "And when he drew near and saw the city, he wept over it, saying, "Would that you, even you, had known on this day the things that make for peace! But now they are hidden from your eyes. For the days will come upon you, when your enemies will set up a barricade around you and surround you and hem you in on every side and tear you down to the ground, you and your children within you. And they will not leave one stone upon another in you, because you did not know the time of your visitation" (Luke 19:41–44).

God's Jonah stewards in Jesus's day could not see that their salvation lay beyond the "visible" securities of their law and temple, false securities that Jesus was replacing with God's kingdom then beginning in him. Paul the Apostle, first introduced in the New Testament as Saul the Pharisee, is an example of one of these who had at first blindly missed Christ's kingdom and zealously held to a sacred canopy to the extent that he was one of the most zealous persecutors of the early followers of Jesus.[23]

Similarly, the "Christian" gospel stewards of today seek through their "holy (culture) war" to restore *their* kingdom. That is why Jesus's call regarding his kingdom is *always* "repent, for the kingdom *of God* is (*always*) at hand." He calls us to change the way we think about everything—since God's kingdom is the ever-new reality. Otherwise, all we will see is our death that will ironically only bring death rather than the new birth God intends. Certainly, Jesus spoke to all of Israel, when he spoke to Nicodemus of the new birth necessary for seeing the kingdom. Jonah only saw death to Israel if salvation would come to the Ninevites. American Christians only see death as "Christian America" dies, but what new birth are they resisting? Nevertheless, God orchestrates the repentance necessary to come to the new birth. Amos Wilder wrote,

---

22. It seems that even the early post-resurrection disciples were at that time still enamored by the pre-Christian hopes of the restoration of a merely Israelite kingdom as evidenced in Acts 1:6. The rest of The Book of Acts provides the answer to the question by showing that national Israel's narrow hope was expanded to the universal hope for the world which at that time had already been accomplished in the gospel's reconciliation of all things in Christ. See Goldsworthy, *The Lamb & The Lion*, 68–69, and Amos Yong, *Who Is the Holy Spirit*, ix–xiv, 3–6.

23. See the narration of Paul's mission as a Pharisee in the chapter titled "Zeal" in, Wright, *Paul*, 27–39.

> Accept no mitigation but be instructed at the null point: the zero breeds new algebra.[24]

The zero of "death" is intended to breed God's "new algebra," of *new thinking* open to a *new possibility*, birthing a previously unknown and unforeseen reality.[25]

What we must now do is somehow imagine a *corporate* repentance of the stewards to further develop their rehabilitation. In a section called "Guilt, Justification, Renewal" in Dietrich Bonhoeffer's magnum opus "Ethics," we see that the "process" embodied in his three words is a corporate "lived appropriation" of the gospel that we discussed in chapter 4. Bonhoeffer shows that the "judgment" of repentance was necessary for the Jonah-church, that wouldn't "come to its birth," to then be vomited from its guilty Sheol-grave onto the land of Nineveh, risen from the dead, embodying and proclaiming God's gospel of the cross and resurrection.

> The issue is the process by which Christ takes form among us. Therefore, the issue is the real, judged, and renewed human being.[26]

Bonhoeffer shows that the issue in repentance is that it is part of the process in which Christ "takes form" (or is embodied or incarnated) among us (or in the worldly reality). So, having now considered repentance somewhat theoretically we now need to consider it more concretely *in process* beginning in confession as the third ingredient of the complex of the steward's repentance.

Confession

Confession, like the words repent, and guilt, is rarely mentioned, viewed positively, or regularly practiced in our culture. But apart from facing the negativity of sin, repentance and confession, any promise of new life is nullified by remaining chained to the old. Repentance and confession

---

24. As cited in Brueggemann, *Reality, Grief, Hope*, 89.

25. "In spite of the changes and regardless of the century, the culture, or the particular emphasis of the evolving proclamation, the dynamics of Christian belief remain constant. As Kierkegaard insists, no generation is allowed a direct, incremental transition to faith. There is always an unbridgeable chasm to overcome. There is always a seeming contradiction or paradox waiting to be embraced." Crump, *Encountering Jesus*, 74.

26. Bonhoeffer, *Ethics*, 134.

are actions in response to the Spirit re-creating the newborn community from the de-created void of sin. We saw above that repentance is "encouraged" by the outward circumstances where God's breath/wind moves "outside" us. Thus, repentance responds to God's outward and inward movements. Therefore, in a sense, the response *visibly* begins with the confession that speaks literally and truly of the old life of "deadly virtues," as the first step that turns from them toward God and the gospel's way. Of course, it does this by the grace of the gospel (Luke 19:1–10).

To illustrate such a confession, we will consider Bonhoeffer's "Jonah-church" confession. It provides an intimate snapshot of the struggle and lament that surely many faithful gospel stewards have experienced in the midst of tragic fallings from true gospel living and witness. That there have been many such fallings is also the case. It is of course a very well-known falling. But it will still be helpful to learn more about its historical context. Bonhoeffer's *Ethics,* narrates his own struggles as a pastor and church leader to chart a course of responsible faith-in-action while living "under" the Nazi regime of "the madman," Hitler.

> Written in the midst of the conspiracy to overthrow the Hitler regime, it discloses to the careful reader the theological-ethics basis of Bonhoeffer's participation in the attempted coup and his approval of tyrannicide in that extreme situation. But it is chiefly concerned with ethics for the postwar time of reconstruction and peace.[27]

Thus, Bonhoeffer's *Ethics* is quite interesting in its historical uniqueness, being "the only ethic written by a Lutheran theologian while engaged in a conspiracy to topple a tyrant."[28] Of course Bonhoeffer never lived to see the postwar situation, having been imprisoned and finally executed by the Nazi regime just several weeks before the war's end as a co-conspirator. The national context of his *Ethics* is more graphically portrayed with the following excerpts from the editor's introduction:

> Understanding Bonhoeffer requires moving from disembodied principles to the concrete situation: confronting the life-destroying warmonger and the murderer of the Jews who had to be stopped. This is the last-resort situation that Bonhoeffer analyzes in discussing "the structure of responsible life.". . . Here discussions about euthanasia, marriage, contraception,

---

27. Bonhoeffer, *Ethics,* from the inside dust jacket flyleaf.
28. Bonhoeffer, *Ethics,* 1.

abortion, sterilization, and suicide are not abstract but highly contextual ... the manuscript present's Bonhoeffer's theological protest against attempts by worldly authorities to decide what is natural, and to exercise control over various bodily rights ... For example, Bonhoeffer was outraged by the government's policy of murdering, under the euphemism "euthanasia," people it deemed unworthy of life ... In Nazi Germany abortion was illegal, but the Law for the Prevention of Offspring with Hereditary Diseases was amended in 1936 to make compulsory the abortion of "genetically unfit" fetuses up to six months in utero. Such Nazi "genetic engineering" is clearly in Bonhoeffer's sights: "this is nothing but murder."[29]

Seeing Bonhoeffer's "corporate confession" helps to further fill in the context and more importantly demonstrates the contours of repentance in taking responsibility for sin. He narrates the acceptance of the judgment of death on the false and dangerous security of "their sacred canopy" which didn't resist entering into collusion with the Nazi regime, and the hope of finding renewal in Christ beyond the confession of "death together." He writes,

> The church confesses its timidity, its deviations, its dangerous concessions ... The church was mute when it should have cried out, because the blood of the innocent cried to heaven ... The church confesses that it has misused the name of Christ ... by not resisting strongly enough the misuse of that name for evil ends ... The church has not opposed contempt for age and the divination of youth [the Hitler Youth] ... The church confesses that it has witnessed the arbitrary use of brutal force, the suffering in body and soul of countless innocent people, that it has witnessed oppression, hatred, and murder without raising its voice for the victims and without finding ways of rushing to help them ... The church confesses that it ... has found no strong or authentic message to set against the disdain for chastity and the proclamation of sexual licentiousness ... The church confesses that it has looked on silently as the poor were exploited and robbed, while the strong were enriched and corrupted ... The church confesses that it has coveted security, tranquility, peace, property, and honor to which it has no claim, and therefore it has not bridled human covetousness, but promoted it ... The church confesses itself guilty of breaking all of the Ten Commandments ... It confesses thereby its apostasy from Christ

---

29. Bonhoeffer, Ethics, 16, 24–25.

... The church calls all to whom it reaches to come under this judgment.[30]

Bonhoeffer presents a highly contextualized confession, but one can easily find systemic failures much the same in the gospel stewards today. We need to consider our failures by juxtaposing this confession beside them, and practice like confession. It is an honest agreement with God, arising from the depths the Spirit has plumbed concerning the real guilt of the stewards. It recognizes failing the gospel's invaluable news and burying it out of sight under the foundation of its sacred canopy.

An image of the stewards that we have not yet considered is that of the NT bride of Christ. Douglas Wilson in his book "Against the Church" brings a prophetic-style covenant lawsuit against her to elicit guilt, repentance and confession.[31] As prosecuting attorney he writes,

> So we need to come to grips with the fact that in North America, the bride of Christ is a hot mess. We live in a time when the charismatics need the Spirit, the Reformed need a reformation, and the evangelicals need to be born again ... A. W. Tozer once cuttingly observed that if revival means more of what we have now, we most emphatically do not need a revival.[32]

All too often, the stewards of the gospel call for revival. But God and the gospel call for repentance, beginning with confession.

One of Dietrich Bonhoeffer's most important books was called *"Life Together."* A recent commentator on Bonhoeffer, Joel Lawrence, has provocatively inverted that title to read "Death Together" to pointedly acknowledge "confession as the heart of death together" because "confession to another human strikes a death-blow to our pride."[33] In short, the stewards of the gospel who are in the dock not only before the culture but primarily before God need to first "die together" in order to live together, and in order to be rehabilitated to the way of faith from their fall to the will to power. Joel Lawrence's commentary on Bonhoeffer explores a major area of Bonhoeffer's theology, ecclesial transformation, which asked *"how the church becomes the church for others."* Lawrence writes,

---

30. Bonhoeffer, Ethics 138–42, parenthesis mine.

31. For a lengthy treatment of the OT covenant lawsuit against unfaithful Israel see Ortlund, *Whoredom*, 25–136.

32. Wilson, *Against the Church*, 7–8.

33. Lawrence, "Death Together," 122, 123.

> It is my proposal that life together in being for others must arise out of an ecclesial transformation from selfishness to selflessness through communal practices by which the church participates in Christ's death. The process of participation in Christ's death is the process that I have termed *death together*. It is through the process of death together that the church is transformed into the image of Christ in her life together. In other words, *apart from the transformative work of death together, there is no life together in being for others*. My aim in these pages is to describe death together and the primary practice by which death together occurs, the confession of sin.[34]

We trust that some promise of gospel life together, *beyond* death together has been intuited through the implicit hope *beyond* the grave of corporate confession that Bonhoeffer was inspired to write in solidarity with the guilty church. For the grain must fall into the ground to be born again and bear much fruit for the watching world, in desperate need of the bread of life. (John 12:24). For that bread is the fruit of the field, growing freely in the world, out from under the sacred canopy that prevents God's true gospel agriculture (Matt 13:38).

In a few short years, Bonhoeffer's was executed by the Nazi's, to seal the witness of his "church" confession against its collusion with that fallen worldly power. Thus, we will move on to the "positive" steps in the repentance/faith complex that the confession was oriented toward.

The Stewards and Lived Faith

Lived faith is another way to phrase Walter Brueggemann's "lived appropriation" of the gospel. This step in the rehabilitation of the stewards represents the transition *from* their wayward Jonah like anti-image of the gospel, *through* their Jonah like death, *to* their Jonah like resurrection as a living image of the gospel.[35] The first three aspects of the *repentance* complex were about what the stewards have too often been, landing them in the dock before all, and especially before God and the gospel. This fourth step of *lived faith* marks the more positive beginning of what they are to be as God's new-creation community. This step aims to see how

---

34. Lawrence, "Death Together," 114–15.

35. Of course, in "the sign of the prophet Jonah," Jonah as the anti-image of the gospel, Jonah in death, and Jonah as the living image of the gospel, are also fulfilled by Jesus who "became sin," "died," and was "raised" for us.

they mirror Christ by incarnating the goodness of his gospel-life in the world. Lived faith joins together the words *lived* and *faith* because they must be conjoined. The steward's faith is not real unless it is lived, and the steward's life is not possible without following the gospel's way of faith and repudiating the "normal" human way of self-love expressed in the will to power.

In this transition we have theoretically moved from the negative mirroring, in contrast to the gospel, to the positive mirroring, by coherence with the gospel. Nevertheless, we will continue to view the stewards as "in the dock" according to the judgment of our Western culture. But the truth is that in many times and places of the world the stewards of the gospel have been demonstrably faithful to the gospel and its way of faith, for the good of humanity. These are the unpublicized and unseen, ignored or forgotten witnesses for the good of the gospel, evangelism, and its evangelizers which, if the "trial" had been held in another venue, we might not be so prejudiced to automatically place them "in the dock."

"The Only Hermeneutic of the Gospel"

A well-known saying, usually attributed to St. Francis of Assisi, exhorts stewards of the gospel with the words: "Preach the gospel, and if necessary, use words." The statement usually resonates with most Christians because it powerfully emphasizes an essential truth about the lived faith of the steward. Some balk at it as nonsense, thinking that it is sentimental drivel used by those that are ashamed of the gospel's *words*. Like many metaphors of life, when pressed too far it breaks down as a false dichotomy. But its emphasis still portrays a powerful truth in a simple and memorable way. The great missionary theologian Lesslie Newbigin wrote of the truth of the statement with a masterful statement of his own:

> How is it possible that the gospel should be credible, that people should come to believe that the power which has the last word in human affairs is represented by a man hanging on a cross? I am suggesting that the only answer, *the only hermeneutic of the gospel, is a congregation of men and women who believe in it and live by it.*[36]

36. Newbigin, *The Gospel*, loc. 4320, Ch. 18, italics mine. All of the citations from Newbigin in these sections will be from chapter 18 of his book and will be indicated by block quotes or in the main text with the use of *italics and quotation marks*. I might add "and boys and girls" to his statement.

Newbigin's thesis implies that without the lived appropriation there is no "show me, don't tell me," no translation of the gospel to human life, no credible witness for the gospel. It remains merely abstract theory floating in the air. He goes on to note that Jesus did not write a book but formed a community. The gospel needs an incarnate community as its witness to demonstrate that it creates a community of persons living in *at-one-ment*. Nothing but a community can bear that witness to the gospel. But nothing can do more damage to that gospel and place it in the dock than a "gospel community" whose "life together" loudly proclaims its denial. This is why in the past few decades there has been an avalanche of books in most church denominations regarding the formation of the "life together" of the gospel stewards. Ray Ortlund has sketched out several possibilities that can occur in the mixture of lived faith and proclaimed words in relation to the gospel. Note that "gospel culture" signifies lived faith and "gospel doctrine" signifies the proclaimed words of the gospel.[37]

Table 5: The Relation of Gospel Doctrine to Gospel Culture

Gospel doctrine	minus gospel culture	equals hypocrisy.
Gospel culture	minus gospel doctrine	equals fragility.
Gospel doctrine	plus gospel culture	equals power.
Right gospel doctrine	plus anti-gospel culture	equals a denial of the gospel.

Hopefully, in light of our discussion the significance of this "flow chart" is fairly self-evident. In sum, the first and last items represent negative outcomes of the stewardship of the gospel, while the second and third items represent positive outcomes, although one is weak because it lacks the words, while the other is strong because it includes the lived appropriation. We must note that the power in the third wholly positive result is certainly not the selfish will to power but the power of gospel faith that works through love (Gal 5:6). It would be a mistake to assume that this chart intends to demonstrate that churches have no culture if they don't have gospel culture. For every church already has *some* formed culture

---

37. Ortlund, *The Gospel*, 23, 88.

but needs to examine its culture in light of the gospel. Thus, Paul told the church in Corinth that they needed to examine themselves "whether they were in the faith" because their present culture was not formed by the gospel but by the culture of Rome (2 Cor 13:5).[38] So today in many churches, due to lack of "self-examination," the "gospel of culture" remains and supplants the gospel culture God intends.

Therefore, we now will consider ten characteristics of God's new community that help form its gospel culture and contribute to the rehabilitation of the stewards "in the dock." The first seven are presented sequentially, with three others added a bit afterwards. The first six characteristics are explicitly derived from Newbigin's thought on what he saw as necessary for stewards to be the hermeneutic, the living explanation of the gospel. (Just as the incarnate life of Jesus was the living explanation of God the Father.)[39]

A Community of Praise

This brings us back to some things we said in Chapter 2 where we spoke of humanity as being stewards of God's breath. God breathed life into the first humans so that their lives would consist of a stewarding of that gift of breath in praise and work to the Creator, and thus serving as the priests of a growing song to extend God's Edenic temple to fill the earth. Newbigin points out the absence of praise in western society due to the skepticism of the "hermeneutics of suspicion" whose gospel of salvation-from-error requires the "liturgics of doubt." The modern French philosopher Paul Ricoeur first called Marx, Freud, and Nietzsche the "masters of the school of suspicion," each of whom with their specific societal interest, has contributed to the pervasiveness of doubt in modern and now post-modern life.[40] Some Christian scholars such as Merold Westphal find the "hermeneutics of suspicion" a useful practice because it can function much as the biblical prophet's messages did in calling out the duplicity of God's stewards. Westphal proposes that the trio ought not be limited to atheists, since Soren Kierkegaard was fully Christian (though reluctant to identify by the term) while also fully the equal to the other masters of suspicion.

---

38. See 1 Corinthians 11:17–34. See Hays, *First Corinthians*, 192–206.

39. See John 1:18. "He has portrayed, detailed, narrated, or exegeted (*exegesato*) the very nature of God for the world." Borchert, *John*, 124.

40. See Westphal, *Suspicion and Faith*, 13.

His "Attack on Christendom" targeted the false heart of "Christian" Denmark.[41] But doubt has its dangers as Westphal notes, in Pharisaism, cynicism, and a sort of fixation on sinfulness rather than cultivating a grace consciousness.[42] This is perhaps a good place, just this side of repentance and the "death" of confession, to consider the danger of a predominant sin-consciousness. Westphal writes of the need for balance:

> In calling Freud, Marx, and Nietzsche the great secular theologians of original sin I have suggested that the hermeneutics of suspicion belongs to our understanding of human sinfulness. The self-deception they seek to expose, like those exposed by Jesus and the Prophets, are sins and signs of fallenness. If we are to deepen our understanding of our sinfulness with their help, we need to remember at the same time the larger theological context in which the doctrine of the fall is properly placed, between creation and redemption . . . Suspicion can be a kind of spirituality. Its goal, like that of every spirituality, is to hold together a deep sense of our sinfulness with an equally deep sense of the gracious love of God.[43]

The danger is to fixate upon and cynically stress human sinfulness, and especially, like the Pharisees, to concentrate on the faults of others. That is why Newbigin stresses that praise and thanksgiving need to be the pre-eminent characteristic of the church. Presently, this side of the redemption of our bodies, we live in the tension and balance between the recognition of both sin and grace. But holding those in the right balance will result in a community being formed as a gospel hermeneutic. Newbigin says,

> The Christian congregation . . . is a place where people find their true freedom, their true dignity, and their true equality in reverence to One who is worthy of all praise that we can offer . . . The Christian congregation meets as a community that acknowledges that it lives by the amazing grace of a boundless kindness . . . In Christian worship we acknowledge that if we had received justice instead of charity we would be on our way to perdition. A Christian congregation is thus a body of people with gratitude to spare, a gratitude that can spill over into care for the neighbor. And it is of the essence of the matter that this

---

41. See Kierkegaard, *Attack on Christendom*.
42. Westphal, *Suspicion and Faith*, 283–89.
43. Westphal, *Suspicion and Faith*, 288.

concern for the neighbor is the overflow of a great gift of grace and not, primarily, the expression of commitment to a moral crusade. There is a big difference between the two.

We saw earlier that the stewards can fall to stewarding *their* established order, their alternate community in which their praise of God is of themselves. Their "virtue" of praise becomes a splendid vice, as Nietzsche said. But through repentance, confession, and thanksgiving for grace their praise may again rise to God. And as faithful stewards they then become a community of praise and a living hermeneutic of the gospel.

A Community of Truth

At the outset we need to present a disclaimer, that a community of truth is not the same as a community of "correct doctrine." Newbigin says that for the stewards to be a community of truth is obvious but needs to be stressed because *"the reigning plausibility structure can only be effectively challenged by people who are fully integrated inhabitants of another."* Our discussion in Chapter 4 on "the gospel of culture" with Walter Brueggemann's work revealing "the dominant script" is at the bottom of what Lesslie Newbigin meant by a plausibility structure. The more plausible a structure the more it is capable of being dominant. He shows that the person in modern society is *"continuously bombarded"* through media that presupposes a *"radically different plausibility structure"* than in the *"Christian understanding of human nature and destiny."* Christians live in an alternate structure through *"constant remembering and rehearsing of the true story of human nature and destiny."* The Christian community is not to use propagandizing techniques but instead have the *"modesty, sobriety, and the realism which are proper to a disciple of Jesus."*

Newbigin's conception of the community of truth is not simply as having been gathered around doctrine, but formed by Christ, becoming a new culture embodying the gospel as its *hermeneutic*. This is not only necessary because the gospel must become "visible," but because only a visible plausibility structure can challenge another one. But this challenge must be made by the life of the community, not merely by its doctrine. Therefore, we need to clarify how all lives are formed by what can be called "life liturgies."

Philosopher James K. A. Smith has done extensive work in relation to this issue and explains how "a community of truth" is integrally based on following an alternative "liturgical practice." This shifts the focus from what we think to what we love, since humans are at bottom "loving animals" rather than "thinking animals."[44] Smith writes of "secular liturgies" that support the culture's dominant plausibility structure, such as going to the shopping mall, as "taught" practices that influence us below the level of conscious thought. The culture knows what really drives us, and so through advertising, peer pressure, and envy, cultivates our subconscious desires, rather than *truly* appealing to our conscious reason. Thus, those living in a culture, follow a Yoda-like dictum: "do not think, . . . do." For the culture drives us by the desires or "loves" its secular liturgies have previously cultivated.[45] This is why Christian discipleship, when it largely consists in a "data dump" into the intellect, so often proves to be ineffectual for transforming life. It aims too much at the head, as though people are for the most part consciously thinking about what they do. But the person's real engine of acting is the heart which has long been colonized by the culture's vision of the good life. We are merely "consumers" to be driven down the path for which we have been carefully conditioned by our culture's "sales department." It is all rather dehumanizing and depressing. Unfortunately, it is also true. The advertising empire of capitalistic consumerism demonstrates how successful is the tag team that "cultivates desire" and "discourages rational thought." Smith explains,

> To be human, we could say, is to desire the kingdom—*some* kingdom . . . To be human is to be animated and oriented by some vision of the good life, some picture of what we think counts as "flourishing." And we *want* that. We crave it. We desire it. This is why our most fundamental mode of orientation to life is love. We are oriented by our longings, directed by our desires.

44. See Smith, *Desiring the Kingdom*, 19–24. For another recognition of how "culture" works see the discussion on the relation between bodily ritual and social belief, in: Butler, *Excitable Speech*, 25, 154–55. Butler invokes the thought of Blaise Pascal on the practice of the ritual of prayer for support. A more philosophically based recognition is given by Paul Tyson who summarizes the underlying truth of myth as "an imaginative and collectively believed story . . . which is assumed by the norms of the everyday way of life of any given human community." and adds "Thus it is necessary to point out that modernity has its own mythos—as do all cultures—and that logos is always derived from mythos, for mythos is more basic than logos as far as human culture (the interpretive lens of all truth discourse) goes." Tyson, *Returning to Reality*, 46, 76.

45. "An NFL football game, a NASCAR race, or an evening at the movies" are other examples of powerfully formative secular liturgies for "The Military-Entertainment Complex." Smith, *Desiring the Kingdom*, 104–5.

> We adopt ways of life that are indexed to such visions of the good life, not usually because we "think through" our options but rather because some picture captures our imagination.[46]

It seems we must agree with Smith's view, no matter how reluctantly. If there is a self-evident truth today this would be the *elephant in the room*. This elephant also evidences why the gospel's stewards must be *a visible* community of truth, with self-evident lives formed by the gospel's vision of the good life. Again, only a life can be a plausible alternative to another life. Mere words, concepts, and theories can't compete. That "the Word became flesh and dwelt among us" attests to the reality that "flesh and blood" living is needed to explain the plausibility of the gospel. Of course, we are speaking of a community here. So perhaps we could summarize by saying that the community that actively and fervently lives, loves, and serves, in gospel-shaped life-together, participates in a "life liturgy" that cultivates desire in relation to truth, to form the community of truth that can be a plausible alternative community.[47] Simone Weil briefly summarizes the need for a humanly holistic orientation to a "vision of the good life" as "the need for roots."

> To be rooted is perhaps the most important and least recognized need of the human soul. It is one of the hardest to define. A human being has roots by virtue of his real, active and natural participation in the life of a community which preserves in

---

46. Smith, *You Are What You Love*, 11. This is a very confusing subject, for "imagination" does not seem much different than "thinking." The difference is that "imagination" is what Rob Moll simply calls "feeling." Everything Smith says of secular liturgies promoting a "vision" is in reality much cruder: "We often think of our brain as the computer that operates a robot. Our consciousness is the interface that allows us to access the programming to tell our bodies what to do. But this analogy is terribly wrong. We think with our feelings, and our feelings are nothing more than the state of our bodies. That's why they're called *feel*ings. This is what scientists call embodied cognition." Moll, *What Your Body*, 57.

47. Newbigin importantly states that in the Christianized secular cultures of the modern West, the church communities did not need to be holistic gospel-shaped communities because the "secular" aspects of church life were "provided" in the larger secular society. "The Churches in most of the countries of Western Europe take it for granted that by far the greater part of the secular affairs of their members are conducted without any direct relationship to the Church . . . The Churches can, without immediate and obvious disaster, confine themselves to specifically 'religious' concerns . . . Membership in a church may often involve only slight and relatively superficial contacts with other members, because the church is—for each member—only one among the many different associations to which he belongs." Weston, *Missionary Theologian*, 117–18.

> living shape certain particular treasures of the past and certain particular expectations for the future . . . Every human being needs to have multiple roots. It is necessary for him to draw wellnigh the whole of his moral, intellectual and spiritual life by way of the environment of which he forms a natural part.[48]

The power of nationalist secular liturgies that can easily capture the gospel stewards was made evident by the catalogue of gospel failures we "witnessed" in the corporate confession of Bonhoeffer. Today's consumerist secular liturgies cultivate our self-love and will to power desires, and rather than alleviate, only exacerbate the anxiety and despair of our Kierkegaardian "sickness unto death." All secular liturgies and cultural gospels operate by *untruth* in regard to the true creational needs of humanity. The gospel-community of truth is meant to embody an alternative plausible way of life that demonstrates the *true* good God intends for all human communities.

To summarize, a plausible "community of truth" lives in and witnesses to the good life that is formed by the gospel as their culture. "The Lord's Supper," as practiced by the early church, was the main *cultural liturgy* that formed each community of Christ. For it was an actual weekly meal for the church community, not merely the five to fifteen minute long sacramental "meal" widely practiced in churches today. But what was especially "formative" in this practice was that the very form of the meal was inherently sociopolitical. The way it was practiced formed the body of Christ according to the truth of the gospel, while at the same time subverting the Roman culture's own "gospel banquet." Each "supper" reflected and reinforced diametrically different visions of "community" with Rome's being that of an enforced social stratification under Caesar's "lordship", and the church's being a liberating social equality under Christ's lordship.[49] Thus the subversive cultural liturgy formed Christ's community as "a community of truth." What this means is that the church needs to realize and follow the dictum of Marshall McLuhan that "the medium is the message" and adopt gospel-culture liturgies that are the medium for the spiritual formation of the community of truth.

Before moving to the next characteristic, we point out that all of these characteristics we are considering "work together" in a holistic "life liturgy" for the gospel-culture community that is the hermeneutic of the

---

48. Weil, *Need for Roots*, 41.
49. See Streett, *Subversive Meals*, 7–51.

gospel. For lack of space, we cannot explicitly detail all the ways they interconnect, but will trust that they may be fairly well intuited through the God-given "tacit knowledge" of the reader.[50]

A Community for Others

Recognizing the contrast between this hermeneutical "community" and the stewards who look after their own interests—succumbing to only caring for their virtues of family, church or nation—is vastly important. Todd Outcalt speaks of the virtue of family as in danger of turning "deadly" and sees the remedy as moving "from focusing on our family to seeing God's family first."[51] The early church had discovered that God's family is ever-growing to include those previously thought to be outsiders. God continues to offer that same basic gospel lesson to his stewards who always need to learn to be a community that exists for others.

Newbigin specifies that the community "*does not live for itself but is deeply involved in the concerns of the neighborhood.*" This neighborly concern embodies the gospel of Christ. Being for the other is the *fractal* pattern of the new life in Christ wherein each one reconciled *in him* is formed to the "cruciform" shape of Christ who lived for others, to result in a cruciform community that lives for others. In Luke 10 we see Jesus's "Parable of the Good Samaritan" which answered the eternal question "who is my neighbor?" Soren Kierkegaard provided one of the best answers saying:

> Christianity, however, teaches a man immediately the shortest way to find the highest good: shut your door and pray to God—for God is still the highest. And when a man will go out into the world, he can go a long way—and go in vain—he can wander the world around—and in vain—all in order to find the beloved or the friend. But Christianity never suffers a man to go in vain, not even a single step, for when you open the door which you shut in order to pray to God, the first person you meet as you go out is your neighbor whom you shall love. Wonderful![52]

Newbigin pointed out the danger when the church exists solely for its present "family" members and "turns its back on the neighborhood

---

50. Polanyi, *The Tacit Dimension*, 4.
51. Outcalt, *Seven Deadly Virtues*, 61.
52. Kierkegaard, *Works of Love*, 64.

that is perceived as irrelevant to its concerns." This is a perennial danger for the stewards, a sort of corporate *homo incurvates in se*—the human turned in on itself.[53] As we have seen throughout this book, inordinate *self-love* is the primal problem of humanity that seeks self-fulfillment in "the will to power" that would even replace God with itself. That is also why the self-giving way of faith, a form of self-death, is implied in every "lived appropriation" of the gospel. Of course, that "death" to self brings birth into the counterintuitive, "kingdom of God" way of love, participating in and becoming perfected in God's love, which is the purpose and ultimate fulfillment of our life (1 John 4:7–12). This is also the counterintuitive truth the church must follow, *through* self-death *to* fruitful life. Inasmuch as the stewards live in Christ, they will always be driven out from "cocooning" together even as Jesus portrayed in another parable *the good shepherd* "leaving" the ninety-nine for the one *other*.

The parable of the *good Samaritan* importantly shows that some of the "others" outside the family, are not "others" to God. For the mark of the Spirit, the giving of self, exists outside "the family" of the stewards. In a discussion of the salvation of the Samaritans in the book of Acts, theologian Amos Yong points toward the need for today's stewards of the gospel to recognize that the spirit breathes upon the waters of humanity, since "*the wind blows where it wishes*" (John 3:8, 4:23–24, 35).

> While the possibility of the salvation of Samaritans would have shocked many Jews, Jesus's own teachings should have prepared them to question their religious assumptions and self-assuredness. Note that Jesus told the famous parable of the good Samaritan (Luke 10:29–37) in response to the Jewish lawyer's attempt to justify himself by asking "Who is my neighbor?" That itself was motivated by his original question about how to inherit eternal life and Jesus's well-known response that it required loving God fully and loving our neighbors as ourselves (10:25–28). This whole episode is just as suggestive today for Christians thinking about religious pluralism as it was two thousand years ago for Jews thinking about Samaritans, religious others, and those whom they thought were demon-possessed . . . the God who shows no

---

53. See Harvey, *Can These Bones Live*, 93–95. Jim Wallis sees "*a practical vision*" of the answer to the question "*Who is my neighbor*" as made possible when "people of faith began transferring their human identities from class, racial, and national loyalties to a global identity in a *new beloved community* created by God." Wallis, *The (Un) Common Good*, 15. The phrase "*homo incurvates in se*" is from Martin Luther and describes how "human egocentricity attempts to dethrone God." See Janz, *Westminster Handbook to Luther*, 127.

partiality is the God who judges impartially as well, condemning unrepentant sinners but also accepting "in every nation anyone who fears him and does what is right" (Acts 10:34–35). To fear God and do what is right is not merely a human accomplishment; rather, these are works of the Holy Spirit.[54]

We include Yong's view, which some may see as overly speculative, merely to make a few remarks regarding the stewards being the "neighborly" community for others. The stewards need to be very careful to not slam the door in the faces of any "Samaritans" who are perhaps demonstrating that *their* love of neighbor is a sign of their love of God and a testimony of response to the Spirit's breathing upon them (1 John 4:7).[55] It is therefore an evangelical tragedy to in effect shut the door on those the Spirit may have brought to the threshold of the visible kingdom, by discounting as false, God's prior work within them through whatever means the Spirit used. We ought to grant the possibility, or knowing God as the good shepherd seeking "the one," the probability of such signs of life in "others." Perhaps our penchant for the "certainties" of human doctrinal *speech* has blinded us to the possibilities of human living *sights*, largely inarticulate in regard to gospel talk yet already demonstrating gospel life, as was the good Samaritan.[56]

Our point here is that the stewards should seek to be the community for others not merely by going out to evangelize them, but by recognizing the extent to which the others are already brought near to God. These "approaching" outsiders threaten to burst our old wineskins of family and church, but they bring with them new wineskins that will help expand the visible gospel threshold of the constantly re-forming community for others. The blindness of the stewards prevents them from seeing the great harvest of ripe and whitened fields that Jesus says are already there, ready and waiting, and even coming (John 4:35; Matt 8:11).[57] Presuming the fields are *not* ready may only demonstrate the old Jonah-blindness. But

---

54. Yong, *Who Is the Holy Spirit*, 93, 117. Cf. Yong, *The Hermeneutical Spirit*, 350–356.

55. See John 4:35; 12:32. We explore these questions fairly extensively in our postscript.

56. Eugene Webb has written a fascinating account of the presence of the sacred in secular literature which represents a different "language" for expressing the holy. See Webb, *The Dark Dove*.

57. Their recognition may be more difficult since the stewards are used to others coming from *within the fields of Christendom*, so that gospel translation and contextualization were easier to navigate.

for Jonah and the stewards today, the conversion of "others" is the opportunity for new conversion.[58] Considered from another angle, if the stewards, like Jonah, are ambivalent toward outsiders and the ripened gospel harvest, then God sends an invitation to them to examine whether they in the faith of the gospel, usually delivered by an interruptive whale (2 Cor 13:5; Jonah 1:17). The community is for others, not for Jonah-like ambivalence toward those *coming* from the East and West to sit with Abraham in the kingdom (Matt 8:11). To mix parabolic metaphors, the stewards must "go out to the highways and hedges and compel people to come in," all the while meeting those already on their way "to sit with Abraham" (Luke 14:23). In short, the *community for others* must be open to *others* in whatever way, shape or form they seem to be, or not be coming to God, and how that relates to the form of their community. Phyllis Tickle summarizes that,

> To that end, it seems to me that we would all be well served at this moment to remember the words of Rowan Williams, the Archbishop of Canterbury. In counseling his flock worldwide, Williams has said repeatedly over the last few years that we are not to read and study and discuss Emergence Christianity in order that we might save the Anglican Church or any other such institution. Rather, he says, we are called to read and study and discuss Emergence Christianity in order that we may discern how to best serve the kingdom of God in whatever form God is presenting it.[59]

The stewards of the gospel need to cultivate new eyes, or at least be ready to be given them, assuming the Spirit's breathing on the ripe fields outside and their call to be a community for them, rather than for the status quo of "their" community. For they are simply part of the one great community of the ages that God is building in Christ, in ways that most often are beyond their capacity of sight, and more tellingly, beyond their desire for biblical hospitality. For to not only see "the kingdom" but to "enter" it," they must "exceed the righteousness" of today's Pharisees inhabiting western liberalism's cardinal doctrine and virtue of "tolerance," with what Ralph Wood calls "ferocious hospitality."[60]

---

58. See Habib, "Who Converts Whom?" 67–75. As we saw above that new conversion entails what appears to be death in regard to old ways and wineskins.

59. Tickle, *Emergence Christianity*, 13.

60. See Wood, *Chesterton*, 125–53. See Matt 5:20. Of course liberalism's "tolerance" turns tyrannical.

A Community of Priests

Lesslie Newbigin writes that the stewards as a hermeneutic of the gospel will be a "*community where men and women are prepared for and sustained in the exercise of priesthood in the world.*" The *priestly* aspect here further defines Newbigin's "community for others" by being "priests" to them. The "preparation" needed for that task reveals an important *positive* nuance regarding the stewards own being that is necessary to its being for others. This preparation is the necessary self-upbuilding of the stewards themselves for the sake of their being for others. Thus, Newbigin shows that preparatory "self-care" of the steward's community is necessary for their "priesthood."

Dietrich Bonhoeffer called this essential practice the "arcane (secret) discipline."[61] This odd sounding term simply means that the gospel community practices relatively *non-public* disciplines to "tone the body" for their *public* priesthood for others. To "translate" the significance of these aspects of "a community of priests" we could say that what most people call "going to church" is the preparation, self-care, or secret discipline. What most people call "the serving church" is the exercise of priesthood." Though we speak of practice and discipline, these activities are the practical aspects of Christ's spiritual formation of the community according to the gospel and enabled by the Spirit. Apart from this preparation, the result would be like when a person solicits a priest or minister to officiate a baptism, wedding or funeral, only to find that the "official" showing up has no preparation or credentials.

Newbigin's gospel call is based on the NT designation of the church as "a royal priesthood" which draws from the OT book of Exodus. Writing on the original significance of Israel as "priests," Brevard Childs writes,

> Israel is God's own people, set apart from the rest of nations. Israel as a people is also dedicated to God's service among the nations as priests function within a society. Finally, the life of Israel shall be commensurate with the holiness of the covenant God. The covenant responsibility encompasses her whole life, defining her relation to God and to her neighbors, and the quality of her existence.[62]

---

61. See Bonhoeffer, *Letters and Papers*, 373. See Lawrence, *Bonhoeffer*, 49–53.
62. Childs, *The Book of Exodus*, 367.

Israel was to be a priestly community for others. Israel was thus to be the hermeneutic of God's OT "gospel" so to speak, for the nations. This brought Israel under the great and humanly impossible task of living "commensurate with the holiness of the covenant God." In Jesus's presentation of the kingdom to Israel the ultimate fulfillment of the priestly call to "Jonah" for the nations had arrived. But "official" Israel rejected the call, Jonah-like, and fled in "self-care" that was not for the sake of being priests for others. Israel's *exclusive* self-care thus became her greatest obstacle to being the living hermeneutic of God's OT community. By the time of Christ, Israel mistook the outward covenantal signs and laws that aided her "self-care" as signs that must be adopted by the nations if they were also to become God's people. Thus their "priesthood for others" was self-serving and in essence was lost.

This problem was also experienced in the early Israelite church and was not settled until the Jerusalem Counsel recorded in Acts 15:1–21 after much conflict and controversy. That counsel was the most important event in the early church period for allowing the new wine of the Jesus-movement to break from the constraining old wineskin of Judaism unto a universal kingdom (Mark 2:22). But this crisis of wineskins is oft repeated in church history. In this scenario, the "community of priests for others" faces the temptation of mediating *their* self-care, *their* forms of expression, *their community, to others,* rather than simply remaining priestly witnesses of Christ who births *new* communities with possibly quite *different* forms of expression. In the controversy of the Jerusalem council, this sort of "false mediation" practice was that the "Judaizers" held that their "self-care" must be followed by the Gentiles. This basically boiled down to the question whether the Gentiles needed to become Jewish, and the Jerusalem counsel's gospel-based determination was, "no." In other words, Christians of different cultures could have different forms of expression. The Jerusalem counsel recognized that a Jewish form and a Gentile form were both bona-fide communities of Christ which could co-exist in Christ.

To translate this to the controversies of today would be to ask, "must a new Christ community follow the forms of self-care of other Christ communities? I realize that my "translation" based on the Jerusalem Counsel is non-equivalent because what believing Israelites wanted to transfer to believing Gentiles were "forms" only necessary for Israel before Christ came and which are fulfilled now apart from those forms. But the gospel-question today is whether the form of gospel-expression needs to be "religiously" followed. It seems that all that needs to be followed is *the dynamic* of the gospel, of which Christ is the mediator. So, it seems that the full *form of expression* of the priest's own community, it's "self-care," does not need to be transferred and can remain in the background. Said in another way, Christ is not a form of religion, and the Christ community is a matter of spirit and truth, not form or place (John 4:20–24). The form need not be transferred and may even be harmful to the new expression of that new gospel community that is becoming.

This perennial temptation and problem are a mistake in conception, combined with a will to power to perpetuate the steward's own form of "self-care." The keys to overcoming the misconception and malpractice are to remember that Christ is the one mediator, the one high priest, of the dynamic life and being of gospel communities (1 Tim 2:5; Heb 4:14). It is, or at least should be, the gospel dynamic, not the subsequent form, which serves as the hermeneutic of the gospel that enables new births of ever-new gospel communities. One might conceive of this by seeing the priesthood community as merely a midwife aiding a birth—in contrast to the mother bearing her child much in the likeness of her very flesh. Gospel evangelism is to be midwife for the birth of new persons in new communities which are born from above, from the gospel through the Spirit and in the new humanity in Christ. In other words, the community of priests must not subtly become priests of *their* form of self-care, but rather be priests of *whatever* form of self-care the Spirit is creating in a new "gospel" community. The given name of every new Christ-community should signify birth in Christ, not the perpetuation of some priesthood perpetuating its priestly gene-pool so that all its "church plants" are named in its own likeness.

A Community of a New Social Order

Newbigin writes "*if the church is to be effective in advocating and achieving a new social order . . . it must be itself a social order.*" A community of a new social order is the most difficult of all these "witness" aspects of the gospel community because it most easily falls into the temptation and problems just discussed. The idea of a social order creates thoughts of a form of being, and that can easily lead to the idea of some ideal form that is to be propagated and perpetuated. But the gospel community is not a matter of form, but a matter of the dynamic presence of the triune

God in the becoming and being of a new social order. Thus, the qualification of "new" is necessary lest gospel evangelism is misconstrued as the steward's propagation of *its* existing social order. And the fact is that all communities, including churches, by default must already have *some* social order, just as it has some culture. But what is needed is a *new* social order formed by the gospel. Therefore, the concern under this heading is with the gospel dynamic of the gospel community, what that dynamic is and how it works.[63] Of course the newness is in contrast to existing communities, and especially merely human non gospel-formed communities. Therefore, we will consider the gospel dynamic of a new social order with a view to its being in contrast to humankind's default social orders.[64] Of course this characteristic is preeminently about "plausibility" since the steward's credibility is based on their demonstration of the gospel's capacity to birth a *new* social order. Thus, Jesus spoke of the social order formed by the gospel which does not "hide its lamp under a basket" and is the "light of the world" and "city on a hill" (Matt 5:14–16). Newbigin called this "city" "*a community of mutual responsibility . . . we grow into true humanity only in relationships of faithfulness and responsibility toward one another*"—which we add, would be a plausibly "new" type of community. We also add that faithfulness and responsibility toward others is a way of describing love for others.

The steward's call to be a new social order of a true humanity, firstly requires faithfulness and responsibility to Christ's gospel mediation, as the only means to faithfulness and responsibility toward others. For truly *loving* human community can only be formed by the priestly mediation

---

63. Peter Leithart calls the specific dynamic the "fundamental physics" that forms every community which is here included for another informative and differently framed view of this complex reality of human social orders: "Locate the sacred center of a group; its boundaries of tolerable and intolerable persons, objects and behavior; its rituals of sacrifice—discover all this and you have got down to the elementary particles that determine the group's chemical composition. Relocate the sacred, rearrange the boundaries of purity and pollution, revise its sacrificial procedure, and you have changed the fundamental physics of the society. A revolution *here* is the most profound of social revolutions, and it is the revolution achieved by Jesus in his cross and resurrection." Leithart, *Delivered from the Elements*, 12. The central element of the change Leithart speaks of, as bringing social revolution, is the mediation of Christ, as we will see.

64. "Without roots that reach into God's gracious purposes, it is not at all theologically obvious that the church is really something theologically necessary, or something that could not be abandoned and replaced by any number of alternative religious or voluntary organizations." Badcock, *House*, 335.

of Christ, and neither the stewards nor the secularists can form the truly human community apart from Christ's mediation. This is all too evident in the coercive and violent "will to power" ways of merely human communities that ultimately only propagate and perpetuate the ways of the cities of Cain and Lamech.

At this point we need to pictorially show the difference between a mediated and non-mediated relationship in relation to love. The first and second rows pictorially demonstrate their difference, while the third row shows that the non-mediated relationship is often not merely a negation, but an attempted replacement.

Table 6: Mediated and Non-Mediated Communities

Mediated community of love	person / Christ / person
Non-mediated community of non-love	person / person
Imitation mediated community of non-love	person / Person / person

This chart may well provoke offense, as Kierkegaard's proposal on this point in his "Works of Love" has done, for its teaching of the insufficiency of human love. This offense is the reason for this entire section on the need of a *new* social order.

Kierkegaard explains the mediated relationship saying: "Christianity teaches that love is a relationship between: a person—God—a person, that is, that God is the middle term."[65] The non-mediated relationship of course leaves God/Christ out as "the middle term" and leads to "direct" or "immediate" relationship person to person and also the replacement of Christ as mediator by a person or the persons with the power to attempt it. Non-mediated and imitation-mediated "loving" attempts at human communities are the poison that invariably sabotages the love in these "communities."[66] Dietrich Bonhoeffer, following Soren Kierkegaard's

---

65. As cited in Ferreira, *Love's Grateful Striving*, 71. See also Ferreira, "Levinas and Kierkegaard," 46–60.

66. M. Jamie Ferreira presents a thorough commentary on Kierkegaard's biblical thought on "God as the Middle Term." She answers objections that "love" mediated by God is not truly loving, showing the opposite to be the case since the God who *is love* is the judge of all "love," and also being the One whose love of all enables that any *true* love in a relation is of God. See Ferreira, *Loves Grateful Striving*, 71–83.

lead, realized that Christ's mediation is the only dynamic of true spiritual community.[67] To try to demonstrate this we will string together several excerpts from Bonhoeffer's classic work, *Life Together*.

> Christian community is not an ideal we have to realize, but rather a reality created by God in Christ in which we may participate... Because Christian community is founded solely on Jesus Christ, it is a spiritual (pneumatische) and not a psychic (psychische) reality. In this respect it differs absolutely from all other communities... Thus in the spiritual community the Spirit rules; in the emotional community, psychological techniques and methods. In the former, unsophisticated, nonpsychological, unmethodological, helping love is offered to one another; in the latter, psychological analysis and design... Within the spiritual community there is never, in any way whatsoever, an "immediate" relationship of one to another.[68]

The substance of Bonhoeffer's thought can be charted as follows with the characteristics of the mediated alternate community of Christ in contrast to the merely human unmediated community:

Table 7: Characteristics of Mediated and Non-Mediated Communities

Mediated "Christ" Community	Non-Mediated Human Community
A reality in Christ	An ideal in the mind
We participate	We "manufacture"
Spiritual	Psychical/emotional
Holy Spirit guidance	Psychological technique/method
Unsophisticated	Analysis
Helping love	Coercive design
Mediate relationships	Immediate relationships

---

67. On Kierkegaard, Bonhoeffer, & community see Kirkpatrick, *Attacks on Christendom*, 216–19.

68. Bonhoeffer, *Life Together*, 39–41.

Rehabilitating the Stewards of the Gospel

Of course, the factor that makes most difference is the last, the mediated or immediate relationships of the persons within the communities. The significance can most easily be seen by considering the following additional chart of the dynamics and results under each type:

Table 8: Dynamics and Results of Mediated and Immediate Communities

Mediated Community	Immediate Human Community
Human / Christ / Human	Human / Human
Christ as a buffer between people	No buffer between people
Protection	No protection
Equality	Non-equality
Mutual responsibility	Dominance/submission
Peace	Conflict
Security of ultimate value	Suspicion of ultimate value
The way of grace and faith	The way of force and the will to power
True love/God's love	Fallen love/human love

One can see the immense differences that follow from the one basic foundational difference of God's or man's mediation. The merely human community essentially consists in power struggles that coerce individual freedom, rather than respect it as given by God and mediated in Christ. The merely human community, or more accurately the societal collectivist struggle, is founded on who prevails to dominate in the ego mix through will to power battles ranging from media technique and sociological pressure to overt societal coercion and violence.[69] In the Christ

69. Several writers recognize varying degrees of violence here. Weil writes ". . . the need of freedom itself, so essential to the intellect, calls for a corresponding protection against suggestion, propaganda influence by means of obsession. These are methods of constraint, a special kind of constraint, not accomplished by fear or physical distress, but which is none the less a form of violence. Modern technique places extremely potent instruments at its service. This constraint is, by its very nature collective, and

community, each person's ultimate value and identity is secure and unchangeable by being derived in relation to Christ alone; in the merely human community each person's ultimate value and identity is suspect and changeable and derives merely from their own self and their valuation by others. The immediate "way" works against the good and freedom of most in the "community" who exist below the higher level(s) of the hierarchical realm of power. Of course, those on the higher levels do so in the name of "love" and depending on their powers of media technique may persuade those on the lower levels of that "love."[70] Bonhoeffer provides a few more specifics on the nature of Christ's mediation and on what I call the merely human attempt at love.

> Because Christ stands between me and an other, I must not long for unmediated community with that person. As only Christ was able to speak to me in such a way that I was helped, so others too can only be helped by Christ alone. However, this means that I must release others from all attempts to control, coerce, and dominate them with my love . . . This is the meaning of the claim that we can only encounter others through the mediation of Christ. Self-centered love constructs its own image of other persons, about what they are and what they should become. It takes the life of the other person into its own hands. Spiritual love recognizes the true image Jesus Christ has formed and wants to form in all people.[71]

What needs to be clarified is that Christians do not automatically practice the Christ community, and therefore their "natural" default setting is the merely human community and the desire to themselves

---

human souls are its victims." Weil, *Need for Roots*, 25. Newbigin writes, "We have witnessed the appalling results of trying to go back to some sort of primitive collectivity based on the total control of the individual, down to the depths of his spirit, by an all-powerful group." But he also shows why, with Weil, he also thought this is perhaps *the* crisis of humankind, saying "Yet we know that we cannot condemn this solution to the problem of men's loneliness if we have no other to offer. It is natural that men should ask with a greater eagerness than ever before such questions as these: 'Is there in truth a family of God on earth to which I can belong, a place where all men can truly be at home? If so, where is it to be found, what are its marks, and how is it related to, and distinguished from, the known communities of family, nation, and culture?'" Weston, *Missionary Theologian*, 117.

70. *Till We Have Faces* by C. S. Lewis demonstrates this top down hierarchical and immediate "way of love" in the coercive violent "love" of Queen Orual for her "lesser" sister Psyche.

71. Bonhoeffer, *Life Together*, 43–44.

"mediate" the community of Christ, as we saw the community of priests tempted to do above. For we cannot create the Christ community. It is already a reality in Christ to be acted upon, not to be created. But Bonhoeffer also says that realizing the unity of Christ through acting upon it can be a rarity. Nevertheless, it is "not the experience of Christian community, but firm and certain faith within Christian community that holds us together."[72] That prevents a false perfectionism from destroying the realization of the loving new social order mediated by Christ.

So where does that leave the prospect of the community of a new social order? Is it merely a hope? As far as in perfection, yes. Bonhoeffer held that the "achievement" of true lived community is the gift of God beyond human appropriation per se, although that doesn't preclude the need for Christians to "practice" the unity in Christ, for practice is the means to realize that particular gift. For otherwise, apart from participating by faith in the gospel's means toward the gift of true community, the stewards will merely fall to the priestly temptation of trying to manufacture community and thereby bypassing the gift to acquire a deadly virtue.

Community is a basic human longing that is perhaps made more conspicuous by its absence. But any strong human longing that is unfulfilled leaves us dangerously open to counterfeits. Eugene Peterson speaks of false means for achieving community and shows their "human, all too human" results."[73]

> Community impoverished Christians are ripe for such exploitation. Our need for community and our dissatisfaction with the community we are in (or looking over) provides a wide open field for the men and women who are selling community." Community as commodity is one of the more spectacular growth industries in North American religion today . . . What is being sold, on inspection doesn't turn out to be community at all. Americans are good at forming clubs and gathering crowds. But clubs and crowds, even when—especially when—they are religious clubs and crowds, are not communities. The formation of community is the intricate, patient, painful work of the Holy Spirit. We cannot buy or make community; we can only offer ourselves to become community.[74]

72. Bonhoeffer, *Life Together*, 47.

73. "Human all too human" is the name of a book by Friedrich Nietzsche and also an oft used (and very useful) phrase of the philosopher Merold Westphal. See Sands, *Reasoning from Faith*, 173.

74. Peterson, "Forward," viii.

True community is an elusive thing because of its connection to the gospel's way of faith that is so *non-immediate*. We think the present community was made by "the God of the gaps" and so think we need to fill those gaps by *our* mediation. But the way of mediated community follows the slow process that daily prays *"forgive us our sins as we forgive those who sin against us,"* an ever-necessary but oft-missing ingredient for communities that wholly consist of *sinners*. But if one does not know of Christ's mediation of a new social order, and does not follow its good means, what community will be found? If God's stewards are "scarcely saved" in regard to community, "where will the ungodly appear?" (1 Pet 4:18).

When one seeks to imagine the "community" that is *perhaps* aimed at by the identity politics and Cultural Marxism of social justice warriors;[75] or when one considers the ways of the anti-fascists; or of well-armed militant religious nationalists; or the violent tribalism of old-school racists; or the implicit will to power as we have seen in many of God's priestly communities of all stripes, what is seen? We cannot yet see their *ends,* but what *means* do we see? What we see are humans against humans with no mediating God in and in-between all. Partisan politics, ad hominem demonization of one's enemies, propagandized legislative wars, psychological manipulations, and what appears to be sheer hatred with merciless judgment, all seem to disclose the will to power's unrelenting quest for dominance over all who "have sinned and fall short of" their version of a new social order. And in such "orders," there is no place for forgiveness, and no need of mediation.

Thomas Hobbes simply replies that this "*is called Warre; and such a warre, as is of every man, against every man.*"[76] What community can possibly form from such means? We are not condemning every social justice, civil right or religious freedom, as illegitimate. Far from it, but

---

75. Douglas Murray notes that Cultural Marxism is incapable of forgiveness, saying "From Michael Foucault these thinkers absorbed their idea of society not as an infinitely complex system of trust and traditions that evolved over time, but always in the unforgiving light cast when everything is viewed through the prism of 'power.' Viewing all human interactions in this light distorts, rather than clarifies, presenting a dishonest interpretation of our lives. Of course power exists as a force in the world, but so do charity, forgiveness and love. If you were to ask most people what matters in their lives very few would say 'power.' Not because they haven't absorbed their Foucault, but because it is perverse to see everything in life through such a monomaniacal lens. Nevertheless for a certain type of person who is intent on finding blame rather than forgiveness in the world, Foucault helps to explain everything." Murray, *Madness of Crowds,* loc. 983.

76. Hobbes, *Leviathan,* 77.

the means of the fallen will to power cannot provide the new social order that, when "finished" would truly be considered a good "society" by all, or in most cases, by most anyone other than the power elites behind each new social order. If there is any hope for true community in society it does not seem to be evident in *the means* being employed for supposed justice that simply look more like *revenge*. Even people that have sought unjust power and done evil deeds, namely those we still call criminals, are provided mediation in a just society which provides it to them because of the image of God in each person. Christ's own attitude toward peoples of different classes remained that of love and forgiveness. But the attitude of "social justice warriors" of all brands appears to be one of endless revenge and "warre."[77] In a discussion on the Christian philosopher Simone Weil, Allen presents some thoughts on large-scale human "justice" movements that are based in the will to power, to reveal their failure to grant essential human independence and uphold justice toward others, which is another way of framing the significance of Christ's mediation:

> Revolutions may topple an unjust social order. But there is no genuine hope unless the "liberators" now exercising power desire that others may exist independently of themselves. This requires self-renunciation rather than self-glorification, and resistance as well to the temptation to impose a prescribed order on others. Weil's fundamental conviction concerning the love of neighbor is that God seeks to enter us so that his love causes us always to consult justice in all our relations with each other, even when we do not have to.[78]

The community of a new social order seems an elusive myth. But is it possible that the *myth became fact* in Christ?[79] Can there be any substantial realization of a communal "lived appropriation" of the gospel of a new social order? As Bonhoeffer said above, *faith* can enter into Christ's gift of community and thus taste of "the powers of the age to come" (Heb 6:5). It seems even *reason* can glimpse the hope by considering *the means*, for is there any better *dynamic* for peace in universal community than

---

77. "In Jesus's concern for the poor and oppressed, he is not tempted to raise these people up by destroying the rich. If Jesus spoke of the evils of wealth, St. Mark tells us that he looked upon the rich young man with love. Jesus criticized the Pharisees, but he did not establish justice by destroying them." Springsted, *Simone Weil*, 44.

78. Allen, *Three Outsiders*, 115.

79. Lewis used the term of Christ. I use it of Christ's body, his new community of humanity. See "Myth Became Fact" in Lewis, *God in the Dock*, 63–67.

can be found in the gospel of a loving transcendent creator and servant king who relinquishes all earthly power for the liberation and uniting of all peoples in love, from the lowest to the highest? Yes, perhaps the stewards need to admit that they have merely tasted of the powers of the world to come, for with Lewis's *Psyche* they confess . . . "*He comes to me only in the holy darkness.*" But a taste is at least the firstfruits of a full harvest to come, especially when the bitter harvest of Hobbes's "warre" has been our basic subsistence sustenance.

We have not described the nature of such a new social order, being occupied with its dynamic of "creation" and some of its characteristics. For we have seen the problem of "forms" and in God's kingdom there is no rigid form of freedom. But what can be assumed in all such orders, though the cultural expression may vary, is a mediated-by-love community where "justice rolls down like waters, and righteousness like an ever-flowing stream, as pictured in Amos 5:24. And we can be sure that God's final community will be fulfilled commensurate with what God has already achieved in the unity of at-one-ment in Christ.

> The church is what it is not because of some program, system of thought, or pattern of practice. It is what it is, in the final analysis, because God graciously chooses to deal with us as sinful creatures . . . What is absolutely required here is neither a theology, or a strategy but what was earlier called "God's lightning," the free action of God that strikes unexpectedly, in ways that surpass what we can ask and in the end is totally independent of our answers and our imaginings.[80]

How then, can any merely human effort create true human community? We again must ask, if God's stewards are "scarcely saved" in regard to community, "where will the ungodly appear?" (1 Pet 4:18). Much of this book has demonstrated that the stewards of the gospel all too often hinder "God's lightening," and dam up God's ever-flowing stream of engulfing love meant to flood them and overflow to those outside, soaking the parched earth and bringing to life the withered and oppressed roots of humanity to break through the hard surface of war in virulent growths of new human community. For the gospel nevertheless remains as the dynamic that mediates true community and a new social order. And as we have elsewhere said, if these proceedings of "The Gospel in the Dock"

---

80. Badcock, *House*, 337. Newbigin similarly writes, "Therefore the nature of the Church is never to be finally defined in static terms, but only in terms of that to which it is going." Weston, *Missionary Theologian*, 126.

were held in another venue, we might see God's lightening striking the rock and the gospel waters flowing forth and watering our desert.

A Community of Hope

Lesslie Newbigin says that *"one of the most striking features of contemporary Western culture is the virtual disappearance of hope."* The main story of the twentieth century was that it was virtually the total repudiation of *"the nineteenth century belief in progress"* that resulted in *"widespread pessimism about the future of 'Western' civilization."* Newbigin notes that the felt *"nihilism and despair"* has driven hope from being this-worldly toward an attempted recovery of some sort of hope in *"the timeless peace of pantheistic mysticism."* We add that much of "evangelical faith" has also lost the eschatological vision of a this-worldly hope and succumbed to an otherworldly "spiritual" hope as we saw in "the gospel of escapism." In response to these losses N. T. Wright's book "Surprised by Hope" demonstrates that the gospel *is* the gospel *because* it is the good news of *the present (and future)* coming of God's kingdom "on earth as it is in heaven." Wright introduces this concern of his book saying,

> This book introduces two questions that have often been dealt with entirely separately but that, I passionately believe, belong tightly together. First, what is the ultimate Christian hope? Second, what hope is there for change, rescue, transformation, new possibilities within the world in the present? And the main answer can be put like this. As long as we see Christian hope in terms of "going to heaven," of a salvation that is essentially *away from* this world, the two questions are bound to appear as unrelated. Indeed, some insist angrily that to ask the second one at all is to ignore the first one, which is the really important one. This in turn makes some others get angry when people talk of resurrection, as if this might draw attention away from the really important and pressing matters of contemporary social concern. But if the Christian's hope is for *God's new creation,* for "new heavens and new earth," and if that hope has already come to life in Jesus of Nazareth, then there is every reason to join the two questions together. And if so, we may find that answering the one is also answering the other.[81]

---

81. Wright, *Surprised by Hope,* 5.

Wright holds, and we believe rightly so, that the gospel is about a "worldly" hope that we could think of as being gained "along the way" to the ultimate hope which as far as specifics goes is largely kept veiled to our understanding. In this regard he clarifies that,

> All language about the future, as any economist or politician will tell you, is simply a set of signposts pointing into a fog. We see through a glass darkly, says St. Paul as he peers toward what lies ahead. All our language about future states of the world and of ourselves consists of complex pictures that may or may not correspond very well to the ultimate reality. But that doesn't mean it's anybody's guess or that every opinion is as good as every other one. And—supposing someone came forward out of the fog to meet us? That, of course, is the central though often ignored Christian belief.[82]

"Supposing someone came forward out of the fog to meet us?" is answered by the coming of Christ. Wright's imagery is identifying the fog as God's future for all things, and Christ as the "someone" from that future. For our purposes at this point we frame Wright's image in this way: "suppose that *some-thing* came forward out of the fog to meet us," namely, *some community* formed according to that future. That community would be the "hermeneutic of the gospel" that Lesslie Newbigin sees as the sign of the kingdom, the sign of the present and the future.[83] In relation to the need for God's stewards to be "a community of hope" he explains that,

> I must repeat again that it is only as we are truly "indwelling" the gospel story, only as we are so deeply involved in the life of the community which is shaped by this story that it becomes our real "plausibility structure," that we are able steadily and confidently to live in this attitude of eager hope. Almost everything in the "plausibility structure" which is the habitation of our society seems to contradict this Christian hope. Everything suggests that it is absurd to believe that the true authority over all things is represented by a crucified man. No amount of brilliant argument can make it sound reasonable to the inhabitants of the

---

82. Wright, *Surprised by Hope*, xiii-xiv.

83. Newbigin writes, "There is no straight line from the politics of the world, from the programs and projects in which we invest our energies, to the kingdom of God. The holy city is a gift from God, coming from above . . . The church exists as sign and foretaste of the gift that is promised; in all its members it is called to act now in the light of the promised future: that is its proper this-worldliness." Newbigin, *Signs*, 106.

> reigning plausibility structure. That is why I am suggesting the only possible hermeneutic of the gospel is a congregation which believes it.[84]

As we have seen, that public hermeneutic consists of communities with certain gospel characteristics, the last of which is hope. Newbigin summarizes his proposal for this hope:

> If the gospel is to challenge the public life of our society, if Christian's are to occupy the "high ground" which they vacated in the noontime of "modernity," it will not be by forming a Christian political party, or by aggressive propaganda campaigns. Once again it has to be said that there can be no going back to the "Constantinian" era. It will only be by movements that begin with the local congregation in which the reality of the new creation is present, known and experienced, and from which men and women will go into every sector of public life to the illumination of the gospel. But that will only happen as and when local congregations renounce an introverted concern for their own life, and recognize that they exist for the sake of those who are not members, as sign, instrument, and foretaste of God's redeeming grace for the whole life of society.[85]

Newbigin's summary also aptly brings together many of the concerns that have been discussed regarding what is necessary in repentance and faith, and that not merely for their own sake, but for the gospel and its concerns for humanity and the world. In coherence with God's self-sacrificial way, the promise of Jesus will hold true so that "death together" leads not only to "life together," but witnesses thereby to life for the world:

> I'm telling you the solemn truth: unless a grain of wheat falls into the earth and dies, it remains all by itself. If it dies, though, it will produce lots of fruit. If you love your life, you'll lose it. If you hate your life in this world, you'll keep it for the life of the coming age.[86]

In light of all these considerations of the stewards as a living "hermeneutic of the gospel," the evidence by which they could become released "from the dock" does not require perfect realization of the community of the future, but rather a credible witness to that hope. It is in this sense that

---

84. Newbigin, *The Gospel*, loc. 4339.
85. Newbigin, *The Gospel*, loc. 4339.
86. John 12:24–25, Wright, *The New Testament*, 2011.

the stewards are the living hermeneutic of the gospel, by witnessing that it *is good for the church community*, and therefore also for the good of the worldwide human community. And this living witness is the apostolic criterion for the faithfulness of the stewards in their gospel mission:

> That which was from the beginning, which we have heard, which we have seen with our eyes, which we looked upon and have touched with our hands, concerning the word of life—the life was made manifest, and we have seen it, and testify to it and proclaim to you the eternal life, which was with the Father and was made manifest to us—that which we have seen and heard we proclaim also to you, so that you too may have fellowship with us; and indeed our fellowship is with the Father and with his Son Jesus Christ. And we are writing these things so that our joy may be complete (1 John 1:1–4).

Writing "at the turn of the past millennium," theologians Richard Bauckham and Trevor Hart show that the steward's connection to the holy "fog" of the future places them in a "testimonial" role between God and the world. They also show that when they are dedicated to the task of witness to what is *beyond* their community, they do not fall to the "deadly virtues" associated with building and maintaining "the sacred canopy" for humanity and the world. Speaking *as stewards of the gospel* they say,

> we shall be a place in the world, which is not properly of the world, the people who live up to the hilt in this life but with their sights set firmly on the horizon lying beyond it, and who therefore model for society how this life may be lived in hope even when hope seems hopeless. In doing so we shall; not, of course, save the world. Only God can do that. But we shall be faithful to our primary calling to bear witness, and to call the world back to a belief in the God with whom alone there is genuine hope for its future.[87]

A half-century earlier, Paul Tillich spoke consciously *from* the place of repentance, *from* the "canopy building and maintaining" of the past, *to* the task of *mere witness*, much as C.S. Lewis spoke *from* the chastened place of the task of Mere *Christianity*. We will end this section with Tillich's restatement of the steward's mission, learned through the pedagogy of the deadly virtues of their past, and their ongoing temptation when the lessons are forgotten, whether willfully or not.

---

87. Bauckham and Hart, *Hope Against Hope*, 210.

Rehabilitating the Stewards of the Gospel

> Don't think that we want to convert you away from your secular state to a religious state, that we want to make you religious and members of a very high religion, the Christian, and of a very great denomination within it, namely, our own. This would be of no avail. We want only to communicate to you an experience we have had that here and there in the world and now and then in ourselves is a New Creation, usually hidden, but sometimes manifest, and certainly manifest in Jesus who is called the Christ.[88]

In a sense, these thoughts on the steward's being a community of hope, given their manifold failures to be the community that is the gospel's "hermeneutic," may reveal that the gospel presents two choices regarding any hope of a viable "life together." One is a hope held against any intimation of hope, for lack of any gospel that can provide a foretaste and is therefore at best a hope *against* hope. The other is a hope that has validity because it has grown from the revealed dynamic that can change the world and has done so "here and there in the world, and now and then in ourselves," and is therefore a hope rooted *in* hope.

A Community of Lament

We add to the first six characteristics Newbigin listed a seventh one, that the stewards of the gospel are called to be a community of lament. For God's community, this side of "kingdom come," lives in a dialectic of suffering and joy.[89] But some steward denominations with their "Christianity and health & wealth" gospel have made exclusive "happy" a gospel inheritance that seems to seek to exclude suffering as a normal aspect of communal life. At worst this is a seriously defective "theology" that much or most of the Bible easily deconstructs. At best the denial of suffering is a theological infection "suffered" by God's community under the influence of "the wishful optimism of our culture" and its underlying cultural gospel of "the modern world."[90] The truth is that God's community,

---

88. Tillich, *The New Being*, 18.

89. Sylvia Walsh provides a thorough discussion of Kierkegaard's biblical dialectic of "Suffering/Joy and Consolation" in her book "Living Christianly—Kierkegaard's Dialectic of Christian Existence."

90. Walter Brueggemann identifies the "wishful optimism" as a sort of existential denial, while N. T. Wright identifies that as rooted in "the competing gospel of the modern world." See Brueggemann, *The Message*, 51–52; Wright, *Simply Good News*, 83–87.

situated in the midst of Western culture, is "notoriously averse to pain and tragedy."[91] We are simply not good at lament *because* the foundation of both praise and lament, is hope, and therefore the loss of hope leads to the loss of true lament.[92] In other words, hope is necessary not only for praise but for true lament, because true lament is not breathed into the void of nothingness but breathed to the presence of God. The title of a book by Walter Brueggemann demonstrates that *grief* is what often lies between *reality* and *hope* since God's people often fall prey to deceptive ideologies such as nationalism so that they then resort to the categorical denial of grief.[93] Brueggemann says that grief is "the long, slow process of loss" which gives way to lamentation as "the liturgical practice of grief."[94]

But grief is not always related to God's judgments on the cultural ideologies of his gospel stewards or humanity in general. Lamentation is therefore also more generally caused by our relation to natural suffering and what Brueggemann calls "disorientation" rather than "equilibrium, coherence, and symmetry" since "life is savagely marked by disequilibrium, incoherence, and unrelieved asymmetry."[95] Which brings us back to the fact of how God's community more often responds to the reality of life:

> It is . . . a frightened, numb denial and deception that does not want to acknowledge or experience the disorientation of life . . . Such a denial and cover-up, which I take it to be, is an odd inclination for passionate Bible users, given the large number of psalms that are songs of lament, protest, and complaint about the incoherence that is experienced in the world. At least it is

91. "Western cultures are notoriously averse to pain and tragedy. We spend an extraordinary amount of money and effort seeking to insulate ourselves against life's vicissitudes. All kinds of precautions are taken to ensure the maximal safety of the environments we must inhabit—our homes, our workplaces, our schools, our social space, our transport, our public places—and, just in case something does go wrong, we are offered just about every type of insurance one could dream of. We do not want sorrow to knock at our doors and, when it does, we do not know what to do with it. Our default mode is to keep it out of sight and pretend it is not there." Parry, *Lamentations*, 1.

92. Brueggemann, *The Message*, 52–58.

93 Brueggemann is specifically considering "grief" as the reaction to God's judgment on ideologies of exceptionalism which disguise reality. Such grief then leads to a "despair that variously produces moralism, hedonism, violence" apart from the prophetic articulation of hope. Brueggemann, *Reality, Grief, Hope*, 1–2.

94. Brueggemann, *Out of Babylon*, 33.

95. Brueggemann, *The Message*, 51.

clear that a church that goes on singing "happy songs" in the face of raw reality is doing something very different from what the Bible itself does.[96]

But Brueggemann's recognition of the place of lament does not stand apart from the place of celebration also. In fact, in his book called "Praying the Psalms" he summarizes this duality of communally breathed expressions saying that,

> *Psalms of lament are powerful expressions of the experience of disorientation . . . Psalms of thanksgiving and hymns powerfully express experiences of reorientation.*[97]

Brueggemann's terms *disorientation and reorientation* convey that what is ultimately in view in celebration or lamentation is the broader creational concern of whether a person or people experience being "landed" or "landless"—which could also be described with the terms "home" or "homeless."[98]

With this wider view of the stewards being a community of lament, we can see how this characteristic surprisingly helps them to fulfill their other callings. They fulfill being "a community of praise" by working through disorientation toward reorientation *through their lamentation*. They fulfill being "a community of truth" by acknowledging *rather than denying* the difficult realities of life so that responsible love and faith in action can be pursued. They pursue that responsibility by being "a community for others" and seeking to help them in their sufferings. Their mournful lament sings in harmony with, and conducts for others, the entire creation's inarticulate groan, as the community of priests for the world (Rom 8:22–23). Their hopeful lament unites a community of a new social order, in redemptive response to the present *disorientation of the world* because of the hope of ultimate reorientation of all things in Christ. Thus, in all these, their being a community of lament *fulfills being a community of hope*—exhibiting living in hope for what is not yet seen (Rom 8:24–25).

In all this, the community of lament participates in the great universal "groaning" of the whole creation for redemption through its own Spirit-beathed "groanings too deep for words" (Rom 8:22–23, 26). In

---

96. Brueggemann, *The Message*, 51–52.

97. Brueggemann, *Praying*, 29–32.

98. Brueggemann says "Land is a central, if not *the central theme* of biblical faith." Brueggemann, *The Land*, 3.

sum, what the community of lament, the community of "the firstfruits of the spirit" testifies to *through lament*, whether in outward breathings or inward groanings, is the redemption of the whole of creation. And this provides a fitting foundation for some further explorations of the rehabilitation of the community of stewards of the gospel in relation to the rest of humanity and the world itself. What we hope to show is that the community of gospel stewards, following Christ the new 'adam,' are both sign and promise of humankind restored to the way of faith from self-love and the way of the will to power. Thus, they set their seal that the gospel is good *for the church*, and so become the living hermeneutic of its goodness for the rest of humanity and the world.

The Stewards and the Gospel of Peace

> And he came and preached peace to you who were far off and peace to those who were near (Eph 2:17).

Peace marks the fifth step in the overall complex of repentance/faith since the gospel is the proclamation of peace to all. In this section we will consider the need of a rehabilitation of the stewards of the gospel in relation to their faithfulness in proclaiming and living by the peace that is part and parcel of the gospel. This is essentially another hermeneutic of the gospel wherein the stewards exist as "a community of peace." Much of the focus of the NT on the peace of the gospel addressed problems of how the peace of the gospel impacted "those who were far off" (the Gentile nations) and "those who were near" (the nation of Israel) and the ongoing relation between them. To consider these issues we will begin by revisiting Jonah, our favorite prophet of "those who were near," who was sent by God to "those who were far off." We also remember that Jesus said Jonah was "the only sign given." This relates to the *sign-ificance* of the *entire* story of Jonah, as we have previously sought to demonstrate. Showing the broad applicability of Jonah as a sign, James Jordan writes,

> Jesus spoke of the sign of Jonah as the ONE sign of His victory. Often, we take this only to refer to His three days in the "heart of the earth" and His resurrection. But it's more than that. Taking the gospel to the gentiles is also part of the sign of Jonah.[99]

---

99. James P. Jordan, "Exile or Ark?" *Biblical Horizons Blog*, April 10, 2008. https://biblicalhorizons.wordpress.com/2008/04/10/exile-or-ark/

Therefore, we will consider more of Jonah's story for the purpose of providing a biblical template for applying the "near" Jonah's relations with the "far off" Ninevites to the contemporary situation, wherein the "near" stewards of God live in relation to those who are presently "far off."

Jonah and the Stewardship of the Gospel

The most obvious thing we see in Jonah's post-fish ministry in Nineveh is his extreme displeasure and anger toward God following the repentance of the Ninevites (Jonah 3:1—4:11). Jonah's reaction, in relation to God's universal purpose for choosing Israel, is on the face of it almost incomprehensible. Shouldn't the repentance of the wickedest nation of Jonah's day have been something he would rejoice over, not only for the sake of the the peoples oppressed by Assyria but the salvation of Nineveh including over 120,000 young children? But the mindset Jonah had all along is finally revealed as he angrily sits following the nation's repentance, saying,

> "O Lord, is not this what I said when I was yet in my country? That is why I made haste to flee to Tarshish; for I knew that you are a gracious God and merciful, slow to anger and abounding in steadfast love, and relenting from disaster" (Jonah 4:1-2).

The mystery of Jonah's anger is revealed in that he did not want Nineveh to repent, since that would spare them from God's judgment. But wouldn't that sparing be a good thing? Does Jonah being angry for that mean that Jonah and the Israel he represented were simply examples of those who enjoy God's judgment on others? Is that not a complete betrayal of Israel's reason for existence as God's "kingdom of priests?" It is, but what we need to consider is that Jonah and Israel feared what might happen if the "gospel of peace" were to be extended to the greatest enemy of all in Israel's known world.

Jonah knew full well that God always "means business" and intended something. Jonah had an idea of what that might be and wanted no part of it. This was because the Assyrians, even if they repented, would still be the greatest threat in the world to Israel. The capital city Nineveh's great wickedness was well publicized, as is recorded in the book of the prophet Nahum. He concludes his oracle by declaring to Nineveh "*upon whom has not come your unceasing evil?*" (Nah 1:1; 3:19). Jonah also knew that God's providential methods include his righteous "use" of evil nations to judge other evil nations, even Israel.[100] So God's mercy to Nineveh was the proximate reason for Jonah's fear, but in essence that was more ultimately a fear of God's judgment, the need of which could have been removed if Israel repented of its own fall to the will to power. Simply put, Jonah and Israel, fell to their fear of God's judgment of their present ways, rather than rising to trust God's gospel for others in faith. The will to power can overcome us not only by enticing us to wield it, but by fearing it to the point of being controlled by it. In short, Israel feared Assyria more than she feared God, and thus "boycotted" the gospel and her call to be a community of peace to those who were far off. In each of the other "hermeneutical communities" the gospel of peace was implicit. But we now need to consider why that was so.

A Community of Peace

We do this first of all by looking more closely at the peace the gospel brings between those estranged from each other, those far off and and those near. That peace is seen in its extremity by considering what was unimaginable to Jonah, namely that the "far off" Assyrians could be brought near, not only to God, but also to Israel. Salvation for those "far off" is one thing, but if that salvation necessitates that the enemies are brought into peaceful *fellowship* with those "near"—well that is another. Of course, I am stretching things a bit here, since before Christ, the true human community of peace was not yet revealed. Israel and Jonah feared peace because the only peace they could conceive of was the removal of their enemies and their installation as the head of all nations under God. What was hidden to them was that Christ would become the head of the kingdom of peace in which they could participate. But that kingdom could only be won by Christ, and participated in by them, by way of the cross.

That way of peace is the scandal—not of particularity which we considered earlier, *but of universality*—the universal way of the cross. Therefore, the way of the cross as the way to the victory of peace is the

---

100. The OT oracle of the prophet Habakkuk is the classic example of that "use" by God although in that case the Babylonian kingdom was in view. On Assyria as "the rod of my anger" see Isaiah 10:5–15. I believe that this "providential use of evil nations as agents of judgment" is what lies beneath the "mark" God placed on Cain in Genesis 4. See discussion of this in our excursus following the introduction. See also Wright, *The Mission of God*, 459–60.

ongoing scandal of the gospel. It also just happens to be the only promise of real hope "come forward from the fog" of the future. The gospel of the cross testifies *historically*, in Christ's cross/victory and the early Church's non-violent settlement of peace the gospel brings for all, in contrast to humankind's tribalistic religious/political ideologies that dangle carrots of hypothetical peace for their own kin. For the gospel way of peace is not merely of personal, tribal, or national peace, but of peace *with* all others. The gospel way of peace also precludes the scapegoating of any other as the rallying point for the unity of the tribe, which must be sacrificed for the benefit of the tribe's "peace" (John 11:45–53).

The problem is that the way of Cain crouches at the door of any would-be social order, even that of the stewards of the gospel. Succumbing to Cain's crouching "sin" to construct "peace" requires dividing and scapegoating others according to the standards of the old creation now abolished in Christ (Gal 3:28). Those conveniently scapegoated then become the inconvenient problem that must be in some manner dealt with in the new social order, possibly even as "the Jewish problem" was dealt with by Nazi Germany. This means of societal formation therefore justifies the exclusion all those deemed unfit for the new order which ultimately is established by scapegoating and then excluding all those deemed deplorable to its "uniting" ideology.

This process is depicted in the NT book of Hebrews when it records the parallel between sacrificial animals being burned outside the camp to the sacrifice of Jesus "outside the gate." But this was part of the perfect storm of atonement, in which Jesus became the ultimate scapegoat to end all scapegoating, and lay the foundation of the life of God's enduring "city to come."[101] And so all of humankind is called to now "go to him

---

101. See Hebrews 13:11–14. The language "scapegoat to end of scapegoating" is derived from what I understand of the thought of philosopher Rene Girard. One writer explains saying: "This (scapegoat) figure Girard terms the 'surrogate victim.' (Of course, this 'single victim' need not be an individual but could be a subgroup within the larger. One can think of the killing of twins in some tribes, for example, or more spectacularly, the Holocaust of European Jewry during World War II or the incarceration of American Japanese descent during the same period. This polarization of violence will have far-reaching effects. Above all, it will transform what had been merely a collection of mutual antagonists into a community united in mutual hatred of a single victim. In their intimations of each other's hatred of the victim they will join in interpreting him as a source of all the previous troubles among them. In addition, the new peace and harmony they experience in this cooperative opposition to a single enemy will make it seem to them as if the expulsion or death of the victim must be its source." Webb, *Philosophers*, 195–96.

outside the camp" of the divisive scapegoating tribalistic ways of the will to power in the merely human "social order" to participate by faith in God's coming community of peace in the "city placed on a hill" otherwise known as "the kingdom of God" that Jesus said was "at hand." Of course, that going to Jesus signifies going to the cross of the scapegoat. Perhaps scapegoating can only end when all are willing to be the scapegoat by not scapegoating others, which is certainly a stark depiction of the way of following a non-violent liberation of humanity. The *foundation* of God's new city, the "house of God," was "dedicated" by the sacrifice of Christ to end Cain's original city, also dedicated by human sacrifice and named Enoch—"*dedicated*" (Heb 10:19–21; 11:10).[102] Altogether, these thoughts reveal the difference between the two ways seeking peace, God's way of offering the scapegoat to end all scapegoating, and man's way of endless violent scapegoating.[103]

How this all relates to the community of peace between those far off and those who are near, is that the merely human community does not seek reconciliation but instead scapegoats those far off for the sake of those near. But the gospel is of the reconciliation of "the near" and "the far" in any one place and in the entire world of peoples. And that "way" of reconciliation is an accomplished reality already won by Christ. Eugene Peterson explains that the community made up of those previously divided as "near" and "far off" simply "practices resurrection" because,

> The *being-ness* of the church is what we are dealing with. Church is not something that we cobble together to do something for God. It is the "fulness of him who fills all in all" (Eph. 1:23) working comprehensively with and for us.[104]

Thus, the task of the stewards of *this* gospel is the "lived appropriation" of the "be-ing" that already is in Christ's "fulness" which is the community of peace. *This* community of peace is not mere theory, it is the accomplished reality of at-one-ment that needs to be lived into as the followers of Christ "go outside" the city of man to the new city of God whose foundations were "dedicated" by the sacrifice of Christ, and thus "designed and built" by God. This city is the gospel's community of peace.

102. See Vos, *Epistle to the Hebrews*, 110; Ellul, *Meaning of the City*, 5–6.

103. "Instead, an odd new counter-community arises, dedicated both to the innocent victim whom God has vindicated by resurrection and to a new life through him that requires no further such sacrifice." Heim, "The End of Scapegoating," 25.

104. Peterson, *Practice Resurrection*, 119.

The community of peace requires sustained attention to its two main aspects: the "inner reality" of the peace of its own community made up of the previously estranged "near and far," and the "outward relation" of that new community toward those *still* "far off." These two aspects will be considered in the following two sections.

A Community of "Those Who Were Far off and Those Who Were Near"

The gospel of peace is most comprehensively explicated in the New Testament in Paul's letter "to the saints who are in Ephesus." The following brief excerpt portrays the depth and significance of the peace of the gospel as it was explained by Paul.

> Therefore remember that at one time you Gentiles in the flesh, called "the uncircumcision" by what is called the circumcision, which is made in the flesh by hands—remember that you were at that time separated from Christ, alienated from the commonwealth of Israel and strangers to the covenants of promise, having no hope and without God in the world. But now in Christ Jesus you who once were far off have been brought near by the blood of Christ. For he himself is our peace, who has made us both one and has broken down in his flesh the dividing wall of hostility by abolishing the law of commandments expressed in ordinances, that he might create in himself one new man in place of the two, so making peace, and might reconcile us both to God in one body through the cross, thereby killing the hostility. *And he came and preached peace to you who were far off and peace to those who were near.* For through him we both have access in one Spirit to the Father (Ephesians 2:11–18).

Paul shows what the gospel has done in regard to the formerly separated "far off" Gentiles and "near" Jews and showed that in that gospel Christ is "preaching peace" to them. "Were" is the definitive term in regard to their former relations of peace with God and with each other. In his letter to the churches of Galatia, Paul further explains how the law divided humanity not only in regard to Israel and the Gentiles, but in regard to more basic categories by which human existence in relation to God and others had been "normally" considered.

> Now before faith came, we were held captive under the law, imprisoned until the coming faith would be revealed. So then,

> the law was our guardian until Christ came, in order that we might be justified by faith. But now that faith has come, we are no longer under a guardian, for in Christ Jesus you are all sons of God, through faith. For as many of you as were baptized into Christ have put on Christ. There is neither Jew nor Greek, there is neither slave nor free, there is no male and female, for you are all one in Christ Jesus. And if you are Christ's, then you are Abraham's offspring, heirs according to promise (Galatians 3:23–29).

In Galatians, Paul used the metaphor of Israel as children under the guardianship of the law looking toward their inheritance to demonstrate the provisional character of the law, showing that its past divisive aspect of them in relation to Gentiles is no longer determinative for the community in which all are now reconciled to God in Christ. L. Ann Jervis writes that,

> The law, which maintains ethnic boundary lines and delineates social and gender distinctions, has no relevance... Through reference to what may have been a widely used baptismal confession, Paul reminds the Galatians of their initial understanding of the faith. Their original commitment was to a worldview in which they understood themselves to have gained a new identity, one rooted in and defined by Christ. This identity transcended all typical social distinctions and the moral distinctions that resulted from such social differentiating... Gentiles are inheritors of the promise to Abraham without following the law."[105]

We could summarize by saying that there are no longer any basic creational human categories that exclude people from salvation in the new community of humanity created in Christ.

The truth that all creational categories of human beings are already reconciled in Christ has obviously not been the basis for the actual constituency of the Christian communities throughout church history. Why this is so probably has more to do with the "gospel of culture" that buttressed the society at large rather than with the gospel itself. The truth of the inclusivity of the gospel is therefore a matter of revelation which can remain unrecognized, or if known, can be resisted.

It is interesting to note that Peter, the Apostle to the Jews, and Paul, the Apostle to the Gentiles both needed *personal revelations* that completely challenged and transformed their views of previously excluded

---

105. Jervis, *Galatians*, 107–8.

"others" leading them to be able see the true nature of God's new community. Peter needed *revelation* to learn *"what God has made clean do not call common,"* namely, the Gentiles to whom "God has granted repentance that leads to life" (Acts 11:9, 18). Paul needed *revelation* to learn that when he was persecuting his fellow Jews who followed Christ, he was persecuting Christ. And so, he heard the voice saying *"Saul, Saul, why are you persecuting me?"* and "saw" the risen Christ (Acts 9:4). In both of these instances Peter and Paul received "new" revelations that shattered their "knowing of persons according to the flesh" which were contrary to God's own view (2 Cor 5:16). Similarly, a counsel of the leaders in the early church in Jerusalem needed *revelation* regarding the place of Gentiles in "the olive tree" of Israel (Acts 15). That counsel is considered to be the all-important event for that, short of the evidential coming of the Spirit on the Gentiles itself seen in Acts 10:44–47, which enabled the gospel to transcend being a merely tribal religion in the near-eastern world.[106]

A reading of Paul demonstrates that his highest priority was simply to *reveal* to the church communities the unity and peace already present in Christ, to which their "life together" should conform.[107] That unity and peace called for their self-presentation to God as their "reasonable" worship, their repentance regarding prior conformity to the world's non-gospel ways, and their subsequent transformation to discern and live in the truth of the gospel (Rom 12:1–2). But the gospel's reality and call do not always find adequate response and gain purchase in the communities of the gospel stewards. Thus, it is undoubtedly true that embedded racism and other "fleshly" attitudes and practices can and do continue and can even prevail. This is partly due to the predominance of "the gospel of correct doctrine." Several theologians point out that,

> It is possible to be excluded from Christian community on the basis of heterodoxy (grave theological error) or heteropraxy (grave moral error) but not, to coin a term, heteroethnicity. That

---

106. Jennings summarizes in a way that demonstrates the epochal shift that must continually be received: "Acts 15 brings us to the interface of creaturely difference and divine desire where God exposes both bound toward each other in ways never before seen in Israel and among the Gentiles. God draws us without destroying us, without eradicating the differences among the creatures. Jews with Gentiles and Gentile peoples with each other, all borne on the wings of God's desire toward life together in the Spirit of God. The single greatest challenge for disciples of Jesus is to imagine and then enact actual together life, life that interpenetrates, weaves together, and joins to the bone." Jennings, W. J. *Acts*, 145.

107. Hays, *Moral Vision*, ch. 1, 2, 10.

some Christians have not understood this, constitutes one of the gravest offenses possible against the gospel.[108]

There are many issues that can divide the gospel community, and the denials of the gospel whether implicit or explicit are tragic offenses against the gospel and indictments upon its stewards. The step beyond denominations to denominationalism presents an equal-opportunity temptation to division. But due to various reasons in both church and society it seems that many church communities are rightfully re-examining their particular denominational policies and attitudes in light of the universal concern of the gospel and the essential unity of the church in Christ. As is always the case, the old wineskins eventually prove inadequate to hold the new wine. Thus, all the denominations need to be "always reforming" their wineskins in seeking to be faithful stewards of the gospel of peace. Some "emerging" groups present great questions of the relation to the old.[109] Some church historians are saying that the world and church are entering a new epoch and call this movement the great emergence or the age of the Spirit.[110] One thing certain is that Jesus prayed for the unity of the community he founded, and that such oneness would evidence the Spirit's testimony to Jesus, Jesus's testimony from God, and God's testimony to the world (John 17:20–23). Therefore, that community needs to be known as peacemakers "for they shall be called sons of God" (Matt 5:9).

A Community for "Those Who Are Far Off"

The peace the gospel brings is not only related to the inner harmony of its present constituency but also relates to those who have not consciously responded to God's reconciliation of them in Christ. In that sense these persons remain "far off" from the visible community of peace which is to extend the peace of the gospel to them. In regard to this responsibility, *"blessed are the peacemakers"* may possibly be the most forgotten Beatitude of church history. For that reason, on a personal note, I was especially overjoyed to learn that our oldest granddaughter's publishing of her first children's book at the age of 14, portrays a small band of children learning to follow the gospel of peacemaking as taught by Christ in

---

108. Gushee and Stassen, *Kingdom Ethics*, 401.
109. See Tickle, *Emergence Christianity*, 181–206.
110. See Tickle, *The Age of the Spirit*, 109–16.

Matthew 5:44, which is Ruthie's book's epigraph.[111] For "peacemaking" often becomes limited to the relationship between individuals and God rather than pertaining to the relationships between people groups.[112] Relationship to others "*so* complicates following Christ" is perhaps the subconscious motivation, and so we often avoid that gospel responsibility.

Many "others" could be considered in this regard, but we will only consider the peacemaking responsibility of the gospel community toward LGBTQI+ persons and how gospel "peacemaking" relates to them. We also consider this question only in relation to the situation in America. We do this to provide an acutely recognized example that demonstrates the need for "peacemaking" and because this particular example is a foremost reason that the gospel is "in the dock" in Western culture. Therefore, we seek to clarify what *is* the *peace* of the gospel that God intends the steward's community to be extending for all LGBTQI+ people. To be more specific, we must define the "good" that atonement brings for "those who are far off," according to the gospel definitions of sin, salvation, and subsequent discipleship. This is necessary because none of these can be defined by one's self, the church, the culture, or the state.

The very idea of a defined "good" goes against the ethos of our culture, wherein "good" is mostly viewed in relation to our consumer culture's supreme value of having *many* "lifestyle" choices available to our expressive individualism.[113] That is the "deadly virtue" of our time and culture in many ways, and especially in regard to sexuality.[114] But to the surprise of many, God does not share this *deadly* virtue with us, since it essentially participates in the egoistic way of the will to power. Of course, there is a proper and necessary individuality of each person because of our given creaturehood. Thus Christ, the new human, delivers us from the will to power to become true selves established by God as "the self rests transparently in the power that established it."[115]

Certainly, as has already been said, no humans are barred from the restoration of human be-ing in Christ's person and work. But that

---

111. Biette, *Battle of Crawdad Hole,* 105.

112. See Gushee and Stassen, *Kingdom Ethics,* 33.

113. See Jardine, *Making,* 91–92.

114. "Similarly, an expressive culture will tend to understand sexuality as a type of aesthetic self-expression, so moral restrictions on sexual activity (including restrictions regarding the results of sexual activity, such as legal prohibition of abortion) will be regarded as oppressive." Jardine, *Making,* 92.

115. Kierkegaard, *Sickness unto Death,* 14.

restoration is not merely a doctrine floating in mid-air for humans to grab for their use. It is *located* in Christ, and more specifically in a life relationship with Christ that is expressed by us through continual repentance and faith. And this is where the definitions of sin, salvation, and discipleship become acute. For Paul is now understood by many as teaching that the gospel provides a "carte blanche" to LGBTQI+ people that affirms their "lifestyle" as acceptable within Christian discipleship. Therefore, the task of this section is to try to rehabilitate the gospel in relation to the thorny question of the gospel's *good* for LGBTQI+ persons, who are in various ways, and by themselves and the gospel stewards, are seen as those "far off," but who the gospel stewards are to be "for." And their being "for" is most perspicuously known, by their "welcome" or not, to the gospel communities.

Sin as the Great Doorway of the Gospel Community

It may seem ironic to many, but sin is like a great universal doorway opened to all to receive all the benefits of the gospel. The only necessary qualification to the atonement is being a sinner, which all are. But it is also a doorway closed to those who want to bring their *practice* of sin into the redeemed life-relationship with Christ. Thus sin "automatically" includes all in the gospel's atonement, but existentially excludes those rejecting the gospel's life by remaining unrepentant towards their sinfulness which is the reason they need salvation. In essence, to desire the gospel's atonement apart from the gospel's life is to desire to be saved and not saved at the same time. We can picture this in the following simple chart of sin in relation to any sinful "identity" or practice, and in relation to LGBTQI+ identity and practice:

Table 9: Sin as the Doorway to the Gospel Community

Sin as our objective access to Christ's atonement	The attitude toward the practice of sin and the new life in discipleship	New life in Christ's disciple community
Any sinner has access to Christ's atonement	Repentant	New life in Christ's disciple community

Sin as our objective access to Christ's atonement	The attitude toward the practice of sin and the new life in discipleship	New life in Christ's disciple community
Any sinner has access to Christ's atonement	Unrepentant	Old life apart from Christ's disciple community
An LGBTQI+ sinner has access to Christ's atonement	Repentant	New life in Christ's disciple community
An LGBTQI+ sinner has access to Christ's atonement	Unrepentant	Old life apart from Christ's disciple community
Objective atonement	Repentance and faith >	Our subjective salvation
God's "yes" of salvation to all	Non-repentance and unfaith >	Our "no" to God's salvation of us

In regard to this chart, we note the following:

- The chart is based on the view of the NT that same-sex practice is sinful, and that there is no salvation from sin apart from faith practiced in discipleship (Rom 1:24–27; 6:1–23; 1 Cor 6:9–11).[116]

- The first pair of lines demonstrate that only non-repentance excludes any sinner from the new life of Christ's disciple community.

- The second pair of lines demonstrates that only non-repentance excludes any LGBTQI+ sinner from the new life of Christ's disciple community (1 Cor 6:11).

- The third pair of lines demonstrates that only the "no" of non-repentance toward the practice of sin excludes anyone from God's "yes" of salvation (2 Cor 5:14–21).

- The chart is also based on the view that Christ's own faith and repentance is included in God's "yes" to all, so that their faith and

---

116. See Hays, *Moral Vision*, 377–405, for what remains one of the best treatments of the subject.

repentance are not based on their own efforts but on God's grace provided in the gospel (John 3:19–21; Phil 2:12–13).

The chart demonstrates why it is so important that God is the one who reveals and defines the gospel in relation to sin, repentance, and discipleship. Otherwise, the gospel becomes co-opted by false gospels of "Culture," "Christianity and," and "cheap grace." For, strictly speaking, the gospel is the cure for sin, not a tonic meant to "manage sin" in what seems a slightly less painful way.[117] Theologian Gary Badcock carefully and sensitively speaks to all these things, in light of forgiveness, discipleship, and the imperfection of the body of Christ. We present a short series of extracts from his concentrated argument of several pages:

> The Son of God, in being "made flesh," established a relationship between himself and *all h*umanity, so that there is no human being and no human nature beyond his reach . . . To be made one with Christ in a saving sense, and to be a member of his ecclesiastical body, requires faith and obedience, participation in the Spirit, and thus the very quality that faith, obedience, and the gift of the Spirit bring—that is holiness. This is the very quality that the homosexual lifestyle is said to compromise—and, I should add, with massive biblical and theological foundation . . . We are the body of Christ in the strict sense only in faith and hope, in the mystery by which we are, in all our sinfulness, incorporated into Christ and made righteous. There is, in the strictest possible sense, no difference between the homosexual "sinner" in this respect and any other. In other words, it is most important for us to say that our place in the church stands on the basis of the forgiveness of sins rather than on the basis of a social liberalism that knows only the value of the individual . . . the humanity with which God in Christ is identified is not some ideal humanity existing beyond the world that we know, but rather a humanity that exists in fragments, in sinfulness, in suffering, and in death . . . in a church that implicitly assumes that there is a humanity not marked by sin, there is in the final analysis room for nobody.[118]

The nature of the gospel is such that there is "room" for everybody in the solidarity of sin, because Christ entered that solidarity and atoned for all. But inside the "room" of at-one-ment also dwells the community

---

117. See "Gospels of Sin Management" in Willard, *Divine Conspiracy*, 35–59.
118. Badcock, *House*, 301–4.

of fellowship in the new be-ing in Christ who has overcome the solidarity in sin. Thus, our existential participation in Christ's new community requires faith and repentance in regard to the old practice in sin and the practice of new life. More specifically, that faith and repentance pertain to our own "wisdom" in regard to the *good* of the discipleship that Christ reveals.

What the entire challenge of discipleship really comes down to for each individual is their reenactment of the primordial scene in Eden, where God's prohibition of the fruit of the tree of the knowledge of good and evil required faith that God's way was good, although the first couple didn't know why. Similarly, it is simply inconceivable to postmodern consumeristic hyper-sexualized expressive individualists that the denial of sexual expression could be good. We will return to this subject below, but here simply say that through the gospel we can participate in Christ's "yes" response to the "good" God intends for us, trusting in God's "fatherly" wisdom.

The LGBTQI+ Quest for Justification within the Present Quagmire of the Will to Power

Though some may disagree with my claim, I nevertheless claim that the LGBTQI+ quest is inherently religious. More specifically, it represents the quest for justification. But Martin Luther, one of the greatest seekers of justification whose quest changed the modern world, demonstrated the nature the quest must take in relation to God:

> It is based on God and solely on God, who is experienced in a unique and personal encounter. The courage of the Reformation transcends both the courage to be as a part and the courage to be as oneself. It is threatened neither by the loss of oneself nor by the loss of one's world.[119]

The quest for justification, because it is inherently and preeminently the quest for justification before God, must find its resolution in God's justification. Thus, the LGBTQI+ quest cannot find what it most desires, though the nature of that quest is veiled to many on that quest, when it does not have the courage to transcend the justification the world might or might not give, and embrace the justification God will give that may

119. Tillich, *The Courage to Be*, 163.

well result in condemnation from the world. In other words, the quest for God's justification can only be resolved by receiving the grace of God being one's *only* criterion. And having God as one's only criterion, means having God as one's criterion of sin. But this must not deflect this justification quest from faith to virtue, but to also establish one's justification in faith, rather than in merely human paganism.

> Faith is: that the self in being itself and in willing to be itself rests transparently in God. Very often, however, it is overlooked that the opposite of sin is by no means virtue. In part, this is a pagan view, which is satisfied with a merely human criterion and simply does not know what sin is, that all sin is before God.[120]

Therefore, the LGBTQI+ quest for justification must rest in faith in *God's* justification in relation to sin.

At the present time, the LGBTQI+ quest, and every other quest for God's justification, has been subverted under the quest for justification with the human community as the criterion of both sin and justification. The result is that the proper "virtue" that gains justification is to submit to the present culture's criterion. And that present culture's motivation is not God's liberation, but rather its will to power that is building and maintaining the present culture's "sacred canopy." Thus the "culture war" over LGBTQI+ issues and most other issues today in the West, is a "justification war" to rival that of the Reformation. *That* war is the quagmire in which church and state collide, and in which all the individuals involved in each are presently the spoils of war.[121] And that war can be waged by each side and all those involved, by the way of the will to power or by the way of faith, and each receives or does not receive God's justification.[122]

---

120. Kierkegaard, *The Sickness unto Death*, 82.

121. From the viewpoint of the gospel's reconciliation this is an unnecessary conflict: "For the religious and the secular realm are in the same predicament. Neither of them should be in separation from the other, and both should realize that their very existence as separated is an emergency, that both of them are rooted in religion in the larger sense of the word, in the experience of ultimate concern." Tillich, *Theology of Culture*, 9. But church and state must both receive God's justification and not replace it with their own.

122. Since judgment begins with the house of God (1 Pet 4:17) we offer the following indictment: "Christians operate with an understanding of power that is derived from the larger and dominant culture of the late modern period." Hunter, *To Change the World*, 100.

We need to turn from this larger quagmirical context in which the quest for justification takes place to the individual persons attempting that quest.

Jesus, the "Eunuch" for the Kingdom, the Gospel of Salvation and Becoming a Self

Klyne Snodgrass narrates why true human identity can only be found in Christ and is not found through any "justification" that one's own self, the civil authority, the culture, or even the church, may promote. We excerpt several of his statements from many pages of his writing on the subject:

> All of life is lived out of a sense of identity, even if one's sense of identity is confused or unconscious . . . The Christian faith says not only can you know yourself, at least at some level, but that you must know yourself, sin and all; that grace makes it possible to look honestly at yourself . . . As for self-centeredness, faith confronts and seeks to overcome self-centeredness, for conversion is about ego transformation and ego management. Faith displaces the ego so that Christ is the primary determiner of the self. In other words, the Christian understanding of the self is found outside the self . . . Displacement of the ego is not about a rejection of one's self—quite the contrary . . . It seeks the glory of God through the ego, as Irenaeus knew when he said, "The glory of God is a living (hu)man." . . . As the Danish philosopher Soren Kierkegaard insisted, Christianity is not a doctrine but an existence-communication. Church is also the place I go to make my protest: against the world, against Christians, and even against the church for its superficiality and for not doing justice to its own gospel . . . Christianity is seen as a minor attachment to their well-guarded identities rather than the ground-shaking transformation of identity it really is . . . Churches have . . . diluted and distorted the Christian message . . . A visit to many churches reveals quickly that people do not want a new identity; they want to feel good about themselves.[123]

The process of "becoming a self" is but one more aspect of the mysterious nature of relation to the triune God of the holy darkness and therefore requires following the way of faith that was abandoned in Eden but was recovered by Jesus. We have continually seen that the way of faith is diametrically opposite to the "normal" way of humankind and

123. Snodgrass, *Who God Says*, 7–8, 30, 34.

its self and cultural quests for justification. In the case of sexual identity under postmodern culture, the way of faith is especially unfathomable. But when God became incarnate as a celibate "eunuch" for the kingdom of God, he effectually deconstructed all the assumptions for a culture living in the ethos and mythos of expressive individualism in regard to sexual "identity."[124] "Creating" our identity whole cloth is the special ethos and familiar spirit of our present age. It is animated by the mythos of autonomous individualism, ours since the temptation of Adam and Eve but especially re-animated by the disembeddedness of modern life.[125] Together, our ethos and mythos confront us with a deadly psychological anxiety, an oppressing burden too great for many to bear, but nevertheless increasingly pressed upon the young at ever-younger ages.[126] Such is the price we pay for the gains of self-justification.

Jesus lived the perfect human life, not without sexual identity, but with his identity found, formed, and focused in relation to the call of his loving transcendent Father. Ultimately the disconnect—between human sexuality and the way of faith *as good* for each and every person—*grows* by not recognizing our relation to God in relationship, calling, and identity. Intimate relation to our loving Father/God provides the security of freedom from the pressure of being "a part," pressed on us by our culture's ethos and mythos. Focus on identity *apart* from God's calling leads to the ever-constricting collapse of the "heart turned in on itself." Flourishing of identity *through* God's calling leads to the establishment of the ever-forming self in Christ. Identity in Christ does not seem like a done deal this side of eternity. For the reception of our complete identity is not at the beginning, but *at the end* of our path of discipleship in the mystery of our self—with the full revelation pictured in the reception of the new

---

124. See Matthew 19:12; See also Bennett, *War of Loves*, 253.

125. "In The Consequences of Modernity, social theorist Anthony Giddens characterizes the technological, consumer-driven culture of modernity as a culture of 'disembeddedness.' Giddens argues that the cumulative impact of the social, economic, technological, and intellectual transformations of modernization has been to extricate the individual self from the traditional bonds of kinship to community, land, and history." Peters, *Logic of the Heart*, 14.

126. "They are doing a kind of metaphysical heavy lifting at an incredibly young age that was not only *not required* by other generations but also nearly unthinkable. Small children are now expected to be able to competently identify their own genders. Young children are expected to discover themselves with almost no education, and with almost no life experience, and they are hyper-aware of their lack of both." Joustra and Wilkinson, *How to Survive*, 186.

name each "overcomer" will receive at the eschaton of all things.[127] And fellowship in Christ-identity brings relationship to the flesh and blood "body of Christ"—the living community of peace which is expanding to fill the earth for the good of others as of yet still "far off."

God's Definition of the Ultimate Good, Love

Implied in our discussion of justification by God alone, and *the good* of the way of repentance and faith in discipleship for each and every person lies the most important question for our present discussion, which is whether *any* humans are capable of *themselves* defining *God's love* for us, or for that matter, defining sin. We humans "naturally" defer to our culture's supposedly "working definitions" that conveniently support the culture's will to power justifications or condemnations. (Perhaps that deference is more accurately submission.) But God has provided a concrete definition, to convey the answers we need, and actually long to know. Allen writes,

> If you want to know what sin is, don't ask for definition, just look at that man on the Cross. If you want to know what love is, look at that man on the Cross. Christianity at its core is neither thoughts nor beliefs, Christianity is deeds: our creation and our redemption by a love that patiently endures our stony hearts, seeking to transform them.[128]

The gospel is rooted in the declaration in 1 John 4:8 that "God is love" and in the fact that humankind has as little capability of defining God's love as it does of defining God or sin. The controversy over defining God's love today is the continuation of the conflict Kierkegaard described regarding Christ's life of love on earth, a conflict that could not be given up for our sake:

> He was, divinely understood, love; he loved in the power of the divine conception of what love is; he loved the whole race. He did not dare—out of love—to give up this conception, for this would mean to betray the race. For this reason, his whole life

---

127. See Rev 2:17. Lewis writes, "What can be more a man's own than his new name which even in eternity remains a secret between God and him?" Lewis, *The Problem of Pain*, 134. See also 1 John 3:2.

128. Allen, *Steps Along the Way*, 44.

was a terrible collision with the merely human conception of what love is.[129]

This also means that humans should accept God's definition of his love for us when *faithfully* expressed by the gospel stewards, including how humans are to live in Christ, in God's love. Christian discipleship, which is a necessity for Christians, is based on the fact that the God who is love is each person's and each church community's "spiritual director." All are called to God's discipleship, not to directing our own path as though *we* define the good our loving God provides for our flourishing. This is indeed the humanly difficult path of discipleship, which is variously and perhaps progressively called the way of faith, the way of the cross, and the way of love. For God's love seeks to deliver us all, no matter our present conception of our identity, from self-directed discipleship. For our natural inclination is of "the heart turned in on itself" in the way of the will to power that seeks fulfillment in egoism.[130] Thomas Merton, the "man of the world" turned Trappist Monk, poignantly narrated the opposite liberating movement from egoism that led to what he called "the four walls of my new freedom."[131] But he moved "from the world only after he had fully immersed himself in it." He wrote,

> Some people may think that Providence was very funny and very cruel to allow me to choose the means I now chose to save my soul. But Providence, that is the love of God, is very wise in turning away from the self-will of men, and in having nothing to do with them, and leaving them to their own devices, as long as they are intent on governing themselves, to show them to what depths of futility and sorrow their own helplessness is capable of dragging them.[132]

David Bennett, a "celibate gay Christian" sensitively and meaningfully narrates his own difficult and eventually liberating path of

---

129. Kierkegaard, *Works of Love*, 115.

130. "There is, therefore, much more in the word of the Cross than the acceptance of suffering or the practice of self-denial. The Cross is something positive. It is more than a death. The word of the Cross is foolishness to them that perish—but to them that are saved 'it is the power of God' (1 Corinthians 1:18)." Merton, *No Man*, 77.

131. Merton, *Seven Storey Mountain*, 410. Ralph Wood discusses the poverty of modern freedom saying, "No longer is freedom understood as obedience to a *telos* radically transcending ourselves and thus wondrously delivering us from bondage to mere-self-interest." Wood, *Chesterton*, 130.

132. Merton, *Seven Storey Mountain*, 136.

discipleship according to the gospel rather than the culture in his 2018 book "A War of Loves."[133] The title of Bennett's book is aptly titled, for the LGBTQI+ controversy in the churches does come down to a "war" of different conceptions of "love" that can only be won when those concerned follow the gospel's revelation of love rather than our culture's. Bennett and other LGBTQI+ Christians following "costly grace" may be the most-needed voice in regard to the church/state conflict between civil rights and religious freedoms. For *his* propagation of the view that homosexual practice *is sin* could be conceived of as supporting "hate crime" by the "rights discourse" and definition of "liberty" in postmodern America.[134] But Bennett *represents* LGBTQI+ Christians who should have the *religious liberty* to follow their faith not only privately but publicly, in relation to following and teaching the word of God. It seems that perhaps the religious liberty of LGBTQI+ people is what needs to inform the present militancy of civil rights over religious freedom.

Bennett relates how his path of discipleship was powerfully catalyzed by hearing a sermon in which Don Carson said, "We must not put ourselves *over* Scripture . . . but we must live *under* the word of God."[135] So Bennett now points the way forward saying,

> God had given me all of himself in his Son and Spirit, and it was time to give him all of myself. My gay identity had to bow to Jesus Christ, and that meant being willing to live without a partner for the remainder of my life. His love calls me to relinquish the desires warring against my repentance. I gave them over to him and was swept into his arms. This was the greater romance, the one true love that could fulfill me, far more than sex or any relationship could . . . God wants all people everywhere to turn from their ways in order to know him. He wants all to adopt an entirely different view of meaning, transcendence, and worship . . . We need a community life like the one modeled in Acts, in which believers lived as a new family in the light of Jesus's life and mission to the nations. We must all humbly name that kind

---

133. For an explanation of Bennett's "descriptive" designation of his identity see: Bennett, *War of Loves*, 18–19, 209–15, 262 n.13.

134. In 1992, the Supreme Court wrote: "At the very heart of liberty is the right to define one's own concept of existence, meaning, of the universe, of the mystery of life." As cited by Wood, *Chesterton,* 130. But Christ's followers will need to accept God's definitions, not their own, as though a state right.

135. Bennett, *War of Loves,* 125.

of life as what we want and be willing to pay the price for it to be reality.[136]

Richard Hays aptly summarizes the way forward for the gospel steward's "stance" and then notes that neither the culture's gospel of self-gratification, nor the church's fall to pandering to those desires, is the truly liberating gospel. He writes,

> Thus, in view of the considerable uncertainty surrounding the scientific and experiential evidence, in view of our culture's present swirling confusion about gender roles, in view of our propensity for self-deception, I think it prudent and necessary to let the univocal testimony of Scripture and Christian tradition order the life of the church on this painfully controversial matter . . . In the midst of a culture that worships self-gratification, and in a church that often preaches a false Jesus who panders to our desires, those who seek the narrow way have a powerful word to speak.[137]

Of course, the state also "panders to our desires" that have been careful cultivated through its secular liturgies. The quasi-religious Orwellian state's "justification" is "graciously" legislated to ennoble its expressive individualist citizens, who have previously been made superfluous and pliably needy by the state's nihilism, to rise in heroic self-creation (read state-creation) to be "born" again in the Huxleyan "Brave New World."[138] We thus present the cultural conspiracy theory that seems too likely the unconscious or conscious blueprint for today's mix of soulcraft and statecraft that militantly preaches its brand of liberty, to enable its quest for self-justification in the totalitarian will to power. That it does so for the sake of "liberty for all" only reveals its hubris that replaces God. Thus, the will to power undoubtedly lurks beneath the state's version of a "gospel

---

136. Bennett, *War of Loves*, 49, 231.

137. Hays, *Moral Vision*, 399, 403. Hays provides in his discussion there a thoughtful discussion of the major practical questions that this "difficult" view of discipleship presents. Thomas Merton's essay "Love and Need: Is Love a Package or a Message?" helpfully engages the commodification of "love" in modern consumer society. See Merton, *Love*, 25–37.

138. In Orwell's "1984" vision of the savior state, "the state, by its constraints, will oblige man to come forth from the nothingness of the anarchy of the passions and lead an upright and even heroic life." Jacques Maritain, as cited in, McGrath, *Heidegger*, 128. In Huxley's savior state of "Brave New World," the constraints are the consumerist enabling of the anarchy of the passions through unbridled sexual expression, the diversion of *the feelies*, and the escapist medication of the perfect social drug *soma*.

crusade," just as it also does for the church that Richard Hays critiqued above. As Jacques Maritain wrote, "Not God, but the state will create man . . . by its constraints," which it gains license to enforce by default, in its denial of the transcendent God who orders creation for the good of all the creatures through both church and state when rightly aligned.[139]

Only the justification of God, such as Luther sought, can result in individuals finding what they truly need. For the justification of God not only frees us from self-justification, but also liberates us from the soulcraft of the state with its "gospel of justification." It seems that Luther's quest for God's justification is still the quest of all. But that justification, and the peace it brings to those consciously following the way of justification, will be God's "peacemakers," welcoming "those who are far off" to find "the tender mercy of our God" who "guides their feet into the way of peace" as they are united in the full fellowship of the gospel community of peace (Luke 1:78–79).

The Stewards and the Question of Beauty

Beauty is the last factor in the complex of repentance and faith in regard to the rehabilitation of the stewards. It thus brings us full circle to where we began in the first "incident" in the mock trial at the beginning of our introduction. Beauty is in a sense the ultimate criterion for their judgment. Here is a fuller citation of the text:

> How beautiful on the mountains are the feet of the messenger who brings good news, the good news of peace and salvation, the news that the God of Israel reigns! The watchmen shout and sing with joy, for before their very eyes they see the Lord returning to Jerusalem (Isaiah 52:7–8, NLT).

In this book, we have proceeded with the awareness that the gospel and its messengers are "in the dock" before our culture and most of us

---

139. As quoted in McGrath, *Heidegger*, 128. At this point we touch upon the inherent contradiction and conflict in Western liberal democracy's statecraft and the church's soulcraft. The conflict is that the state, meant to be a relative authority under God, according to the First Amendment's non-establishment of religion, "effectively sequesters one of the 'principalities and powers' from submission to the reign of Christ." Smith, *Awaiting the King*, 102, n. 19. Thus "civil rights" and "religious liberty" inevitably "compete" in the Liberal secular democracy wherein the state and the church have different visions of Augustine's principle, "that a people was a multitude defined by the common objects of their love." As cited in Biden, "Inaugural Address."

are not watching for signs that they bring good news and therefore have beautiful feet. We have attempted to rehabilitate the stewards as good for their relation to the gospel, no matter their grave failings of the gospel. But have we seen any real possibility of beauty yet? Perhaps we need to briefly review what we have seen so far.

In Chapters 1 and 2 we saw something of the depths and complexities of the gospel itself, showing the immensity of the steward's responsibility to be its bearers. As Jesus himself was fully immersed in God's redemptive mission for the world, so also are the stewards as they participate in Christ's mission. In fact, as was Jonah, they are immersed, baptized, whether they are faithful or not "for the gifts and calling of God are irrevocable" (Rom 11:29). Mere participation in *this* redemptive mission of the triune God is in itself *terribly* beautiful, bearing the costly "weight of beauty." And God's irrevocable calling of them, issuing in their judgement, testifies to God's costly love for the world that gives his only Son, with his adopted sons and daughters, unto such depths for the life of the world. Only Jesus was fully faithful, but God's other sons and daughters were nevertheless caught up into God's unfolding movement to redeem and reconcile and restore the rest of humanity. They gave what they willingly gave, or were given in what God willingly gave, or both gave and were also given. For in God's costly redemption of humanity, where "any man's *death* diminishes *me*," they became redemptively "involved in *Mankinde*."[140] Such terrible costs of redemption reveal an inscrutable beauty.

In Chapters 3 and 4 we only really glimpsed the outskirts of the sorts of myriad places and murky swamps the stewards traverse as they bear the terrible glorious burden of the gospel. They struggled in those "sloughs of despond" and vanity fairs" against their chief adversaries, the Devil, their own natural "self-love," and their "will to power." Thus, some reduced and distorted the gospel to serve their means for their own ends. They faced a world of adversaries who were armed with hidden "gospels" to capture or mislead them, and to make merchandise of the ones they were to help with the gospel. The immensity of the task—in struggles "against enemies foreign and domestic"—when recognized in all its gravity and grace, calls for acclamations that "heroes" of any other such story would readily be given considering their human (all too human) frames.

---

140. Moses, *One Equal Light*, 127. Strictly speaking, they participated in the redemption of Christ.

It would seem that some sympathy for such burdened Jonahs might admit some semblance of a valiant, though damaged beauty.

In Chapters 5 and 6 our gaze turned even more directly upon the stewards, though their shadow had preceded them beforehand. We saw much to deeply lament, but also the hope their better selves promised through connection to the gospel. Dietrich Bonhoeffer's church-confession of solidarity in sin revealed the tragic depths of our failure, rightly culminating the repentance of death-together. But such slashing and burnings of the weeds and tares feeds the gospel ground for the sake of life-together in the time of re-planting. Confession yielded the strange glory of beauty present in the rarified air of honesty and the true contrition shed of false fig leaves, coming out from hiding before God and the watching world. Thus, the grain of wheat falls into the ground and dies to bring forth fruit in the bread given for the life of the world. For that bread ultimately signifies the table of community welcome to those coming from far off. The table is set for sinners coming from the east and the west, to sit with the sinful stewards, whose bread and cup proclaim the Lord's death for their sin and that of the world's, until he comes (1 Cor 11:25).

Our admittedly imaginatively embellished revisiting of earlier scenes has been portrayed as it was to convey the conflicted beauty of the stewards of the gospel. For even their damaged beauty magnifies the beauty of the gospel's central proclamation that "though your sins be as scarlet, they shall be as white as snow; though they be red like crimson, they shall be as wool" (Isa 1:18, KJV).

Soren Kierkegaard's understanding of his total and extensive authorship illustrates the gospel good in God's greatest "scandal of particularity," the stewards, and their imperfect words and ways. Of this Barnett writes,

> Kierkegaard compares his authorial task to that of a seamstress, who "works on a cloth for sacred use." The seamstress by no means disdains the attempt to make her art beautiful. However, its beauty is to serve as a channel by which the observer comes into contact with the holy, not as an object of contemplation in and of itself. The seamstress would be "deeply distressed if anyone were to make the mistake of seeing her artistry instead of the meaning of the cloth or were to make the mistake of seeing a defect instead of seeing the meaning of the cloth." Rather, the seamstress and her skill are to be detached from, even "infinitely forgotten."[141]

141. Barnett, *From Despair,* 122. Our only caveat is to say that the "infinite

In sum it seems more than merely possible, even eminently plausible, that God's stewards, Jonahs though they be, nevertheless *beautifully* bear the gospel burden as wounded healers of humankind. Jesus himself was, of course, the wounded gospel healer *par excellence*. But the stewards can and do participate in Christ's suffering, healing mission. Paul wrote "*I am glad when I suffer for you in my body, for I am participating in the sufferings of Christ that continue for his body, the church*" (Col 1:24). So also, the stewards participate in the sufferings of God in Christ for the sake of the church and the world. Salvation is partaking in a stewardship of "wounded healing" for the world. Paul elaborated more upon this saying,

> We are pressed on every side by troubles, but we are not crushed. We are perplexed, but not driven to despair. We are hunted down, but never abandoned by God. We get knocked down, but we are not destroyed. Through suffering, our bodies continue to share in the death of Jesus so that the life of Jesus may also be seen in our bodies (2 Cor 4:8–10, NLT).

The steward's troubles and sufferings, that accompany their following of Christ, declare the gospel of *his* redemptive troubles and sufferings. This is also beautiful, because from the sins of human conflict which even result in death, God has brought and continues to bring the gospel of forgiveness and life through Christ. And that is because the love, of the God *who is love,* is "as fierce as death."[142] N. T. Wright says that,

> The good news that Jesus put into practice during his public career and that he enacted as he went to his death is this: love, faced with rejection, overcomes it with yet more love.[143]

Perhaps God's stewards are not meant to be what we thought they needed to be, perfect mouthpieces of God. If they were, they would no longer be human. In fact, their very humanity seems to be the precise reason why they can be more than mere mouthpieces by participating in God's *pathos* in their persons, incarnating God's *life* in their living bodies

---

forgetting" of the seamstress (steward) is only relative, because as God's icons they remain, themselves caught up into God's incarnate mission into the world. It is interesting that Kierkegaard's "seamstress" finds corroboration in Muslim carpet weavers: "They deliberately incorporate a flaw into each work of art that they create. Only God, they say, is flawless. Only God can create flawlessness. So, they do not strive for flawlessness; they strive, instead, for beauty." Tutu & Tutu, *Made for Goodness*, 48.

142. Bloch and Bloch, *The Song*, 111, 213. (See Song 8:5.)

143. Wright, *Simply Good News*, 140.

in the world. Abraham Heschel provides us with an invaluable picture of God's prophets of old. We propose that Heschel's view of the prophets holds true for God's stewards.

> The prophet is not a mouthpiece, but a person; not an instrument, but a partner, an associate of God . . . The prophet is no hireling who performs his duty in the employ of the Lord . . . The task of the prophet is to convey the word of God. Yet the word is aglow with the pathos . . . the fundamental experience of the prophet is a fellowship with the feelings of God, a *sympathy with the divine pathos,* a communion with the divine consciousness which comes about through the prophet's reflection of, or participation in, the divine pathos . . . Prophetic sympathy is a response to transcendent sensibility. It is not, like love, an attraction to the divine Being, but the assimilation of the prophet's emotional life to the divine, an assimilation of function, not of being.[144]

We don't intend trying to understand or discuss all of the theology or philosophy implicit in Heschel's statement. Instead, we point out that the stewards are akin to Heschel's view of the Prophets as those who have been caught up in the *personal pathos* of the triune God though their reconciliation in Christ. The work of the Spirit in them and the transformation of their minds through the Scriptures forms and images the redemptive pathos of God revealed in the gospel for the world. What could be more beautiful, though also *terrible* in relation to *normal* human life, than that imaging? For fellowship in that *pathos* unites them to participate with Christ *in the beginning* of God's *new creation*. These are but "beginnings"—but they breath in the approaching air of the future heavenly atmosphere. "He has made everything beautiful *in its time.*" There is beauty *in* the suffering of the humble beginnings. And all to come lies *in* the beauty of God's suffering love, in *that* means to the end of fully-grown beauty that can be seen through the veil by those with eyes touched with Christ's spittle, and lives newly breathed into the dust of the ground (John 9:1–7; Gen 2:7).[145]

---

144. Heschel, *The Prophets,* 25–26.

145. Ecclesiastes 3:19. Note that the text does not read "will make everything beautiful in time" (in the end.) The French activist/philosopher Simone Weil wrote that all creation was like a musical string attached at the two end poles of God's love, and Christ's suffering. Thus, every point of *the present life* pressed between those poles resonates with the musical vibration of the string so that everything, "in its time" can be harmonized in the divine love of the Father in heaven and the Son on the cross. See Springsted, *Simone Weil,* 50.

Before moving to another major aspect regarding the stewards and beauty, it seems necessary to tie up what seems a loose thread that was dangling above, which is the contrast between the gospel's "approval" of imperfection and the perfectionism of a cultural gospel of today. I have not specifically named that "gospel" until now but see its perfectionistic will to power driving much of politics today. We noted near the end of Chapter 4 that a poisonous perfectionism has developed through "the immanentization of the Christian eschaton," caused by the culture's nearly complete loss of any plausible future age of God's consummate justice and peace, that has been replaced by the obsessive desire of a utopian "just" society achieved by the Cainite will to power.[146] This immanentized eschaton was the engine driving the totalitarian and genocidal utopian quests in Soviet Russia, China, and Nazi Germany. A similar ethos has grown and animated the social justice "puritanism" of today's political correctness, identity politics, and partisan legislation of liberal "morality" and "liberation" that breeds the intolerance of a quasi-religious establishment.[147] Ralph Wood thus rightfully bemoans "the triumph of an intolerant tolerance" and "the rise of despotic liberty" in American Liberalism.[148] The intolerable by-products of such legislated freedoms reveal that the citizen's "impulse buying" relies on the mercy of the political establishment's salespersons, which generally does not exist when both buyer and seller are enthralled to the self, its consumerism, and their false "liberty."[149] Of course perfectionism may simply be the modern/postmodern Cainite ethos grown from the tempting successes of technology, so that whatever party finding itself empowered may be "unable" to resist the perfectionistic application of its political will to *further* power. Thus, the real political problem of today may simply be that "the human being

---

146. See Voegelin, *New Science*, 117–32; Polanyi, *Personal Knowledge*, 226–35; Van Leeuwen, *Critique of Heaven*, 145–206.

147. Tolerance, as the "cardinal Liberal practice" of modern Western "statecraft," is increasingly proving to be problematic. See Moore, *Limits*, 139. Bernard Williams also admits to the problems of the tolerance doctrine and sees it as only "an interim value" needed before a better future arrives. For the time being "the belief in autonomy . . . skepticism against fanaticism" are resources against "the manifest evils of toleration's absence; and quite certainly, power." Williams, *Philosophy*, 134.

148. Wood, *Chesterton*, 125–32.

149. "Thus, people in present-day Western societies, who think of themselves as being the freest people in human history by virtue of the extensive consumer choice they enjoy, might well be regarded by other cultures as the most abject slaves of a pathetically limited understanding of human existence." Jardine, *Making*, 91.

is thrown back on his own resources. He has learned to cope with everything except himself."[150] And that inability does not bode well for those other than the particular "himself" that is in power.

In sum, the main point of this depressing digression is that the gospel way does not seek societal perfection through political, economic, social, religious, or any other means of coercion. As we saw earlier, the gospel community of a new social order is non-coercive. So, to clarify, the gospel response to the modern post-Christian problem of "the immanentization of the eschaton" is not to wholly deny any immanentization of God's will for justice. For that would be the gospel of escapism, and the gospel is that "the kingdom is at hand." Therefore, in accord we are to pray, work, and hope that God's will be done "on earth as it is in heaven."[151] But an important caveat *against* perfectionism is that God's will for justice is qualified as justice *and mercy* (Mic 6:8; Matt 23:23). Thus, the modern problem of seeking the immanentization of the eschaton is its post-Christian east of Eden ethos which fully inhabits the will to power, the way of the Cainite builders of the city of man. In essence, the modern builders of the eschaton pridefully and vainly attempt the impossible, since they are themselves merely "of the old world . . . of Adam . . . claimed, formed, and driven by its constellation of overlapping and mutual consenting sovereignties . . . possessed by the 'ravishing and enslaving powers' of the rebellious creation."[152] The way of faith through the gospel is the better way that is *already but not yet* "come . . . to the city of the living God" (Heb 12:22). Thus, it does not fall to the perfectionism that invariably oppresses others in its means toward the desired end on earth as in heaven, *because* the city to come (Heb 13:14) still grounds the future hope in *the means and ends* of faith, hope, and love (1 Cor 12:31; 13:10, 13).

---

150. Bonhoeffer, Letters and Papers, 500

151. Middleton, *A New Heaven*, 241–82; Wright, *Surprised by Hope*, 189–289; for biblical treatments of the proper *partial* or "already-not yet" view of the future immanentization of the eschaton.

152. Ziegler, *Militant Grace*, 45.

Jonah and the "Plant" of Nineveh, Its Livestock, and All of Creation

We would be somewhat remiss if we didn't address something in the last chapter of Jonah that also portrays the beauty of the gospel. But in that chapter the prophet Jonah is *quite ironically* un-beautiful—though "resurrected" from the fish onto the land of the living. But again, if we seek to understand him a bit, we may find it possible to find some *sympathy* for his truly *pathetic* endurance of quite a lot as God's prophet called for the sake of others. Beginning with stomach-acid bleached Jonah lying in a vomitous mass on the sand of the beach, before what he estimates was a four-hundred-mile trek inland to Nineveh, David Benjamin Blower narrates Jonah's missionary experience proper in what seems anything but, a heroic tale:

> Rather, there was a very long walk to hell, during which every terrifying possibility might present itself to the desperate man's mind. As he lay there vomited up on the beach, did he feel saved, as he had done in the belly of the whale? Or did he feel doomed? We then read of his lonely entry to the City of Blood; the epicenter of darkness, a place filled with the stories and images of beheadings, impalings and skinnings, where nothing was familiar, and every sound and every person was strange, malicious and other. And he spends a day walking around in, I suppose, terrified anticipation of the moment when he will have to open his mouth and speak his foreign tongue against this irresistible force of triumphalist terror. There is no promise given in the story that he will not end up being burned or mangled or buried alive, and I should think it would be difficult to imagine any other outcome. And then after taking in his last miserable day of life, he says this: "Yet forty days and Nineveh shall be overthrown!" And then he waits to have his throat cut.[153]

Or is it a heroic tale after all? Suddenly Jonah seems transformed into an action hero with nerves of steel and no regard for his own life to solitarily face the universally dreaded bloodthirsty Assyrian scourge of the ancient world.

So, after Jonah traveled its great breadth of a three-day's journey preaching *"Yet Forty Days, and Nineveh shall be overthrown,"* following which all Nineveh repented, he sat on the ground to the east of the city

---

153. Blower, *Sympathy for Jonah*, 24.

to see what would happen (Jonah 3:1—4:11). As Jonah sat there under a booth he had made, "the Lord God appointed a plant and made it come up over Jonah, that it might shade his head, to save him from discomfort." We have already seen that this plant symbolized Nineveh and God's pity for the "great city" that Jonah in his understandable drawing back from a dangerous enemy love—*for the sake of those he did love*—did not pity. But God's reckless and relentless love nevertheless did, since it was a city of "*more than 120,000 children and much cattle*" (Jonah 4:11). Nineveh represented a microcosm of the world, and as is often the case in the OT, God expresses an intimate focus on "natural" concerns also. Probably due to a neglect of the OT perspective, an inadequate theological reconciliation of creation and redemption, and the "gospel of escapism," many Christians overlook God's redemptive concern for the whole of creation. Therefore, the mention of "cattle" represents the non-human creation and God's concern for it. In the NT this concern and hope is everywhere implied since everything in the OT will be fulfilled in Christ in some way (Matt 5:17–18; 2 Cor 1:20). Paul expresses this creational concern, writing,

> For I consider that the sufferings of this present time are not worth comparing with the glory that is to be revealed to us. For the creation waits with eager longing for the revealing of the sons of God. For the creation was subjected to futility, not willingly, but because of him who subjected it, in hope that the creation itself will be set free from its bondage to corruption and obtain the freedom of the glory of the children of God. For we know that the whole creation has been groaning together in the pains of childbirth until now (Rom 8:18–22).

Paul admits what the Scriptures nowhere deny. The present age is *characterized* by suffering. But it will give way to "the glory" to come. What is often overlooked is that the entire creation is *eagerly longing* for "the revealing of the sons of God." For with that day the creation's release from corruption will arrive. Paul is recognizing the "longing" of creation for that day when humankind is fully restored in its worship/work in the stewardship of God's image in the whole earth/temple as God's visible icon. That is why humans were prohibited from "making idols" of God, since humans were meant to be the only visible icon of the invisible God.

This means that the stewardship of the gospel is not the first stewardship God has entrusted to humans. The explicit gospel stewardship is in fact the second, although they are entwined in God's overall plan.

Therefore, the reconciliation of all things in the gospel includes that of humankind to the natural world and restoration in the first stewardship of humankind. We cannot enter into any detailed treatment of this first stewardship, but certainly need to consider to some extent this primal responsibility.[154] But we will do so by first revisiting those of the second stewardship.

The "resurrected" Jonah, waiting outside Nineveh after his preaching, is still backwards to God's purposes of redeeming all people and his whole creation. He would settle for the preservation of the part already "redeemed"—Israel—which under *normal reasoning* could be gravely endangered by the *worst* unredeemed part, which was Assyria. Jonah could also have been concerned for any of "the poor and oppressed wind-blown pattern of humanity," which was already or may well have become oppressed by Assyria. This is quite understandable to normal people. But as we have already seen, "normal" falls short of God's "radical" intent to redeem all of creation, *including* those who were the enemies of God's steward people, other peoples, and even the natural creation itself. So, when we look at the stewards of God at the present day, what "Jonah" do we see? The Jonah who most desired the cheap-grace preservation of the present concerns, or the Jonah/Christ who would not retreat from the costly-grace of the ultimate concern of the salvation of all? For the immediate concern may sabotage the ultimate one, while the ultimate concern in reality includes the immediate one.

This scenario, and its implied choice regarding ultimate concern, may well be being played out before our eyes in "the existential crisis" humankind now faces, according to the consensus of climate-change scientists. So, as we look for evidence of what would now be termed the "ecological" concerns of the stewards in history do we see any? I believe there is undoubtedly much more than might be supposed, especially given the fact of the connection of science itself to Christianity. Christians who devalue science in relation to the stewardship of creation, and are pessimistic regarding the future of natural creation, are signs of a fall from the faithful Christian responsibility. It is a fall which we briefly narrated in the "gospel of escapism" in Chapter 4. Some such escapists may be surprised that there is evidence for a very positive view of creation from early in the Christian era. One recent lengthy study demonstrates that throughout the first millennium after Christ, at least part of the

---

154. For a basic overview see "Mission and God's Earth" in Wright, *The Mission of God*, 397–420.

church saw itself as "a paradise in this world," planted by the Resurrection of Christ as the citation from Irenaeus, (c. 130 to 200) quoted at the head of the introduction of this book reads,

> The Church has been planted as a *paradisus* in this world.[155]

The authors of that study see evidence in the New Testament and early church that contains this focus. But the escapist gospel has popularized a false view of the end of the world. The view reads "apocalyptic texts," which were a literary genre of *symbolic language*, as positing that the present earth is to become *literally* destroyed at the return of Christ.[156] This reading of ancient texts through modern eyes which equate the ancient genre of apocalyptic to the genre of modern news, creates and perpetuates the "gospel of escapism."[157] The authors of the aforementioned study provide this overview of a better and more biblical view:

> In sum, the early church—before and after Constantine—taught that paradise was a place, a way of life, even an ecosystem. The church as a community that dispensed "the medicine of life" nourished human life in paradise. The church was a concentration of paradise, a place where the strengths, weaknesses, needs, and contributions of each member could compliment the others. Their life in paradise was a shared accomplishment in which the exercise of human powers and the imperatives of human need worked together to save and sustain life for all members together.[158]

Perhaps the way forward for today's stewardship of paradise is something of a return. For the modern-day stewards of the gospel are thought by some to be part of the ecological problem today. What is now a fairly early study called "The Historical Roots of Our Ecological Crisis" from 1967 by Lynn White Jr. says,

> More science and more technology are not going to get us out of the present ecological crisis until we find a new religion or rethink our old one.[159]

---

155. Brock & Parker, *Saving Paradise*, 84.

156. On the genre of apocalyptic see: Boring, *Revelation*, 1–62; and Gorman, *Reading Revelation Responsibly*, xi–80.

157. For scriptural critique of this view see: Hoekema, *Bible* 274–87; Middleton, *A New Heaven*, 283–312.

158. Brock and Parker, *Saving Paradise*, 106.

159. Walker-Jones, *The Green Psalter*, 1.

Unfortunately, ecological concerns and the stewardship of the earth have become entangled in the political, cultural, and scientific wars of the last several decades or more. Therefore, the stewards of the gospel are divided amongst themselves and against others on many issues including whether there is any such thing as climate change, whether humankind is the main or even an important contributing factor of causation *if* it is real, and if so whether humankind has a responsibility of stewardship to try to alleviate its "existential" danger. As we have been seeking to demonstrate, any denial of the last statement is overtly unbiblical. But in our time, the group most militantly claiming to be biblical, by identifying as "evangelical," is, as of this writing, perhaps the leading edge of Christians who think that human-made climate change is complete political fabrication. Many of the same also ironically affirm the probably soon coming destruction of the earth, rendering the question quite moot. (Although many of the same also believe in a "literal" thousand-year millennium following the return of Christ so I suppose they simply assume that Christ will clean up any mess they have irresponsibly "left behind.") If they are wrong on the reality of climate change, that may encourage a self-fulfilling prophecy of the coming destruction. As we have seen, God's stewards can be very wrong, and this could contribute to a global tragedy in motion since Christianity *is* a very influential and ever-growing global force. That danger is certainly among the "reasons" that creation groans for the sons of God to get their heads on straight and become the better Jonah never seen in *his* story but hinted at by God's questioning of his sub-gospel posture, and even as redeemed in Jesus, the faithful Jonah. Paul's words in Romans are indeed eschatological, about the glory to come beyond the age of suffering. But the stewards are to live in the present according to that future. Jonah's ambivalence to the greater redemption exhibits a very dangerous posture that will be perilous if the stewards do not at the least take the challenge of this potential global crisis seriously. For when God's earthly plant that shades "Jonah's" head withers away he may finally try to do something about it, but by then it may be too late for repentance, though it is sought Esau-like, with tears (Heb 12:17). But present-day Jonah ought to learn from the first Jonah that being backwards to the call is never much fun and may in fact be disastrous for more than his understandable but proximate concerns.

At this point we can return to our discussion of the first stewards of the earth. If we simply think about it, it is quite obvious that all of humankind is always involved in the exercise of dominion on the earth, for better or for worse. Just as "evangelizers always evangelize" for better or for worse, so also stewards always steward. Of course, we have seen Paul's declaration of the coming *restoration* of humankind *in* that calling. This means that the restoration is a *character renovation* of humankind in this call and task to fulfill their identity as the image of God. For being God's image cannot be escaped from, "for the gifts and calling of God are irrevocable" (Rom 11:29).

Thus, the rise of explicit modern ecological concern is an instance of "stewards always stewarding" but seeking to do so better. Some do it in conscious relation to God the Creator, some perhaps in unconscious relation, and some in relation to "Mother Earth." Though these conceptions may differ, the matter of fact is that humans are stewards and there ought to be collaboration between the gospel stewards and earth stewards. In 2008 Arthur Walker-Jones reported that,

> Several years ago, the Union of Concerned Scientists released a video that made a direct appeal to people of faith for help. Science, they said, had identified the problems, but science could not respond to the environmental crisis because the issue was a moral and behavioral one. They appealed to communities of faith for help in changing values and behavior.[160]

Is it possible that a growing storm on the earth—climate change—may necessitate a collaboration between Jonah and his Gentile mariners in the earth ship to seek to alleviate their common destruction in a growing storm? Indeed, the call of the Union of Concerned Scientists recognized the necessity of collaboration. Otherwise, one could consider an alternate scenario wherein there is a new "casting of lots" to determine who should be "sacrificed" to the storm god. Some, or perhaps even many, see that lot as already falling on "white evangelicalism" for its seeming unconcern regarding the potential catastrophe of global warming due to their *escapist gospel*, the support of shortsighted economic policies, and other factors.[161] But from their view the politicization of the issue is already paving the way for the Cainite builders of a new social order that scapegoats those it considers deplorable to its desired order which is always more than mere altruism toward all of humankind. In the reality

---

160. Walker-Jones, *The Green Psalter*, 2. Just as with church/state issues, division of stewardship labors is necessary; over-division because of an overt rejection of stewardship under God is counter-productive.

161. Tad Delay writes, "white evangelicalism . . . far and away the most dangerous faith the world has yet known." Delay, *Against*, 13.

of our post-truth culture, all that can be said for sure is that the will to power always lies crouching at the door that opens to the right or the left.

At any rate, a better future could come through a "partnership" between the secular earth stewards and the gospel stewards. That could be a beginning of the fruition of the "cosmic" gospel and the restoration of the stewardship of the earth that creation groans for. The truth is that all the stewards need to move toward "life together" because of the gospel that is good for the church, humanity, and the world. The alternative is the bad form of "death together." Desmond and Mpho Tutu write of the South African concept of *ubuntu*:

> *Ubuntu* recognizes the interconnectedness of life. My humanity, we say, is bound up with your humanity. One consequence of *ubuntu* is that we recognize that we all need to live our lives in ways that ensure that others may live well. Our flourishing should enhance the lives of others, not detract from them.[162]

It seems that God's providence may be orchestrating the necessity for cooperation, for that reveals the necessity of the gospel.

Another somewhat related possibility of God's orchestration that is scripturally hinted at, at the least, is that world circumstances may also contribute to the *Israelite stewards* of God and the *Christian stewards* of God also finding themselves brought together in some common cause for the sake of the world, thus finding themselves both rooted together in the olive tree they are both in different senses related to already. (Of course, that common cause may simply be that they are both "people of the book" along with Muslims also, since the phrase comes from the beginning of the Koran.) Something like this seems to have been in Paul's purview in Romans 11 which is probably informed by OT texts that Paul saw as speaking to the inter-relation of these stewards of God's one olive tree. One thing is also certain, that Paul saw all of history past, present and future as God's tapestry of human history wherein he would bring to pass Christ's universal reconciliation.

> For God has consigned all to disobedience, that he may have mercy on all. Oh, the depth of the riches and wisdom and knowledge of God! How unsearchable are his judgments and how inscrutable his ways! (Rom 11:32–33).

---

162. Tutu and Tutu, *Made for Goodness*, 47.

It seems that in more ways than one, creation waits with eager longing and groans in the pains of childbirth looking to be set free from its bondage to corruption and obtain the freedom of the glory of the children of God (see Rom 8:19–21). In that future day all humanity on the new earth will have been reinstated as its renewed stewards, and the stewards of the gospel will have finished bearing the news of their weighty and glorious, terrible and beautiful gospel in the outworking of God's plan for the glory that was to come. For then, the gospel news will have become unnecessary in the face of the full realization of the gospel reality. God's breathed out breath, forming his stewards as God's image bearer in the earth will then have moved from faith to faith and from glory to glory in the inheritance of all things reconciled in Christ. In the meantime, God is orchestrating all things toward that end, through the inscrutable ways that subvert the viral contagion of the will to power.[163] For "He has made everything beautiful in its time" (Eccl 3:11).

---

163 "The righteous inherit the destiny prepared for themselves, the truly human destiny (Matt. 25:34), for which their names have been written in the book of life (Rev. 20:12, 15), but the wicked are left to the fate they have chosen by identifying themselves with evil . . . the destiny prepared for the devil and his angels . . . throwing in their lot with the evil that God must finally remove from his good creation." Bauckham and Hart, *Hope Against Hope,* 141, 145.

Conclusion
"God's Purification of Means"

> And the Lord appointed a great fish to swallow up Jonah. and Jonah was in the belly of the fish three days and three nights.
> —JONAH 1:17

"The Prosecution's Closing Statement in Humankind vs. The Gospel of Jesus Christ"

JUDGE WILL T. POWER: "The prosecution may begin its closing statement."

Pilate H. Cain: "Your Honorable Judge Will T. Power, ladies and gentlemen of the jury, the proceedings of this court have been long and laborious as my esteemed colleagues and I have presented before the jury much evidence of the multitude of offenses against humanity and the world committed by the infamous trio of the gospel, evangelism and its evangelizers. I will seek to draw all that has been presented to a conclusion that ought to make the correct verdict self-evident. I will revisit the five incidents mentioned in our opening argument for the purpose of reconsidering them in light of what we have since learned about this crafty trio, namely that their intention has always been to "turn the world upside down" as was reported by unbiased observers not many years after the public appearance in the world of their infamous ringleader, Jesus of Nazareth, and his band of deceivers.[1] For their gospel stories were "an invention of those stewards. All made up to keep the rest of us under their thumb . . . They are a shrewd lot, those stewards. They know which

---

1. See Acts 17:6

side their bread is buttered on, all right. Clever fellows. Damn me, I can't help admiring them."[2]

The First Incident Revisited: The Report of Isaiah

The first incident we had heard about was Isaiah's depiction of the beauty of sweaty messengers bearing good news. This picture was what birthed the name of this whole so-called "revolutionary" movement, "the gospel." In light of all we have heard we can now summarize that the gospel itself presents a confusion of categories and therefore evangelism and its evangelizers can only fail at being the bearers of such a confused notion of "good news." For here's the rub, to be blunt. The feet of the bearers of this "gospel" are supposed to be beautiful for "turning the world upside down!" How can such anarchy be seen as beautiful? It is no wonder that the accused trio meet with denunciation rather than acclamation. Furthermore, even if one could accept that in some manner this revolutionary gospel was actually good for us all, we have heard a preponderance of evidence that its evangelism and evangelizers so often fail to challenge our system. Instead, they covertly operate by the same means of our beloved will to power, while claiming to represent a new revolution of faith! At times the defense has pathetically asked us to have some sympathy for them, even see some beauty in the feeble attempts that we admit at times may contain a bit of courage, albeit a manifestly foolhardy bit. Perhaps, in their Babel of voices we must admit we catch a hint of the charisma of the founder. But his own confusion of tongues, speaking out of one side of his mouth of saving the world, and then *condemning* our universally beneficent order out of the other, invariably demonstrates that justice was served when his proposed gospel of lunacy was answered by his own trial and *condemnation*. It seems that we humans, as the ultimate measure of all things, can only conclude that *our* justice was served, just as *our* justice must be served again, regarding the troublesome trio in the dock before us.

The Second Incident Revisited: Jonah and the Ancient Mariners

The second incident of Jonah being cast overboard in the storm at sea, for being its cause, was just the tip of the iceberg of his story, especially as told by the trio in the dock before us. For the bare facts of his story,

2. Lewis, *The Pilgrim's Regress*, 35.

in relation to the alleged meaning this trio attributes to them, simply boggles the mind of any reasonable person. For the plain fact of the matter is that Jonah, strange as he was by being a prophet of God and all, was in actuality a misunderstood witness for *our* side. For from what we can see he clearly opposed God's dangerous gospel from the beginning to the bitter end! For Jonah had the courage to stand against this God and his gospel of "forgiveness" for the veritable Nazi's of his day! But the defendants claim him as the star witness for *their* side, by first admitting that Jonah was guilty of following *our gospel* of the will to power, by which, we note in passing, we have now created the most just order of the ages! Second, the infamous trio try to spin Jonah's story so that his *near-death experience* and virtual resurrection in the "great fish incident" was *the preeminent* sign of the death and *alleged* resurrection of Jesus of Nazareth, to vindicate Jesus's wimpy way of faith. This is simply sleight of hand! For it is obviously impossible since the vindication of Jesus condemns our beloved way of the will to power! Furthermore, we *know* that resurrection is impossible. So, we must stand our ground on the tried and tested way of reasonable people (of whom we are the most reasonable) in the will to power that rightfully condemned Jesus and vindicated our beloved Jonah! As for the alleged idea that somehow, through what happened to *our* Jonah and *their* Jesus, forgiveness was won for all humankind, well I have to admit that we would all like to be given such a gift . . . if it were true that we needed it! For our way of the will to power is not merely seeking crude power such as these Ninevites did. No, we aren't such heathens, for we have *our* religion and can humbly *confess* the sins of imperfection that appear in our established order and *atone* for them by ever striving for its complete perfection by removal of whatever deplorable scapegoats blemish *our* moral righteousness!

The Third Incident Revisited: The Supposed Paradise of Irenaeus.

In my introductory arguments I showed that Irenaeus's statement "The Church has been planted as a paradisus in the world," was self-evident evidence otherwise. In part of the trial, we heard the defendants' claim that the gospel's way of faith provides God's mediation between human relationships to enable the formation of true human community rather than the coercive and violent ways of the will to power. We also heard the claim that the evangelizers were supposed to be the living paradigm of a new social order based in forgiveness and living for the good of others. These are of course lofty goals that our own established order also lives by, with the only difference of note being that we do this by our own unfailing light of reason and inherent goodness. For we live together by forgiving ourselves simply because our basic goodness and humility demand it. We live for others as did the founder of our city-model, Cain, who has been zealously followed, resulting in the establishment of our beneficent fortress cities, in which we can realize our God-ness. Our accused trio claim that paradise was always meant to be based in humankind's simple faith in the mysterious God. *This* was the "original sin" to our way. For our way is to boldly venture forth *not* as those dependent on a Creator who would keep us in the cradle, but *by ourselves* to become the Lords of the cosmos! Our way began when we heard from an alternate but completely reliable and *agreeable* source, that the claim of God's gospel of faith to be good was a thinly disguised power play seeking to keep us from becoming like God, and therefore our own God. Therefore, though Irenaeus and his kind speak of the church as the real beginning of the "paradise" God originally intended, those of our way saw through its trickery. And so, we ought to judge this "paradise" as an invasion of squatters, whose only claim here is unwarranted "faith." They invade the "promised land" Cain provided, which is always "east of Eden" and its degrading faith system of subservience. For we enjoy the plenteous fruits of *our labors* in our will to power *in* the good of *our fortress city*, securely housing *our tribe* safely inside from all those "others" who would threaten us. Thus, the guilty verdict on the gospel trio ought to be the foregone conclusion. Otherwise, we may find ourselves in "at-one-ment" with deplorable and other unsavory specimens of so-called humankind! Our father Cain dedicated his heir and his city to this glorious destiny of salvation from God and others, unless of course the others can be made subservient to our will to power. "Gospel" talk of a better way of faith simply repeats the attitude of the first heretic to our way, useless Abel. Need I say more to appeal to the legitimacy of our common cause of universal brotherhood in the will to power? (Never mind any crude literalism of the idea of brotherhood.)

The Fourth Incident Revisited: Orual and Psyche, Two Pagan Sisters

This peculiar quasi-historical story sounds like myth to anyone with modern sense. But in the course of this trial the defense appealed to it to demonstrate some of the supposedly difficult extenuating circumstances of the evangelizers of this "gospel," such as that they have never "seen" God, in order to raise sympathy for them. Of course, this appeal can only make sense if we ignore the vast advances of humankind, having "come of age" in our self-assured certainty that we have seen and are ever arriving at our glorious destiny. There is no gospel other than what we declare to be gospel, especially when the supposed "gospel" of Christ is admitted to only provide us with "seeing through a glass darkly." Let us judge rightly as to the fate of the accused "gospel in the dock," so that we can live in the way of full sight through our pure powers of reason. Let us be delivered from the primitive instincts of myth and meaning, which lead beyond the horizon of our beloved immanent frame toward the dreaded realm where so-called transcendental truths like beauty and love can invade and disturb the tranquility of our diversion from our selves. C. S. Lewis, a ringleader of these evangelizers and a veritable dinosaur from medieval times, had the audacity to propose that we moderns of enlightened times would be closer to truth if we became Pagan again. For that would bring us closer to the "reality" of the world replete with transcendental truths of God and of course, the dreaded God of holy darkness! Let us not forget that our modern enlightenment has made us realize *our* Godlike stance of knowledge rooted in our pure reason. Of course, a newer and most disturbing trend in many of our own philosophers, secret traitors to our will to power if you ask me, call that knowledge "the view from nowhere" and criticize it as impossible! That a few of our defendant's philosophers claim that only a universal God could have a view from nowhere, and that such a God has revealed some of that view through Christ and in the Scriptures, again demonstrates that this trio indeed seeks to subvert our enlightened philosophy that supports our will to power and thus turn our world upside down. Their guilt in this is beyond question! For how could such treasonous subversion of our better way be good?

The Fifth Incident Revisited: Cain and Abel, the First Two Brothers

In my original presentation of this incident, after my initial gracious neutral report of the facts, I asked whether Cain has been misjudged by subsequent history. Perhaps now we need to consider this a bit further than we did there. Certainly, those who settled in his highly successful city considered him worthy to break the ground of the first glorious city of man. We may ask where any supposed "city of God" can be found or what it has done for humankind. Never mind the idea that all our real progress has been due to our following the gospel's idea that a divine Creator's words imbued creation with intelligibility and enabled the possibility of science. Or that transcendent values and the linear view of history, derived from the same notion of creation and the gospel's influence in Christendom, enabled moral and societal progress and the first true humanism.[3] For our will to power has been able to grow and flourish simply because it is our practical reality, and we can't help it if some ultimate fact of reality has enabled our success. For the only proof that matters is our achievement, the city of man. Some think that such a city ought to be built on "brotherhood." But Cain showed the better way, and he and Abel as "brothers" ought not be taken too literally, as implying some top-down theory of a universal brotherhood imposed by "God." For God asked Cain where his brother was, and so Cain rightfully responded by asking whether *he* was "his brother's keeper" since that "keeping" was God's responsibility, not his. But Cain showed himself the better, and "went the extra mile" at God's suggestion and so his city has "kept" many a slave . . . er . . . I mean . . . brother, though some such as Abel, were kept out. Of course, he and his kin in the way of faith, could never fit in anyway which is the real problem with this trio in the dock and all their breeding of discontent toward our city of man. This trio has never aimed to wholly "fit in" and therefore we call on the members of the jury to render the only just verdict, and cast them out, and will leave it to our esteemed judge's just judgment regarding their sentence which will effectually remove them from "the dock" to "the outer darkness" to save us once and for all time from their dreaded salvation. Of course, knowing their sleight of hand, we expect to hear from them again, claiming that their way is that of resurrection.

3. On the Biblical vs. Greek conception of time and history see Hoekema, *The Bible,* 305; on humanism see Zimmermann, *Incarnational Humanism,* 52–162.

Concluding Summary of These Five incidents

I conclude by simply pleading with the jurors to rely upon their pure reason though it has been greatly assaulted by the defense and ask whether or not humanity ought to bear with this accused trio's way of faith, or whether to say, by borrowing one of their Bible's most unusual sayings, "the violent bear it away!" To bear this "gospel" away from humanity, for the sake of the common good of flourishing through our tried and tested "will to power" that has always provided for us and especially so in our darkest times.[4] But this so-called "gospel" only turns the world upside down. Our gospel has proven to be adept at turning every crisis "right-side up" through our ever-ready, efficient and gracious Leviathan.[5] So I appeal to you, my eminently reasonable comrades in arms, to render the warranted just verdict upon these religious fanatics whose subversive way of faith cannot take root in our swamp, nor overcome the world for its good as we can through our untethered will to power. Faith corrupts, but absolute power liberates absolutely. "Down, down with the defeated! Victory is the only ultimate fact."[6] Long live the way of Cain! All hail Leviathan!"[7]

On "Pilate H. Cain" as Prosecutor

My "mock trial's" opening and closing statements have sought to imitate the diabolical voice of C. S. Lewis's "Uncle Screwtape" in the prosecutor Pilate H. Cain as I have been able, though certainly falling far short of the master craft of Lewis.[8] A psychological evaluation of Pilate H. Cain would reveal that he is more conflicted than his will to power shows. The will to power is obviously more fully personified in the judge, "Will T. Power," showing that the will to power itself contains no conflict. But Cain and Pilate both did. Sin was "crouching" at the door of Cain's soul,

---

4. "Perhaps . . . from the perspective of mankind, war has never 'paid.' Yet war recurs. The beast in man may glory in the carnage; the reason in man rebels." Waltz, *Man, the State, and War*, 224.

5. See Higgs, *Crisis and Leviathan*.

6. From "The Ball and the Cross" by G. K. Chesterton, as cited in Wood, *Chesterton*, 144.

7. "*Art* goes yet further, imitating that Rationall and most excellent worke of Nature, *Man*. For by Art is created that great LEVIATHAN called a COMMON-WEALTH, or STATE." Hobbes, *Leviathan*, xxxiii.

8. Lewis, *The Screwtape Letters*.

and Pilate anxiously sought to release Jesus but could not, showing that the will to power had more control of him than he had of it. Therefore, humanity is represented by the conflicted Pilate H. Cain, not by Will T. Power. And our way of the will to power is always haunted by our primal relation to God.

This manner of presentation was used for what seemed a theopoetical way of using satire and exaggeration to portray the ethos we guiltily will against the gospel. As we discussed earlier that ethos is largely ours through "unconscious" formation in the cultural rituals of our shared modern life rather than through conscious reasonable thought.[9] Thus our method sought to make our cultural unconsciousness, more visible. It is hoped that this theopoetical method was to some measure effective. One of the lessons of this aesthetic method is simply to note the truth that Jesus brought to bear on the reality of our human ways of judging: "When you say what is wrong in others, your words will be used to say what is wrong in you" (Matt 7:2, NLV). Judging the gospel is therefore a self-incriminating endeavor since all already live according to other "gospels" and our judgment of *the true gospel* will reveal the "gospel" we actually live by and thus provide the grounds for our being judged.

In the mock trial it may be noticed that to Pilate H. Cain the end justifies the means. We have discussed means and ends earlier in the book and now want to show how "the purification of means" is a unitive factor in all of God's redemptive purposes for humankind, and how that relates to the gospel being in the dock.

"The Purification of Means"[10]

The "Jonah" text at the head of this conclusion, showing Jonah in the belly of the fish for three days and nights, under the sign of the prophet Jonah signifies the stewards being in the dock as God's means of bringing the gospel. This is because Jonah epitomizes and symbolizes the Israelite and

---

9. See Smith, *Desiring the Kingdom*, 19–24; Butler, *Excitable Speech*, 25, 154–55. (See above in Chapter 4 under the subheading "A community of truth."

10. Eugene Peterson writes, "Jacques Maritain, one of our more prescient and incisive prophetic voices from the twentieth century, continues to call on all of us who have taken up membership in the Christian community to be vigilant and active in what he called "the Purification of Means." He saw this as urgent work, about which we should not procrastinate if we are to follow Jesus in the freedom where he leads us, and if we are not to end up as slaves in a de-souled culture." Peterson, *The Jesus Way*, 3–4.

Church stewards who do not view the gospel as good and for that reason place it in the dock. This is why we have needed to seek to rehabilitate the gospel from the dock for *them,* while also seeing to rehabilitate "their" gospel for the rest of humanity and the world. Thus, our task has been to see God's purification of them as God's scandalous means for bringing the gospel to the world. Therefore, an understanding of "The Purification of Means" is necessary to better understand the means God uses toward the ends of the gospel. For in essence, the gospel is God's means toward God's ends and just as the gospel is one, so also are the means and ends. Soren Kierkegaard writes,

> Eternally speaking, there is only one means and there is only one end: the means and the end are one and the same thing. There is only one end: the genuine Good; and only one means: this, to be willing only to use those means which genuinely are good—but the genuine Good is precisely the end. In time and on earth one distinguishes between the two and considers that the end is more important than the means. One thinks that the end is the main thing and demands of one who is striving that he reaches the end. He need not be so particular about the means. Yet this is not so, and to gain an end in this fashion is an unholy act of impatience. In the judgment of eternity, the relation between the end and the means is rather the reverse of this.[11]

A point that we stressed earlier is that means are the visible signs of the unseen ends. This is also why those means must be in harmony with their intended end. And when there is a perceived lack of such congruity in the manner of the gospel, its evangelism and evangelizers, we are faced with the problem of the gospel in the dock.[12] The problem of the gospel in the dock is in a sense caused by God's use of seemingly insufficient means for the ends of the reconciliation of humanity and the world. This is the essence of every "scandal of particularity" that we considered in Chapter 4. And the question therefore is whether or not God's use of the particular means of the gospel, namely evangelism, and the stewards, is sufficiently congruous with the end of reconciliation. The answer is that there is congruity, simply because God is continually purifying the gospel-means of the stewards toward the gospel-end of the purification

---

11. Kierkegaard, *Purity of Heart,* 202.

12. "Across the centuries, the consensus has been that if the nature of the means has been compromised and is in contradiction to the nature of the end, the end is desecrated, poisoned, and becomes a thing of horror. Peterson, *The Jesus Way,* 7.

of all of humanity, to be restored as God's good-image bearer in the world. Since the focus of this book has mostly been in the rehabilitation/purification of the gospel stewards, we have not focused on the gospel end itself, which is the rehabilitation/purification of the creation stewards, humanity at large.

Therefore, we will now consider the relation between the "purification" of God's means, *the gospel stewards* and God's "purification" of God's first stewards, the *creation stewards,* considered at the end of the last chapter. This will demonstrate more fully the interconnectedness of all of humanity in relation to the gospel, and show that that when we place the gospel stewards in the dock, we also place the gospel for the stewards of God's image in creation, and therefore ourselves, in the dock.

The Rehabilitation of All God's "Gospel Stewards" and "Image Stewards"

The various Jonahs that we have seen throughout the book were instances of varying degrees of purified stewards. At this point we need to consider the "resurrected" and "purified" Jonah standing on the shore of Nineveh in contrast to the "dead to God's mission" Jonah sleeping in the ship and swallowed by "Leviathan."[13] In the typology of the sign of Jonah, this Jonah on the shore signifies a restored adamic image of God as the steward of creation. This is because Jonah is *firstly* human, and as such was to be an image steward, and only *secondly* an Israelite to be a gospel steward. This "resurrected" Jonah on the shore is "restored," grudgingly but nevertheless participating, in both offices of stewardship. For this Jonah-steward on the shore, in "the sign of the prophet Jonah," signifies Jesus the restored adamic "gardener" of God's new Eden, and therefore also the first *human* fully restored in the stewardship of the image of God in creation. Corroborative biblical/theological tracing of the development of this image-bearing motif is beyond our scope here.[14] We can only summarize that it seems to be verified in the gospel account when the risen Christ was mistaken as "the gardener."[15] But to gener-

13. We are contrasting the Jonah of Jonah 4 with the Jonah of Jonah 1, to be clear.

14. Hebrews 2:5–18 and Romans 8:12–30 certainly summarize much of this biblical motif of the restoration of God's image bearers to steward creation.

15. See John 20:15. The otherwise unimportant detail in John where everything has typological significance seems to demonstrate that this case of mistaken identity intentional alludes to the stewardship of creation. See Zahnd, *Mistaken As the Gardener.*

ally clarify, we will narrate God's progressive purification of means from 'adam' through Jonah, and because of the sign of Jonah, this signifies *the gospel's* restoration of God's *image stewards* in Christ. This progression is best arranged as a chiastic structure:

Table 10: God's Purification of Means in the Sign of Jonah.

1a) 'adam' as the means of God's image.

    2a) 'adam' as fallen from being the means of God's image.

        3a) Jonah as 'adam'/Israel as the intended means of God's image/gospel.

            4a) Jonah as 'adam'/Israel *in process* as the means for God's image/gospel.

                5a) ***Jesus as "Jonah" as the fulfilled means of God's image/gospel.***

                5b) Jonah as Humankind/Israel/Church as the fulfilled means of God's image/gospel.

            4b) Jonah as Humankind/Israel/Church *in process* as means of God's image/gospel.

        3b) Jonah as Humankind/Israel/Church as the intended means of God's image/gospel.

    2b) Humankind as fallen from being the means of God's image.

1b) Humankind as fulfilling the means of God's image.

This chiastic structure shows God's continual purification of gospel-means toward God's gospel-ends from the creation of humankind to the consummation of God's purpose. It shows humankind as a whole as both fallen and fulfilled stewards of God's image. It shows Israel and the church elected from humankind at large to serve as the gospel stewards for the restoration of the image stewards. It also shows Christ at the center as the ultimate means for the purification of the gospel stewards and the image stewards. It essentially demonstrates the inner logic of the outworking of God's gospel-scandal of particularity toward the gospel-good of universality.

Therefore, in light of all this, we can summarize that most of this book has been an attempt to see the purification of the *means* of the gospel's scandal of particularity, for the sake of the *end* of the gospel's good of universality. After the work of the first creation, God saw it all and declared that "it was very good." So also, when God's purification of means is completed in the new creation, it will be said "it was very good," or perhaps, "it is even better" as Revelation 21:1—22:5 seems to testify. Hopefully, through gospel-formed eyes, we can "see" even now, something of that end "coming forward from the fog" of God's future. For what we see now is God's purification of means toward God's good ends in the restoration of the image stewards in the new garden-temple in Christ that will fill creation.

Reconciled in the Way of Faith

What all the stewards of God need is to swim in the new current, flowing towards the centripetal center of life, the reconciliation already accomplished in Christ. Ironically, the gravity of creation propels us to move away from Christ the center in the will to power as the "solution" to the mysteries and sufferings of creation. This movement results in increased suffering and grows the "city of Cain" to fill the earth. And we are all good Cainites, seeking God's protection, using God as means to *our* ends. Simone Weil humorously and tragically pictures the manner of "seeking God" through the fallen desire of humankind in this context of suffering:

> There are people whose manner of seeking God is like a man making leaps into the air in the hope that if he jumps a little higher each time, he will end up staying there and rising to heaven.[16]

Of course, the problem is the *gravity of suffering* that continually pulls us down. But the gospel of God is the news that God entered the suffering of the world in the flesh-and-blood man Jesus, to the point of death on the cross but then rose again because the powers of sin and death could not hold the Holy author of life. Simone Weil's illustration is reminiscent of Paul's text where the righteousness of faith necessary for the proper relation to God "comes down" to us in Christ rather than requiring our needing to leap up to heaven to bring Christ down to us (Rom 10:6–13). Our alienation from God's transcendent presence,

---

16. As cited in Springsted, *Simone Weil*, 53.

originally "available" in the Garden in Eden through the tree of life, is thus provided by Christ "coming down" from the transcendent realm to become the gravitational center of the new creation in which nothing, including suffering, can separate us from the love of God.

The suffering of Christ, the new 'adam,' on the cross, is *the ultimate means* that brings our life and all our sin and suffering together with the life of God. For in Christ, God fully entered into our life, bringing *the ultimate gospel-end* of the reconciliation of all things in Christ. Thus now, to be "pulled down" by suffering is to move *nearer* to Christ the reconciling center of the new cosmos. This signifies the purification of creational suffering as a gospel-end of God. Because of Christ, all of life is now lived within the poles of both *gravity and grace*, always pulled "down" to the center of God's love in the suffering Christ.[17] The dream to leap into heaven *is* a pipe dream, conditioned by the old way of understanding the cosmos, because the gospel *is* the inbreaking of the heavenly dimension of God's love, God's eternal life, God's way of power, God's Christ, the new human, *already come*.

Thus, each and every individual and community of the world, can live *now* in God's *future eschaton*, which has already provisionally come to earth in Christ. And if this is the firstfruits of the gospel in the world where suffering is still the context of life, what will be the full harvest when suffering itself "is no more" and the only context of life is to fully partake of the tree of life—the ever-present God who *is love* and *eternal life* (1 John 4:8; 5:20). For the fruits of the gospel that all human stewards can presently participate in, is "The *beginning* of the gospel of Jesus Christ, the Son of God" (Mark 1:1). The gospel-ends have never been fully revealed, and what has been seen is only the beginning of what cannot even be imagined (1 Cor 2:9). It seems that Irenaeus was correct, the church has been *planted* as a paradise in the world, albeit with seedlings and saplings that grow *by* grace, *because of* the gravity (Mark 4:26–29). And the fruits from Christ's new garden, though only partly received and shared, are nevertheless seen

---

17. We are relying here on the thought of Simone Weil, and her conception of the twin poles of "gravity and grace." Springsted explains, "Normally we tend to see affliction as a condition that not only brings a crashing halt to human purposes, but also gives us reason to think that the world of force in which we live is completely alien to our hopes for any good whatsoever. When affliction is found to have a use, however, we can see that our hopes and the world are not necessarily at cross purposes, for we can see a side to the natural world, even in affliction, that signals another dimension to our lives. Force does not have to thwart us; it may be the very gateway to what we have longed for." Springsted, *Simone Weil*, 55.

by those who do so, as good for humanity and the world. For the healing leaves of the garden are for all the nations, when they cease their prosecution of the planted paradise in the world, and instead find therein their own reconciliation and restoration in God's image.

And though we cannot imagine the full reality of God's gospel of euchatastrophe, it may well be that the gospel "in the dock" will be to the church, all of humanity, and the entire cosmos, the impossible shadow in the gospel's fullness of eternal day. And but for the scars of Christ, something no longer possible to even imagine, in that now unimaginable day, the inverse of our time when it is nearly impossible to imagine otherwise.

Unscientific Exegetical Postscript
Is there a "Dark Side" of the Gospel?

> This is the message we have heard from him and proclaim to you, that God is light, and in him is no darkness at all.
>
> —1 JOHN 1:5

> He is the propitiation for our sins, and not for ours only but also for the sins of the whole world.
>
> —1 JOHN 2:2

> And Jesus, perceiving in himself that power had gone out from him, immediately turned about in the crowd and said, "Who touched my garments?"
>
> —MARK 5:30

> *"Here, it becomes clear that speaking about the mystery of Christ means speaking about the mystery of life."*
>
> —KARL BARTH[1]

THIS "UNSCIENTIFIC EXEGETICAL POSTSCRIPT" is presented with a nod to Soren Kierkegaard's over 600 page "Concluding Unscientific Postscript to Philosophical Fragments." My postscript is fortunately not nearly as long. It is "unscientific" simply for the fact that I am no philosopher, as

---

1. Barth, *Epistle to the Ephesians*, 139.

one of Kierkegaard's many pseudonymous authors, "Johannes Climacus," also supposedly was not.[2] But I use the word mainly because I admit that this postscript is in the main "speculative" although I believe it has merit by following what may be called "theological instinct," which will be discussed below. This postscript is further defined as "exegetical" not because of my exegesis, which is also "unscientific," being no proper biblical scholar or theologian, but because of a preeminent *exegesis of existence* that Christ provides, which I will propose in and as the core of this postscript.

The three texts above present, for our purpose here, a microcosmic view of the gospel of Christ in relation to all the people of the world of all times and places. A historically prominent view of the church, known as the exclusivist view of salvation, holds that apart from a conscious faith response to Jesus, there is no possibility of salvation. A view that challenges this, known historically as the inclusivist view of salvation, holds that people of any time or place can possibly be saved *by* Christ, but apart from their conscious knowledge *of* Christ. The exclusivist view presents what we call here a potentially "dark side of the gospel" because the "good news" of God's reconciliation of the world through Christ results in the condemnation of multitudes of those who never hear such "good news." Do God's *means* of salvation through Christ alone, due to the seeming lack of saving *ends*, need *purification*? The exclusivist's and inclusivist's "short answers" are "no," because God's means of Christ as the only way is the wholly pure means to God's wholly pure ends (Gen 18:25). For "God is light, and in him is no darkness at all." The inclusivist would add that Christ is the propitiation not only for conscious "believers" but "for the sins of the whole world," so *perhaps* God's reconciliation of the world in Christ results in the universally beneficent situation where from the midst of the undifferentiated "crowd" of the world, any individual may grasp after God and touch the salvific garment of Christ. This "perhaps" leads to the need of our "long answer" to the question which is this postscript.

The "long answer" to the question of a potentially "dark side of the gospel" therefore poses the need for additional rehabilitation of the gospel. For the prominent exclusivist doctrine of the definite need of conscious faith in Christ for anyone to be saved presents perhaps the greatest "scandal of particularity" before the religiously diverse peoples

2. On the purposes of Kierkegaard in his title and "Postscript" see Backhouse, *Kierkegaard*, 237.

of the world, resulting in a deadly serious "stumbling block" for them being able to accept the gospel with this "dark side" of condemnation "hidden" in its fine print. We will begin this rehabilitation by looking at the well-known—because oft used "evangelical" text, John 3:16.

What's the Problem with John 3:16?

> For God so loved the world, that he gave his only begotten Son, that whosoever believeth in him should not perish, but have everlasting life (KJV).

The short answer is, of course, that there is no problem with John 3:16, which is perhaps *the verse* for "Evangelicals." Unfortunately, at the present time, that does not bode well for John 3:16. Nevertheless, Andreas Kostenberger summarizes the past "fame" of the text, saying,

> John 3:16 is one of the most beloved verses in all of Scripture. Its declaration of God's love for the world, its depiction of Jesus's vicarious sacrifice, and its promise of eternal life for all who respond to God's offer of salvation in Christ through faith have brought hope and comfort to many. In addition, John 3:16 poignantly encapsulates the message of John's entire Gospel and provides a window into the heart of his theology.[3]

What may not be obvious to those not well versed in modern evangelical theology is that John 3:16 is not without problems of interpretation leading to what could be seen as "bad publicity" for the gospel—indeed—what seems a veritable "dark side of the gospel." This is because the text contains an obvious disconnect between *what* "God so loved," namely, "the world," and the "whosoevers" that "believe in him" *from* or *in relation to* that world. It is obvious that the entire *world* and the *whosoever* within it are not necessarily coextensive. This may be simply because John's gospel is itself evangelical, representing the sharing of the good news as providence will allow with people *within* the world so that *whosoever* of those hearing of salvation in Christ *may* believe in him, and have *eternal life*. But historically, more elaborate theological gymnastics have been practiced for bridging the disconnect. Here is one attempt by the historic Calvinist view:

---

3. Kostenberger, "Lifting Up," 141.

> "The 'World' does not signify all people universally, but only all types of people; therefore 'whosoever' signifies 'the elect' personally and unconditionally chosen by God from the world for irresistible redemption."

It is not possible to fully answer this within the scope of this postscript, but it seems fairly likely that "world" signifies the undifferentiated mass of people of the world, not the different types of people.[4] 1 John 2:2 seems to plainly verify this view of the world, viewed as a whole, rather than as a collection of various types or classes of peoples (see 1 Tim 4:10). What is even more certain is that God's saving action focused on the world as a whole, not on individuals within it. In other words, the "whosoevers" were loved and atoned for *while in* "the world."[5] Another attempted bridge is the exclusivist view:

> "The 'World' does signify all people universally but only those hearing the gospel can believe in it and benefit from it."

This idea is even more common than the Calvinist view, and is widely held in evangelicalism. It is an expression of "The Conditional Gospel" that we discussed in Chapter 4 above. It seems to be explicitly contradicted by Paul in 1 Timothy 4:10 where Paul writes, "*For to this end we toil and strive, because we have our hope set on the living God, who is the Savior of all people, especially of those who believe.*" The exclusivist view emphasizes the way any "whosoever" comes to consciously "believe" but makes that a deterministic law that requires hearing and believing to be saved, rather than a report of historical providence. But John 3:16 is simply declaring the logical connection between conscious faith and the faith object that allows it to become "belief."

What I seek to challenge is the belief that there is *no benefit* to any and even all of the people of "the world" apart from conscious faith in Christ. Stated positively, I propose that *any* person from the world, *who* Christ became incarnate for, and atoned for, may "feel their way toward him and find him" and "touch the garments" of Christ (Acts 17:26–28; Mark 5:28) *because* of the gospel that God is already reconciled to them

---

4. T. F. Torrance presents an important critique of the Calvinistic views, partly based in the idea that there could be no divide between the love-motivated election of the whole world by God and the love-in-action work of Christ for the whole world. See Torrance, *Atonement*, 183, 187.

5. See Andreas J. Kostenberger, *Understanding the Times*, 156.

in Christ. This will require us to focus more on the significance of the disconnect between John's "world" and "whosoever."

On Connecting John's Disconnect between "the World" and "Whosoever Believes"

It seems that the exclusivist view has misconstrued the significance of the logical necessity presented in the evangelistic situation, wherein when the good news of salvation in Christ is made known, a positive response to it requires conscious faith. The exclusivist turns this logical necessity into an over-determinative requirement concerning what goes on "outside" of the evangelistic situation. The exclusivist understands John 3:16 to be speaking beyond the proper scope of its evangelistic concern, as though it says,

> "For God so loved the world, that he gave his only begotten Son, that *only* those who believe in him should not perish, but have everlasting life."

It seems that there is a serious disconnect between the gospel's "whosoever" and the exclusivist's "only." It is a disconnect which denudes the goodness of the gospel, adding a "dark side" which seems far from the intent of John 3:16, and more importantly then, at complete odds with the declared intent of the God who "so loved the world." The exclusivist's "dark gospel" says,

> For God so loved the world, that he gave his only begotten Son, that only those who *consciously hear of him* should not perish but have everlasting life.

This "new gospel" with a hidden dark side also seems to manifestly contradict the very next statement of John following 3:16:

> For God sent not his Son into the world to condemn the world; but that the world through him might be saved (John 3:17, KJV).

Strangely, the exclusivist gospel has derived the condemnation of multitudes of the world from the gospel that defines itself as the exact opposite. An exclusivist paraphrase of John 3:16–17 could very well read like this:

> For God so loved the world, that he gave his only begotten Son, *that only those who consciously hear of him* should not perish but have everlasting life. For God sent not his Son into the world

to condemn the world; nevertheless, the majority of the world remains under God's condemnation.

John's gospel does indeed *often* speak of a condemnation that *follows* the conscious rejection of the gospel. But the exclusivist gospel posits a condemnation that both *excludes* the gospel's specific news that God *no longer condemns* the world and continues to *dominate* the entire world "outside" of the evangelistic situation. The very news that God has through Christ removed the world's condemnation has been removed from the gospel, as though it has not yet come. But the question is how the world can still be construed as condemned? It seems that the answer is exceedingly ironic, only to be found in the minds of the "evangelical" exclusivists, as well meaning as they seek to be in "following Scripture." For somehow "the supreme and all-sufficient manifestation of God's love . . . directed toward sinners (the world)" is marred by the exclusivist gospel's manifest insufficiency to do anything for anyone apart from the evangelistic situation.[6] The exclusivist's "scandal of particularity" is a scandal that remains in place no matter the apologetic gymnastics presented to rehabilitate it.

It seems that the disconnect of John 3:16 between "world" and "whosoever" is only exacerbated in the exclusivist "solution" of connecting "world" to their interpretive "only." But the inclusivist can connect "world" and "whosoever" by leaving them in the evangelistic situation where John presupposes them to be. As for the fate of "the world" that remains "outside" of John's application of the gospel in the situation that his evangelistic gospel book itself creates, the world is nevertheless *still* "so loved" by God and *still* atoned for by Jesus who in John 4:21–22 is called "the Savior of the world" by Samaritans who heard the gospel and believed. Therefore, we will consider several other important texts that reveal problems of the exclusivist position and serve to begin to set forth a positive case for the inclusivist view.

Texts toward an Inclusivist Gospel

John 14:6

Another beautifully memorable and well-known text that is thought to support the exclusivist view is where Jesus says,

---

6. The words in quotation are from Kostenberger, *Understanding the Times*, 157.

> I am the way, and the truth, and the life. No one comes to the Father except through me.

C. S. Lewis, probably one of the most well-known Christian inclusivists of the modern era explains why the exclusivist view "puzzled" him, saying,

> Here is another thing that used to puzzle me. Is it not frighteningly unfair that this new life should be confined to people who have heard of Christ and been able to believe in Him? But the truth is God has not told us what His arrangements about the other people are. We do know that no man can be saved except through coming through Christ; we do not know that only those who know of Him can be saved through Him.[7]

The view of Lewis questions the exclusivist view by looking a little past the "surface" meaning so that he can apply God's word regarding the universality of God's reconciliation in Christ. Lewis's conversation about Jesus's proclamation of being "the only way" is paradigmatic of all conversations about Jesus in a world redeemed through Christ where there are multitudes that never had or never will have *any* conversations *about* Christ, while nevertheless living in *relation to Christ* through relation to the Father, Son and Spirit *because of* creational relation to the Father, general revelation of the Spirit, and the universal election in both the incarnation and atonement of Christ for all.

What Lewis saw in this text is the foundation of the inclusivist view, that any and all that are saved, are saved by coming to God through Christ whether they consciously know it or not. All salvation is based on the universal love of God's electing intent acting in the incarnate person and atoning work Christ for all humanity that provided reconciliation for all. In other words, any and all salvation is based on the gospel, whether the gospel is consciously known or not. Lewis clarifies this by saying that,

> What then is the difference which He (Jesus) has made to the whole human mass? It is just this; that the business of becoming a son of God, of being turned from a created thing to a begotten thing, of passing over from the temporary biological life into timeless "spiritual" life, has been done for us. Humanity is already "saved" in principle. We individuals have to appropriate that salvation. But the really tough work—the bit we could not have done for ourselves—has been done for us. We have not got

---

7. Lewis, *Mere Christianity*, 50.

to try to climb up by our own efforts; it has already come down into the human race.[8]

Another thing we can note was also stated explicitly by Lewis, that God has *not* "told us what His arrangements about the other people are." The assumption that God has *very plainly* told us is perhaps one of the largest mistaken assumptions of the exclusivist position.[9] Examples of this "very plain" revelation of God's arrangements for those who never hear are found in texts that are mistakenly thought to be about those who have *never heard* the gospel and are nevertheless condemned in relation to the gospel, when they are actually about those that *have heard* the gospel and rejected it, and are therefore condemned in relation to the gospel. We could diagram this as follows:

Table 11: The Exclusivist vs. Biblical Views of the Gospel, History, and Condemnation

Views	Gospel	Historical Experience	Condemnation
Exclusivist view of texts on condemnation	Many never hear the gospel	Many have not believed	Many are condemned in relation to the gospel
Biblical text's views on condemnation	Many heard the gospel	Many rejected the gospel	Many are condemned in relation to the gospel
Exclusivist view of texts on the gospel	The gospel does not remove condemnation	Many never heard the gospel	Many are condemned in relation to the gospel

---

8. Lewis, *Mere Christianity*, 141. We note that his view seems much the same as that of Torrance's "unconditional gospel" we consider in Chapter 4.

9. We say "very plainly" because it may well be that the answer is not so much found in a supposedly very plain system of "proof texts" but rather in a more "organic" system of textual interpretation. We tried to demonstrate the latter "system" above on John 3:16–17, just as Lewis aptly demonstrated it in his brief comment on John 14:6 which shows that a little "integrated" interpretation opens doors of possibility in contrast to the "plain" surface value "interpretation" that "simply" shuts doors on deeper thought on the subject. In other words, to the exclusivist, when the truth is *so obvious*, why look for more? But are we really fit judges of *God's word* when we see only surface value "obvious" meanings which are very likely seen as such because of what is called "confirmation bias?"

Views	Gospel	Historical Experience	Condemnation
Biblical text's views on the gospel	Gospel removes the condemnation of all	Many never heard and never explicitly rejected the gospel	Many are not condemned in relation to the gospel
Exclusivist view of the gospel	The gospel's removal of condemnation *depends* on human response	There is no opportunity for human response to the explicit gospel	The gospel is *ahistorical* and leaves multitudes in condemnation
Biblical view of the gospel	The gospel removes condemnation *before* any human response	**Human response to the explicit gospel is not always necessary**	The gospel is *historical* and universally removed the condemnation of all
Biblical view of the gospel in regard to those who never hear	The gospel removes condemnation *before* any human response	**Human response to God because of the unconditional gospel is always possible**	The gospel is *historical* and universally removed the condemnation of all

It seems that the exclusivist view misses the implied narrative and therefore the significance of the historical experience of people in relation to the gospel, while the actual texts and the inclusivist view recognizes it. The exclusivist view "reads" condemnatory "gospel" experience into the historical experience of those who never heard, while the texts and the inclusivist view do not. The exclusivist view also ignores or negates the gospel's accomplishment of removing the condemnation of all which is in fact what the "good news" is, that "in Christ God was ... not counting their trespasses against them" (2 Cor 5:19). Thus, the fifth row demonstrate that the exclusivist view wholly depends on the conditional gospel and make the gospel essentially ahistorical and wholly insignificant in regard to those who never hear it.[10] The two highlighted third columns in the bottom two rows essentially presents the basis of the inclusivist view, which at this point, for the sake of argument, is presented as the "biblical view of the gospel in regard to those who never hear." The full defense of this chart will be made in the rest of this postscript.

10. The "gospel of conditionality" was discussed in Chapter 4.

The primary text which becomes paradigmatic of others with that same family resemblance of supposed condemnation to those never hearing is actually John 3:16–17 within its larger context up to verse 21.

John 3:16–21

We have already seen that John 3:16 with its emphasis on conscious belief in Christ ("whosoever believes") becomes a support for the view that it is *always* necessary. But as we have seen one can ask whether the text *requires* belief for any or all people to be saved whether they hear it or not, or only acknowledges the necessary response for those who *actually* hear the gospel. We have already considered that John 3:17 seems on the face of it to preclude that condemnation is in any way the intent of the gospel and perhaps also an indication that condemnation is not its main result. The universal intent to not condemn, but to save, could not be emphasized more strongly:

> 18Whoever believes in him is not condemned, but whoever does not believe is condemned already, because he has not believed in the name of the only Son of God.

I say "strongly" because this text introduces the *surprising* news of condemnation, that could not have been more clearly precluded in the texts before it. How this condemnation relates to the gospel is the question. The exclusivists make several assumptions regarding this text which for them *ironically* and *flimsily* becomes foundationally determinative for all other NT texts linked to "condemnation." The exclusivists explicitly and blatantly contradict the gospel which says that God was, in Christ removing the very ground of the condemnation of all humanity by,

> ". . . reconciling the world to himself, not counting their trespasses against them" (2 Cor. 5:19).

So, one could rightly ask, "How could God's *declaration of universal reconciliation,* that is the message of the gospel to be proclaimed, become transmogrified, into a message of near universal condemnation for the multitudes of all time who never heard the gospel?" It was done by exclusivists mistakenly believing that John's "whoever does not believe is condemned already, because he has not believed in the name of the only Son of God" is speaking about people *irrespective* of their having heard the gospel or not. And the logic then requires that the "condemned already" even *precedes* hearing and rejecting the gospel, making null and void the gospel's declaration that the condemnation of all was *already* and *universally* taken away *in Christ*. But the phrase "already" in John 3:18 simply indicates *when* some are "condemned." People who have *now* consciously rejected the gospel of God's non-condemnation, are *"already i.e., at the present time,* condemned." It signifies being condemned "ahead of time" just as in John's "realized eschatology," eternal life is received "ahead of time."[11] It is not about people remaining condemned apart from even hearing the gospel. But contrary to this, in what seems to be an example of the mistake, Gerald L. Borchert writes:

> People without Christ are by their basic commitments oriented actively to sin. Accordingly, the Johannine term "reject" or disobey (apeitho) here is operative for the whole human race. Something positive therefore needed to be done to reverse the sinful way of humanity. The means God provided to overcome the existing state of condemnation is for people to believe the Son. Failure to do so is not to become condemned; it is to continue in condemnation.[12]

If the gospel is that God was "reconciling the world to himself, not counting their trespasses against them" as Paul says, then Borchert's interpretation of John 3:18, wherein all of humanity is still condemned before God, is simply a denial of Paul's gospel. The next words of John reveal implied historical sequence that this interpretation misses, and therefore posits that though Christ's atonement has been made, it has actually done nothing. It has left all of humanity condemned beforehand, and apart from, hearing the gospel.

> **19**And this is the judgment: the light has come into the world, and people loved the darkness rather than the light because their works were evil.

John had already shown in his Gospel that "the true light, which gives light to everyone, was coming into the world" (1:9). According to John this "light" was the eternal *logos*, translated "word," in whom "was

---

11. See Carson, *John*, 97–98.

12. Borchert, *John*, 195. Borchert demonstrates the "theological" move wherein a simple time designation indicating when some are condemned in reaction to their hearing the gospel becomes a systematic theology positing that all of humanity, condemned *before* the gospel event, remain so *after* it, *even if they never hear it or consciously reject it.* This seems to be a reading into the text what a theological system requires than reading out of the text its simple meaning.

life," the life which "was the light of men." So, the light coming into the world was not his "first" appearance but had already and always been the light of all humankind. In John 3:19 then, we see that light coming into the world in a different way, as flesh. The logos/light "became flesh and dwelt among us" (1:14). So, the judgment John is speaking of in 3:19 *follows* the fleshly appearance of the light, since "people loved the darkness rather than the light." This simply repeats what John had previously narrated in 1:9–13 about the coming of Jesus the logos/light to the world and Israel:

> [9]The true light, which gives light to everyone, was coming into the world. [10]He was in the world, and the world was made through him, yet the world did not know him. [11]He came to his own, and his own people did not receive him. [12]But to all who did receive him, who believed in his name, he gave the right to become children of God, [13]who were born, not of blood nor of the will of the flesh nor of the will of man, but of God.

This seems to clearly indicate that John 3:16–21 is parallel with John 1:9–13. This also means that in John 3 the encounter with Christ *and his grace* by segments of humanity resulted in the rejection of God's grace in Christ by some or many thereby bringing about a *new* condemnation. But John also shows that not all rejected Christ, but instead believed and received the reconciliation and salvation God had *already* won for them. Before Christ came, John seems to clearly imply that there was also rejection of the logos/light when he writes that "the light shines in the darkness, and the darkness has not overcome it" (John 1:5). But this does not necessarily imply a universal rejection of the logos/light just as when the logos/light became flesh and was received by some.

> [20]For everyone who does wicked things hates the light and does not come to the light, lest his works should be exposed. [21]But whoever does what is true comes to the light, so that it may be clearly seen that his works have been carried out in God."

These two texts reveal something of the inner dynamics of rejection or response to Jesus the enfleshed light. Those rejecting Jesus hate the light because he exposes their works. Those receiving Christ are said to be "doing the truth" by allowing themselves to be exposed by the light, and whose "works" of response are said to be "carried out in God." It is interesting that their response itself is "in God"—fully in congruence with what we saw in Chapter 4 when we discussed the view of Torrance that the human response is provided in the person and work of Christ. In other words, those responding did so "in Christ." In the exclusivist view, the response is what *causes* one to become "in Christ" which is out of sync not only with Torrance, but with John 3:21 and the gospel itself as *finished* apart from any human response.

We might also point out that just as some positively responded after Christ the logos/light became flesh, there may be no good reason to reject the view that some could positively respond to the logos/light of Christ, before Christ came. In this sense the logos/light could provide sufficient "revelation" to respond to the Christ to come, just as Israelites responded to the logos/light before Christ came. In other words, John may be revealing that the logos/light of Christ is all of one, since the triune God has been actively seeking to save that which was lost from the beginning of humankind. The exclusivist view seems to unbiblically restrict the triune God who works within all of history with what seems in that sense an *ahistorical* existential gospel that restricts the efficacy of the gospel event to human knowledge of Jesus, when the reality is of an eternal indivisible logos/Christ/Spirit soteriology.

So, at this point we have hopefully sufficiently considered the context of the "exclusivist" Gospel of John and seen the possibility of inclusivism instead. What we will now try do is expand the context of the gospel of Christ as revealed in the NT so that it is rightly seen as the narrative of the known "cure" against the larger backdrop of the hidden "unknown" cure of the same triune God who certainly didn't begin his salvific work at the time of the historical Christ. When we do this, we may see that the answer to the question of the fate of those who never hear is not their certain death in sin, but the hope of the salvation of some or possibly many based upon the universal possibility of response *to the "unknown"* person and work of the triune God. We will seek to further expand and explain this context, filling it in with some of these "hidden" salvific ways of the God who *so loved the world* that we probably ought not expect anything less.

At the same time, we may need to narrate something we alluded to before when we said that the exclusivist view may have erred mostly by believing that God revealed his plan for "others" *very simply*—basically with a "proof text system." But the answer is to be found in the broader and more "organic" harmony of God's gospel plan, and a theological instinct, a hermeneutic to follow what would most plausibly cohere with that revealed harmony. Therefore, we need to consider the nature of

God's *general* salvific purposes, *apart* from the historical particularities of the main scriptural focus upon Israel, the historical Christ, and the church. We have already seen that Jesus, the enfleshed logos/light was active as the logos/light from the beginning of creation. As we said a bit earlier, this means that God's purposes in Christ are "all of one" and should not be separated through unbiblical thinking about God's relation to the world. The NT certainly emphasizes that the revelation of Christ is greater than God's revelation that came before, but does that mean that the pre-Christian light was not sufficient for salvation? We have already mentioned that Israel had sufficient salvific light. What may be helpful to begin to unravel these questions is to first consider how Paul viewed the history of Israel in the light of Christ who was *active* but not known.

1 Corinthians 10:1–4

Paul seemed to adopt the interpretive method Jesus "outlined" for several disciples on the road to Emmaus following his resurrection (Luke 24:25–27). This is evident when Paul in his letter to the Corinthians says,

> For I do not want you to be unaware, brothers, that our fathers were all under the cloud, and all passed through the sea, and all were baptized into Moses in the cloud and in the sea, and all ate the same spiritual food, and all drank the same spiritual drink. For they drank from the spiritual Rock that followed them, and the Rock was Christ.

Paul continues on to apply the experience of Israel with Christ to the Christians in Corinth, exhorting them to not "put Christ to the test" as Israel did (1 Cor 10:9). The point is that Paul saw Christ as "spiritually" active with Israel before he became historically incarnate. Gospel commentators have increasingly seen that the gospels present Jesus Christ as the organic fulfillment of God seen in relation to Israel in the OT. Thus, the Gospel of Mark is spoken of as an "enacted Christology" in which the actions more than the words of Jesus portray his fulfillment of the role of Yahweh, although the Gospel of John brings Jesus's words to more explicitly support this fulfillment Christology.[13] The difficulty with this is that it simply does not easily fall into our "scientific" notions of space and time. But Colin Gunton explains why our views "that in effect remain

---

13. See Garland, *A Theology*, 261–316; Borchert, *John*, 61–63; Carson, *John*, 98.

imprisoned in ideologies that make our space and time absolute" need to be overcome and re-conceptualized through the gospel by saying,

> By contrast, if we are to achieve a positive Christology that does not fall prey to the absolutism of time or eternity, we must hold firmly to the bipolarity of the New Testament's approach: that this life is both temporal and yet is the place where the eternal is present . . . What happens with Jesus of Nazareth is first of all to be understood as the good news of the movement into time of the eternal.[14]

Allen explains this typological relationship between the OT and NT scriptures saying,

> For example, Matthew shows the correspondence between Jesus and the Jewish people: Jesus, after his baptism, is tempted in the wilderness for forty days and nights, as the Jews, after they were baptized by passing through the Red Sea, were tempted in the wilderness for forty years . . . Such a reading of the Old Testament assumes that throughout biblical history God has been acting for human redemption, showing only in part what was to come in Christ. It assumes a divine sovereignty over history, so that people, events, and writings have a significance beyond what they were thought to have at earlier times.[15]

But we need to try to broaden this picture some, since so far, we have mostly drawn upon the OT Scriptures relating to Israel. Gunton helps expand our view with a bigger picture of God's work in relation to creation.

> The logic of divine love becoming present in Jesus is, indeed, continuous with the saving activity of God elsewhere. That should not, however, be identified with the cosmic process in general, but with the way in which in the past God has freely related himself to the created order.[16]

Lest we miss something of vital significance we note that Gunton is contrasting the logos become flesh with the pre-incarnate *activity* of the

---

14. Gunton, *Yesterday and Today*, 127–28. Similarly, philosopher Charles Taylor, writing on a different Christological correspondence says, "The sacrifice of Isaac was seen as a type of the sacrifice of Christ. In this outlook, two events are linked through something outside history, when the symbolical affinity reflects some deeper identity in regard to Divine Providence . . . In spite of the immense temporal gap, there is a sense in which they are simultaneous." As cited in Allen, *Spiritual Theology*, 135.

15. Allen, *Spiritual Theology*, 134, 135.

16. Gunton, *Yesterday and Today*, 127.

logos/light. He emphasizes the free relation of God to the created order, not merely some abstract identification of God with the cosmic order. This is necessary because we moderns have adopted a Deistic universe where God's Spirit is for the most part thought of as distant and impersonal. B. B. Warfield notes the OT perspective is sacramental by writing, "'Whither shall I go,' asks the Psalmist, 'from thy Spirit? or whither shall I flee from thy presence' (Ps. cxxxix.7)?" and concerning the Spirit says,

> In the very phraseology of Genesis i.2, for example, the moving Spirit is kept separate from the matter to which He gives movement; He *broods over* rather than is merged in the waste of waters; He acts upon them and cannot be confounded with them as but another name for their own blind surging. So, in the 104th Psalm (verses 29, 30) the creative Spirit is *sent forth* by God and is not merely an alternative name for the unconscious life-ground of nature. it is a thing which is *given* by God and so produces life (Isa. xlii. 5). Though penetrating all things (Ps. cxxxix. 7) and the immanent source of all life activities (Ps. civ. 30), it is nevertheless always the *personal* cause of physical, psychical and ethical activities.[17]

Warfield helps provide more definition to the activities of the triune God before the incarnation of Christ and apart from Israel in what is usually called by theologians "general revelation" but might better be called "Spirit revelation." Warfield was of course no "Dispensationalist" that sees little or no "continuity" between God's redemptive eras, as demonstrated by his observations of the Spirit in the OT.[18] And it may be that exclusivism is overly dispensational in regard to the agency of the Spirit before Christ came in the flesh. In his discussion of the "new dispensation" as "the dispensation of the Spirit" and Jesus's promise and giving of the Spirit, Warfield writes that,

> It cannot be meant that the Spirit was not active in the old dispensation. We have already seen that the New Testament writers themselves represent Him to have been active in the old dispensation in all varieties of activity with which He is active in the new ... The old dispensation was a preparatory one and must be conceived as such. What spiritual blessings came to it were by way of prelibation. They were many and various, The Spirit worked in Providence no less universally then than

---

17. Warfield, *Biblical*, 136–37.
18. Feinberg, *Continuity and Discontinuity*.

now. He abode in the Church not less really then than now. He wrought in the hearts of God's people not less prevalently then than now. All the good that was in the world was then as now due to Him.[19]

Thus, Vos writes that "Christ is the *core* of the heavenly, spiritual world. Therefore, a *real contact* existed between that world and the Old Testament house. The Old Testament house was therefore also in vital contact with the heavenly, spiritual reality."[20]

The things we have considered thus far ought to provide an adequate basis in God's presence for salvific activity from the beginning of creation. What we must now do is turn to a consideration of the nature and efficacy of that saving activity. For most exclusivists will at the least grant that God's universal activity as narrated in the OT had always intended salvation, if only humans would respond. The only, and quite large caveat that exclusivists posit, is that apart from the *special revelation* of Christ, humankind *universally* thwarts God's intent. Of course, we have already seen that some of John's teaching of the pre-incarnate logos mitigates against this universal rejection. The problem and origin of the caveat is that Paul seemed to state the opposite when he wrote of God's universal pre-incarnate revelation to humankind.

Romans 1:18–21

For the wrath of God is revealed from heaven against all ungodliness and unrighteousness of men, who by their unrighteousness suppress the truth. For what can be known about God is plain to them, because God has shown it to them. For his invisible attributes, namely, his eternal power and divine nature, have been clearly perceived, ever since the creation of the world, in the things that have been made. So, they are without excuse. For although they knew God, they did not honor him as God or

---

19. Warfield, *Biblical*, 154–55. In a footnote Warfield writes, "Smeaton (The Holy Spirit, 49) comments on John vii.37 *sq.* thus: 'But the apostle adds that "the spirit was not yet" because Christ's glorification had not yet arrived. He does not mean that the Spirit did not yet exist—for all Scripture attests His eternal preexistence—nor that His regenerate efficacy was still unknown—for countless millions had been regenerated by His power since the first promise in Eden—but these operations of the Spirit had been but an anticipation of the atoning gift of Christ rather than a giving. The apostle speaks comparatively, not absolutely."

20. Vos, *Epistle to the Hebrews*, 67.

give thanks to him, but they became futile in their thinking, and
their foolish hearts were darkened.

It seems that Paul's universal statement of humankind's rejection of God's natural revelation in creation is contradictory to John's universal statement of humankind's reception of the light of the logos. But is this really the case? We note two possible answers to this question.

First, Paul and John may be speaking of somewhat different revelations, with the "perceived" creational revelation perhaps externally oriented but the "logos" revelation perhaps internally so. Thus, creation is most likely the external medium through which the internal revelation of *God* comes to the souls of humans.[21] In other words, the external revelation of creation reveals God *perceptually* as the external creator of the world, but the internal revelation of the logos reveals God *spiritually* as the internal "mover" of the soul. Thus, Paul is not necessarily contradicting John as far as some manner of revelation to a sensical or spiritual faculty of humans is concerned. But he still seems to be contradicting John in regard to revelation adequate to the *volitional* faculty which can induce response, or in Paul's thought—*rejection*—of the revelation.

Second, Paul and John may in fact be in agreement regarding the reception, but how so, remains our question. Based on Romans 1:18–21, the exclusivist view holds that there is indeed universal revelation, along with universal rejection of God's saving intent. So also, John 1 also implies universal but universally non-saving revelation apart from the explicit gospel. The problem with this view is that John seems to say otherwise as we saw earlier, and Paul himself seems to admit the possibility of a positive response in Romans 2.[22]

> [6]He will render to each one according to his works: [7]to those who by patience in well-doing seek for glory and honor and immortality, he will give eternal life . . . [13]For it is not the hearers of the law who are righteous before God, but the doers of the

---

21. This is the view proposed and defended by Johnston that general revelation is "not about that which can be known about God from the divine 'footprint' left by God at creation" but about "those divine encounters that many witness to having only occasionally, but significantly, in their lives." Johnston, *Wider Presence*, 120–21.

22. C. Stephen Evans, under a heading "Achieving an Absolute Relation to What is Absolute," presents his (and Kierkegaard's) belief that "the person who recognizes the absolute character of 'living well' in the Socratic sense is someone who has an awareness of the divine, even if the person does not realize this" in a way that does not mention Romans 2 but seems to breath it's truth, especially as Evans goes on to discuss the "reward" of "eternal happiness." Evans, *Kierkegaard and Spirituality*, 68–73.

law who will be justified. **14**For when Gentiles, who do not have the law, by nature do what the law requires, they are a law to themselves, even though they do not have the law. **15**They show that the work of the law is written on their hearts, while their conscience also bears witness, and their conflicting thoughts accuse or even excuse them **16**on that day when, according to my gospel, God judges the secrets of men by Christ Jesus (Romans 2:6–7, 13–16).

There are many views of these statements of Paul in regard to what they mean and how they relate to Paul's statements in Romans 1. The most common exclusivist interpretations are that Romans 2 speaks of a "hypothetical" possibility that *never* becomes reality, or that Paul has in mind Gentile Christians who have responded to the explicit gospel. The problem is that these interpretations are themselves hypothetical, lacking evidence of demonstration. Paul simply didn't "flesh out" what exactly he had in mind regarding these people positively responding to God.

There may be a solution though, which we propose through a theoretical statement which can be supported by a concrete historical example from Paul. The theorem is this: Paul's speech in Romans 1 of universal human suppression of "natural revelation" reveals a universally subsidiary part of the human/divine interactive reality but not the whole of that reality. In other words, humans do universally and "naturally" suppress the revelation of God, but some do not continually persist in rejecting such revelation and therefore suppression is not the final word on that interaction since many do eventually respond positively. In fact, this pattern of rejection/reception would hold for the post-Christ historical situation also, as is evidenced by the majority of the NT's anecdotal evidence wherein many or most "disciples" come to follow Christ through a suppression/reception pattern. This pattern of suppression/reception, seems the dominant pattern of the entire human/divine encounter portrayed in all the Scriptures.

This means that Paul, along with other Scriptures, present a "dialectic" wherein two seemingly contradictory truths are both presented as parts of the whole. Paul and the Scriptures therefore speak of humans as universally *not* seeking God, while also speaking of many humans as seeking God. For the non-seeking side, we see Paul affirming the words of the Psalmist:

> As it is written: 'None is righteous, no, not one; no one understands; no one seeks for God. All have turned aside; together they have become worthless; no one does good, not even one'" (Romans 3:10–12).

But as we have just noted above, Paul seems to affirm otherwise in Romans 2: 6–7:

> "*He will render to each one according to his works:* ⁷*to those who by patience in well-doing seek for glory and honor and immortality, he will give eternal life.*"

If there is a dialectic in Scripture regarding these two aspects of human seeking after God apart from the explicit revelation of Christ, it may be helpful to move from that abstract dialectic to a concrete example where perhaps both are seen in relation to each other. We believe we find such an example in the record of Paul's missionary visit to Athens presented by the gospel writer Luke.

Acts 17:16–34.

> ¹⁶*Now while Paul was waiting for them at Athens, his spirit was provoked within him as he saw that the city was full of idols.*

Paul's provocation in reaction to the city's idolatry presupposes that the "general revelation" to humankind is powerful enough to transmit knowledge of the only true God which nevertheless results in suppression and distortion of that knowledge when humans both resist but also conceptualize that knowledge, as Romans 1:18–32 states. This points to what we mentioned above, the suppression/response pattern, albeit with the response yielding "distortion." What may also be necessary to point out is that the distortion factor is a perennial problem even for Christians, if we are to consider the reality of God and that reality as conceptualized by humans. In other words, there is actual contact with the reality of God that coexists with "human-all-to-human" idolatrous conceptions of God.[23] Merold Westphal shockingly confesses this truth

---

23. Contact with, and knowledge of, are two relations to reality. Contact seems to have the preeminence in the reality of human experience and God's grace in Christ has "endorsed" that preeminence. As Michael Polanyi wrote, "we know more than we can tell" through "tacit knowledge" which differs from linguistic knowledge. Polanyi, *The Tacit Dimension*, 4. A hundred years before Polanyi's writings John Henry Newman

when he readily admits that he has possibly or probably "never prayed to God" in a way such that his conception of "God" came near to "capturing"—the reality of God.

> Discussing the hermeneutics of suspicion with students at a Christian college, I once said that I suspected I had never prayed to a God who wasn't an idol. They were horrified, but they began to see my point when I explained that (1) I believed the God who hears my prayers was no idol, but the living God, and (2) that God as I intended, represented, conceived of God was always an imperfect, distorted approximation, not only in relation to God's inherent reality but even in relation to God as we humans ought to think of God. Not only the finitude of our createdness but also the fallenness of our current conditions keeps our God-talk from being the mirror of divine nature.[24]

Westphal's honest, disturbing, but wholly necessary admission reveals the point of Paul's overall argument regarding any and all knowledge of God, both Pagan and Jewish, through general and special revelation: "that every mouth may be stopped and the whole world may be held accountable to God" (see Romans 3:19; 11:32). This understanding of Paul's argument of suppression and distortion properly relativizes the human seeking of God such that the result does not need to be "perfect" to be saving, for if it did, *none* would be saved. This understanding of the limitation of accurate conception of God can also apply to human response to God, to the conceptual precision, or lack thereof, in our language when we speak to and of God. In one of his deepest descriptions of the life in the Spirit, Paul speaks of the "weakness" of knowledge in our speaking to God and declares that "the Spirit himself intercedes for us with groanings too deep for words" (Rom 8:26). This also points toward the fact that any and all human response is not conditioned on the ability or cognitive quality of our response to God, but on Christ's work for us and the Spirit's work in us, just as our repentance and faith in God participates in Christ's incarnate response, as we saw in the unconditionality of the gospel in Chapter 4.

> [17]*So he reasoned in the synagogue with the Jews and the devout persons, and in the marketplace every day with those who*

---

posited much the same idea and called it "illative knowledge." Newman wrote, "the human mind in its present (earthly) state is unequal to its own powers of apprehension; it embraces more than it can master." Harrold, *A Newman Treasury*, 15–16, 119.

24. Westphal, "Theological Anti-Realism," 147.

> *happened to be there.* **18***Some of the Epicurean and Stoic philosophers also conversed with him. And some said, "What does this babbler wish to say?" Others said, "He seems to be a preacher of foreign divinities"—because he was preaching Jesus and the resurrection.* **19***And they took him and brought him to the Areopagus, saying, "May we know what this new teaching is that you are presenting?* **20***For you bring some strange things to our ears. We wish to know therefore what these things mean."* **21***Now all the Athenians and the foreigners who lived there would spend their time in nothing except telling or hearing something new.*

Paul always sought to share the gospel with the Jews and the Gentile "God fearers" in every place he went in the marketplaces and synagogues, but now he had the opportunity to share with the Pagan philosophers in Athens. Luke presents these philosophers as "seekers," but seems to imply that much of their seeking was perhaps due to the novelty of such entertainment. But Paul who "hopes all things" (1 Corinthians 13:7) hoped that perhaps some were more seriously seeking after God and proceeded to probe their religiosity for a potential sincerity therein on the part of some of these Epicureans and Stoics.

> **22***So Paul, standing in the midst of the Areopagus, said: "Men of Athens, I perceive that in every way you are very religious.*

Paul is accommodating to their religiousness, even granting that they are "very" religious. Paul does not denigrate them on this account. This is probably because he recognizes that their "religious" response *is a response*, no matter its distortion, to the one and only God who is universally active and, as Calvin conceived it, is graciously accommodating toward all because of our finitude. And such a recognition serves to Paul not as the *barrier to* witnessing of Christ, but as the *bridge* for the gospel. Paul seems to model what ought to be the approach of all evangelical people toward peoples whether religious or irreligious, assuming that God's general revelation is "operative" in them and that any truth in whatever "construct" they consciously or unconsciously adopt is nonetheless some manner of response to God's truth. This is a different approach than some "evangelicals" take, when they seem to assume that non-Christians have absolutely no truth and that there is no truth in their "religion" or even their "atheism." Paul seems to exemplify a practical adoption of the truth of John's gospel prologue wherein the "life" of the Word/Logos in creation was the "light of men" and "enlightens everyone." It seems that a disbelief in some truth in what pre-Christian Pagans "saw" is a denial of the pre-Christian "activity" of the Logos of God. It is also important to note the NT doctrine of the Logos is not that people could "see" the Logos, so much as that they only see anything truly, to any extent, *by* the Logos which is the reality that alone makes existing things intelligible.[25] Also, through that "sight" some intuited the reality of the Logos which is why John's use of the term would be familiar to many even though John's use is also derived from the OT Scriptures and not merely or even primarily from philosophy.[26]

> [23]*For as I passed along and observed the objects of your worship . . .*

Paul speaks of the "objects of your worship" showing that their religiosity was not merely hypothetical but practical, and "worship" rather than "works" based. This is also something that needs to be recognized and thought through when considering the question of the "response" of non-Christians to what they intuit of God apart from God's scriptural revelations. In his "existential phenomenology of religion," *God, Guilt, and Death,* Merold Westphal demonstrates that "natural" human religion can be universally understood as the dual reaction of both human repulsion and attraction in relation to "the Holy" which becomes formulated into three main types of response according to the basic worldview of the practitioners. These three types of response are based on conceptions of the relation of God to the world and history and therefore also based in humanity's relation to those. Westphal calls them the exilic, mimetic, and covenantal types of religion.[27] What is most interesting is that the human response to God is based on a hope or trust in the grace or mercy of God, as "God" is conceived in relation to the world. Hence "salvation"

---

25. Charlie Starr makes this point in his discussion of a probable allusion to John's Logos in C. S. Lewis: "In trying to describe the God who is love in *The Four Loves*, Lewis notes that any precision we apply to knowing God will be but a 'model or a symbol'—that we can understand the 'ultimate being' only by 'analogies.' And of this he concludes, 'We cannot see light, though by light we can see things.' Lewis is doubtless echoing Scripture. 'The true light that gives light to every man was coming into the world,' and 'in your light we see light.' Lewis twice refers to God as 'Father of Lights' and both times in the context of the reaches of human knowledge." Starr, *Light*, 58–59. On the logos and intelligibility see Tyson, *Returning to Reality*, 93–95.

26. See Carson, *John*, 111–17.

27. See Westphal, *God, Guilt, and Death*, ix. Each signify dramatically different conceptions of the nature of God and the world and their inter-relation. The exclusivist view oversimplifies and thus restricts whether or not covenantal salvation in Christ can savingly reach those in history living under the exilic and mimetic types.

is not trying to "manipulate" God/the world through "merit" but rather intends to become correctly aligned, or responsive, and participate in the way guilt and death are overcome in relation to them.

It seems that Westphal's study reveals that a trust in human "works," as conceived of in Protestant or even Catholic religion, is not the basic practice of all "types" of religion other than their covenantal type of religion, Christianity.[28] The point is that Paul's recognition of their "worship," however distorted, witnesses against the assumption that all "merely" human religion is always based on a merit system of works to achieve salvation. This recognition ought to inform the statement of Peter recorded in Acts 10:34–35: "So Peter opened his mouth and said: *"Truly I understand that God shows no partiality, but in every nation anyone who fears him and does what is right is acceptable to him."* In accord to what we have just proposed, "does what is right" does not indicate a merit-based practice of works but rather the life-response of "faith" to God/the world from the interiority of the person to which God speaks, no matter how faulty the "hearing" or conception.[29] Otherwise we will need to accuse the gospel as itself proclaiming a works-based religion as viable.

> *I found also an altar with this inscription: 'To the unknown god.' What therefore you worship as unknown, this I proclaim to you.* ²⁴*The God who made the world and everything in it, being Lord of heaven and earth, does not live in temples made by man,* ²⁵*nor is he served by human hands, as though he needed anything, since he himself gives to all mankind life and breath and everything.* ²⁶*And he made from one man every nation of mankind to live on all the face of the earth, having determined allotted periods and the boundaries of their dwelling place,* ²⁷*that they should seek God, and perhaps feel their way toward him and find him. Yet he is actually not far from each one of us,* ²⁸*for "In him we live and move and have our being'; as even some of your own poets have said, "'For we are indeed his offspring.'*

---

28. Westphal writes "ambivalence vis-a-vis the Sacred as the *mysterious tremendous at fascinans* is involved in the religious life as such and not just in particular forms of it . . . guilt and death have the importance they do in biblical religion because it is religious and not because it is biblical." Westphal, *God, Guilt, and Death*, 114,

29. The phenomenologist Michel Henry writes, "One does not gain access to life, to one's own life, to that of others, or to that of God, by means of the senses." Henry, *The Word of Christ*, 107. Henry verifies the view of Johnston that "rather than simply conveying new information that is then ignored, general revelation instead involves numinous encounter, one that is often transformational." Johnston, *God's Wider Presence*, 9.

Paul now reveals his positive method of approach to the Pagan philosophers. He not only presupposes that general revelation provides a bridge of connection between Christ and their "faith," he finds an implicit point to explicitly bring Christ into their distorted faith. Paul proclaims to them that their "unknown god" not only points toward Christ but *is* Christ. *What* they worship as unknown, Paul proclaims to them. In his "Confessions" Augustine speaks *to God*, of his relation to him *before* he was converted from the false religion of Manichaeism to true Christianity, demonstrating that the distorted (and unrighteous) views people have of God are indeed distorted views *of God*.

> And how could anything be more proud than to assert, as I did in my incredible folly, that I was by nature what you are? . . . I preferred to think that you were also subject to change rather than I was not what you are.[30]

Our point is merely that Augustine believed that the God he held false views of was indeed God, just as Paul seems to be saying that the Athenian's "unknown god," known in his Manichaean "exilic" type of religion, was indeed the covenantal God, albeit "known" in distortion. This reveals the same principle of contact with God/distortion of God we saw above in Westphal's Christian but idolatrous prayers to God. But note that we are not here implying that such distorted knowledge is "saving," we are merely pointing out the possibility of real contact with God. For Augustine spent over a decade in Manichaeism and only "salved his potentially troubled conscience with these ideas."[31] The salvific nature of any knowledge of God, is not whether one has any contact with God through it but depends on what that contact with God signifies in regard to the response Paul posited as saving in Romans 2:7–8.

It is informative to note that Paul does not follow this explicit connection to the true God who was hidden in their admission of ignorance, "the *unknown* god," with explicit scriptural revelation. Rather, Paul continues to mainly explain this unknown God to them as *already* known through general revelation by speaking of God as the Creator of the world and humankind, the provider and determiner of the parameters

---

30. Westphal, *God, Guilt, and Death*, 181.

31. Westphal, *God, Guilt, and Death*, 182. The "exilic" type of religion posit an essential dualism of physical and spiritual reality that views the world as a place of exile of the human soul. It is thus anti-worldly, in comparison to the creational covenantal religion which affirms the world of history and nature. The mimetic type "affirms the world as nature (but not as history)" See Westphal, 165.

of life for all, and the intended goal of their seeking. He also speaks of God as "intimately" related to all and does so by quoting Greek poet/philosophers to them. The ambivalence of the poetry—*that they should seek God, and perhaps feel their way toward him and find him*—seems to speak more to the real possibility of "finding" God than exclusivist theology has been willing to admit, especially given Paul's mention that God mercifully "overlooked" these past "times of ignorance."[32] That "mercy" for the peoples of the world during these "times of ignorance" probably means that God delayed the still coming judgment. Thus, it seems unwarranted to suppose that such "mercy" meant that all those who lived apart from God's special revelation to Israel would be automatically and universally separated from God in eternity, especially in light of God's stated intent for humankind to "seek" and "*find*" the God who *was* "not far from each one" so that they lived "in him," and whose "offspring" they were. In a sense we see the same problem that is presented in gospel exclusivism when we consider the dialectical statements of God's giving of Christ to universally reconcile all, with those that seem to imply that only those who hear (and positively) respond can be actually reconciled. In essence, in the exclusivist view we have a contradiction between what we seem warranted to expect from the God who "shows no partiality," and texts that seem to say otherwise to those never having the opportunity to hear and respond to God's declared beneficence.[33]

> **29** *Being then God's offspring, we ought not to think that the divine being is like gold or silver or stone, an image formed by the art and imagination of man.* **30** *The times of ignorance God overlooked, but now he commands all people everywhere to repent,* **31** *because he has fixed a day on which he will judge the world in righteousness by a man whom he has appointed; and of this he has given assurance to all by raising him from the dead."* **32** *Now when they heard of the resurrection of the dead, some mocked. But others said, "We will hear you again about this."* **33** *So Paul went*

---

32. See Bruce, *Acts*, 340.

33. In a footnote of his commentary on Acts 10:34 "I realize that God has no favorites," F.F. Bruce seems to show that God's non-partiality is part and parcel of the gospel itself, simply because to think that God would not be impartially (universally) gracious in the opportunity of his salvation is pictorially horrifying to consider. In such cases, God can be viewed as literally refusing to "lift the faces" of those downtrodden that the gospel claims God "so loved." Bruce writes "('respecter of persons,' lit. 'lifter of faces') reflects the Hebrew idiom *nasa panic*, 'lift (someone's) face' and hence 'show favor' or, in a pejorative sense, 'show favoritism.'" Bruce, *Acts*, 211.

out from their midst. **34***But some men joined him and believed, among whom also were Dionysius the Areopagite and a woman named Damaris and others with them.*

Paul says that the philosophers can see what God is like by considering what humankind is like as the image of God, "God's offspring." Paul thus expounds on the "inspired" words of their poet/prophet to show that if humans are God's offspring, then we will mirror the nature of God in contradistinction to other images formed of God through the imaginations of humans. Interestingly, Paul's response to their "images" may have been somewhat passe for these sophisticated Athenian philosophers who distinguished between forms and essences, although it might be appropriate for the probably illiterate Greeks Paul encountered not much earlier in Lystra (Acts 14:8–18). The Athenians may have had less crude views of "the gods" so that the Zeus being referenced in Paul's citation of the Greek poet is quite possibly "the Stoic reinterpretation of Zeus as a life force in Greek philosophy."[34]

Paul's introduction of a day of judgment through an appointed man who God resurrected from the dead and a call to "repentance" in light of such show how he moved to scriptural revelation and the explicit revelation of Christ. At this point it seems that Paul perhaps "lost" most of his audience, but not all as some wanted to hear more and some came to join Paul in believing the gospel of Christ. Paul sets the demand for "all people everywhere to repent" in response to the coming judgment in contrast to the former times when God overlooked humankind's "ignorance," which raises the question whether God's lenient "times of ignorance" can coexist in the present in *places* where people never hear God's "command to repent."[35] In other words, is there any overlap of these two ages so that places where the gospel is not proclaimed are essentially still existing chronologically "before Christ," so to speak.[36] It certainly seems

---

34. See Johnston, *God's Wider Presence*, 111–16.

35. "It is important to note that Christians often imagine now as a time of grace compared to the old covenant's *past* time of justice . . . Now is still the time of mercy, but judgment is coming, before which all humans should tremble." Byassee, *Psalms*, 3.

36. Brunner writes, "History, in the proper strict sense of the word, has only existed since, and by means of, Jesus Christ. Only since He came has human time become time of decision, in the full grave sense of the word, because only since He came is there the possibility of deciding in view of the challenge to decision with which we are confronted . . . With Jesus Christ, wherever His Word, or the news about Him, has come, directly or indirectly, there a new consciousness of existence has begun, both for

puzzling that God's former leniency in the times of ignorance would be removed where such ignorance continues, by no fault of their own, *after* Christ came for the salvation of all humankind. At any rate, the Athenian philosophers were then duly *updated* in regard to God's "new" arrangement, and therefore it may be unwarranted to hold that this command, regarding the update, is "enforced" where the memo is yet to be given. Paul's memo/proclamation, of the relation of the past "times of ignorance God overlooked" to the coming fixed "day on which he will judge the world in righteousness," is something we will consider below in our main proposal. Paul seems to provide an essential bridge connecting all the eras of human history, hinting at some integral commonality in all human existence: before Christ came, at the present, and in the future, in the "man he has appointed . . . by raising him from the dead."

We have considered to some depth several important texts for what they may contribute toward an inclusivist understanding of the gospel. So now we will present our prospective theology of inclusivism which we call "The Existence-Revelation of Christ."

A Theology of Inclusivism: "The Existence-Revelation of Christ"

The term "existence-revelation" is similar to Soren Kierkegaard's term "existence communication" which he coined to describe what the gospel actually is, namely the communication from God to humans of a certain "existence" which is otherwise more abstractly called "salvation." For the bare term, *salvation*, is easily domesticated as a *possession* and accommodated to common cultural "gospels" that serve man's consumerism and will to power rather nicely. Thus, to Kierkegaard, this form, content, and manner were encapsulated in Christ himself, the God-man who had entered human existence for the purpose of communicating (bringing) a new type of existence to humanity. Christopher Ben Simpson clarifies that,

> Kierkegaard's theological method serves to define Christian existence. By 'definition' we here mean the setting forth of the virtues, qualities and activities that define Christian existence. It is this movement that is present in Kierkegaard's intent to introduce Christianity not as a doctrine but as an

---

believers and unbelievers." Brunner, *Man in Revolt*, 456–57.

'existence-communication' (CUP 383). The end goal of the 'existence-communication' is to elicit a certain kind of existence.[37]

Kierkegaard's intent was to combat the cheap grace of Christianity as doctrine. This *gospel of correct doctrine* is an important ingredient to our "existence-revelation" term and project here, since exclusivism is based in restricting the person and work of Christ to the times and places where the "doctrine" of Christ is revealed. We hold that the communication of an existence related to the person and work of Christ should not be so restricted and aim to show that our prospective "theology" is also based in existence itself—unrestricted by the "doctrine" of Christ—but rather and nevertheless "revealed" by the person and work of Christ. Hence our term, "existence-revelation," or in other words, *the revelation of human existence that was made possible through the incarnate person and work of Christ*. We hold that this may provide the answer needed: the interpretation of *all* human life in relation to God, regardless of whether the "doctrine" of Christ has been made known. For the substance of Christ's person and work for all human existence *always precedes* any historical "arrival" of the doctrine and is thus *already* "there," *whether or not* the doctrine "follows," because of the unconditional gospel. For it must be stressed that because of the unconditional gospel, "we have an obligation to see the world differently . . . as saved in principle."[38] And therefore, that obligation requires the application of the "existence-revelation" of Christ, no matter whether this may seem "reckless" or "heretical." Wilson writes,

> Just as grace does not mean antinomianism, but will provoke charges of antinomianism, so also an understanding of the incarnation as *God's reckless grace to the whole universe* will provoke charges of some heresy or other. And perhaps some will veer off into those heresies, but it cannot be unorthodox to say that our orthodoxy has been too small and that we need a whole lot more of it.[39]

Thus, we hope to somewhat expand the border of orthodoxy *against* the boundary of heresy, even if it has been thought "orthodox," as an application of the existence-revelation of Christ, for God's reckless grace seems to warrant the risk.

---

37. Simpson, *The Truth is the Way*, 17. CUP signifies Kierkegaard's "Concluding Unscientific Postscript."

38. Wilson, *Against the Church*, 109.

39. Wilson, *Against the Church*, 64–65.

Quite possibly the problem that has largely prevented a recognition of Christ's "existence-revelation" is because the Scriptures mainly reveal and narrate the *explicit* "history of redemption" rather than the *implicit* nature of human existence. But this concentration on the explicit does not mean that the implicit does not exist or is not implied even in the Scriptures. One example of this is the book of Proverbs which according to Roland Murphy presents a "kerygma of life" rather than the "usual" kerygma as the proclamation of God's saving acts in redemptive history.[40] Robert Johnston writes,

> As I have begun to reread the Bible with my experience of general revelation as my "spectacles," new texts have come to life. A beginning point has been the Wisdom literature of the Old Testament. Here the focus is reflection on the goodness of created life, not the narration of the story of salvation.[41]

Thus, the Scriptures can and will augment such a project, and help one interpret the "kerygma of life" from the viewpoint of the gospel movement of God. Jason Byassee captures the essence of our view in this brief excerpt that serves as a preview of the notion of the "existence revelation of Christ." Exhibiting the revelatory movement from Scripture to life that parallels this *existence- revelation*, Byassee writes,

> The motion of Christological exegesis is from befuddlement ("this passage makes no sense") to slow illumination ("wait, I think I see the contours of God in Christ even here') to delight ("wow, the Lord was in this place and we didn't know it!"). This is the same motion of every sermon, of every soul, of every particle of the created universe: We expect initially that we are on our own, without meaning and lost. We find that, in fact, God has already come close, even here.[42]

We believe that Christ presents himself as the key to interpreting the implicit nature of human existence and thus to some extent at least exegetes the details of how the Logos/Word was *and is* "the life" and "the light of men" (John 1:4) and whether that life-reality of Christ in all human life can lead to salvation. Though we will present our proposal on this interpretive key as a sort of *phenomenology of life* we admit that this

---

40. See Murphy, "The Kerygma." 1, 3–14.

41. Johnston, *God's Wider Presence*, 71. (See above under #4 on reading with new spectacles.)

42. Jason Byassee, *Psalms 101–150*, xxii.

"existence-revelation of Christ" largely remains "the undiscovered country" due to the proper and natural historical predominance of Christian theology upon explicit "redemptive history."[43] But that is the reason that the gospel stewards, including this author, in regard to a theology of inclusivism, are still only at the beginning.[44]

It seems that the apparent divide between the redemptive-historical trajectory that necessarily emphasizes *outward particularity* (and exclusivity) and the existence-revelation of Christ that illuminates *inner spirituality* (and inclusivity) comes to this:

1. The *redemptive-historical* trajectory is *the explicit story* of the coming of God's *historical* kingdom.

2. The "redemptive-creational" trajectory is *the implicit story* which constantly runs "beneath the lines" of the "historical" story.

But in Christ's gospel, the implicit story became more fully and historically illuminated by giving definition through Christ, the implicit "logos" and "mystery" of human existence, to provide invaluable light on the fate of the unevangelized, under-evangelized and over-evangelized masses of humanity regardless of their relation to the "visible" kingdom.[45]

---

43. It seems that Michel Henry's *phenomenology* of the words of Christ is based in this *existence-revelation of Christ*, though we cannot here even begin to trace the similarities: "For the human being, belonging to the truth means to be born of Life, or the only Life that exists: the all-powerful Life which engenders itself. It is the Son of this unique Life who can alone give life: 'You have only one Father.' Because life is self-revelation, it is Truth, the original and absolute Truth, in relation to which any other truth is merely secondary. Because they are sons of this Life which is Truth, human beings belong to the Truth." Michel Henry, *The Words of Christ*, 116.

44. This certainly also applies to even beginning to adequately consider Christian practice that ought to follow upon the descriptive revelation of life that this *existence-revelation of Christ* posits. Merold Westphal's presents the goal of his voluminous phenomenological hermeneutics: "The time has come for understanding the world to become the guide for changing it." Cited in Sands, *Reasoning from Faith*, 163.

45. By speaking of these two explicit and implicit stories, we don't mean that the explicit one deals mostly with humanity at large while the implicit one only deals with individuals "within" that story. For the "existence-revelation of Christ" is not only about how Christ relates to individuals but is also how Christ relates to humanity apart from the explicit knowledge of the kingdom. We are only applying the "existence-revelation of Christ" to individuals for the sake of the question of inclusivism. In her book on Simone Weil's view of "force," E. Jane Doering relates that Weil believed that she had discovered "a message of pure gold for humankind" and demonstrates in her book on Weil that her views didn't merely posit the possibility of individuals implicitly responding to the hidden Christ, but also that societies are also engaged in the same

In other words, there is an "above the surface" story line narrated in the Bible, along with an "under the surface" un-narrated story line, and the final kingdom is the only place where those two stories, and the fates of all those living in relation to one or the other or both, *visibly* come together. This coming together can also be considered as the ultimate historical meeting of the universal *extra*-incarnate work of Christ (or the triune God) and the incarnate work of Christ, which is the *basis* of God's *final* judgment at the end that Paul preached in Acts 17:30–31. These "works" of Christ find their ultimate culmination in what already calls for the repentance of all who hear, and the judgment of all whether hearing or not, because of the coming of the existence-revelation of Christ that defines all human existence of all times and places. Willie James Jennings writes,

> This way of repentance invites peoples and nations to see a future that is moving irrevocably toward this new human, the judge of the living and the dead.[46]

A biblical-theological view would see this as the coming of God's visible and historical kingdom against the backdrop of God's eternal and universal kingship. One could also consider these two revelations as the concrete linear narrative of existence and the abstract non-linear reality of existence. This is the thesis we will present, and this also indicates the challenge to discern the explicit and implicit, and the exclusive and inclusive, in God's truly universal story that encompasses both. For both stories *must* somehow work together in the warp and woof of God's universal tapestry whereby all things are woven together in Christ.

It may be that a discovery of the underlying narrative may in fact be more a rediscovery, because it seems that the nascent early church was required by history to more fully consider the place of the gospel in

---

struggle and possibility. Doering writes that "Because knowledge of the supernatural is transmitted through all the great traditional religions and their cultures, concern for the well-being of one's neighbor means that everyone has the obligation to preserve these civilizations from annihilation." Doering, *Simone Weil*, 12. Eric O. Springsted also discusses that Weil's thought was not merely about a problematic "inward turn" of individualism but is rather that the "one who dwells in the inner is the one who has overcome the distinction . . . Her 'spiritual knowledge' is the way she looks at the world as a whole. This does not mean that the knowledge of God is nothing more than a way of looking at the world; but it does mean that it is linked and inseparable from it. Looking at the world attentively and wisely, one participates in God. That is why it is linked and inseparable." Springsted, "I Dreamed I Saw St. Augustine," 223.

46. Jennings, *Acts*, 178.

relation to the previous religious and philosophical forms of existence in the Greco-Roman world where the Son arrived, in the fullness of time (Gal 4:4). But that task may have waned as Christianity became established and largely defined itself apart from relation to others and the "life-existence" of humanity "outside" it. In a sense then, modern *pluralism* may well be God's means for pressing the gospel's stewards to plumb the line of Christ's "existence-revelation" to the redemptive historical narrative that they could not bear before Christ's resurrection, and perhaps fell from after Christendom became established.

The Basis of the Existence-Revelation of Christ

The basis of this revelation in and by Christ is largely based on two key texts, Colossians 1:15–20 and Luke 24:27. We say revelation "in and by Christ" because Christ revealed himself *as the content* of the revelation as Colossians 1 notes; and Christ revealed himself as *the key* for seeing and interpreting the revelation as Luke 24 notes. We look first at the *existence* part of "existence-revelation." Colossians 1:15–20 reads as follows:

> [15]He is the image of the invisible God, the firstborn of all creation. [16]For by him all things were created, in heaven and on earth, visible and invisible, whether thrones or dominions or rulers or authorities—all things were created through him and for him. [17]And he is before all things, and in him all things hold together. [18]And he is the head of the body, the church. He is the beginning, the firstborn from the dead, that in everything he might be preeminent. [19]For in him all the fullness of God was pleased to dwell, [20]and through him to reconcile to himself all things, whether on earth or in heaven, making peace by the blood of his cross.

From Paul's summary statement of Christ, we will only touch on several things. Paul claims that Christ is the center of all God's creative and redemptive purposes. For the contours of this "theology" we emphasize that Christ is the center of "new creation"—of God's "reconciling all things" to himself through Christ. We could paraphrase this according to the theology we are presenting to say that Christ is *and always was* the significance of human existence, the center that in time became explicitly known in the incarnate person of Christ. We now look at the *revelation* part of "existence-revelation." Luke 24:27 reads as follows:

> ²⁷And beginning with Moses and all the Prophets, he interpreted to them in all the Scriptures the things concerning himself.

At this point we need to consider the full significance of what "the things concerning himself" in all the Scriptures means. For this does not merely mean that Christ is the key to "all the Scriptures" although it does not mean less than that. What it signifies is much more than that, because the entire scriptural narration from creation to redemption "concerns himself" as Colossians claims, and as we saw earlier in 1 Cor 10:1–4. And the Scriptures do not testify to themselves as mere abstract truth, as if to say that a "message" about Christ is simply *in* all the Scriptures. Rather Colossians and Luke seem to testify of Christ as their very substance. In other words, the Scriptures testify not of life "containing" Christ in some manner, though again we don't deny that, but of life being in Christ because he is the very center of all that was narrated in the scriptures. Taking this one step further, the scriptural narrative was not to merely reveal "abstract" knowledge of certain historical events, but about the very nature of existence that the scriptural history tells the story of. This means that Christ is the very center of the life that was narrated through all the Scriptures. If we fail to see this, we can fall to thinking that the significance of Christ is limited to a specific *way* of life, perhaps only applicable to the specific covenantal relation of God to the covenant people, since the Scriptures for the most part narrate *this* relation. But Colossians shows Christ as the center of *all* human life and existence, and only in Christ can such life "consist," (KJV) or "hold together" (ESV). We hold that this does not only point to the *mechanics* of the cosmos as though Christ is the glue holding all things together, but as also pointing to the *meaning* of the cosmos, holding together the ultimate meaning of existence. One commentator writes that,

> *In him all things hold together,* literally, "stand together," cohere . . . he imposes upon all things their pattern and inner coherence, and so their meaning. In the last resort, it is the presence of Christ in history that makes the universe intelligible.[47]

This seems to certainly demonstrate that Christ was and is the logos continually "holding all things together" and therefore providing *intelligibility* and "light" to all humankind as John's gospel prologue says in

---

47. White, "Colossians," 227. See Newbigin on "Christ as the clue to history" in Weston, *Missionary Theologian*, 54–65.

1:1–18.⁴⁸ Thus it seems that Christ's own interpretation of himself as the key to the ultimate meaning of all the Scriptures is required by Colossians to signify that Christ is the exegetical key of all human existence. This does not mean that the historical coming into the world of the logos made flesh was not as the sunrise is to the previous darkness of night, for it was after all, Christ who revealed the significance of all things. But it does mean that the logos was and remains always already there in the world, giving the light of *some* intelligibility and the warmth of *some* meaning, in coherence to Christ, though not yet fully known apart from Christ's existence-revelation.⁴⁹ We know that if the darkness of night signified the complete absence of the sun, then life would not exist on the earth. Similarly, the darkness of the world before the sun of Christ arose, so to speak, did not prevent Christ from holding all things together. Therefore, any and all true meaning, any and all true light of men, cohered in Christ the center, although the name of the center was unknown by title, and the significance was not yet explicitly revealed.

Stated more positively, there already was significance and implicit revelation in all of existence. And those provide the basis for the "usage" of the existence-revelation of Christ for the question of inclusivism. For the "light" was known by the character and structure of creation, and historically/narratively speaking, those creational qualities *preceded* their naming, just as the natural qualities of many biblical characters *preceded* their naming.

Hopefully we have adequately conveyed the proposal that the nature and substance of life for all humans of all times and places "consists" in Christ the center of all existence, "in whom we live and move and have our being." But that existence can only be rightfully interpreted through Christ the *hermeneutical* key since Christ is eternally the center not only of redemption but of creation.⁵⁰ Dietrich Bonhoeffer wrote powerfully of Christ the center and all his theological understanding of human life and reality itself was based upon it.

48. Colin J. D. Greene says that "Nowhere are the cosmic dimensions of Christology stated more unequivocally than in the christological hymn of Colossians 1:15–20. Greene, *Christology*, 32–33.

49. See Dembski, *End of the Beginning*, 96–106, who writes: "All the information in the universe is, in the end, mediated through the divine *Logos*, who is before all things and by whom all things consist (Col 1:17).

50. The Greek word translated as Jesus "interpreted" (to them) in Luke 24:27 is the word "hermeneuo" which can obviously be seen as transliterated into the English "hermeneutic," and signifies interpretation.

> There are not two realities, but *only one reality,* and that is God's reality in Christ in the reality of the world. Partaking in Christ, we stand at the same time in the reality of God and in the reality of the world. The reality of Christ embraces the reality of the world in itself. The world has no reality of its own independent of God's revelation in Christ . . . there are not two realms, but only *the one realm of the Christ-reality* . . . in which the reality of God and the reality of the world are united . . . the whole reality of the world has already been drawn into and is held together in Christ. History moves only from this center and toward this center.[51]

Commenting on Ephesians 1:10 and also on Bonhoeffer's words just noted, Barry Harvey adds that,

> God identifies the risen Christ as the center of all things, the one in whom all things in heaven and earth are to be gathered up. The movement of time—the complex rhythms, harmonies, and recapitulations of history—can therefore be comprehended only in relation to this center, from which all things have their being, and toward which all things tend.[52]

William Lynch discusses Christ as the new revelation of the "old" creation in a way that helps us to grasp what is the all-important point of this conception of Christ as the "existence-revelation" of all human existence, saying,

> For Christ, we have said, is not another item of the first creation, to be used as any other item by the old imagination. The real point is ever so much more crucial. For he has subverted the whole order of the old imagination. Nor is this said in the sense that he replaces or cancels the old; rather, he illuminates it, and is a new level, identical in structure with, but higher in energy than, every form or possibility of the old.[53]

---

51. Bonhoeffer, *Ethics,* 58. See also Bonhoeffer, *Berlin,* 324–27 where he discusses Christ as "the center of human existence, of history, and of nature." The editors of Bonhoeffer's *Creation and Fall* explain in the Afterward that Bonhoeffer's usage of Christ as the center is "not the central point on a straight line but rather the center of a circle or, better, a point in space from which every direction radiates out. No outward limit is in view, but only one point, namely, the center of everything." Bonhoeffer, *Creation and Fall,* 165.

52. Harvey, *Can These Bones Live?* 157.

53. Lynch, *Christ and Apollo,* 185–87, as cited in Desmond, *Risen Sons,* 27.

John Desmond sees this "illumination" of the old brought by Christ as inestimably increasing the meaningfulness of any and all analogies between Christ and creation. But for our purpose here we need to remember that our focus is on the potentialities that were always already sown into creation by the triune God, before and apart from the explicit historical knowledge of Christ and the revelation of the gospel, since it is easy to forget the seed from which the fully formed fruit becomes visible. Desmond writes,

> With Christ's immersion into history, a new dimension is added to the analogical ... The different elements and acts in creation and history are gathered up in him and linked together meaningfully. His analogical union with creation is complete; it fulfills all the possibilities in existence, such as time, death, rebirth, mystery, identity, and the hypostatic union of spirit and matter. This is the mystery of the Incarnation. With this total analogical identity of a specifically historical Christ and specific human history, things and acts in creation are raised to a new level of meaning, and the precise sense of the concept of providence becomes clear; that everything in existence "counts"; nothing is neglected in the redemptive perspective.[54]

We could summarize by simply stating that before the incarnate Christ came everything "counted," and the task of understanding the existence-revelation of Christ is to show how and why this has always been so, by revealing the purpose and meaning of human existence through the interpretive lens of Christ.[55]

We now move from an introduction of the *basis* of the "existence-revelation of Christ" to the *basic contours* of all human existence that "count" toward a theology of inclusivism.

---

54. Desmond, *Risen Sons*, 28.

55. We note that this project is the opposite of Marx's view of the purpose of philosophy in the service of history to remove "religion as the illusory sun which revolves around man" so that any idea of existing things "counting" would be purely derived from life solely in relation to the world which has been "disenchanted" from any notion of transcendent meaning from a transcendent God. See Van Leeuwen, *Critique of Heaven*, 11.

Basic Contours of Life Contributing to a Theology of Inclusivism

To discuss the basic contours of human existence for a theology of inclusivism means that we need to interpret all of life *as implicitly related to Christ as its center* rather than life *as only related to him through explicit outward knowledge of him historically* as in exclusivism. We seek to discover how person's lives can cohere and hold together in Christ apart from a conscious knowledge of the person and work of Christ, and how such lives might possibly respond positively to Christ, the center of those lives. Our hypothesis is that humans may positively respond *in* the basic contours of life in the world in such a way that they are positively responding *to* God.[56] We need to remember what we mentioned earlier, that all Westphal's "types" of religion are based on human relation and response to some synthesis of God and the world, even in the biblical, covenantal type of religion.

In our studies of the question of inclusivism it seems that the thought of Simone Weil, the French political activist, philosopher, and convert to Christianity from the secular "freethinking" Judaism of her parents, provides a helpful framework for the basics of this theology.[57] Her essay "Forms of the Implicit Love of God" similarly sets forth much of what will be presented.[58] I will present much of the substance of her "forms" within three "basic contours of creation," which are: 1) *the nature of creation*—in which are the realities of a natural/spiritual "order of gravity," along with God's spiritual "order of grace," and God's love; 2) *the cross of Christ in creation* (or suffering); and 3) *the universal opportunity*—to respond to God through those realities of creation and the cross in creation. The reader may easily note that this follows Colossians 1:15–20, by drawing together creation and Christ's cross, but also adding the element of human response to Christ the center of human existence of all times and places which of course was implied by Paul and made

---

56. Similarly, Vincent G. Potter writes "The Absolutely Exalted is present in these experiences, and the task of rational reflection is the recovery of that presence through the discovery that those marks are indeed genuine marks of God." Potter, *John E. Smith*, 15.

57. Her parents are considered to have been "freethinking" in relation to religion in general. See McLellan, *Utopian Pessimist*, 3; Nevin, *Simone Weil*, 1.

58. Weil, *Waiting for God*, 83–142. Her "forms" were: "The Love of Our Neighbor; Love of the Order of the World; The Love of Religious Practices; Friendship." Diogenes Allen presents his own synthesis of Weil's inclusivism in his valuable essay which we will also be referring to here. See Allen, "A Christian Theology," 305–13.

explicit in the following words wherein he exclaims how fully his positive "toil" manifests the life of Christ the center by "his energy that he works powerfully in me" (Col 1:21–29). Of course, this also follows the basic view of Christianity that God is first the Creator and then the Redeemer while also recognizing that Christ is the Redeemer from before the foundation of the world. As we look to Weil's insightful thought, I believe we can see that she expounded the nature of human existence on the basis of Christ, following Christ's model of "existence-revelation" to show its true coherence and reveal its true meaning along with the potential for response to him at the center.[59]

The Nature of Creation

In Weil's thought, the created existence, in which "operate" the realities of gravity, grace, and God's love, provides the basic framework for an inclusive theology. She held that God was the Creator who had the power to command things into existence. God "created through love and for love . . . God did not create anything except love and the means to love."[60] But God's creation was "not an act of self-expansion but of restraint and renunciation" in which "God permitted the existence of things distinct from himself and worth infinitely less than himself."[61] In her view these created things all operate in the realm of what she called "gravity." Most would simply understand this as "nature." All things naturally and necessarily operate in the domain of nature and according to its "given" laws.[62] But Weil held that within the world of gravity human beings were "at least one kind of creature" that can follow the principle of grace rather than only that of gravity.[63] Weil's view of human life in gravity is reminiscent

---

59. We rely heavily on Weil's thought here, but her views of existence did not make her merely an outlier from basic Christian interpretation. Her difference was to explicitly draws out the possibility of saving response to God's reality. Bradley Green demonstrates that interpreters as diverse as C. S. Lewis, Geerhardus Vos, and Augustine, would assent to the truth that "all created reality is made up of signs—and these signs, each in its own unique way, proclaims something about the God who made them." Green, *Gospel and Mind*, 133, (see 127–32). The truth that creation "speaks" has been generally recognized, but our specific question is whether Creation ever speaks or brings "gospel." See Vos, *Biblical Theology*, 355.

60. Weil, *Waiting for God*, 72.

61. Weil, *Waiting for God*, 89.

62. See Allen, *A Christian Theology*, 306–7.

63. Allen, *A Christian Theology*, 307.

of the view of Thomas Hobbes wherein life *according to the state of nature* consists of "warre, as is of every man, against every man."[64] The observation of Weil is similarly corroborated in the 2011 film "Tree of Life" directed by Terence Malick, which a commentator summarizes by saying,

> The essence of nature then is self-assertion, self-willing, self-expansion; while the essence of grace is self-denial in the name of the glory of God.[65]

Weil's views were partly informed by her study of Homer's *Iliad* which resulted in her 1939 essay "The Iliad: Poem of Force." Eric Springsted summarizes that,

> The essay is an understanding of the world and our place within it without reference to anything beyond the world of nature. In this sense it is the lesson we *ought* to learn from the Trojan War and is a lesson about our relations to the world of nature. These relations only appear larger in the case of war. The key to the lesson of the *Iliad,* Weil contends, lies in understanding that the true hero of that poem is not Achilles, Agamemnon, Hector and any other character. The hero is force. The force of which Weil speaks is not only coercion and compulsion, but also prestige; all of these things, she says, have their roots in the actions and reactions of brute matter. It is force alone, and thus matter, she says, that ultimately determines the thoughts and actions of the men and women of the Trojan War. By analogy, Weil bids us see that same quality in our relations in areas of human life other than war, and this despite our belief that we direct our own destinies. Force can reduce us to little more than inanimate matter.[66]

We can see that Weil presented a relational view of human life informed by Christian theology, so that creation itself consisted of "gravity and grace" to therein frame human life in relation to God and self, with the choice of the self being, biblically speaking, the fall to "sin." John Desmond summarizes Weil's basic metaphysical view saying,

> For her, man is a metaphysical unity of spirit and matter, a being constituted *by nature* to seek his ultimate meaning in the

---

64. Hobbes, *Leviathan,* 77. Weil's view of "gravity" can seem much like the views of Schopenhauer and Nietzsche in which all of nature operates, apart from "choice" in a "will to power." But Weil's view of "grace" provides the possibility of faith and prevents Weil from falling into an unbiblical dualism.

65. Chisney, "All the World," 222.

66. Springsted, *Simone Weil,* 19.

transcendent good. His value as a creature is defined by that end. He lives in the *metaxu*, i.e., between the transcendent and the earthly.[67]

In Michael Federici's book on the thought of philosopher Eric Voegelin, the unfamiliar but inestimably important term "metaxy" is defined as,

> The permanent in-between structure of existence. Sometimes referred to as the between or in-between, meaning that humans live in a structure of reality that is between the poles of existence (the *Apeiron* and the Beyond).[68]

Thus, in Weil's view all human existence is necessarily lived in a world where all choices and acts are made in relation to gravity and grace, sin and God, and in response therein to God, the self and the other. In fact, because of this creational "set up," the world itself is "a series of *metaxu*, or bridges, between us and God."[69] But here we need to remember that Christ is "the logos" of the world, so that Weil was expounding the "existence-revelation" according to Christ. Diogenes Allen discusses that in Weil's view God created the order of gravity because of love and as a means by which humans could learn to love by choosing to belong to the order of grace.[70] When humans live only in gravity their life is servile. God's love desired us to obey as God's children through *voluntary* consent to the order of grace as well as the order of gravity.[71] The choice for humans is whether to try to fill the emptiness of the servile life through living in the will to power in "the order of gravity" or "force," ("falling short of the glory of God") or to live by faith in "the order of grace," ("being justified freely by his grace through the redemption that is in Christ Jesus") as Paul wrote in Romans 3:23. Weil thought that the *renunciation* of self-effort to give ourselves "fulness," *imitated*, whether consciously or not, "the very love of God which created the universe." Allen writes that the "faith performance" of this renunciative act was to yield to grace as

---

67. Desmond, *Gravity and Grace*, 20.

68. Federici, *Eric Voegelin*, 226. "Apeiron" is "A pole of the structure of reality (*metaxy*) that indicates the origin or beginning of existence and living things. Voegelin locates the *apeiron* as the opposite pole of existence to the Beyond." (208)

69. Gabellieri, "Reconstructing Platonism." 138.

70. This is similar to the view of T. F. Torrance we discussed earlier wherein what is "objective" to us (the order of grace) needs to be received as "subjective" by us.

71. Allen, *A Christian Theology*, 308.

a principle within us and thereby to allow grace and God's love to find a "lodging" in the realm of gravity and the creature of gravity.[72]

We could surmise that in this "lodging" the human being is "participating" in Christ the center, according to the truth of the atonement of Christ especially as we discussed in Chapter 4 when we considered the views of T. F. Torrance. It seems that Weil is expounding Christ's "existence-revelation" of human life, presupposed in the event of humankind's "fall" from the grace of the tree of life to the ways of mere gravity and force.

To further demonstrate this existence-revelation of all human life we need to consider Weil's second basic contour of human existence.

The Cross of Christ in Creation

The cross of Christ in creation provides the redemptive basis which is efficacious in all of human history and thus provides the basis for an inclusive theology as expounded in Weil's "existence-revelation." In Weil's thought the cross demonstrates the universality and "mediation" (or metaxy) between gravity and grace. The cross exhibited historically that the use of "force" in the will to power in the order of gravity was overcome by Christ's faith in and obedience to the order of grace. More specifically, Christ's renunciation of self on the cross was in harmony with and thus revealed the renunciation of "self" that "first" occurred in God's initial creation of the world. Allen explains that in the incarnation in Christ, God entered the order of gravity and became subject to its workings to the point of suffering the destructive powers of creation, exhibiting Weil's view that in the cross the forces of gravity and grace conclusively met.[73] This means that the Cross is not merely "applied" to all of history by God, but that the Cross re-enacts *the central cosmic drama of all history* and therefore all people have to some extent *experienced* the cross of Christ in their life experience. Whether suffering at the hands of nature, others, or causing the suffering of others, the common experience of all humanity evokes in people a knowledge that their life yearns for something beyond such *gravity*. Thus, their life experience in suffering witnesses *through hope* to the absolute good of Christ who by faith voluntarily *suffered* the force of the order of gravity and *procured* the grace of the order of grace

---

72. Allen, *A Christian Theology* 309.
73. Allen, *A Christian Theology* 310.

for all humanity. Perhaps a brief definition/description of "force" by Weil will help show how force "produced" the cross:

> To define force—it is that x that turns anybody who is subjected to it into a *thing*. Exercised to the limit, it turns man into a thing in the most literal sense: it makes a corpse out of him. Somebody was here, and the next minute there is nobody here at all; this is the spectacle the *Iliad* never wearies of showing us.[74]

But the cross, that de-foliated tree, because of Christ and the resurrection, also reveals the redemptive content at the center of all human life, *the tree of life* in its midst, even planted as the cross/tree of life in the midst of the *Iliad*. It also reveals through the mystery of life that finite creatures live in, the need of faith and hope which presents the temptation of *the tree of the knowledge of good and evil* that is always present in the experience of life. The temptation is to grasp after complete knowledge through the will to power, to secure life. Thus, God's way of redemption that is "implicit" *in* life rather than "explicitly" understood *of* life, brings together the redemptive situation that was and is always at the center of human existence. Of course, the existence-revelation of Christ and the existence-revelation *hidden* in the Edenic situation, both "stipulate" that redemption is *only* efficacious through *faith* in the order of grace.

For Christ's cross in creation is of *judgment* on the order of gravity at the center of creation. It means that humans are not to live as though they are at the center, deriving their life from *their own* center in a self-grasping will to power. Dietrich Bonhoeffer said that Christ's cross of grace at the center means that "the tree of life, that is, the very God who gives life . . . is at once the boundary and center of our existence."[75] Similarly, Eric O. Springsted explains that,

> There is a sanctity to human life, Weil taught, not derived from a "spark" of the divine at the center of our being, but rather because "at the center of the human heart, is the longing for an absolute good, a longing which is always there and is never appeased by any object of this world."[76]

Therefore, human suffering at the hands of nature (or the force of gravity) "consists" in and is "held together" by the "metaxy" or *mediation*

---

74. Weil, *War and the Iliad*, 3.
75. Bonhoeffer, *Creation and Fall*, 86.
76. Springsted, *Simone Weil*, 17–18.

of the cross of Christ, providing the existence-revelation of the two poles of the "gravity and grace" of human existence.[77] It should be obvious that suffering at the hands of nature appears to signal the absence of God, and that the suffering from absence is also the common experience of life in the order of gravity. How this coheres in Christ is through the absence of God to Christ that he experienced pre-eminently at the cross apparently forsaken as though all that existed was the order of "force" (or gravity) so that the oppressors themselves are manifest aspects of malevolent matter to reduce us to suffering non-persons in a universe with no meaning. But Christ committed his spirit to his Father, fully trusting in the order of grace and the love at the core of creation.[78] And we see through this another instance whereby human existence is revealed through Christ the center, showing that human life has always been lived in proximity to God who at times is seemingly absent but can yet be the anchor beyond the veil (Heb 6:19). Paul's quoting of Pagan poets that we saw above, essentially seems to be an example of Paul's own use of the existence-revelation of Christ:

> The God who made the world and everything in it, being Lord of heaven and earth, does not live in temples made by man, nor is he served by human hands, as though he needed anything, since he himself gives to all mankind life and breath and everything. And he made from one man every nation of mankind to live on all the face of the earth, having determined allotted periods and the boundaries of their dwelling place, that they should seek God, and perhaps feel their way toward him and find him. Yet he is actually not far from each one of us, for "'In him we live and move and have our being'; as even some of your own poets have said, "'For we are indeed his offspring' (Acts 17:24–28).

In light of Colossians 1:15–20 it seems that Paul potentially saw the "closeness" and "availability" of God to humans of any time and era as based in the reality of Christ the center of existence and that was also the reason why Paul proclaimed the greater light of Christ come in the flesh as the fulness answering to the measure of light they previously had, a

---

77. "Gravity and Grace" is the title of a collection of selections from the diaries of Simone Weil. See Weil, *Waiting for God*, xii. In his book of the same name, John Desmond chillingly states Weil's view of a life lived only in "gravity" apart from grace: "Man has become or is in danger of becoming 'a thing,' a slave to the forces of gravity." Desmond, *Gravity and Grace*, 20.

78. See Allen, *Suffering at the Hands*, 183–91; Springsted, *Simone Weil*, 39–52.

fullness of light to which they would come if indeed they were responding to God in Christ *before* they had heard of him. In regard to the reality of Christ at the center of all human existence, Torrance writes,

> And so we must think of the cross and its reconciliation as the deepest secret and the ultimate secret of all that happens in human history, for it is in and through the cross that now all things are made to cohere and to work together in God's cosmic purpose of reconciliation. Thus, the supreme act of the divine judgement in the cross lives on in the person of Christ, the same yesterday, today and forever, and remains an abiding force determining all history and every crisis in human affairs falls under its action and reflects its meaning—but in the nature of the case, that is to be understood not with observation, but eschatologically, that is apocalyptically. That is what we glimpse in the book of the revelation of Jesus Christ, in which the apocalyptic vision is all focused ultimately upon the enthroned lamb. [79]

One inestimably important aspect of the cross in creation that could be overlooked in our concentration on Christ's "cosmic" significance to all human life, is that the cross was that of the incarnate human Jesus. Thus, it is the *human* Christ, who allows "the existence-revelation" of *all* human life.[80]

This leads us to our third point in outlining the contours of an inclusivist theology based in the existence-revelation of Christ.

The Universal Opportunity.

The universal opportunity to respond to God through the redemptive realities of creation and Christ provides the possibility of a saving response to Christ as he that is implicitly embedded in existence. In our first two points we have endeavored to demonstrate that the existence-revelation of Christ reveals that humankind of all times and places has lived in relation to Christ at the center of the contours of created life. This

---

79. Torrance, *Atonement*, 170. Similarly, Simone Weil also saw "the lamb that had been slain from the beginning of the world" in the text of the Revelation as revealing the cross as central in God's creation from its beginning. Weil, *Waiting for God*, 89.

80. Badcock therefore sees the humanity of Jesus as a major key for a necessary shift for the gospel's missional extension in the world, moving beyond the rationalistic theology of the West, which is "quite alien to much of the rest of the world." Badcock, *Light of Truth*, 268.

implicit relation provides an opportunity for response in several ways. These ways of response include: *some* manner of "recognition" of the realities of creation which brings them into a relation of "accountability" to realities greater than themselves; *some* manner of "expression" of the way of renunciation and self-denial in relation to their reliance on the will to power in "force" against everything "other" than self that would otherwise seek to secure their self-interests in the order of gravity; and *some* manner of "faith" that is presupposed in these first two "ways of response" that "hope" for *some* provision of "grace" that will mediate life or even death against the dominance of "gravity."[81] Thus we see a negative side which might be called "repentance" regarding the ways of gravity, and a positive side that might be called "faith" that such a renunciation exhibits. This "repentance" and "faith" participate in Christ's incarnate atonement that he universally procured for all in the way of faith under the order of grace, which also presupposes God's love for others, instead of the fallen way of self-love in the will to power.

The reality of the cross of Christ in creation demonstrates that Christ exists in a form of hidden solidarity with all "others" suffering under force in the order of gravity. This means that these *others* in solidarity with the hidden Christ, nonetheless, *represent* Christ. This also means that the person renouncing self-interest, force, and the mere ways of gravity to voluntarily show compassion and love to these visible *others,* is thereby *responding* to Christ. This seems much the same as what Christ reveals as the criterion for the judgment of the nation's when Christ returns, as narrated in Matthew 25:31–45:

> [31]"When the Son of Man comes in his glory, and all the angels with him, then he will sit on his glorious throne. [32]Before him will be gathered all the nations, and he will separate people one

---

81. How "accountability" relates one to God, and in a sense provokes faith in mediation through the human insufficiency to eradicate real guilt in relation to the past and present life, is discussed by C. Stephen Evans, whose discussion seems to evoke the struggle of Romans 2:6–11, and also demonstrates how hope and faith are born from the "massive 'contradiction' between the ideals we humans strive for and the actuality of our lives" in which "the person perceiving the contradiction" gains a hope for some "solution." See Evans, *Kierkegaard and Spirituality,* 86–89. Emmanuel Gabellieri, while discussing Weil's views in comparison to Maurice Blondel, posits more technically that "there is a connection between a phenomenology 'of insufficiency' and an ontology of mediation" that provides for "the intrinsic incompleteness of being and acting . . . the 'crack,' the 'gap,' the 'void' inherent in natural and spiritual being . . . suggesting that being and acting have a hidden relation to the Incarnation (and not only to the creator God)." Gabellieri, "Reconstructing Platonism," 147.

from another as a shepherd separates the sheep from the goats. ³³And he will place the sheep on his right, but the goats on the left. ³⁴Then the King will say to those on his right, 'Come, you who are blessed by my Father, inherit the kingdom prepared for you from the foundation of the world. ³⁵For I was hungry and you gave me food, I was thirsty and you gave me drink, I was a stranger and you welcomed me, ³⁶I was naked and you clothed me, I was sick and you visited me, I was in prison and you came to me.' ³⁷Then the righteous will answer him, saying, 'Lord, when did we see you hungry and feed you, or thirsty and give you drink? ³⁸And when did we see you a stranger and welcome you, or naked and clothe you? ³⁹And when did we see you sick or in prison and visit you?' ⁴⁰And the King will answer them, 'Truly, I say to you, as you did it to one of the least of these my brothers, you did it to me.' ⁴¹"Then he will say to those on his left, 'Depart from me, you cursed, into the eternal fire prepared for the devil and his angels. ⁴²For I was hungry and you gave me no food, I was thirsty and you gave me no drink, ⁴³I was a stranger and you did not welcome me, naked and you did not clothe me, sick and in prison and you did not visit me.' ⁴⁴Then they also will answer, saying, 'Lord, when did we see you hungry or thirsty or a stranger or naked or sick or in prison, and did not minister to you?' ⁴⁵Then he will answer them, saying, 'Truly, I say to you, as you did not do it to one of the least of these, you did not do it to me.' ⁴⁶And these will go away into eternal punishment, but the righteous into eternal life."

Comparing this judgment of people of the *Christian era* who apparently did not consciously know Christ, to the scenario we just described above, it seems possible to posit that God's judgment of the peoples of the *pre-Christian era* may be the same, based in their treatment of "Christ" who they could not have known consciously, but was nevertheless present in the oppressed they did know.[82] The criterion of these future and past judgments seems to be based on humans' compassionate treatment, or lack thereof, in relation to "others" in hidden solidarity with Christ's

---

82. Though not applying this passage to the time before Christ came, Brunner still shows how it may well be applicable: "The parable of Jesus of the paradoxical world Judgment upon the unbelieving believers and the believing unbelievers remains as a warning, above all confessions and creeds, and as a reminder of the hidden judgement of God, above all unbelief. The kingdom of God is indeed invisible in the midst of the godless world; and even of the godless world it is said that 'God so loved the world . . .' Even there, when the veil is drawn back the first will become the last and the last the first." Brunner, *Man in Revolt*, 460.

suffering. This means that there have always been visible "Christs" to respond to, even apart from the historical appearance of Christ. It also means that the "final judgment" of each human being is a judgment based on one's relation to Christ because each one actually had *some* relation to Christ, known through suffering "others."[83] Allen summarizes this by explaining that humankind of every era and locality have been universally given two opportunities, with the first being to know gravity and the second being a refusal to live according to it but instead live compassionately toward those that suffer.[84] Weil's thought, in light of Jesus's teaching on the future judgment seems to show that all humankind invariably has ample opportunity to know gravity and grace, and respond in life to God's "Christs," whether they be individuals or communities. The incarnation and cross of Christ were the necessary events for revealing the truth of Christ's implicit solidarity with universal human suffering under gravity. It is an event not limited in its time and space effect since Christ, as the center of creation, is "before all things, and in him all things hold together" (Colossians 1:17). The principle of incarnation was enacted by God in creation as we saw in the first point above. Weil explains, "that is why Saint John says that the Lamb had been slain from the beginning of the world."[85]

Weil presented "The Love of Our Neighbor" as the first of the "Forms of the Implicit Love of God" that she intuited from the existence-revelation of Christ.[86] What was just discussed above concerns that first

---

83. M. Jamie Ferreira presents several scripturally based comments of Soren Kierkegaard along with her own comments that serve to corroborate our thought here: "How can a man say he loves God whom he does not see, if he does not love his neighbor, whom he sees (p. 155). There is no doubt about the coincidence between love of God and love of neighbor: "'He who sees his brother in need, yet shuts his heart'—yes, at the same time he also shuts out God. Love to God and love of neighbor are like two doors that open simultaneously, so that it is impossible to open one without opening the other, and impossible to shut one without also shutting the other." The point of the story of the final judgment, in which people are told that they fed and clothed God when they fed and clothed "the least" of their neighbors (Matthew 25:34–45), is made explicitly by Kierkegaard, who repeats the words "what you do for them, you do for me" (p. 160). Ferreira, *Loves Grateful Striving*, 80. The parenthetical references refer to the Princeton edition of "Works of Love."

84. Allen, *A Christian Theology*, 312.

85. Weil, *Waiting for God*, 89. The translation Weil followed has been questioned, but the sense she understood in that text is accurately conveyed in 1 Peter 1:19–20. On the text in Revelation 13:8 See Mounce, *Revelation*, 256; Beale, *Revelation*, 701–3.

86. Weil, *Waiting for God*, v.

implicit form. Eric O. Springsted elaborates a bit more on the dynamics of this form, saying,

> According to Weil, there are four forms of the implicit love of God: the love of neighbor, . . . the love of the world's beauty; the love of religious practices; and the love of friends, . . . Each of these is a love "in which God is really though secretly present." (WG, 137). God is secretly present because we cannot know, in the fullest sense, his presence; he is really present because the nature of these loves can only become self-sacrificial (rather than self-centered) through his grace. Each of these loves, even the happiest of them, shows the marks of sacrifice. It is those marks too, which express the divine nature of these loves, and which allows them to bestow a goodness both to us and to the world that could only come from God.[87]

We won't enter into an elaboration of these other forms of the implicit love of God, mainly because they were implicitly included in the "basic contours of life" presented above.[88] The specifics of each therefore participate in the same dynamics, namely a prevenient grace that enables one to self-denial for the sake of concentrated "attention" to something outside our narrow self-interests in gravity and toward the signs of beauty in the world and even in its oppressed others. This outward focus toward the creation and the needy others ultimately directs the seeker beyond the present order of the world and all it can offer to the way of faith. That longing which cannot be presently fulfilled, even for Christians with the knowledge of Christ, is what ultimately must drive any person from the safety of an "abstract" God of earthly satisfactions, to some manner of faith in the "concrete" God of mystery and grace who *for that reason* has made existence to speak of the "heavenly satisfactions" that alone can satisfy.[89] For in every era before the final eschaton, Christ is the cen-

---

87. Springsted, *Simone Weil*, 85. Note that "WG" refers to Weil's *Waiting for God*, which includes her essays on these "Forms of the Implicit Love of God." See Weil, *Waiting for God*, 83–142.

88. Allen, undoubtedly in "conversation" with Weil, frames our reception and response to the love of God under a trifecta of wounds: ". . . the wounds of repentance, compassion, and longing. The first wound is caused by awareness of how much and in many ways, we have disappointed God . . . the second wound of compassion . . . when we see the needs and suffering of people . . . the third wound is caused by our hunger and thirst for God." Allen, *Steps Along the Way*, 83.

89. Allen shows that the problem of all, with or apart from explicit knowledge of Christ, is that ". . . we have a *need* for God, but not a *desire* for God. At first, we seek to satisfy our many wants, needs, desires, hopes, and fears by what we find on earth . . .

ter of existence in the present vaporous cross-shaped world described by Ecclesiastes, which also and always sacramentally points toward the future fulfillment of the resurrection-shaped new creation of all things brought together in Christ.

For God's prevenient grace flows from the atonement of Christ's cross at the center of human existence, and from the assumption of human nature by the incarnate Christ to enable voluntary participation in the life that is symbolized at the final consummation in the hidden manna (bread) of the earth, fulfilling what was symbolized at the beginning in the tree of life's fruit in the garden.[90] Faith in the unknown hope of satisfaction anticipates final participation in what God has already provided in the shape of life redeemed by Christ. In a sense, the ultimate discovery of *any* redeemed life, and therefore the ultimate sign of *any* redeemed life, is the recognition, renunciation, and hope that our *present* "flesh and blood *cannot* inherit the kingdom of God" (1 Cor 15:50).[91] But this trifecta of recognition, renunciation and hope leads to a better way of presently navigating our temporality/eternity in this world and the world to come. Allen writes of the results of this trifecta of grace that effectually narrates the overcoming of the way of the will to power which as we have seen throughout this book, brings the opposite of what we intend to gain by it. Faith is indeed the only way to life in this world that will endure "in the coming ages" (Eph 2:7). And this could perhaps signify reaching the very pinnacle of our rehabilitation of the gospel as good for humanity and the world though we cannot here linger to enjoy the view.

> A kind of love fills us at times which we did not even know existed. The world does not give us this love; it arises precisely because we have turned from all that we can imagine giving us fulness of life in this world. And now because of this love, we

---

The discovery of God begins when we realize that there is nothing in this world that can fully satisfy us ... We remain unsatisfied because we have been made for so much more than this world." Allen, *Steps Along the Way*, 92. It seems that Allen is describing the patient seeking "for glory, honor and immortality" that God grants "eternal life" to for the faith seeking "already" partakes in the life to come (Rom 2:7).

90. Revelation 2:17. God's "manna," and fruit of the tree of life, are hidden to those living only according to "the order of gravity" and by their way of force and the will to power. But they are "known" and "fed" upon by those living in the way of faith, as Adam and Eve were meant to, in "the order of grace."

91. Perhaps the ultimate significance of Weil's book. See Weil, *Waiting for God*, 139.

find ourselves able to love other people as our neighbors. We find ourselves kinder people, more thoughtful people, more gentle people, more forgiving people, happier people. And oddly enough, we also find ourselves loving this world and all that it has to give. But we no longer need to be grasping and anxious, seeking to possess all we can. We know the world's goodness is limited, and precisely because our deepest hunger is being fed, we can enjoy the things of this world with an ease and freedom we never had before.[92]

It seems to us, and obviously to a few scholars who have studied the thought of Simone Weil, that in her short life she was able to mine some of the depths of human existence, exhibiting an exegesis of the existence revelation of Christ that we believe Christ himself gave warrant to explore as disclosed in Luke 24:27. Eric Springsted discusses the cross-centered focus that enabled Simone Weil, this young Jewish convert to Christ's love, to do such deep exegesis of the contours of human existence, saying,

> Weil's claim is clearest when we understand the centrality of the cross for all her theological thinking. When theologians talk about God, they often assume a sort of chronological exposition that begins by considering the nature of God, then Creation, and then the mysteries of the faith such as the Incarnation, Crucifixion and Trinity. This scheme is to some degree a convenient device for textbooks. In Weil, however, there is a clear sense in which her understanding of the nature of God and the creation depends on the cross, for she understands God's goodness and the method of creation as a similar renunciation of power.[93]

We hope that we been able to convey that Weil's interpretations of creation and the cross reveal the existence-revelation of Christ in its "basic contours toward a theology of inclusivism." It seems that Weil's meditation on the Cross of Christ enabled her to understand how and why Christ is the center of all human existence, from love exhibited in God's original creation of the order of gravity to the fulness of love exhibited in the new creation's ordering of all things in grace. Moreover, she shows how human existence of all time consists of life lived in relation to Christ, for "all things were created through him and for him . . . and in him all things hold together" (Colossians 1:17).

---

92. Allen, *Steps Along the Way*, 94.
93. Springsted, *Simone Weil*, 47.

The Open Doorway

We need to emphasize that our theoretical consideration of Weil's contours of life needs to be recognized as a descriptive doorway that opens upon an expansive universe of reality. This emphasis is made because we are so prone to rational argumentation that we can easily miss the forest for the trees, and also think that our previous understanding of "doctrines" of *creation, the cross, and opportunity,* can perhaps easily debate Weil's "doctrines." But viewing Weil's contours of life for what they are opens up an expansive world which is not easily understood by doctrinal abstractions. The human being of Romans 2, "seeking for glory, honor, and immortality," needs to be seen as fully existing beyond the abstraction of our doctrinal understanding of "humanity." For the mystery of human existence in God's creation is not so easily grasped or catalogued. McGrath writes that,

> At "the core" of the human being resides a mystery that images the divine. Like the tabernacle in the Jewish Bible, the human being is a site for the unveiling of God.[94]

The reason for our emphasis here is to point out that Weil's contours could be supplemented by many other ways of understanding the salvific possibilities of existence because of Christ and the nature of created existence. Therefore, we will briefly narrate a few other aspects of human life explored by theologians which could be expanded to provide additional support for our thesis of the implicit Christ. Of course, Weil's views themselves were only minimally introduced and could be greatly expanded.

Karl Barth, considered by many to have been the greatest protestant theologian the twentieth century, may have much to offer.[95] The quota-

---

94. McGrath, *Heidegger*, 127.

95. Barth may seem an odd theologian to set forth here, to any who are familiar to his definitive "Nein!" in response to Emil Brunner's positing of a natural theology. (See Mangina, *Karl Barth*, 4.) But Barth's emphasis on the transcendent God made known in the human Jesus offers much. Todt has shown how Barth's thought, that might seem to be all "nein" to a project such as proposed here, can be mitigated through Bonhoeffer's development of Barth, and Barth's own developing thought. (Todt, *Authentic Faith*, 30–39.) Similarly, Macquarrie has brought Barth's basic and developing thought into conversation with the question of an "anthropological approach to theology" that demonstrates how Barth's thought could in the main help, rather than hinder Macquarrie's view of "openness" toward religions other than Christianity because of the Logos. See Macquarrie, *Theology, Church, & Ministry*, 48–68; 125–54. Finally, Badcock

tion of his at the head of this postscript is in itself an apt summary of the existence-revelation of Christ: "*Here, it becomes clear that speaking about the mystery of Christ means speaking about the mystery of life.*"[96] To Barth, the mystery of life is revealed thus:

> It is as if God had said to humanity, "Now things are based not on you, but on me! Based on you, on your thought and actions, there was *sin*; based on me, there is forgiveness and the power of a new life. Based on you, there is *distress and affliction;* based on me there is help and salvation. Based on you, there is always *opposition, one against the other;* based on me, there is togetherness and being for one another.". . . In the Savior an *understanding*, a perceiving recognition of true life, has come to humanity.[97]

It seems that if Weil provided us with a basic exegesis based on the existence-revelation of Christ, Barth provides the theological basis of that revelation. For Barth was preeminently a theologian of revelation, and more specifically of the revelation of Christ.[98] To Barth, the revelation of Christ provides the bridge over "the ugly, broad ditch which I cannot get across . . . Lessing's ugly ditch between eternal and rational truth and contingent historical truth."[99] And that is essentially what the existence-revelation of Christ also provides. Barth says that "the power of the resurrection is neither a contingent historical truth nor an eternal rational truth . . . it is most emphatically *revelation.*"[100] Thus Barth saw *the event of Jesus of Nazareth* as the bridge that *reveals* the nature and meaning of creation and human existence, what we call "the existence-revelation of Christ.[101]

---

has proposed that the later Barth saw the need for a theology of the Holy Spirit that would seem to be open to "the question of the human being" in our "existence-revelation of Christ," not as "anthropocentrism," but as "simply good theology." See Badcock, *Light of Truth,* 6–8. Badcock's own "Theology of the Holy Spirit" has much to offer to our proposal. (See especially 1–7, 257–73.)

96. Barth, *Epistle to the Ephesians,* 139.

97. Barth and Willimon, *The Early Preaching,* 70–71.

98. Being a theologian of revelation meant that Barth was a theologian of exegesis: "Throughout his career Barth claimed that biblical exegesis remained the presupposition and goal of all his work." Burnett, *Karl Barth's Theological Exegesis,* 23.

99. Barth, *Epistle to the Ephesians,* 172–73, n. 181; Mangina explains, "Jesus Christ is the human being made in the image of God. *He* inhabits the boundary between heaven and earth. Mangina, *Karl Barth,* 97.

100. Barth, *Epistle to the Ephesians,* 140.

101. "Only in *Him* can we understand creation. And when Barth says, 'only in *him*' he does not mean the creation of all things through the second person of the trinity,

For the sake of brevity, we will only provide several thoughts of Barth that depict how his thought provides the theological basis of this postscript:

> In him, the non-given is given; God is revealed. In him, the Spirit broods upon humanity, and God turns toward humanity in grace. In him, both the relativity of all things and their relation to the absolute are one . . . In Christ, almighty God, the giver of life and the source of all blessings, becomes the basis of our existence in the *past* as well as the future . . . Christ constitutes the living relation of humanity to God, the cornerstone, the crisis as well as the ground of our existence . . . not that the living relation between God and man is created or made possible for the first time . . . God's wisdom is manifold, polyvalent, and perdurable . . . we can regard gentiles as future Christians and the godforsaken as anonymous children of God.[102]

Diogenes Allen has presented a Christ-centered way, which according to our thesis can therefore be fully applicable to all of human existence. He writes, "In the Christian religion our knowledge of divine love causes three wounds—the wounds of repentance, compassion, and longing."[103] The wound of repentance is "to encounter something that measures and judges our lives;" The wound of compassion is the "pain when we see the needs and suffering of people;" The wound of longing "is caused by our hunger and thirst for God."[104] We can see how these three "wounds" cohere with Weil's contours, and as we consider other examples we will see how expansive they are in relation to truth that God has embedded in existence and brought to light in Christ.

C. S. Lewis, in his entire corpus exhibited his life-long quest that is perhaps best summarized as a life of insatiable longing for *something* and the actual promise death brings for that *something* that cannot be fully given in this life. That something turned out to be God and heaven. He writes,

> There have been times when I think we do not desire heaven but more often I find myself wondering whether, in our heart of hearts, we have ever desired anything else . . . The thing you long for summons you away from the self. Even the desire for the thing lives only if you abandon it. This is the ultimate law—the

---

but through Jesus of Nazareth." Berkouwer, *The Triumph of Grace,* 53.

102. Barth, *The Epistle to the Ephesians,* 124, 140–42.
103. Allen, *Steps Along the Way,* 83.
104. Allen, *Steps Along the Way,* 83, 88.

seed dies to live, the bread must be cast on the waters, he that loses his soul will save it.[105]

This brief excerpt from Lewis demonstrates how closely entwined human existence is with heaven and the cross of self-denial, simply because of the deep and universal realities of longing and death because of the reality of "gravity and grace" in the present world.

Merold Westphal further elaborates on the life-long search of Lewis with his insights on "the existential meaning of death." He points out that in Tolstoy's *Death of Ivan Ilyich,* death is "a mirror that challenges and tests my life" and is "the test that proves Existenz and relativizes mere existence," as Karl Jaspers wrote.[106] Mere existence is life in its "objective functions and processes." But,

> Death is the test that proves Existenz. It does so in two ways, if we look it in the face. It asks us whether we have made the leap to Existenz, whether we have acknowledged and accepted the freedom that we are and the responsibility which goes with it, and it asks whether we have exercised such freedom wisely, lovingly, and honestly. Have you fulfilled the task of becoming a self and have you used the gift of self-hood rightly?[107]

This sounds much like the accountability to God that death brings to all according to Psalm 90:10–12. It also sounds much like the necessary prerequisite for the "patience in well-doing" of Paul's candidate for "eternal life" in Romans 2:7, which also "relativizes mere existence"—the "self-seeking"—that does not "obey the truth" but rather "unrighteousness" and brings God's "wrath and fury" (Rom 2:8).

Soren Kierkegaard's thought on death provides a further elaboration of this. Simon Podmore presents the view that Kierkegaard conceived of human existence as in relation to three spheres of death which necessarily condition the knowledge of self and God:

> Insofar as Kierkegaard's vision of the self can be described as a modern inheritor of the Christian belief in the immortality or eternity of the soul, his writings relate a consequent rhetorical blurring of any absolute distinction (or difference) between life and death—particularly where the struggle for subjectivity is

---

105. Lewis, *The Problem of Pain*, 130, 134. See also "Preface to Third Edition" in Lewis, *The Pilgrim's Regress*, 5–14; and his autobiography, Lewis, *Surprised by Joy*.
106. Westphal, *God, Guilt, and Death*, 100.
107. Westphal, *God, Guilt, and Death*, 100.

described. The contemplation of death in all its poetic, spiritual, and visceral forms thereby becomes a mysterious and fecund wellspring of hidden self-knowledge and knowledge of the divine.[108]

Podmore calls these three spheres, *the living death of despair, the theophany of death,* and *Spirit is to will to die.*[109] It is of immense interest and significance that death is seen as a "Theophany"—an appearance or manifestation of God. Podmore summarizes by saying,

> The death, resurrection, and life of selfhood are, from beginning to end, determined by the inescapable and often harrowingly inexorable veracity of the immortality of the soul. And yet it is in the light of the eternal that the self must recontemplate the meaning of the shadow of death in life. The self's authentic self-becoming "before God" is ultimately characterized by a decisive deliverance of the self from the fatalism of despair and the theophany of death. And yet it is a deliverance from death before God, which finds new life in the act of dying to one's (sinful or despairing) self. It is therefore, through the harrowing yet "upbuilding" struggle with *Anfaegtelse,* implicit in becoming a self before God, that one may begin to see how the dreadful theophany of death becomes supplanted by the divine promise of forgiveness and reconciliation as the self's deliverance, not only from the fear of death or annihilation before the Holy, but also from the melancholy dis-ease of a living death.[110]

There is undoubtedly much that could be unpacked from these summaries of very complex realities Kierkegaard posited. One extremely important point is that what most see as the greatest obstacle to finding God and meaning in life—*death*—is a revelatory theophany of *life,* in relation to Christ, as the existence-revelation of Christ posits. Another important point is to recognize that the theophany of death is related to seeing God's face.[111] This recognition can serve to demonstrate how the existence-revelation of Christ opens a doorway for viewing all of human existence as lived in relation to God's face, and the struggle to see God's

---

108. Podmore, "Die and Yet Not Die," 45–46.

109. Podmore, "Die and Net Not Die," 47–59.

110. Podmore, "Die and Yet Not Die," 62. The term *Anfaegtelse* means "spiritual trial" (58).

111. Kierkegaard's "theophany of death" was based in the scripture when God says to Moses: "you cannot see my face; for no one shall see me and live" (Ex 33:20. NRSV). This is why annihilation was an issue of concern in Podmore's summary. Podmore, "Die and Yet Not Die," 45.

face of grace in natural revelation. "The face of the Lord is against those who do evil," says Psalm 34:16, which is the reason one cannot see God's face and live (Ex 33:20). Yet in Christ, God's face of grace and truth was made fully known, against the backdrop of the revelation of God in the law of Israel and the law known in every conscience (John 1:16–18; Rom 2:12–16). Humankind then, invariably struggles to discern God's true face, fully made known in Christ. We struggle to discern God's true face behind the "crosses" of creation, the frowning providences. The insatiable longing that Lewis spoke of impels us, to look for the "chinks" through which we might see past the cross that towers over all creation, to see the "gold" of our "daily scene" which even at times "looks big with its secret" but does not let it free until "the large dimensions of death" release it.[112] Thus God's "face" behind the world is difficult to "read," just like that of the "leather-face people" that Huck Finn knew, and also knew that Miss Mary Jane did not have. For her face, "a body can set down and read it off like coarse print."[113] The face of God in Christ is the face that can be read like the print in a book. This struggle of reading God's face is the struggle of every person of all times and places. It was even Christ's struggle on the cross when God's face would say that he was forsaken and accursed by God. This all illustrates how the existence-revelation of Christ opens the door on human life as the seeking of God's holy face, the *mysterium et fascinans* that both terrifies and attracts and therefore must nevertheless be sought if we are to find the source of life's good that seeps through the chinks in the world's firmament.

These several examples help to demonstrate that the existence-revelation of Christ is an open doorway to view God's redemptive possibilities in God's creation. Perhaps possibilities should be called probabilities to give due significance of God's creative redemptive work. The *doctrine* of Christ is indeed necessary to the existence-revelation of Christ, but what is found by it cannot be reduced to doctrine(s). What is found should perhaps be considered "A Table in the Mist," below the firmament, where weary travelers patiently seeking for wisdom and well-doing, and longing for glory, honor, and immortality, find precious life-giving sustenance, provided by their loving Creator beyond the mist, for their long journey home.[114] Jeff Meyers writes,

---

112. Lewis, *Problem of Pain*, 133
113. Twain, "The Adventures," 514–15.
114. Meyers, *A Table in the Mist*.

Life in itself is unable to supply the key to the questions of identity, meaning, purpose, value, destiny. Only God holds the key, and he must be trusted with it. He does not make copies of the key for us to use. You do not get to keep God's key in your back pocket.[115]

Through Christ, the "table in the mist" of Ecclesiastes has become more solid, and provided more sustenance than Solomon could know or partake in. But this "existence-revelation" of Christ is God's key, and even still only God fully knows the empirical truth *of* each person. The key is only provided that we may trust Christ's truth and grace *in* existence. For God's grace and truth, now made incarnate, also implicitly incarnates "the way and the life," and no-one comes to the Father in any other way (John 14:6). Christians tend to under-emphasize that mist still pervades the character of our lives in response to God and can't conceive how faith could be born in the mist apart from knowing the explicit incarnation or lead anyone toward its implicit hope that God grants eternal life to. But the NT exhorts us to remember the misty character of our lives, and not to suppose that sight has replaced faith, as it proclaims the human journey to the unseen New Jerusalem as the only way of all God's pilgrims of any era (Heb 11:13–16; 12:22–24).[116]

Texts in Genesis That Demonstrate the "Existence-Revelation" of Christ

To this point we have concentrated on the "exegesis" of life itself in regard to the "existence revelation" of Christ. But to follow Luke 24:27 we ought to be able to find that the OT Scriptures themselves reveal this revelation of human existence in the "mist" of life before Christ became explicit. If treated properly this hypothesis would require a thorough "exegesis" of the entire OT itself. But all that can be provided at this point towards the end of this unwieldy postscript to what became a Kudzu-like book is a consideration of a few additional approaches to Scripture,

---

115. Meyers, *A Table in the Mist*, 16–17.

116. Vos notes that the faith community the letter to the Hebrews addresses was seeking to replace faith by sight in a religious "externalism" that overly sought to find "realistic" manifestations of the spiritual realities of the New Covenant in things like the temple in Jerusalem and its institutions of Israel's law. Vos, *Epistle to the Hebrews*, 20–23, 51–53.

and interpretations of early sections of Genesis that demonstrate that the Scriptures do yield the existence-revelation Christ proclaimed.

To begin we will consider a book called "GodStories—New Narratives from Sacred Texts" by H. Stephen Shoemaker. The author considers his re-presenting of the Scriptures of both Testaments to be a Christian form of Rabbinic "*Haggadah,* which was the imaginative re-telling of biblical narratives so as to teach us the way of God" and was a Rabbinic exercise of "relaxation and amusement."[117] Shoemaker's "Christian Haggadah" signifies that "the Christ event is the key to unlocking the Scriptures."[118] Of course this is the "ardent pursuit" of all Christian interpreters and also is only to follow Christ's own lead recorded in Luke 24:27.

But Shoemaker's treatment of the early chapters of Genesis also demonstrates that his re-narration is essentially an exegetical example of following the existence-revelation of Christ in those early texts. His treatment of these stories reveals the categories of life that Simone Weil saw as always inherently related to God. Thus Shoemaker's "GodStories" is aptly named since these stories of basic human struggles with dysfunctional families and providential blessings and cursings, these "HumanStories" so to speak, are nevertheless *GodStories*. Given that these "Human/GodStories" are those of the first human family, these stories also are meant to portray the stories of all humanity for all times and places, setting the context for the nature of that existence to be revealed by Christ's existence-revelation.

Providential blessings and cursings are mentioned because that is a strong theme in these early accounts of humanity, wherein the blessing of one seemed to signify the cursing of the other.[119] These range from the "acceptance" of Abel's offering and rejection of Cain's to the rival warring wives of Jacob seen in the naming of Leah's firstborn, Reuben, which means "See, a son," and which "no doubt echoed like a taunt in Rachel's ears."[120] Much of the problem of human dysfunction, sin and conflict

---

117. Shoemaker, *GodStories,* xv-xvii. Shoemaker writes that *Haggadah* is in contrast to the more normative Rabbinic "ardent pursuit" of *Halakah* which was "the exposition of the Law of Moses into rules for daily living." (xvi).

118. Shoemaker, *GodStories,* xvii.

119. A theme with important consequences seen in today's violent "religious" conflagrations, which is explored by Rabbi Jonathan Sacks's 2015 book, *Not In God's Name—Confronting Religious Violence.* Writing of Jacob's night of wrestling, Sacks says "The truth at which Jacob finally arrived, to which the name *Israel* is testimony, is that to be complete we need no one else's blessings, only our own." (138)

120. Shoemaker, *GodStories,* 54.

stems from the *misinterpretation* of life and God's providence within it, so that a bad providence simply *means* God's rejection.[121] But life and the providences of God are no simple matters to understand. Nevertheless, these contours of life are the means God uses so that the HumanStories are also, *always* GodStories of some sort. Shoemaker narrates this mistake of equating providence with God's complete attitude toward one's person:

> Abel's offering, the text says, was acceptable to God, but Cain's was not. What if this is how it happened: Cain and Abel made their offerings. Afterward, Abel's flocks prospered, and Cain's crops flopped. What we may well be observing is the relative good and bad fortune of the brothers. How they read this inequality of fortune was that God accepted one's offering but not the other's.[122]

Yoram Hazony, another interpreter with a unique approach to the Scriptures, similarly expands on this "reading" and offers a fascinating account of God's rejection of Cain's sacrifice as a challenge to Cain's overwillingness to submit to a life of subservience to the cursings related to farming in comparison to the innovative Abel's way of shepherding flocks.[123] Abel thus seems akin to the Jacob who always seeks the better deal than what's offered by providence. This reading presents a sort of twist on the question of what living by faith vs. the will to power is, and who is doing which. For God seems to accept such "wrestlings" with "life"—because they wrestle through "gravity" to find the God of grace at the center rather than what "God" could appear to be—Simone Weil's "force" of nature—"a capricious reality without tendency or direction at all."[124] Hazony writes,

---

121. The fact of "misinterpretation" demonstrates the practical need of the existence-revelation of Christ.

122. Shoemaker, *GodStories*, 28–29.

123. Hazony, *Philosophy*, 105–10. These departures from traditional understandings, rather than being seen as "playing loose" with the accounts, seem rather to signify the richness of the texts which do not fill in much of the context and allow for such readings. Also, biblically informed readings of such texts help readers to rightly "read" their own lives—not in regard to having what Meyers called a "key" to keep in one's pocket to "divine" the meaning of events, but to recognize the inscrutable nature of God's relation to "providence" so we will focus on our creative responsibility/faith response to God's revealed will, rather than "the secret things" (Deut 29:29).

124. Hazony, *Philosophy*, 247. This "wrestling" might seem to some an exercise of "the will to power" but it is seems more accurately to be "a will to grace." For God's "cure" of the will to power is not negation of will but direction toward God and the

The account of Jacob's wrestling with God at the ford of the Yabok thus reprises crucial themes that first appeared in the story of Cain and Abel. Jacob, like Abel, is a man who refuses the hand he has been dealt and is willing to take enormous risks to try to improve things for himself and his posterity—even if these risks involve dissenting from what appears to be God's manifest will. And like Abel, he finds that God admires and cherishes those who defy the decree of history and dare to better things for themselves and their families in ways that conflict with the order that has been created for them by king and state, by their fathers, by God himself. Indeed, we are to understand that it is just such individuals who gain God's blessing.[125]

Some may object that Abel's sacrifice was simply accepted by God because it was offered in faith as the NT states in Hebrews 11:4.[126] But it seems that Hazony's view is not at all contradictory to Abel and Jacob exercising "faith." In fact, a case can be made that they had true faith that "wrestled with God" rather than slavishly obey "the letter of the law." Perhaps this is why Jesus himself commends the "shrewd manager" in his parable in Luke 16:1–9 and even provides the unusual recommendation of "shrewdness" to his disciples at the end which seems to more easily harmonize to Hazony's view of the Bible's Jacobs and Abels than the slavish Cains.

Jacob wrestled with life and thereby wrestled with God, obtaining God's blessing in "the order of grace." True to Kierkegaard's understanding, Jacob became a self by being "established by God," and so was named God's Israel.[127] *Jacob's* transformative HumanStory/GodStory wrestling

---

good so that the will does not become the demonic "heart turned in on oneself" as the center.

125. Hazony, *Philosophy*, 138. Hazony translates God's challenge to Cain as "Why are you angry, and why is your face fallen? If you improve (*teitiv*), will you not be lifted up?" and goes on to say "God accepts the offering of a man who seeks to improve things, to make them good of himself and his own initiative. This is what God finds in Abel, and the reason he accepts his sacrifice." (108)

126. Others simply object that Cain's was rejected for being a bloodless sacrifice. Waltke answers that "Cain's flawed character led to his feigned worship." It was not that it was his "bloodless sacrifice." See Waltke, *Dance*, 227–36. Walton notes that "no major evangelical commentary in the last several decades endorses it" (the "bloodless sacrifice" view). Walton, *Genesis*, 261.

127. "It was Kierkegaard more than any other author who helped me to understand the tension between the sense that we are responsible for shaping or authoring our own lives, and the sense that there is something distinct and definite about ourselves that has to be accepted as simply given." Rudd, *Self, Value, & Narrative*, 3.

with life/wrestling with God enabled him to say to Esau, "To see your face is like seeing the face of God." Shoemaker writes,

> The wrestling during the night and the embracing by day were joined as one in Jacob's mind. He had met God in the river and in his brother's arms. And God's name and face was grace.[128]

Jonathan Sacks sees Jacob's wrestling as his "battle with existential truth" because Jacob's essential battle was with who he was, whether the man "who longed to be Esau . . . or the man called to a different destiny, the road less travelled."[129] Shoemaker poignantly portrays the Jacob who does not know the name of God and yet wrestles to sees God's face, and survives, and so becomes *Israel* (Gen 32:28–30):

> Jacob limped toward the dawn bearing the wound of blessing. Can we speak of a diminishment that blesses? A blessing that leaves us with a limp? Some wounds in life are what C. S. Lewis called a "severe mercy." Some nights of our lives we find ourselves wrestling in the river Jabbok, in that stream called "Struggle" (for that's what the name "Jabbok" literally means). Is it a human person we wrestle with? an angel? a demon? God? Is it life itself, with all its fierce and frightening power? Is it death we wrestle with there in the waters? Whoever it is we have hold of, or Who has hold of us, we find ourselves hanging on for dear life and crying, "I will not let you go until you bless me!" This is not an act of defiance but an act of *faith* in God, a faith that refuses to give up on life's goodness, and God's, a faith that believes that somewhere in the midst of the struggle, darkness and pain, there is blessing.[130]

It seems thus quite possible if not probable that many in the course of human history, whose lives have been created—"*that they should seek the Lord, if haply they might feel after him, and find him, though he be not far from every one of us*"—have had the opportunity for such *faith*, in response to the contours of life that centripetally surround the life-giving source at the center, which is and has always been Christ, thus finding their lives in the Lamb *"foreordained before the foundation of the world"* who was prefigured in "the tree of life" in Eden (Acts 17:27; 1 Pet 1:19–20;

---

128. Shoemaker, *GodStories*, 57.

129. Sacks, *Not In God's Name*, 138.

130. Shoemaker, *GodStories*, 58. For an in-depth study of faith which is like Jacob's, an embodied moral quest in what Kierkegaard called "existence-communication" see, Springsted, *The Act of Faith*; and Evans, *Kierkegaard and Spirituality*.

KJV). For, the existence-revelation of Christ reveals the reality of Bethel, "the house of God," where stands the ladder between earth and heaven, and of Peniel, "the face of God" (Gen 28:12–19; 32:30). And though many will not wrestle *through* life to see the angels of God ascending and descending, obtain the blessed limp, receive the new name, and see the face and live, some will, because of Christ at the center of life. For the heavenly realm that co-mingles with the terrestrial one is always part of the whole sacramental tapestry of reality:[131]

> "Surely the Lord is in this place, and I did not know it." The next morning, he took the rock that had been his pillow, poured oil on it, and named the place *Bethel*, which means "house of God," for this, he said, "is none other than the house of God and the gate of heaven."[132]

We don't doubt that "Christian Haggadah," or *the way of God*, can be found throughout the entire Old Testament as Jesus says in Luke 24:27, because of the existence-revelation of Christ. It is also interesting that two of the interpreters we have cited are Jewish interpreters who perhaps have been more adequately formed to enter into the contours of the ancient strange world of the Bible and be able to narrate the existence-revelation of Christ, though they may not name it as that. As we proposed earlier, this may be the be the largely undiscovered country because the key Christ gave in Luke 24:27 has not been enough put to that purpose, perhaps especially not by Evangelical exclusivists.[133]

It may be helpful at this point to clarify what our conception of the "existence-revelation of Christ" is and is not. It is not claiming to be a tool for historical research with which one can infallibly discover how Christ was existentially related to *any* particular historical events, or *the whole* of human history. It is claiming to be merely the opening of a window of possibility through which the existential reality of Christ can be conceived of as related to the lives of human beings apart from their conscious knowledge of the historical person of Christ and his gospel significance. The exegesis of the existence-revelation of Christ is thus a sort of ahistorical knowledge which only speaks of the theoretical, theological

---

131. See Boersma, *Heavenly Participation—The Weaving of a Sacramental Tapestry*.

132. Shoemaker, *GodStories*, 53.

133. It may well be "old hat" to many in other faith traditions. In that case I merely offer this work as supportive with perhaps a few insights and descriptions of the "existence-revelation of Christ" that may be of value.

significance of the existential lives of humankind in mundane history. In other words, the existence-revelation of Christ only reveals that human life in all of mundane history was and is pregnant with the immanent reality of the transcendent Christ. Only in the fulfilled eschaton of God could it be possible that even one could know any or all of the details of Christ's existence-revelation, if it is granted within the promise that "I will know fully even as I have been fully known" (1 Cor 13:12).

Thus, our task was merely to seek to sufficiently present what seems to be warranted by the nature of Christ's creation and the trajectory of redemption. That warrant was given by the event of Christ that reveals all events, the reality of the redemption implicit in creation from the beginning.

> An entirely new *critical discernment* about the nature and destiny of humankind, not to mention the general order of things, once and for all is untethered. The event is not fully disclosed; it is still on its way, yet remaining to be fully disclosed.[134]

On Counterintuitively Proclaiming the Gospel

We return now to the broader context of this postscript, our discussion of exclusivism and inclusivism and the present concern of what we hold to be an unnecessary offense—a seemingly "dark side of the gospel." Exclusivists fear that an opening up of the possibility of salvation apart from conscious response to the name of Christ will only result in a loss of the gospel itself, and a lesser harvest for the gospel because the missionary motivation will be removed by inclusivism.[135] This supposition misunderstands that inclusivism as described above does not in the least change the impetus for missions which is based on the commands of Christ in relation to the agency of the church in the visible historical outworking of "thy kingdom come on earth as in heaven." As to the "size" of the harvest, obviously, what the gospel is cannot be changed for the sake of a supposed greater harvest. Nevertheless, we hold that the

---

134. Raschke, *Critical Theology*, 148.

135. It is interesting to note that Billy Graham held to inclusivist views and may have preached to more people in more countries than anyone else in history, showing that his view did not sever the missionary nerve. Graham said, "I think that many millions of Americans are searching for God. And I think that many are finding God in our various religions in this country." See Frost, *Billy Graham,* loc. 244.

visible harvest of an inclusivist gospel could prove to be counterintuitively greater than exclusivists think. For the gospel is always surprising, and requires imaginations open to the deep workings of the Father, Son and Spirit in the lives of all people.

Exclusivists today may be similar to Peter in the scene that unfolds in Luke 5:1–11 when the expert fisherman and his team's night-long expedition surprisingly yielded only empty nets. But Jesus told him to cast out again "into the deep." It is beyond doubt that Peter balked at this suggestion, the lifelong fisherman who knew that field of the sea like the back of his hand being instructed by a carpenter now turned controversial Rabbi and part-time fishing advisor. Peter was seeing this as advice from someone out of their proper field and was surely thinking, "Jesus . . . leave the fishing to me!" But Jesus knew what lay hidden in the deep, the great harvest of fish that signified the peoples of the gospel harvest. The exclusivist's belief is that the deep of human life apart from the explicit knowledge of the gospel simply holds no possibilities for God or the fishers of men.[136] When this belief inevitably accompanies their gospel proclamations, it often results in driving from their nets the very "fish" they mean to "catch" due to its backhanded offense to the naive yet tacit theological instincts of their hearers. But a proclamation of the gospel that is open to the possibilities lying hidden from them in the deep may find the gospel is freed from any "dark side," resulting in a surprisingly counterintuitive greater harvest. This "imaginative" illustration hopefully reveals that my concern is for those the gospel aims to reach, and that faith in our own fishing expertise regarding the mysterious migrations of fish in the depths beyond our reach needs to give way to the master fisherman's greater knowledge of the mysteries and providences of the deep. For the gospel itself reveals that the full harvest *always* lies beyond the range of view of its faithful stewards, "fishing" out over the vast depths, "out on seventy thousand fathoms of water."[137] Within the "visible" realm of the West the process of conversion in response to explicit gospel proclamation may well consist of much more of what goes on "below the surface,"

---

136. *Possibility* is the need for the evangelizer and the evangelized. As Kierkegaard wrote, "When someone faints, we call for water, eau de cologne, smelling salts; but when someone wants to despair, then the word is: Get possibility, get possibility, possibility is the only salvation. A possibility—then the person in despair breathes again, he revives again, for without possibility a person seems unable to breathe." Kierkegaard, *Sickness unto Death*, 38–39.

137. A favorite expression of "the apostle of possibility," Soren Kierkegaard. See Kierkegaard, *Concluding Unscientific Postscript*, 204.

in the very contours of life we have been discussing. Certainly, proclaiming life as it is now revealed to be through the existence-revelation of Christ would seem to hold an even greater promise for those who explicitly discover what their "wrestling" with life means. This is only to bring to the table of discussion what Flannery O'Connor said of people coming to the church as probably holding true for those consciously coming to Christ:

> I think most people come to the Church by means the Church does not allow, else there would be no need their getting to her at all."[138]

The point is that conversion is always more about the iceberg below the surface and the wind blowing where it wishes (John 3:8), than a simple "call and response" view that most exclusivists will rightly reject. Alexander wrote: "Surely then there must be mystery in the second birth!"[139] In other words, if the depths are not touched and disturbed, the resulting "conversion" will generally prove to be the seed sown on the highway or shallow soil which cannot germinate or grow any root. Christ's call to become successful "fishers of men" is based on his prior deep-sea plunge into the flesh of all humanity, not merely those who have lived since the time of his incarnation. And so, the net of Christ's flesh encompasses all, though we will ask "when did we see you?" (Matt 25:39). For Christ has long labored in the depths of the sea of humanity.

> One has the picture of someone going right down and dredging the sea-bottom . . . Or else one has the picture of a diver, stripping off garment after garment, making himself naked, then flashing for a moment in the air, and then down through the green and warm and sunlit water into the pitch black, cold, freezing water, down into the mud and slime, then up again, his lungs almost bursting, back again to the green and warm and sunlit water, and then at last out into the sunshine, holding in his hand the dripping thing he went down to get. This thing is human nature; but associated with it, all nature, the new universe.[140]

---

138. O'Connor, *Collected Works*, 945.

139. Alexander, *Thoughts*, 23. "Conversion is a mystery of God, and the varieties of conversion experiences testify to that divine initiative seeking out those who are lost, finding them, and bringing them home." Kerr and Mulder, *Conversions*, xii-xiii.

140. Lewis, *God in the Dock*, 82. "It is a matter of God having plunged into life in our flesh to subdue the enemies of creation and establish a way between God and humanity that cannot be undone." Byassee, *Psalms*, 76.

If Christ had not previously dove into the very flesh of humanity to bring it up in "a new universe," the gospel net would have come up empty. It would never have caught up a Nicodemus, a band of fishermen who turned the world upside down, or much of Israel and the Samaritans, Paul and the Gentiles, as the net was cast ever deeper and further.

Escaping "the Dark Side" to Uncover the Gospel of God Who Is Only Light

I begin to bring this lengthy postscript to a conclusion where I began, with the three texts that together present a microcosmic view of the gospel:

> This is the message we have heard from him and proclaim to you, that God is light, and in him is no darkness at all (1 John 1:5); He is the propitiation for our sins, and not for ours only but also for the sins of the whole world (1 John 2:2); And Jesus, perceiving in himself that power had gone out from him, immediately turned about in the crowd and said, "Who touched my garments?" (Mark 5:30.)

It is hoped that our "Unscientific Exegetical Postscript" has perhaps at the least provoked thoughts of God's possibility and the incarnate gospel's propriety for all of humanity. John 3:16 seems to require a plan that is equal to God's overflowing active pursuing love. If God gives compassionate "attention" to even the sparrow, will he not give attention to,

> "a little piece of flesh, naked, inert, and bleeding beside a ditch; he is nameless, no one knows anything about him. Those who pass by scarcely notice it, and a few minutes afterward do not even know that they saw it. Only one stops and turns his attention toward it."[141]

Perhaps the "existence-revelation of Christ" may reveal the possibility that God is not simply another who merely passes by even one person discarded as nothing and lying by the side of history's long road between Jerusalem and Jericho. Perhaps God has always used "good Samaritans" and "victims" to graphically reveal the need and way of gospel to those willing to pay attention to *life* set before them. Perhaps even multitudes "paying attention" to *life* may reach forth to touch the hem of Christ's

---

141. Weil, *Waiting for God*, 90. The illustration is from Jesus's "parable of the good Samaritan," the one "traveler" who alone paid attention to the man lying along the road robbed, naked and beaten, and left for dead. See Luke 10:25–37.

garment that lies within their grasp—so that even Christ may ask "who touched my garments?" For we have seen that this is a question of finding Christ *incognito*—such that even the "Christ" that may be touched, and the one touching, do not know they are Christ for the other in the hidden depths of the human story. For we have also seen that it is always also God's story. Christ was ordained as God's incarnate Lamb from the foundation of the world, and God's redemptive journey into the depths of human life ought not be restricted to Christ's time on the cross, or the time of his earthly life. For the triune God has inhabited the depths of human life from the beginning, providing life and hope in the valley of the shadow of death.

What is beyond any doubt is that Christ's descent into the deep does not diminish the light of God, in whom is no darkness at all. Instead, the separating darkening veil of the temple is torn open so that the light may shine out from the cross planted in the center of the earth, from the tree of life, promising freedom from the way of gravity by participation in the order of grace. And if there is no darkness in God, then there can be no darkness in his gospel. If there *seems* to be darkness in the gospel, we can be *sure* that it is not on God's account, but on account of the gospel's stewards, or misunderstood by those hearing it, or rejected by those "whose deeds are evil and therefore hate the light" (John 3:19–20).

East of Eden we "naturally" participate in the will to power and the ways of force under the old world of gravity. But the tree of life/cross of Christ has nevertheless always stood at the center of creation, for the good of the church, humanity and the world, bringing *resurrection* for all those who participate in Christ's own *practice* of God's new reality.[142] God has reconciled all things in Christ, and will bring all things together when the kingdom is fully realized. Then and there, the explicit and implicit kingdom of God will be known as one, when those who saw, and gazed upon, and touched the manifest life (1 John 1:1–2), and those who desperately grasped after his trailing garment, feeling their way toward him and finding him (Acts 17:27) will together partake of the hidden manna.[143] Until the final unveiling of Christ, the bread of life remains hidden in the world

---

142. Eugene Peterson aptly summarizes the gospel imperative in the title of his 2010 book *Practice Resurrection*.

143. See Revelation 2:17. The manna remains "hidden" in the heavenly reality even during the present era, signifying that the comparative fullness of the revelation of Christ, in relation to the preceding limited era, nevertheless remains a seeing and partaking of Christ "through a glass darkly" (1 Corinthians 13:12).

in both trajectories of God's kingdom. In the coming daybreak, any hint of a "dark side" of the pure gospel will be shown to have been the figment of a fleeting shadow that was only seen through eyes that were "bad" and saw darkness where there was only light (Matt 6:22–23). God asks, "is your eye evil because I am good?" (Matt 20:15). And so once again, we see the sign of the prophet Jonah in some overshadowed stewards of the gospel, reluctant to allow the gospel's light free reign. "And the light shineth in darkness; and the darkness comprehended it not" (John 1:5).

It may be helpful to consider one more text, to supplement the three we began our postscript with. The text narrates the content of the faith of the king of Nineveh which issued in his own repentance and that of the Ninevites:

> Who knows? God may turn and relent from his fierce anger, so that we may not perish (Jonah 3:5).

What is interesting for our purpose is to notice that the *content* of this faith and repentance is summarized by the King's words, "*who knows?*" In other words, God's only explicit revelation to the Ninevites was the announcement of their impending doom: "Yet forty days, and Nineveh shall be overthrown!" (Jonah 3:4). All that the Ninevites "believed" (Jonah 3:5) was that this God, who they didn't actually know, was their judge, and that they were accountable to him, and that they were guilty of great evil against humanity. No intimation of mercy was given, no hint of grace that would spare them. Their judgment was announced as *inevitable*. But in some way, they intuited that "God is not the God of the inevitable but of the unforeseeable."[144] To apply this to the existence-revelation of Christ we note several things.

First, there is little difference between God's explicit announcement of judgment, and "the cross" in creation wherein humans all find their ways invariably at *cross-purposes* with the providence of life, with inevitable death, and with the pangs of conscience which speak of our accountability to "the unknown God." Whether an explicit declaration of inevitable judgment, or the impending doom of the cross in creation, the basis for faith in some "salvation" can only be implicit.

Second, therefore the "basis" of faith must be *read into* our accountability, by reading a hope of *some* salvation into it.

Third, we note that according to other scriptures, Nineveh's repentance proved to lapse after a generation or so, and therefore did

---

144. Shoemaker, *GodStories*, 134.

not positively bring Nineveh into the broader historical scope of God's explicit redemptive purposes, at least not until the time of Christ.[145] In other words, the "salvation" of Nineveh at that time was more like the form of salvation that the inclusivist view posits, what we earlier called the "redemptive-creational trajectory," *the implicit story* which constantly runs "beneath the lines" of the "redemptive-historical trajectory," *the explicit story* of the coming of God's *historical* kingdom.

This unique OT account of repentance among those with no explicit revelation of salvation, seems to provide an example of "salvation" which is better understood through the inclusivist view than the exclusivist. The exclusivist view might be better able to argue for its case, if Nineveh had followed the exclusivist view that there can be no positive response to mere "accountability." Thankfully, they did not follow that view and instead intuited the gospel because of Christ's deep atoning dive into their humanity.

Revelation, the Mysteries of Human Personality, and the Mystery of God

It seems that the greatest obstacle to being receptive to this proposition, is the conflict that has ironically been caused by the entrance of "the Word" as flesh so that "the way, the truth, and the life" could be *seen,* or more accurately "comprehended" in the lives of others *to some measure.* This *seeing* is of course necessary due to the historical coming of the visible kingdom of Christ which finds a "normative" use of *sight* for viewing the church itself. The problem is supposing that the revelation provided to see the church reveals the final results of the hidden reality of people living apart from the conscious knowledge of Christ. The existence-revelation of Christ does reveal the nature of that *being-in-relation* to Christ, but it does not save or reveal the saved. It only reveals the nature of life that provides the "universal opportunity." In regard to the exclusivist view, my proposal could be rephrased as,

---

145. Blower presents the fascinating history of how the dispersed Assyrians became "among the first peoples to embrace Christianity" and that Jonah's "City of Blood has become a city of blood once again . . . it is none other than Jonah's Assyrians—the Christians of Mosul on the Northern Plains—who are now being brutalized by Islamic State militants." Blower, *Sympathy for Jonah,* 36, n.8.

> "The light shines in the darkness of those living apart from the explicit gospel, but *the* exclusivist's gospel light has not comprehended or overcome it."

The existence-revelation of Christ merely reveals the possibility of all lives because there is a "universality of human experience" and a "mystery of the human personality, operative at all times and all places . . . and the holiness it harbors."[146] But the specific revelation of particular lives lived apart from the conscious knowledge of Christ are only fully knowable by God, just as the lives of those who consciously follow Christ are only fully known to God, for "we know in part" and "see in a mirror dimly" as Paul wrote (1 Cor 13:12).

This lengthy postscript has been presented as a necessary sub-hearing of "The Gospel in the Dock" by trying to show that the gospel is wholly good even in its multifaceted mystery, in contrast to exclusivism's mystery removing/good reducing understanding whereby it can simply posit the damnation of all those who never hear the gospel. In sum, the existence-revelation of Christ does not reveal "dogma" with which the stewards can infallibly exegete the mysteries of each and every human life. Instead, it reveals the possibility God has embedded in all of life, of human being-in-relation to God, of the mysterious goodness of God, who *is* love, and eternal life (1 John 4:8, 5:20). And because of Christ, present in all of human life, any human life can reach forth and touch the hem of his healing garment. For one touching Christ, incarnate in all of life, touches eternal life."

---

146. O'Donnell, *Flannery O'Connor*, 123. The existence-revelation of Christ is the basis of O'Connor's revelational writing: "O'Connor's art is an act of faith—a means through which she glimpsed the human, the divine, and the invisible nexus that connects the two—and then she passed those glimpses on to her readers" (123).

Epilogue
"The Beginning of the End of Adversaries"

> The Lord is good, a stronghold in the day of trouble; he knows those who take refuge in him. But with an overflowing flood he will make a complete end of the adversaries, and will pursue his enemies into darkness.
>
> —NAHUM 1:7-8

THIS "EPILOGUE" WILL REVISIT a "Jonah" text we saw in Chapter 2, from Nahum, having to do with Nineveh, one of many historic enemies of God, in order to end on the positive note of two of the gospel's *otherworldly* ways of liberation, ways that ironically provide the gospel's true *worldly good* for humanity and the world.[1]

God's Stronghold of Refuge

The Lord is Good, a stronghold in the day of trouble; he knows those who take refuge in him.

---

1. The gospel's "otherworldly" ways are ironically beneficial to the world: "If you read history you will find that the Christians who did the most for the present world are just the ones that thought the most of the next. The Apostles themselves, who set on foot the conversion of the Roman Empire, the great men who built up the Middle Ages, the English Evangelicals who abolished the Slave Trade, all left their mark on Earth, precisely because their minds were occupied with Heaven. It is since Christians have largely ceased to think of the other world that they have become so ineffective in this. Aim at Heaven and you will get the earth "thrown in": aim at earth and you will get neither." Lewis, *Mere Christianity*, 104.

God is *the* good stronghold *from* the ways of force in the order of gravity, the self and others following the self-enslaving others-oppressing ways of the will to power. The fortress cities of Cain do not provide refuge from these fallen ways but rather "settle" themselves and their inhabitants "East of Eden" "away from the presence of God." But God "knows those who take refuge in him." Though Cain and his kind, in some sense move away from the presence of the Lord, Christopher Hitchens viewed God's presence as a tyrannical "cradle to the grave" surveillance.[2] It is difficult to know whether this was a mistake in metaphysics or a truth of human psychology that followed Hitchens. But as for God, both Scriptural testaments instead reveal God as overwhelmed by intimately "knowing" the sufferings of humanity and therefore bending all his efforts to *become* the stronghold for humankind to find refuge in.[3] What Hitchens and others like him consider God's cold, heartless, totalitarian surveillance, contrarily demonstrates the love in God's attention, grief, regret, suffering, and compassion:

> *The voice* of your brother's blood is *crying to me* from the ground (Gen 4:10) . . . The Lord *saw* that the wickedness of man was great in the earth, and that every intention of the thoughts of his heart was only evil continually. And the Lord *regretted* that he had made man on the earth, *and it grieved him to his heart* . . . (Gen 6:5–6) . . . What troubles you, Hagar? For God has *heard the voice* of the boy where he is. Up! Lift up the boy, and hold him fast with your hand, for I will make him into a great nation (Gen 21:17–18) . . . Then the Lord said, "I have surely *seen the affliction* of my people who are in Egypt and have *heard their cry* because of their taskmasters. *I know their sufferings*, and I have come down *to deliver them* out of the hand of the Egyptians and to bring them up out of that land *to a good and broad land, a land flowing with milk and honey* (Ex 3:7–8) . . . Now the word of the Lord came to Jonah the son of Amittai, saying, "Arise, go to Nineveh, that great city, and call out against it, for their evil has come up before me." (Jonah 1:1–2) The Lord is Good, a

---

2. Hitchens, "I am not even."

3. Terrence Fretheim writes of some of the depictions of God in the OT: "God is thus portrayed not as a king dealing with an issue at a distance . . . God sees suffering from the inside . . . God is internally related to the suffering of the people. God enters fully into the hurtful situation and makes it his own . . . for God to bear the sufferings of the people had a negative effect on God. God's life was somehow expended because of his internalization of the sufferings of the people; God suffered because they were suffering." Fretheim, *Suffering of God*, loc. 1740.

stronghold in the day of trouble; *he knows those who take refuge in him* (Nah 1:7).[4]

Certainly, we must therefore also believe that God *saw, and heard, and knew*, the suffering and inarticulate unspoken cries of Christopher Hitchens. It seems that perhaps the overly formulaic notions of a distant judgmental, contractual God, too commonly the picture propagated by God's stewards, continue to lead many such as Christopher Hitchens to reject the God who does not exist.[5] Living our lives in its many sufferings of body, soul, and spirit may lead us to "close the book" on the God we think we see in the Bible and in Christ. But a closer and more faithful "reading" tells us that God never closes the book on us. For the sufferings of Christ, "hidden" in the sign of the prophet Jonah, and missed by all humankind including God's "Jonahs," speak better things of God's caring attention and intimate knowledge of each fallen sparrow and person (Matt 10:29–30). For the sign reveals in its veiling the solidarity of the triune God with the suffering people of all times. Jonah's three days in the Sheol-belly of the beast signified more than three calendar days of Christ's sufferings with humankind. We can in no way fathom the suffering of God, the eternal dance of divine love, *entering creation* to dwell in, and ultimately redeem, the sufferings of humanity *as* its hungry, its thirsty, its strangers, its naked, its sick, its imprisoned.[6] Indeed, "the Lord is Good."

God's Pursuit of Enemies

But with an overflowing flood he will make a complete end of the adversaries and will pursue his enemies into darkness.

---

4. This narration of God certainly runs through the entire Bible in one way or another, and even so we but glimpse the hem of the garment of God's full character. In regard to the narration of God *as a character in Genesis*, Humphreys writes, "There is an openness to him as a character as well. He seems more than the sum of what is narrated . . . We clearly sense that not all is known about him." Humphreys, *Character of God*, 21.

5. See Radcliff, *Claim of Humanity*, 15–47. Jacques Maritain says, "there are *pseudo-atheists*" because "the God whose existence they deny is not God but something else." Maritain, *Social and Political Thought*, 171.

6. C. S. Lewis writes, "God is not a static thing—not even a person—but a dynamic, pulsating activity, a life, almost a kind of drama. Almost, if you will not think me irreverent, a kind of dance." Lewis, *Mere Christianity*, 136.

The gospel is "the beginning of the end of adversaries."[7] Traditionally, in most Christian belief, the *end* of the end of adversaries transpires in the final day of God's wrath to be brought upon his adversaries. But does that act of God, like the notion of a gospel that leads to the condemnation of those never hearing it, seem to be true to what has been revealed of God's ways that were made evident in the gospel? We have seen that the cross was a different type of victory, the overcoming of God's enemies through Christ being overcome by the demonic and human forces aiming to wholly negate God. Again, the sign of the prophet Jonah reveals the otherworldliness of the gospel in its way of self-emptying faith. For that gospel was the only hope, for something other than the sheer "will to power," to become an established and available reality for the good of humankind and the world. The gospel is the self-emptying of the way of faith that ironically, counterintuitively, and justly leads to participation in the truly liberating power of God. In contrast, the self-embrace of the will to power in the way of force ironically, counterintuitively, and justly turns the soul in on itself and ends in self-perpetuating self-destruction.[8] This is the gospel's way of euchatastrophe that is wholly good, bringing blessed catastrophe upon the final adversaries bent on self-love that oppresses all and ends in their own self-destruction (Luke 1:51–55; 68–75).

God's Sign of the Prophet Jonah

This is the choice that still remains "hidden" for humankind in the sign of the prophet Jonah, "the only sign given to this generation"—which means *all* generations. The sign, despite the manifold ways that its intricacies can be imagined and understood, ever remains a sign and that calls for faith to be "seen." The sign includes God's fleshly enactment of all eventualities of sin and death, resurrection and life, that lay hidden in the bare command given in Eden. The sign shows God in Christ pursuing his enemies, us, into the darkness around and in us. The sign perennially offends our "reason," because to participate in its veiled good, requires entering into

---

7. Our thoughts in much of this epilogue largely echo what was presented in our excursus which followed our introduction.

8. The prophecy of Obadiah 15 pictures the "automatic" reciprocity of force used to gain power over others as the grounds of the inevitable self-judgment of God's counterintuitive power-relinquishing kingdom: "For the day of the Lord is near upon all the nations. As you have done, it shall be done to you; *your deeds shall return on your own head.*" (Emphasis added.)

its apparent death. The sign reveals God's high dive into the cold heart of darkness, to overcome it through the non-grasping self-existent being of God who consists in the eternal triune dance of self-giving love.

In sum, God's gospel reveals "the beginning of the end of adversaries" by *mediating* their adversity. That way has sometimes been discovered, albeit only "here and there in the world and now and then in ourselves . . . usually hidden, but sometimes manifest" by blessed peacemakers.[9] But it is only discovered because God has woven it into the very fabric of the transcendent order of grace which cannot be overcome by evil, but overcomes evil with good (Rom 12:21). Each person throughout the ages has alternatively thrust away and grasped for this gospel, for there are only these two ways. God's stewards of the gospel have alternatively thrust away and grasped for this gospel. All societal groups have alternatively either thrust away and grasped for this gospel. For this is "the sign of the prophet Jonah—the only sign given" to humankind in the valley of decision between the will to power against the face of the other and way of faith and peace toward the face of the other. And only the one way can see God's face and live.

Ultimately, God's *overflowing flood* that will *make a complete end of the adversaries* is seen in the vision of Ezekiel, as the water flowing from God's new temple becomes a great river flowing into the sea and transforming its salt waters to fresh water (Ezek 47:1–12). Therefore Revelation 22:17 says,

> The Spirit and the Bride say, "Come." And let the one who hears say, "Come." And let the one who is thirsty come; let the one who desires take the water of life without price.[10]

God's gospel words to humankind conclude with an open invitation to those remaining "outside." The end of adversaries is already accomplished "from God's side." To put it in modern jargon, God says, "the ball is in your court." The Scriptures present no tidy end of a universal homecoming for true home only exists where all *want* to be welcomed.

Humanity ever stands "in the valley of decision." Will "the gospel in the dock" prove to be our ultimate way of self-salvation, our ultimate way of self-damnation, or under the sign of the prophet Jonah, our way

---

9. Tillich, *The New Being*, 18.

10. Note that "the Bride" signifies God's gospel stewards viewed as finally faithfully breathing the gospel words of God's Spirit, demonstrating the ideal accomplishment of "God's purification of means."

of God's salvation? For in that sign, the power-relinquishing Christ has "pursued us into darkness," into "the belly of the beast," raising us from its cavernous depths of power and futility, to surface in a new world, where Christ's new human community rises on the shoreline to grow into a living holy temple of God's Spirit.

> "I called out to the Lord, out of my distress, and he answered me; out of the belly of Sheol I cried, and you heard my voice. For you cast me into the deep, into the heart of the seas, and the flood surrounded me; all your waves and your billows passed over me. Then I said, 'I am driven away from your sight; yet I shall again look upon your holy temple' (Jonah 2:2–4).

God's Sign of Isaac

The story of Jonah, the long-time occupation of this book, might be seen as a tragedy or a comedy. But it *is* a comedy, because "it pokes fun at our human foibles and has a happy ending. Tragedy is about the inevitable, says novelist Frederich Buechner, and comedy is about the unforeseeable. And the story of Jonah is full of the unforeseeable."[11] The end of the narrated story of Jonah leaves him, and therefore leaves God's stewards, ambivalent before God, humankind, and the world, just sitting there between the inevitable he thought he wanted, and the unforeseeable he longed for, but couldn't quite surrender to. The glory of humanity is the possibility of the unforeseeable, and God only allows that to those beloved creatures. But the temptation of humanity is to grasp after the inevitable, and to always end in tragedy. For we think we can clearly see our way ahead of us, beckoning us from our *self-conceived* future. But only God can call us *from* the truly good and possible, unforeseeable future, *from* our new humanity in Christ.

In the sign of Jonah, we can either sit with Jonah *tragically*, in *anxiety* waiting for the inevitable, under the meager yet sufficient shade in the desert where God graciously enabled Jonah's comfortable observation of "the gospel in the dock."

Or we can sit with Jesus *comedically*, in *faith* waiting for the unforeseeable, under the plenteous shade of the tree of life "on either side of the

---

11. Shoemaker, *GodStories*, 128.

river ... with its twelve kinds of fruit yielding its fruit for each month ... the leaves of the tree for the healing of the nations" (Rev 22:2).[12]

For truly, the mirth of God's originary youngness, exulting in the earth's cross and comedy, jubilant in the eucatastrophe of Christ's cross, will wipe away every tear from the epoch of weeping, turning its mourning into dancing.[13] No wonder that Abraham and Sarah, the new Adam and Eve, patriarch and matriarch of the faith of all humankind, were "surprised by laughter" and told by God to name the child of promise given for them and for the church, humanity, and all the creatures of the world, *Isaac*, or "he laughs."[14] Thus the dark mystery of the sign of the prophet Jonah, the only sign given to humanity, is ultimately fulfilled by the bright sign of *Isaac*, the mirthful laughter of the mysterious God become flesh, to catch all creation up together in God's eternal joyous dance. To borrow several phrases from Pierre Teilhard de Chardin, "everything that rises must converge" in *the divine milieu* of God's eternal joy.[15]

---

12. By faith we can now "see" the unforeseeable, and the comic quality, the euchatastrophe of life because of Christ's gospel. Flannery O'Connor wrote, "Only if we are secure in our beliefs can we see the comical side of the universe." As cited by Lindvall, *Surprised by Laughter*, 79.

13. "It may be that He has the eternal appetite of infancy; for we have sinned and grown old, and our Father is younger than we." Chesterton, Heretics/*Orthodoxy*, 218. See Eccl 3:4

14. See Gen 17:15–21; 21:1–7; Rom 4:11–16. "Surprised by laughter" is from Lindvall, *Surprised by Laughter*.

15. The quoted phrase is from Teilhard de Chardin, *The Future of Man*, 186; and the italicized phrase is from Teilhard de Chardin, *The Divine Milieu*.

Bibliography

Alexander, Archibald. *Thoughts on Religious Experience*. Edinburgh: Banner of Truth Trust, 1978 [1844].
Allen, Diogenes, "A Christian Theology of Other Faiths," *Theology Today* 38:3 (1981) 305–13.
———. *Steps Along the Way: A Spiritual Autobiography*. New York: Church, 2002.
———. "Suffering at the Hands of Nature," *Theology Today* 37:2 (1980) 183–91.
———. *Spiritual Theology: The Theology of Yesterday for Spiritual Help Today*, Boston: Cowley, 1997.
———. *Three Outsiders: Soren Kierkegaard, Blaise Pascal, Simone Weil*. Boston: Cowley, 1983
Anderson, Joel Edmund. "Jonah in Mark and Matthew: Creation, Covenant, Christ, and the Kingdom of God" *Biblical Theology Bulletin* 42:4, (2012) 172–86.
Backhouse, Stephen. *Kierkegaard: A Single Life*. Grand Rapids: Zondervan, 2016.
Badcock, Gary. *The House Where God Lives: Renewing the Doctrine of the Church for Today*. Grand Rapids: Eerdmans, 2009.
———. *Light of Truth & Fire of Love: A Theology of the Holy Spirit*. Grand Rapids: Eerdmans, 1997.
———. *The Way of Life: A Theology of Christian Vocation*. Grand Rapids: Eerdmans, 1998.
Baggett, John F. *Seeing Through the Eyes of Jesus: His Revolutionary View of Reality & His Transcendent Significance for Faith*. Grand Rapids: Eerdmans, 2008.
Baker, Hunter. *The End of Secularism*. Wheaton: Crossway, 2009.
Barnett, Christopher B. *From Despair to Faith: The Spirituality of Soren Kierkegaard*. Minneapolis: Fortress, 2014.
Barnett, Paul. *Finding the Historical Christ*. After Jesus, Volume 3. Grand Rapids: Eerdmans, 2009.
Barth, Karl. *The Epistle to the Ephesians*. Translated by Ross M. Wright. Grand Rapids: Baker Academic, 2017.
Barth, Karl., and William H. Willimon. *The Early Preaching of Karl Barth: Fourteen Sermons with Commentary by William H. Willimon*. Translations by John E. Wilson. Louisville: Westminster John Knox, 2009.
Bauckham, Richard., and Trevor Hart. *Hope Against Hope: Christian Eschatology at the Turn of the Millennium*. Grand Rapids: Eerdmans, 1999.
Beale, G. K. *The Book of Revelation*. New International Greek Testament Commentary. Grand Rapids: Eerdmans, 1999.

———. *The Temple and the Church's Mission: A Biblical Theology of the Dwelling Place of God.* New Studies in Biblical Theology. Downers Grove: InterVarsity, 2004.

Beale, G. K., and D. A. Carson. *Commentary on the New Testament Use of the Old Testament.* Grand Rapids: Baker Academic, 2007.

Beeby, H. D. *Hosea—Grace Abounding.* International Theological Commentary. Grand Rapids: Eerdmans, 1989.

Belmonte, Kevin. *Defiant Joy: The Remarkable Life & Impact of G. K. Chesterton,* Nashville: Thomas Nelson, 2011.

Bennett, David. *A War of Loves: The Unexpected Story of a Gay Activist Discovering Jesus.* Grand Rapids: Zondervan, 2018.

Berger, Peter L. *The Sacred Canopy: Elements of a Sociological Theory of Religion.* Kindle Edition. New York: Open Road Integrated Media, 2011 [1967].

Berkouwer, G. C. *The Church.* Studies in Dogmatics. Translated by James E. Davison. Grand Rapids: Eerdmans, 1976.

———. *The Providence of God.* Studies in Dogmatics. Translated by Lewis B. Smedes. Grand Rapids: Eerdmans, 1983

———. *The Triumph of Grace in the Theology of Karl Barth,* Grand Rapids: Wm. B. Eerdmans, 1956.

Biden, Joseph R. Jr. "Inaugural Address by President Joseph R. Biden Jr." https://www.whitehouse.gov/briefing-room/speeches-remarks/2021/01/20/inaugural-address-by-president-joseph-r-biden-jr/

Biette, Ruthie L. *The Battle of Crawdad Hole.* Crawdad Kids, Book 1. Greenville SC: Ambassador International, 2020.

Bloch, Ariel., and Chana Bloch, *The Song of Songs: A New Translation.* Berkley: University of California Press, 1995.

Blower, David Benjamin. *Sympathy for Jonah: Reflections on Humiliation, Terror and the Politics of Enemy-Love.* Eugene OR: Resource Publications, 2016.

Bock, Darrell L. *Luke.* IVP New Testament Commentary Series. Downers Grove: InterVarsity, 1994.

Boersma, Hans. *Heavenly Participation: The Weaving of a Sacramental Tapestry.* Grand Rapids: Eerdmans, 2011.

Bonhoeffer, Dietrich. *Berlin: 1932–1933,* Translated by Isabel Best and David Higgins. Dietrich Bonhoeffer Works 12. Minneapolis: Fortress, 2009.

———. *Creation and Fall,* Translated by Douglas Stephen Bax. Dietrich Bonhoeffer Works 3. Minneapolis: Fortress, 1997

———. *Discipleship,* Translated by Barbra Green and Reinhard Krauss. Dietrich Bonhoeffer Works 4. Minneapolis: Fortress, 2001.

———. *Ethics,* Translated by Reinhard Krauss, Charles C. West, and Douglas W. Scott. Dietrich Bonhoeffer Works 6. Minneapolis: Fortress, 2005.

———. *Letters and Papers from Prison,* Translated by Isabel Best, Lisa E. Dahill, Reinhard Krauss, and Nancy Lukens. Dietrich Bonhoeffer Works 8. Minneapolis: Fortress, 2010.

———. *Life Together—Prayerbook of the Bible,* Translated by Daniel W. Bloesch and James H. Burtness. Dietrich Bonhoeffer Works 5. Minneapolis: Fortress, 1996.

Borchert, Gerald L. *John 1–11.* The New American Commentary, Nashville: Broadman & Holman, 1996.

Boring, M. Eugene, *Revelation.* Interpretation: A Bible Commentary for Preaching and Teaching. Louisville: John Knox, 1989.

Brock, Rita Nakashima and Rebecca Ann Parker. *Saving Paradise—How Christianity Traded Love of This World for Crucifixion and Empire.* Boston: Beacon, 2008.

Bruce, F. F. *The Book of the Acts*. The New International Commentary on the New Testament. Grand Rapids: Eerdmans, 1988.

Brueggemann, Walter. *Biblical Evangelism—Living in a Three-Storied Universe*. Nashville: Abingdon, 1993.

———. *Genesis*. Interpretation. A Bible Commentary for Preaching and Teaching. Kindle Edition. Louisville: John Knox, 2010.

———. *The Land: Place as Gift, Promise, and Challenge in Biblical Faith*. Overtures to Biblical Theology. Philadelphia: Fortress, 1977.

———. *Mandate to Difference—An Invitation to the Contemporary Church*. Louisville: John Knox, 2007.

———. *The Message of the Psalms—A Theological Commentary*. Minneapolis: Augsburg, 1984.

———. *Out of Babylon*. Nashville: Abingdon, 2010.

———. *Praying the Psalms*. Winona MN: St. Mary's, 1982.

———. *Reality, Grief, Hope—Three Urgent Prophetic Tasks*. Grand Rapids: Eerdmans, 2014.

Bruner, Michael Mears. *A Subversive Gospel: Flannery O'Connor and the Reimagining of Beauty, Goodness, and Truth*. Downers Grove: IVP Academic, 2017.

Brunner, Emil. *Man in Revolt: A Christian Anthropology*. Translated by Olive Wyon. Philadelphia: Westminster, 1947.

Burnett, Richard E. *Karl Barth's Theological Exegesis: The Hermeneutical Principles of the Romerbrief Period*. Grand Rapids: Eerdmans, 2004.

Butler, Judith. *Excitable Speech—A Politics of the Performative*. New York: Routledge, 1997.

Byassee, Jason. *Psalms 101–150*. Brazos Theological Commentary on the Bible. Grand Rapids: Brazos, 2018.

Calvin, John. *Institutes of the Christian Religion, Volume 1*. Translated by Ford Lewis Battles. The Library of Christian Classics. Philadelphia: Westminster, 1960.

Caputo, John B. "Beyond Sovereignty: Many Nations Under the Weakness of God" *Soundings* 89:1–2 (2006) 21–35.

Carson, D. A. *The Cross and Christian Ministry: Leadership Lessons from 1 Corinthians*. Grand Rapids: Baker, 1993.

———. *The Gospel According to John*. Grand Rapids: Eerdmans, 1991.

———. "What is the Gospel?—Revisited" in *For the Fame of God's Name: Essays in Honor of John Piper*, edited by Sam Storms et al., 147–70. Wheaton: Crossway, 2010.

Catherwood, Christopher. *The Evangelicals—What They Believe, Who They Are, and Their Politics*. Wheaton: Crossway, 2010.

Caws, Peter. et al., *The Causes of Quarrel—Essays on Peace, War, and Thomas Hobbes*, edited by Peter Caws, 78–127. Boston: Beacon, 1989.

Chester, Tim. *Good News to the Poor—Social Involvement and The Gospel*. Wheaton: Crossway, 2013.

Chesterton, G. K. *The Everlasting Man*. San Francisco: Ignatius, 1993 [1925].

———. *Heretics/Orthodoxy*. Nelson's Royal Classics. Nashville: Thomas Nelson, 2000 [1905, 1908].

Chenavier, Robert. "Simone Weil: Completing Platonism Through a Consistent Materialism" in *The Christian Platonism of Simone Weil* edited by E. Jane Doering et al., 61–76. Notre Dame: Notre Dame Press, 2004.

Childs, Brevard S. *The Book of Exodus*. The Old Testament Library. Philadelphia: Westminster, 1974.

Chisney, Vernon W. "All the World is Shining, and Love is Smiling through All Things— The Collapse of the 'Two Ways' in *The Tree of Life*" in *The Way of Nature and the Way of Grace: Philosophical Footholds in Terrence Malick's The Tree of Life*, edited by Jonathan Beever et al., 213–32. Evanston IL: Northwestern University Press, 2016.

Cole, Allen Hugh Jr. *Be Not Anxious: Pastoral Care of Disquieted Souls.* Grand Rapids: Eerdmans, 2008.

Crump, David. *Encountering Jesus, Encountering Scripture—Reading the Bible Critically in Faith.* Grand Rapids: Eerdmans, 2013.

Dark, David. *The Gospel According to America—A Meditation on a God-blessed, Christ-haunted Idea.* Louisville: Westminster John Knox Press, 2005.

Davids, Peter H. *The First Epistle of Peter.* The New International Commentary on the New Testament. Grand Rapids: Eerdmans, 1990.

Dawkins, Richard. *The God Delusion.* Boston: Houghton Mifflin, 2006.

Delay, Tad. *Against: What Does the White Evangelical Want?* Eugene OR: Cascade, 2019.

Dembski, William A. *The End of Christianity: Finding a Good God in an Evil World,* Nashville: B&H Academic, 2009.

Desmond, John F. *Gravity and Grace—Seamus Heaney and the Force of Light.* Waco TX: Baylor University Press, 2009.

———. *Risen Sons—Flannery O'Connor's Vision of History,* Athens: University of Georgia Press, 1987.

Dillard, Annie. *An American Childhood.* New York: HarperPerennial, 1987.

———. *Pilgrim at Tinker Creek.* New York: Bantam, 1974.

Doering, E. Jane. *Simone Weil and the Spectre of Self-Perpetuating Force.* Notre Dame: University of Notre Dame Press, 2010.

Eagleton, Terry. *Reason, Faith, and Revolution: Reflections on the God Debate.* The Terry Lectures Series. London: Yale University Press, 2010.

Easley, Kendell. *Revelation*—Holman New Testament Commentary. Nashville: Broadman & Holman, 1998.

Ellison. H. L. "Jonah." In *The Expositor's Bible Commentary*, edited by Frank L Gaebelein et al., 7:361–91. Grand Rapids: Zondervan, 1985.

Ellul, Jacques, *The Meaning of the City.* Biblical and Theological Classics Library. Grand Rapids: Paternoster, 1970.

Endo, Shusaku. *Silence.* Translated by William Johnston. New York: Picador, 2016 [1966].

Evans, C. Stephen. *Faith Beyond Reason: A Kierkegaardian Account.* Grand Rapids: Eerdmans, 1998.

———. *Kierkegaard and Spirituality: Accountability as the Meaning of Human Existence.* Kierkegaard as a Christian Thinker. Grand Rapids: Eerdmans, 2019.

———. *Soren Kierkegaard's Christian Psychology—Insight for Counseling and Pastoral Care.* Vancouver: Regent College Publishing, 1990.

Federici, Michael P. *Eric Voegelin: The Restoration of Order.* Library of Modern Thinkers. Wilmington DE: ISI, 2002.

Feinberg, John S. ed. *Continuity and Discontinuity—Perspectives on the Relationship Between the Old and New Testaments.* Wheaton: Crossway, 1988.

Ferreira, M. Jamie. "Levinas and Kierkegaard on Triadic Relations with God" in *Gazing Through a Prism Darkly*, 46–60, edited by B. Keith Putt. Perspectives in Continental Philosophy. New York: Fordham University Press, 2009.

———. *Love's Grateful Striving: A Commentary on Kierkegaard's Works of Love,* New York: Oxford University Press, 2001.

Ferry, Luc. *A Brief History of Thought: A Philosophical Guide to Living.* New York: Harper Perennial, 2011.

Ferguson, Harvie. *Melancholy and the Critique of Modernity: Soren Kierkegaard's Religious Psychology.* London: Routledge, 1995.

Fretheim, Terrence E. *Exodus.* Interpretation: A Bible Commentary for Preaching and Teaching. Louisville: John Knox, 1991.

———. *The Suffering of God: An Old Testament Perspective.* Overtures to Biblical Theology, Philadelphia: Fortress, 1984.

Frost, David. *Billy Graham: Candid Conversations with a Public Man.* Kindle Edition. Colorado Springs: David C. Cook, 2014.

Gabellieri, Emanuel. "Reconstructing Platonism: The Trinitarian Metaxology of Simone Weil" in *The Christian Platonism of Simone Weil,* edited by E. Jane Doering et al., 133–58. Notre Dame: University of Notre Dame Press, 2004.

Garland, David E. *A Theology of Mark's Gospel.* Biblical Theology of the New Testament, Grand Rapids: Zondervan, 2015.

Geldenhuys, Norval. *The Gospel of Luke.* The New Testament Commentary on the New Testament, Grand Rapids: Eerdmans, 1993.

Goldsworthy, Graeme. *The Lamb & The Lion—The Gospel in Revelation.* Nashville: Thomas Nelson, 1984.

Golka, Friedemann W. "Divine Repentance: Commentary on the Book of Jonah" in, *Revelation of God: The Song of Songs & Jonah,* by George A. F. Knight et al., 65–136. International Theological Commentary. Grand Rapids: Eerdmans, 1988.

Gorman, Michael J. *Reading Revelation Responsibly—Uncivil Worship and Witness—Following the Lamb into the New Creation.* Eugene OR: Cascade, 2011.

Green, Bradley C. *The Gospel and the Mind: Recovering and Shaping the Intellectual Life,* Wheaton: Crossway, 2010.

Greene, Colin J. D. *Christology in Cultural Perspective—Mapping Out the Horizons.* Grand Rapids: Eerdmans, 2003.

Grindheim, Sigurd. *Living in the Kingdom of God—A Biblical Theology for the Life of the Church.* Grand Rapids: Baker Academic, 2013.

Gunton, Colin E. "The Doctrine of Creation" in *The Cambridge Companion to Christian Doctrine,* edited by Colin E. Gunton, 141–57. Cambridge Companions to Religion. Cambridge: Cambridge University Press, 1997

———. Gunton, Colin E. *Yesterday and Today: A Study of Continuities in Christology.* Grand Rapids: Eerdmans, 1983.

Gushee, David P., and Glen H. Stassen. *Kingdom Ethics—Following Jesus in Contemporary Context,* Second Edition. Kindle version. Grand Rapids: Eerdmans, 2016.

Habib, Sandy. "Who Converts Whom? A Narrative-Critical Exegesis of the Book of Jonah" Biblical Theology Bulletin 44:2 (2014) 67–75.

Hall, John Douglas. *Confessing the Faith: Christian Theology in a North American Context.* Minneapolis: Fortress, 1996.

Harrold, Charles Frederick, ed. *A Newman Treasury: Selections from the Prose Works of John Henry Newman.* New Rochelle NY: Arlington House, 1943.

Harvey, Barry. *Another City—An Ecclesiological Primer for a Post-Christian World.* Christian Mission and Modern Culture. Harrisburg PA: Trinity Press International, 1999.

———. *Can These Bones Live? A Catholic Baptist Engagement with Ecclesiology, Hermeneutics, and Social Theory.* Grand Rapids: Brazos, 2008.

———. *Taking Hold of the Real: Dietrich Bonhoeffer and the Profound Worldliness of Christianity.* Kindle version. Eugene OR: Cascade, 2015.

Hauerwas, Stanley. "Preaching as Though We Had Enemies." *First Things* (May 1995). https://www.firstthings.com/article/1995/05/preaching-as-though-we-had-enemies

Hays, Richard B. *First Corinthians*. Interpretation: A Bible Commentary for Preaching and Teaching. Louisville: John Knox, 1997.

———. *The Moral Vision of the New Testament: Community, Cross, New Creation—A Contemporary Introduction to New Testament Ethics,* Kindle version. New York: Harper One, 1995.

Hazony, Yoram. *The Philosophy of Hebrew Scripture*. Cambridge: Cambridge University Press, 2012.

Heim, S. Mark. "The End of Scapegoating." *Patterns of Violence*. Institute for Faith and Learning at Baylor University (2016) 20–27. https://www.baylor.edu/content/services/document.php/264317.pdf

Henriksen, Jan-Olav. *Desire, Gift, and Recognition—Christology and Postmodern Philosophy*. Grand Rapids: Eerdmans, 2009.

Henry, Carl F. H. *The Uneasy Conscience of Modern Fundamentalism*, Grand Rapids: Eerdmans, 1947.

Henry, Michel. *Words of Christ*. Translated by Christina M. Gschwandtner, Interventions. Grand Rapids: Eerdmans, 2012.

Heschel, Abraham J. *The Prophets—An Introduction, Volume 1*. New York: Harper, 1969.

Higgs, Robert. *Crisis and Leviathan—Critical Episodes in the Growth of American Government*. New York: Oxford University Press, 1987.

Hitchens, Christopher. "I am not even an atheist so much as an antitheist." https://www.goodreads.com/quotes/473943-i-am-not-even-an-atheist-so-much-as-an

Hobbes, Thomas. *Leviathan or The Matter, Forme & Power of a Common-wealth Ecclesiasticall and Civill*. The Barnes & Noble Library of Essential Reading. New York: Barnes & Noble, 2004 [1651].

Hoekema, Anthony A. *The Bible and the Future*. Grand Rapids: Eerdmans, 1979.

Humphreys, W. Lee. *The Character of God in the Book of Genesis: A Narrative Appraisal*. Louisville: Westminster John Knox, 2001.

Janz, Denis R. *The Westminster Handbook of Martin Luther*. The Westminster Handbook to Christian Theology. Louisville: Westminster John Knox, 2010.

Jardine, Murray. *The Making and Unmaking of Technological Society: How Christianity Can Save Modernity from Itself*. The Christian Practice of Everyday Life Series. Grand Rapids: Brazos, 2004.

Jennings, W. J. *Acts*. Belief: A Theological Commentary on the Bible. Logos Library System Version. Louisville, KY: Westminster John Knox Press, 2017.

Jervis, L. Ann. *Galatians*. New International Biblical Commentary. Peabody MA: Hendrickson, 1999.

Jewett, Robert, *Mission and Menace—Four Centuries of American Religious Zeal*. Minneapolis: Fortress, 2008.

Johnston, Robert K. *God's Wider Presence: Reconsidering General Revelation*. Grand Rapids: Baker Academic, 2014.

Jordan, James. "Exile or Ark?" *Biblical Horizons Blog*, April 10, 2008. https://biblicalhorizons.wordpress.com/2008/04/10/exile-or-ark/

———. *Primeval Saints: Studies in the Patriarchs of Genesis*. Moscow ID: Canon, 2001.

Joustra, Robert., and Alissa Wilkinson. *How to Survive the Apocalypse—Zombies, Cylons, Faith, and Politics*. Grand Rapids: Eerdmans, 2016.

Bibliography

Keller, Timothy. *Center Church: Doing Balanced, Gospel-Centered Ministry in Your City.* Grand Rapids: Zondervan, 2012.

Kerr, Hugh T., and John M. Mulder., eds. *Conversions: The Christian Experience.* Grand Rapids: Eerdmans, 1983.

Kierkegaard, Soren. *Christian Discourses and The Lilies of the Field and the Birds of the Air and Three discourses at the Communion on Fridays.* Translated by Walter Lowrie, London: Oxford University press, 1940.

———. *The Concept of Anxiety: A Simple Psychologically Orienting Deliberation on the Dogmatic Issue of Hereditary Sin.* Translated by Reidar Thomte, Kierkegaard's Writings, VIII. Princeton: Princeton University Press, 1980.

———. *Concluding Unscientific Postscript to Philosophical Fragments, Volume I.* Kierkegaard's Writings, XII.1. Translated by Howard V. Hong and Edna H. Hong, Princeton: Princeton University Press, 1992.

———. *Fear and Trembling/Repetition,* Kierkegaard's Writings, VI. Translated by Howard V. Hong and Edna H. Hong, Princeton: Princeton University Press, 1983.

———. *For Self-Examination/Judge for Yourself!,* Kierkegaard's Writings XXI. Translated by Howard V. Hong and Edna H. Hong, Princeton: Princeton University Press,1990.

———. *Kierkegaard's Attack Upon "Christendom" 1854–1855.* Translated by Walter Lowrie, Princeton: Princeton University Press, 1946.

———. *Practice in Christianity,* Kierkegaard's Writings, XX. Translated by Howard V. Hong and Edna H. Hong, Princeton: Princeton University Press, 1991.

———. *Purity of Heart is to Will One Thing: Spiritual Preparation for the Office of Confession.* Harper Torchlight Books. Translated by Douglas V. Steere, New York: Harper & Brothers, 1956.

———. *The Sickness unto Death: A Christian Psychological Exposition for Upbuilding and Awakening.* Kierkegaard's Writings, XIX. Translated by Howard V. Hong and Edna H. Hong, Princeton: Princeton University Press, 1980.

———. *Soren Kierkegaard's Journals and Papers, Volume 3.* Translated by Howard V. Hong and Edna H. Hong, Bloomington: Indiana University Press, 1975.

———. *Spiritual Writings—Gift, Creation, Love: Selections from the Upbuilding Discourses.* Translated by George Pattison. Harper Perennial Modern Thought. New York: HarperPerennial, 2010.

———. *Works of Love.* Translated by Howard V. Hong and Edna H. Hong, Harper Perennial Modern Thought. New York: HarperPerennial, 2009.

———. *Works of Love.* Kierkegaard's Writings, XVI. Translated by Howard V. Hong and Edna H. Hong. Princeton: Princeton University Press, 1995.

Kirk, Connie Ann. *Critical Companion to Flannery O'Connor: A Literary Reference to Her Life and Work.* New York: Facts on File, 2008.

Kirkpatrick, Matthew D. *Attacks on Christendom in a World Come of Age—Kierkegaard, Bonhoeffer, and the Question of "Religionless Christianity."* Princeton Theological Monographs Series. Eugene OR: Pickwick, 2011.

Kostenberger, Andreas J. "Lifting Up the Son of Man and God's Love for the World: John 3:16 in its Historical, Literary, and Theological Contexts" in *Understanding the Times—New Testament Studies in the 21st Century,* edited by Andreas Kostenberger et al., 141–59. Wheaton IL: Crossway, 2011.

Law, David R. "Cheap Grace and the Cost of Discipleship" in *For Self-Examination and Judge for Yourself!* International Kierkegaard Commentary, Volume 21, edited by Robert L. Perkins, 111–42, Macon GA: Mercer University Press, 2002.

Lawrence, Joel. *Bonhoeffer: A Guide for the Perplexed.* T & T Clark Guides for the Perplexed. New York: T & T Clark, 2010.

———. "Death Together—Dietrich Bonhoeffer on Becoming the Church for Others" in *Bonhoeffer, Christ and Culture,* edited by Keith L. Johnson et al., 113–29. Downers Grove: IVP Academic, 2013.

Leithart, Peter J. *Against Christianity.* Moscow ID: Canon, 2003.

———. *Between Babel and Beast: America and Empires in Biblical Perspectives.* Theopolitical Visions 14. Eugene OR: Cascade, 2012.

———. *Delivered from the Elements of the World: Atonement, Justification, Mission.* Downers Grove: IVP Academic, 2016.

———. *A House for My Name: A Survey of the Old Testament.* Logos Library System Version. Moscow ID: Canon, 2000.

———. *Solomon Among the Postmoderns.* Grand Rapids: Brazos, 2008.

———. *The Theopolitan Vision.* West Monroe LA: Theopolis, 2019.

Lewis, Alan E. *Between Cross & Resurrection: A Theology of Holy Saturday.* Grand Rapids; Eerdmans, 2001.

Lewis, C. S. *The Abolition of Man or Reflections on Education with Special Reference to the Teaching of English in the Upper Forms of Schools.* New York: Macmillan, 1947.

———. *God in the Dock: Essays on Theology and Ethics.* Grand Rapids: Eerdmans, 1970.

———. "The Great Divide" *Christian History Magazine, The Great Divide,* https://christianhistoryinstitute.org/magazine/article/lewis-great-divide

———. *The Great Divorce.* New York: Macmillan, 1946.

———. *The Last Battle.* Book Seven, The Chronicles of Narnia. New York: HarperCollins, 1956.

———. *The Lion, the Witch, and the Wardrobe.* Book One, The Chronicles of Narnia. New York: HarperCollins, 1950.

———. *Mere Christianity.* New York: Macmillan. 1978 [1943, 1945, 1953].

———. *Perelandra, A Novel.* New York: Scribner, 1944.

———. *The Pilgrim's Regress: An Allegorical Apology for Christian Reason and Romanticism.* Grand Rapids: Eerdmans, 1958 [1933, 1943].

———. *The Problem of Pain.* New York: Simon & Schuster, 1996 [1940].

———. *Selected Literary Essays.* Kindle version. New York: Harper One, 2013 [1955].

———. *Surprised by Joy: The Shape of My Early Life.* San Diego: Harcourt Brace, 1955.

———. *The Screwtape Letters and Screwtape Proposes a Toast.* Annotated Edition by Paul McCusker. New York: HarperOne, 2013 [1942, 1959]

———. *Till We Have Faces: A Myth Retold.* San Diego: Harcourt Brace, 1956.

———. *The Weight of Glory and other Addresses.* Revised and Expanded Edition. New York: Macmillan, 1949.

———. *The World's Last Night and Other Essays.* San Diego: Harcourt Brace, 1960.

Lilje, Hanns. *The Last Book of the Bible: The Meaning of the Revelations of St. John.* Translated by Olive Wyon. Philadelphia: Muhlenberg, 1957.

Lindvall, Terry. *Surprised by Laughter: The Comic World of C. S. Lewis,* Nashville: Thomas Nelson, 1996.

Longman, Tremper III., and Daniel G. Reid. *God is a Warrior.* Studies in Old Testament Biblical Theology. Grand Rapids: Zondervan, 1995.

Lopez, Davina C. *The Apostle to the Conquered: Reimagining Paul's Mission.* Paul in Critical Contexts. Minneapolis: Fortress, 2008.

Lynch, William F. *Christ and Apollo: The Dimensions of the Literary Imagination.* New York: Sheed and Ward, 2004.

Macquarrie, John. *Theology, Church, & Ministry.* New York: Crossroad, 1986.
———. *Two Worlds Are Ours: An Introduction to Christian Mysticism.* Minneapolis: Fortress, 2005.
Mangina, Joseph L. *Karl Barth: Theologian of Christian Witness.* Louisville: Westminster John Knox, 2004.
Maritain, Jacques. *The Social and Political Philosophy of Jacques Maritain: Selected Readings.* New York: Charles Scribner's Sons, 1955.
Markos, Louis. *Atheism on Trial—Refuting the Modern Arguments Against God.* Eugene OR: Harvest House, 2018.
Marsden, George M. *Fundamentalism and American Culture: The Shaping of Twentieth-Century Evangelicalism. 1870–925.* New York: Oxford University Press, 1980.
McGrath, Alister E. *A Scientific Theology, Volume 2: Reality.* Grand Rapids: Eerdmans, 2002.
———. *Why God Won't Go Away: Is the New Atheism Running on Empty?* Nashville: Thomas Nelson, 2010.
McGrath, S.J. *Heidegger: A (Very) Critical Introduction,* Interventions. Grand Rapids, Eerdmans, 2008.
McLellan, David, *Utopian Pessimist—The Life and Thought of Simone Weil.* New York: Poseidon, 1990.
Mendenhall, Allen. "Cultural Marxism is Real." *The James G. Martin Center for Academic Renewal.* https://www.jamesgmartin.center/2019/01/cultural-marxism-is-real/
Merton, Thomas. *Love and Living.* San Diego: Harcourt Brace Javanovich, 1979.
———. *No Man is an Island.* San Diego: Harcourt Brace, 1955.
———. *The Seven Storey Mountain: An Autobiography of Faith.* San Diego: Harcourt Brace, 1948.
Meyers, Jeffrey. *A Table in the Mist: Meditations on Ecclesiastes.* Through New Eyes Bible Commentary. Monroe, LA: Athanasius, 2006.
Middleton, J. Richard. "Created in the Image of a Violent God?" *Interpretation,* 58:4 (2004), 341–55.
———. *A New Heaven and a New Earth: Reclaiming Biblical Eschatology.* Grand Rapids: Baker, 2014.
———. "Reading Genesis 3 Attentive to Human Evolution—Beyond Concordism and Non-Overlapping Magisteria" in *Evolution and the Fall,* edited by William T. Cavanaugh et al., 67–97. iBooks Edition. Grand Rapids MI: Eerdmans, 2017.
Miller, Johnny V., and John M. Soden. *In the Beginning We Misunderstood: Interpreting Genesis 1 in Its Original Context.* Grand Rapids: Kregel, 2012.
Mitchell, Mark T. *Michael Polanyi: The Art of Knowing.* Library of Modern Thinkers. Wilmington DE: ISI. 2006
———. *Power and Purity: The Unholy Marriage That Spawned America's Social Justice Warriors.* Washington DC: Regnery, 2020.
Moll, Rob. *What Your Body Knows About God: How We Are Designed to Connect, Serve, and Thrive.* Downers Grove: IVP, 2014.
Moore, Charles E. ed. *Provocations: Spiritual Writings of Kierkegaard,* Walden NY: Plough, 2002.
Moore, Scott H. *The Limits of Liberal Democracy: Politics and Religion at the End of Modernity.* Downers Grove: IVP Academic, 2009.
Morris, Leon. *Expository Reflections on the Letter to the Ephesians.* Grand Rapids: Baker, 1994.
Morrow, Jeffrey L. *Seeking the Lord of Middle Earth: Theological Essays on J. R. R. Tolkien.* Eugene OR, Cascade, 2017.

Moses, John. *One Equal Light: An Anthology of the Writings of John Donne.* Grand Rapids: Eerdmans, 2004.
Motyer, J. Alec. *The Prophecy of Isaiah: An Introduction and Commentary.* Downers Grove: IVP Academic, 1993.
Mounce, Robert H. *The Book of Revelation.* The New International Commentary on the New Testament. Grand Rapids: Eerdmans, 1977.
Murphy, Roland E. "The Kerygma of the Book of Proverbs," *Interpretation*, 20:1 (1966), 3–14.
Murray, Douglas. *The Madness of Crowds.* Kindle version. London: Bloomsbury Continuum, 2019.
Myers, Ched. *Binding the Strong Man: A Political Reading of Mark's Story of Jesus*, Maryknoll NY: Orbis, 1988.
Newbigin, Lesslie. *The Gospel in a Pluralist Society.* Kindle version. Grand Rapids: Eerdmans, 1989.
———. *Proper Confidence—Faith, Doubt and Certainty in Christian Discipleship.* Grand Rapids: Eerdmans, 1995.
———. *Signs Amid the Rubble—The Purposes of God in Human History.* Grand Rapids: Eerdmans, 2003.
Nevin, Thomas R. *Simone Weil—Portrait of a Self-Exiled Jew.* Chapel Hill NC: University of North Carolina Press, 1991.
O'Connor, Flannery. *Collected Works.* The Library of America. New York: Library of America, 1988.
———. *Complete Stories,* New York: Farrar, Straus and Giroux, 1971.
O'Donnell, Angela Alaimo. *Flannery O'Connor: Fiction Fired by Faith.* Collegeville MN: Liturgical, 2015.
O'Donovan, Oliver. *The Problem of Self-Love in St. Augustine.* New Haven and London: Yale University Press, 1980.
Ortlund, Raymond C. *The Gospel: How the Church Portrays the Beauty of Christ.* Building Healthy Churches. Wheaton IL: Crossway, 2014.
———. *Whoredom: God's Unfaithful Wife in Biblical Theology.* New Studies in Biblical Theology. Grand Rapids: Eerdmans, 1996.
Oswalt, John N. "Golden Calves and the 'Bull of Jacob': The Impact on Israel of Its Religious Environment" in *Israel's Apostasy and Restoration: Essays in Honor of Roland K. Harrison,* edited by Avraham Gileadi, 9–18. Grand Rapids: Baker, 1988.
Outcalt, Todd E. *The Seven Deadly Virtues: Temptations in Our Pursuit of Goodness.* Downers Grove: IVP, 2017.
Parry, Robin A. *The Biblical Cosmos: A Pilgrim's Guide to the Weird and Wonderful World of the Bible,* Eugene: Cascade, 2014.
———. *Lamentations.* The Two Horizons Old Testament Commentary, Grand Rapids: Eerdmans, 2010.
Pascal, Blaise. *Pensees.* Translated by A. J. Krailsheimer. London: Penguin Group, 1966
Peters, James R. *The Logic of the Heart: Augustine, Pascal, and the Rationality of Faith.* Grand Rapids: Baker Academic, 2009.
Peters, Ted. *God—The World's Future: Systematic Theology for a Postmodern Era.* Minneapolis: Fortress, 1992.
Peterson, Eugene H. *Christ Plays In Ten Thousand Places: A Conversation in Spiritual Theology.* Grand Rapids: Eerdmans, 1999.
———. *Eat This Book: A Conversation on the Art of Spiritual Reading.* Grand Rapids: Eerdmans, 2006.

Bibliography

———. "Forward" in *The Safest Place on Earth,* by Larry Crabb, vii-viii. Nashville: W. Publishing Group, 1999.

———. *The Jesus Way: A Conversation on the Ways that Jesus is the Way.* Grand Rapids: Eerdmans, 2007.

———. *Practice Resurrection: A Conversation on Growing Up in Christ.* Grand Rapids: Eerdmans, 2010.

Podmore, Simon D. "To Die and Yet Not Die: Kierkegaard's Theophany of Death." *Kierkegaard and Death,* edited by Patrick Stokes et al., 44–64. Indiana Series in the Philosophy of Religion, Bloomington: Indiana University Press, 2011.

Polanyi, Michael. *Personal Knowledge: Towards a Post-Critical Philosophy.* Chicago: University of Chicago Press, 1958.

———. *The Tacit Dimension.* Chicago: University of Chicago Press, 1966.

Polk, Timothy Houston. *The Biblical Kierkegaard: Reading by the Rule of Faith,* Macon GA: Mercer University Press, 1997.

Potter, Vincent G. "John E. Smith and the Recovery of Religious Experience." *Reason, Experience, and God—John E. Smith in Dialogue,* edited by Vincent M. Colapietro, 7–18. American Philosophy Series. New York: Fordham University Press, 1997.

Poythress, Vern S. *Understanding Dispensationalists,* Second edition. Phillipsburg: P & R, 1994.

Punt, Neal. *A Theology of Inclusivism: A Treatise on the Generosity of God.* Kindle version. Allendale MI: Northland, 2008.

Radcliff, Alexandra S. *The Claim of Humanity in Christ: Salvation and Sanctification in the Theology of T. F. and J. B. Torrance.* Princeton Theological Monograph Series. Eugene OR: Pickwick, 2016.

Raschke, Carl. *Critical Theology: Introducing an Agenda for an Age of Global Crisis.* Downers Grove IL: IVP Academic, 2016.

———. *GloboChrist: The Great Commission Takes a Postmodern Turn.* The Church and Postmodern Culture. Grand Rapids MI: Baker Academic, 2008.

Ridderbos, Herman. *Paul—An Outline of His Theology.* Translated by John Richard De Witt. Grand Rapids: Eerdmans, 1975.

Rigney, Joe. *The Things of Earth—Treasuring God by Enjoying His Gifts.* Wheaton: Crossway, 2015.

Roades, David, et al., *Mark as Story: An Introduction to the Narrative of a Gospel.* Third Edition. Minneapolis: Fortress, 2012.

Rosas, L. Joseph III. *Scripture in the Thought of Soren Kierkegaard.* Nashville: Broadman & Holman, 1994.

Ross, Hugh. *Improbable Planet: How Earth Became Humanity's Home.* Grand Rapids: Eerdmans, 2016.

Rudd, Anthony. *Self, Value, & Narrative: A Kierkegaardian Approach.* Oxford: Oxford University Press, 2012.

Rutledge, Fleming. *The Crucifixion: Understanding the Death of Jesus Christ.* Kindle version. Grand Rapids: Eerdmans, 2015.

Sailhamer, John H. *Genesis,* The Expositors Bible Commentary, edited by Frank E. Gaebelein et al., 2:1–284. Grand Rapids: Eerdmans, 1990.

Sacks, Jonathan. *Not in God's Name—Confronting Religious Violence.* New York: Schocken, 2015.

Sandner, David. "Between Euchatastrophe and Grace: J.R.R. Tolkien and Flannery O'Connor." *Soundings,* 89:1–2 (2006), 171–98.

Sands, Justin. *Reasoning from Faith: Fundamental Theology in Merold Westphal's Philosophy of Religion.* Bloomington: Indiana University Press, 2018.

Scheler, Max. *Ressentiment.* Translated by Louis A. Coser. http://www.marquette.edu/mupress/Ressentiment.shtml

Shoemaker, H. Stephen. *GodStories: New Narratives from Sacred Texts.* Valley Forge PA: Judson, 1998.

Simpson, Christopher Ben. *The Truth is the Way: Kierkegaard's Theologia Viatorum.* Eugene OR, Cascade, 2011.

Smith, James K. A. *Awaiting the King: Reforming Public Theology.* Cultural Liturgies Volume 3. Grand Rapids: Baker Academic, 2017.

———. *Desiring the Kingdom: Worship, Worldview, and Cultural Formation.* Cultural Liturgies Volume 1. Grand Rapids: Baker Academic, 2009.

———. *How (Not) To Be Secular: Reading Charles Taylor.* Grand Rapids: Eerdmans, 2014.

———. *Who's Afraid of Relativism: Community, Contingency, and Creaturehood.* The Church and Postmodern Culture. Grand Rapids: Baker Academic, 2014.

———. *You Are What You Love: The Spiritual Power of Habit.* Grand Rapids: Brazos, 2016.

Smith, Scotty., and Michael Card. *Unveiled Hope—Eternal Encouragement from the Book of Revelation.* Nashville: Thomas Nelson, 1997.

Smith, Wilfred Cantwell. *Faith and Belief.* Princeton: Princeton University Press, 1979.

Snodgrass, Klyne R. *Who God Says You Are—A Christian Understanding of Identity.* Grand Rapids: Eerdmans, 2018.

Sponheim, Paul R. *Existing Before God: Soren Kierkegaard and the Human Venture.* Mapping the Tradition. Minneapolis, Fortress, 2017.

———. *Love's Availing Power: Imaging God, Imagining the World.* Minneapolis: Fortress, 2011.

Springsted, Eric O. *The Act of Faith: Christian Faith and the Moral Self.* Grand Rapids, Eerdmans, 2002.

———. "I Dreamed I Saw St. Augustine . . ." in *The Christian Platonism of Simone Weil,* Edited by E. Jane Doering et al., 209–27. Notre Dame: University of Notre Dame Press, 2004.

———. *Simone Weil and the Suffering of Love.* Cambridge MA: Cowley, 1986.

Sprinkle, Preston., and Andrew Rillera. *Fight: A Christian Case for Non-Violence.* Colorado Springs: David C. Cook, 2013

Starr, Charlie W. *Light: C. S. Lewis's First and Final Short Story.* Hamden: Winged Lion, 2012.

Steinbeck, John. *East of Eden, Steinbeck Centennial Edition.* New York: Penguin, 1952.

———. *Journal of a Novel: The East of Eden Letters.* New York: Penguin, 1969.

Streett, R. Alan. *Heaven on Earth: Experiencing the Kingdom of God in the Here and Now.* Eugene OR: Harvest House, 2013.

———. *Subversive Meals: An Analysis of the Lord's Supper under Roman Domination during the First Century.* Eugene OR, 2013.

Teilhard de Chardin, Pierre. *The Divine Milieu,* Perennial Classics. New York: Harper Perennial, 2001 [1960].

———. *The Future of Man,* New York: Doubleday, 2004 [1959].

Tickle, Phyllis., and Jon Sweeney. *The Age of the Spirit: How the Ghost of an Ancient Controversy is Shaping the Church.* Kindle version. Grand Rapids: Baker, 2014.

———. *Emergence Christianity: What It Is, Where It Is Going, and Why It Matters.* Grand Rapids: Baker, 2012.

———. *The Great Emergence: How Christianity is Changing and Why.* Emergent Village Resources for Communities of Faith. Grand Rapids: Eerdmans, 2008.

Tietjen, Mark A. *Kierkegaard—A Christian Missionary to Christians*. Downers Grove: IVP Academic, 2016.
Tillich, Paul. *The Courage to Be*. Second Edition. New Haven: Yale University Press, 1952.
———. *The New Being*. New York: Charles Scribner's Sons, 1955.
———. *Theology of Culture*, New York: Oxford University Press, 1959.
Todt, Heinz Eduard. *Authentic Faith: Bonhoeffer's Theological Ethics in Context*. Translated by David Stassen and Ilse Todt. Grand Rapids: Eerdmans, 2007
Tolkien, J. R. R. *The Tolkien Reader*. New York: Ballentine, 1966.
Torrance, Thomas F. *Atonement: The Person and Work of Christ*. Downers Grove: IVP Academic, 2009.
———. *The Doctrine of Jesus Christ*. Logos Library System Electronic Edition. Eugene OR: Wipf and Stock, 2002.
———. *Incarnation: The Person and Life of Christ*. Downers Grove: IVP Academic, 2008.
Tutu, Desmond., and Mpho Tutu. *Made for Goodness: And Why this Makes the Difference*. New York: Harper One, 2010.
Twain, Mark, "The Adventures of Huckleberry Finn" in *Mark Twain: Five Novels*, 355–594. Library of Essential Writers. New York: Barnes & Noble, 2006
Tyson, Paul. *Kierkegaard's Theological Sociology: Prophetic Fire for the Present Age*. Eugene OR: Cascade, 2019.
———. *Returning to Reality—Christian Platonism for Our Times*. Kalos Series 2. Eugene OR: Cascade, 2014.
Vanauken, Sheldon. *A Severe Mercy*. New York: Harper & Row, 1977.
VanGemeren, *Willem A. Psalms*, The Expositors Bible Commentary, edited by Frank E. Gaebelein et al., 5:1–880. Grand Rapids: Zondervan, 1991.
Van Leeuwen, Arend Theodoor, *Critique of Heaven: The First Series of the Gifford Lectures entitled "Critique of Heaven and Earth."* New York: Charles Scribner's Sons, 1972.
Voegelin, Eric. *The New Science of Politics*. Chicago: University of Chicago Press, 1952.
Vos, Geerhardus. *Biblical Theology: Old and New Testaments*. Grand Rapids: Eerdmans, 1991 [1948].
———. *The Teaching of the Epistle to the Hebrews*, Phillipsburg, NJ: Presbyterian and Reformed, 1956.
Walker-Jones, Arthur. *The Green Psalter: Resources for an Ecological Spirituality*. Minneapolis: Fortress, 2009.
Wallis, Jim. *The (Un)Common Good: How the Gospel Brings Hope to a World Divided*. Grand Rapids MI: Brazos, 2013, 2014.
Walsh, Sylvia. *Living Christianly: Kierkegaard's Dialectic of Christian Existence*. University Park: Pennsylvania State University Press, 2005.
Waltke, Bruce K. *The Dance Between God and Humanity: Reading the Bible Today as the People of God*. Grand Rapids: Eerdmans, 2013.
Walton, John H. *Genesis*. The NIV Application Commentary. Kindle version. Grand Rapids: Zondervan, 2001,
Waltz, Kenneth N. *Man, the State and War: A Theoretical Analysis*. New York: Columbia University Press, 2001 [1954, 1959].
Warfield, Benjamin B. *Biblical and Theological Studies*. Phillipsburg NJ: Presbyterian and Reformed, 1968.
Webb, Eugene. *The Dark Dove: The Sacred and Secular in Modern Literature*. Seattle: University of Washington Press, 1975.

———. *Philosophers of Consciousness: Polanyi, Lonergan, Voegelin, Ricoeur, Girard, Kierkegaard.* Seattle: University of Washington Press, 1988.

Weil, Simone. *The Need for Roots: Prelude to a Declaration of Duties Toward Mankind*, Translated by A. F. Wills, London: Ark, 1987 [1952]

———. *Waiting for God*, Translated by Emma Craufield. New York: HarperPerennial, 2009 [1951]

Weil, Simone., and Rachel Bespaloff. *War and the Iliad*. Translated by Mary McCarthy. New York: New York Review of Books, 2005.

Wells, Albert N. *Pascal's Recovery of Man's Wholeness.* Richmond: John Knox, 1965.

Weston, Paul ed. *Lesslie Newbigin: Missionary Theologian—A Reader.* Grand Rapids: Eerdmans, 2006.

Westphal, Merold. *God, Guilt, and Death: An Existential Phenomenology of Religion.* Studies in Phenomenology and Existential Philosophy. Bloomington: Indiana University Press, 1984.

———. *Kierkegaard's Concept of Faith.* Kierkegaard as a Christian Thinker. Grand Rapids: Eerdmans, 2014.

———. *Kierkegaard's Critique of Reason and Society.* University Park: Pennsylvania State University Press, 1987.

———. *Overcoming Onto-Theology: Toward a Postmodern Christian Faith.* Perspectives in Continental Philosophy. New York: Fordham University Press, 2001.

———. "Paganism in Christendom: on Kierkegaard's Critique of Religion" in *Christian Discourses and The Crisis and a Crisis in the Life of an Actress.* International Kierkegaard Commentary, Volume 17, edited by Robert L. Perkins, 13–33. Macon GA: Mercer University Press, 2007.

———. *Suspicion & Faith: The Religious Uses of Modern Atheism.* New York: Fordham University Press, 1998.

———. "Theological Anti-Realism" *Realism and Religion: Philosophical and Theological Perspectives* ed. by Andrew Moore and Michael Scott. Aldershot, UK: Ashgate, 2007.

———. "The Philosophical/Theological View." in *Biblical Hermeneutics: Five Views*, edited by Stanley E. Porter. Spectrum Multiview Books. Downers Grove: IVP Academic, 2012.

White, R. E. O. *Colossians*, The Broadman Bible Commentary, edited by Clifton J. Allen et al., 11:217–56. Nashville: Broadman, 1971.

Wikipedia, "Alfred Loisy." https://en.wikipedia.org/wiki/Alfred_Loisy

Willard, Dallas. *The Divine Conspiracy: Rediscovering Our Hidden Life in God*, San Francisco: HarperSanFrancisco, 1998.

Williams, Bernard. *Philosophy as a Humanistic Discipline.* Edited by A. W. Moore, Princeton: Princeton University Press, 2006.

Williams, Rowan. *The Lion's World: A Journey into the Heart of Narnia.* New York: Oxford University Press, 2012.

Wilson, Douglas. *Against the Church*. Moscow ID: Canon, 2013.

Wilson, Gerald H. *Psalms Volume 1, The NIV Application Commentary.* Grand Rapids: Zondervan, 2002.

Wolf, Carl Umhau. "The Continuing Temptation of Christ in the Church: Searching and Preaching on Matthew 4:1–11" in *Interpretation*, 20:3 (1966), 288–301.

Wood, Ralph C. *Chesterton: The Nightmare Goodness of God.* The Making of the Christian Imagination. Waco: Baylor University Press, 2011.

———. *Contending for the Faith: The Church's Engagement with Culture.* Waco: Baylor University Press, 2003.

———. *Flannery O'Connor and the Christ-Haunted South.* Grand Rapids: Eerdmans, 2004.

Wright, Christopher J. H. *The Mission of God: Unlocking the Bible's Grand Narrative.* Downers Grove: IVP Academic, 2006.

Wright, N. T. *The Day the Revolution Began: Reconsidering the Meaning of Jesus's Crucifixion.* New York: HarperOne, 2016.

———. *Judas and the Gospel of Jesus: Have We Missed the Truth of Christianity.* Grand Rapids: Baker, 2006.

———. *The New Testament for Everyone.* London: SPCK, 2018.

———. *Paul: A Biography.* New York: HarperOne, 2018.

———. *Paul for Everyone: 2 Corinthians.* Louisville: Westminster John Knox, 2004.

———. *Simply Good News: Why the Gospel Is News and What Makes It Good.* New York: HarperOne: 2015.

———. *Simply Jesus: A New Vision of Who He Was, What He Did, and Why He Matters,* New York: HarperOne, 2011.

———. *Surprised by Hope—Rethinking Heaven, the Resurrection, and the Mission of the Church.* New York: HarperOne, 2008.

———. *Judas and the Gospel of Jesus: Have We Missed the Truth about Christianity?* Grand Rapids: Baker, 2006,

Yoder, John Howard. *The Politics of Jesus.* Grand Rapids: Eerdmans, 1972.

Yong, Amos. *The Hermeneutical Spirit—Theological Interpretation and Scriptural Imagination* for the 21st Century. iBooks Edition. Eugene OR: Cascade, 2017.

———. *Who is the Holy Spirit? A Walk with the Apostles.* A Paraclete Guide. Brewster MA: Paraclete, 2011.

Zahnd, Brian. *A Farewell to Mars—An Evangelical Pastor's Journey Toward the Biblical Gospel of Peace.* Kindle version. Colorado Springs: David C. Cook, 2014.

———. "Mistaken as the Gardener" https://brianzahnd.com/2018/03/mistaken-as-the-gardener/

Ziegler, Philip G. *Militant Grace—The Apocalyptic Turn and the Future of Christian Theology.* Grand Rapids: Baker Academic, 2018.

Zetterholm, Magnus. *Approaches to Paul: A Student's Guide to Scholarship.* Minneapolis: Fortress, 2009.

Zimmermann, Jens. *Incarnational Humanism: A Philosophy of Culture for the Church in the World.* Strategic Initiatives in Evangelical Theology. Downers Grove: IVP Academic, 2012.

Index

1 Corinthians, 22, 57–58, 61–62, 279–82
2 Corinthians, 54–55

Abraham/Sarah, 12, 32, 56, 77, 196, 222, 343
Acts, 60–61, 72–74, 87, 198, 223, 285–93
Adam/Eve, 9, 12, 65, 105, 111, 157, 232, 243, 261, 343
Allen, Diogenes, 45, 207, 233, 280, 303–4, 306–7, 313–16, 319
anxiety, 11, 13, 21, 112, 123, 157, 192, 232
Attack on Christendom, 43n18, 118–19, 176, 188
atonement, 52–54, 75–76, 81–90, 129–46, 226–27
Augustine, 10, 237n139, 290

Backhouse, Stephen, 267n2
Badcock, Gary D., 65n23, 128n47, 200n64, 208n80, 228, 310n80, 317n95
baptism, 50, 108–9, 112–14, 118, 122, 123, 125, 127, 129, 144, 145, 156, 158, 222, 280
Barth, Karl, 46, 63, 83, 116–17, 266, 317–19
Bauckham, Richard, 212, 251n163
Beale, G. K., 27, 67n27, 80, 114n15, 124n37, 313n85
beauty, 3, 85n49, 171, 237–44, 253, 256, 314
Bennett, David, 232n124, 234–36
Berger, Peter L., 146n79, 175–76

Berkouwer, G. C., 29–30, 129n48, 143n74, 318n101
Bible, 12, 14n28, 31, 36–39, 42–43, 44n20, 55n12, 68, 83–84, 121, 123, 139, 140–46, 149, 171, 213–15, 295–302
birth, 52, 198–200, 245, 251
Blower, David Benjamin, 42, 113–14, 172, 244, 335
Boersma, Hans, 100n8, 328n131
Bonhoeffer, Dietrich, 83n41, 118–19, 127, 165–66, 180–84, 192, 197, 201–7, 239, 243n150, 300–301, 308
Borchert, Gerald L., 141, 187n39, 276, 279n13
breath of God, 46, 63–68, 70, 75, 81, 88, 105, 181, 187, 194–96, 214–16, 241, 251, 341n100
Brueggemann, Walter, 19–20, 35, 37, 132–34, 149–53, 184, 213n90, 214–15, 347
Buber, Martin, 12
Brueghel, Pieter, 20
Byassee, Jason, 292n35, 295, 331n40, 347

Cain/Abel, 6–10, 14, 18, 20–21, 25, 47, 58, 111, 114, 151, 255, 257, 324–26
Calvin/Calvinism, 101, 137, 142, 178n20, 268–69, 287
Caputo, John B. 33n22
Carson, D. A., 117, 1289n45, 134–35, 141, 235, 276n11, 288n26, 347

361

cattle (representing non-human creation), 80, 107, 125, 245
Chesterton, G. K., 24, 173, 178, 258n6, 343n13
Childs, Brevard S. 197
Chisney, Vernon W. 305n65
church as a community,
   for others, 193–96
   for those far off, 224–37
   of hope, 209–13
   of lament, 213–16
   of new social order, 199–209
   of peace, 218–37
   of praise, 187–89
   of priests, 197–99
   of truth, 189–93
city, 7, 10, 19–21, 27–28, 92, 108, 147–48, 162, 164, 173, 179, 200, 210n83, 219–20, 243–45, 255, 257, 285
civil religion, 2, 119–20, 156, 178–80
climate change, 247–51
Colossians, 56–57, 62, 298–300, 303, 309
confession, 29–30, 157, 171, 180–84, 188–89, 192, 239, 290
condemnation, 230, 233, 253, 267–79, 340
cosmos, 53, 57, 88, 93, 98, 255, 264, 265, 299
creation, 14, 20 n. 42, 31–35, 64–67, 70–71, 81, 100, 105, 113, 155, 215–16, 222, 236–37, 244–51, 257, 280–283, 296–318, 322
cross, 18–19, 23, 33, 37–40, 55, 86, 87, 147–48, 172, 200n63, 218–20, 233–34, 307–11, 316, 322, 333–34, 343
cultural Marxism, 150–52, 206,
culture 18, 114–15, 117–19, 146–55, 162–65, 186–87, 189–92, 198, 225, 230–237
culture war, 114, 115, 153–54, 179, 230

Dark, David, 148,
Dawkins, Richard, 63

death, 11, 35, 38–41, 44–45, 49–50, 54–61, 74–75, 81–89, 109, 171–73, 178–80, 182–84, 250, 319–22
Desmond, John F., 302, 306, 309n77
Devil, 19, 56, 62, 73–74, 80, 82, 86
Dillard, Annie, 13–14, 42–43, 105
discipleship, 118–19, 190, 225–29, 233–36
disembeddedness, 232
disorientation, 162–64, 214–15
dispensationalism, 122–26, 281
diversion, 104, 154, 236n138, 256

East of Eden, 20, 26–27, 243, 255, 333, 338
Ecclesiastes, 10, 166nn8–9, 249n145, 315, 323
Eden, 11, 28, 46, 64, 88, 102, 146–47, 154–55, 162, 187, 229, 261, 264, 308, 327, 340
Ellul, Jacques, 20n42
Endo, Shusaku, 5
enemy-love, 76, 81, 172, 217, 245
Ephesians, 84, 113, 137, 147, 156, 216, 220–221, 301
euchatastrophe, 52, 61, 68 n. 29, 88, 265, 340
evangelicalism, 122, 249, 269
evangelism, 91–159
evangelizers, 160–251
Evans, C. Stephen, 65n25, 283n22, 311n81, 327n130
exclusivism, 96–99, 266–336
existence communication, 231, 293–94
existence revelation of Christ, 293–336
exodus, the, 12, 39–40, 59, 77, 88, 197–98
expressive individualism, 225, 229, 232, 236

faith, 6–22, 29–30, 43–48, 50, 55, 57–59, 65, 108–9, 140–44, 174–77, 184–87, 226–32, 263–65, 266–336
Federici, Michael P., 306
Ferreira, M. Jamie, 201n65, n66, 313n83

force, 8, 12, 18–22, 25–33, 56, 62–63, 66, 68–70, 79, 86, 109–12, 305–11
forgiveness, 27, 59, 138nn57–58, 151–52, 206–7, 228, 254, 318, 321
fortress church, 125
fortress city, 7, 125, 164, 255, 338
foundationalism, 101–2
Fretheim, Terrence E., 39n13, 338n3
fundamentalism, 121–23, 126–29, 140n3

Galatians, 32, 151–52, 186, 219, 221–22, 298
Galatianism, 151–52
Garland, David 35n3, 279n13
God, 10–12, 63–66
God in the Dock, 15–19
gnosticism, 48, 124
Genesis, 11–13, 34–35, 64–67, 323–29
gospel, 34–90
    culture, 155, 156, 184, 185–92
    events, 35
    focus, 37–39, 57–58
    narrative, 36–37
    of kingdom of God, 155–57
    of peace, 216
gospels of,
    cheap grace 118–20
    Christianity and, 115–18
    conditionality, 129–46
    correct doctrine/practice, 127–29
    culture, 146–55
    escapism, 122–26, 246
    reaction, 120–22
    war, 111–14
great reversal, the, 123–26
groaning, 215–16, 245, 286
Gunton, Colin, 100n8, 279–80

Hart, Trevor, 212, 251n163
Harvey, Barry, 113, 164–65, 301
Hays, Richard B., 23n45, 227n116, 236–37
Hazony, Yoram, 325–26
hell, 27–28, 87–88, 138–39
Henry, Carl, 122

Henry, Michel, 86, 136n55, 289n29, 296n43
Heschel, Abraham, 241
Hebrews, 7, 56, 88, 219–20, 261n14, 323n116, 326
hermeneutic of the gospel, 185–237
history, 47–48, 279–80, 285–93, 296–302, 307, 310, 327–29
Hitchens, Christopher, 338–39
Hobbes, Thomas, 22n44, 76, 153, 206, 208, 258n7, 305
Holy Spirit, 60, 195, 202, 205, 282
hope, 20–21, 39–40, 57, 87, 125, 178–79, 205–7, 209–16, 311, 315
human judgment, 167–70
humanity, 66–76, 244–51, 261–65

identity, 231–37, 342
immanentization of the eschaton, 242–43
inclusivism, 266–336
interruption, 42–45, 164, 169, 172
Irenaeus, 4–6, 9, 21, 231, 247, 254–55, 264
Isaac, 342–43
Isaiah, 3–4, 70–71, 74–75, 77–78, 237, 253
Islam, 240, 250
Israel, 12, 32, 38–41, 45–46, 59–61, 77–80, 178–79, 197–98, 217–18, 221–23, 262, 279, 327

Jardine, Murray, 225n113, 242n149
Jennings, Willie James, 148, 223n106, 297
Jervis, L. Ann., 222
John, 34, 124–26, 128, 141–44, 268–79, 283
Johnston, Robert K., 283n21, 289n29, 295
Jonah, 3–4, 10, 15–19, 74–84, 87–90, 161–62, 171–74, 217–18, 261–62, 342
joy, 104, 342–43
judgment of God, 19, 25–33, 54, 152, 173, 178, 217–18, 311–13, 334, 339
justice, 109–11, 206–9

justification, 26–27, 121, 133, 140, 180, 229–33, 236–37

Kierkegaard, Soren, 14n28, 43n18, 65n25, 101–3, 118–19, 121, 174, 176, 193, 201, 231, 260, 293–94, 320n83, 320–321
kingdom of God, 18, 62, 92, 109, 117–18, 122–26, 155–57, 163, 177–79, 190, 231–32, 296–97, 311–12
Kirk, Connie Ann, 86
Kirkpatrick, Matthew D., 118–19, 202n67
Kostenberger, Andreas J., 268–69, 271n6

Lamech, 25–27
Lawrence, Joel, 183–84, 197
Leithart, Peter J., 92n1, 101n9, 113n11, 151, 152n100, 153n102, 200n63
Leviathan, 73, 76, 80, 82, 87, 115, 172–73, 258, 261
Lewis, C. S., 2, 3, 5–6, 8, 15–18, 24, 28, 37–38, 41n16, 44n21, 83–85, 104, 115–16, 139, 151, 154, 163n3, 167–68, 256, 258, 272–73, 288n25, 319–20, 337n1, 339n6
logos, 276–83, 287–88, 295–96, 299–300
longing, 104–5, 155n107, 190, 205, 245, 308, 314, 319–20, 322
Lopez, Davina C., 20n42, 32
Lord's Supper, 22, 108–9, 118, 125, 145, 154, 192
love, 9–10, 15, 33, 64–65, 84, 143, 169, 172, 190–95, 201–4, 207–8, 233–37, 240–241, 264, 268–71, 304–7, 311–16
Luke, 17, 39–40, 44, 50, 68–69, 193–94, 298–99, 323–24, 328, 330, 340
Luther, Martin, 65n23, 121, 194n53, 229, 237
Lynch, William, 301

Macquarrie, John, 11, 317n95
Malick, Terrence, 305
Maritain, Jacques, 236n128, 237, 259n10, 339n5

Mark, 10, 35, 50n1, 68, 72, 138n57, 155, 264, 266, 269, 279
mark of Cain, 25–27, 218n100
Markos, Louis, 104, 109–10
Marx, Karl, 150, 176, 187–88, 302n55
Marxism, 150, 152, 206
Matthew, 49, 58–59, 73, 76, 82, 92–94, 280, 311–13
McGrath, Alister E. 101, 151n95
McGrath, S. J., 105n21, 236n138, 237n139, 317
mediation, 85, 198, 200–207, 254, 307–8, 311n81
Merton, Thomas, 234, 236n137
Meyers, Jeffrey, 10n19, 166n8, 322–23, 325
Middleton, J. Richard, 31, 39n13, 67n27, 70n31, 125n42, 162n2, 243n151, 247n157
miserable sinner Christianity, 67–68
Mitchell, Mark T. 150–51
modernism, 100–103, 123, 141n67, 153n102
moral inversion, 150, 152
Motyer, J. Alec, 71nn32–33
Murphy, Roland E. 295
Murray, Douglas, 150n90, 206n75
Myers, Ched, 35n2, 68n28, 173
mysterium tremendum et fascinans, 65, 322
mystery, 11–14, 30, 65, 74–75, 97, 137–38, 142, 169, 232, 235n134, 266, 296, 302, 308, 314, 317–18, 331, 335–36, 343

Nahum, 337–40
nationalism, 92, 117, 152, 192, 206, 214
nature, 29–30, 244–51
natural revelation, 280–293, 335–36
neighbor, 98, 149, 193–95, 313–14
new birth, 46, 177–80, 302, 331
new creation, 21, 23n45, 31–33, 52–53, 55, 57, 85, 87–88, 98, 109, 133, 136, 155, 162–64, 209, 213, 222, 241, 251, 263–64, 298
Newbigin, Lesslie, 96n4, 98, 116, 185–213, 299n47
Newman, John Henry, 142, 285n23

Index

Nietzsche, Friedrich, 1n1, 150–51, 176, 187–89, 205n73, 305n64

O'Connor, Flannery, 8n15, 46n25, 52, 85–86, 331, 336n146, 343n12
O'Donnell, Angela Alaimo, 336n146
Old Testament, 58, 63, 150, 280–282, 295, 328
Ortlund, Raymond C., 183n31, 186
Outcalt, Todd E., 175–77, 193

paradise, 4–5, 7, 9, 21, 247, 254–55, 264–65
parables, 50–51, 193–94, 312n82, 316, 332n141
Pascal, Blaise, 9n18, 104, 116, 142, 154, 160n44
Paul, apostle, 22–23, 32, 36, 38, 40, 55–58, 62–63, 94, 130, 133, 221–23, 240, 245, 279–93, 298, 309, 320, 336
peace/peacemaking, 3, 57, 112, 114, 164, 178–79, 216–25, 237, 341
perfect storm, 51–54, 63–65, 75, 78, 80–82, 84–86, 88–89, 219
perfectionism, 128, 152, 205, 242, 243
Peter, apostle, 26, 61, 112, 222–23, 289, 330
Peterson, Eugene H., 35n2, 205, 220, 259n10, 260n12, 333n142
Philippians, 23, 38
philosophy, 61–62, 101, 107–8, 140–46, 256, 285–93
Pilate, Pontius, 2n3, 72, 74, 157, 163, 258–59
Plato/Platonism, 100, 109–10
Podmore, Simon D., 320–321
Polanyi, Michael, 120n29, 150–52, 242n146, 285n23
politics, 92, 113, 120, 150–52, 206–8, 210n83, 242–43
poor, the, 68–71, 73, 75–76, 80–81, 112, 177, 182, 207n77, 246
possibility, 85, 97, 101–4, 180, 194–95, 237–43, 257, 330n136, 266–336
postmodernism, 41, 99–103, 103, 153n102

preaching, 29, 61–62, 111, 135, 221, 244, 285–93, 329–35
Proverbs, 295
providence, 11, 18, 25–27, 29–30, 177–78, 234, 250, 269, 281, 302, 322, 324–25, 330, 334
Psalms, 64, 70–72, 87, 89, 214–15, 281
purification of means, 252, 259–64, 267, 341n10

Raschke, Carl, 93, 329n134
reality, 43, 100–105, 167–70, 210, 256–57, 279–82, 288, 300–301, 304–10, 328–29
reconciliation, 53–57, 75–84, 105, 129–30, 220–221, 267–77, 310
rehabilitation of the gospel, 22–24, 39–45, 47–48, 49, 89–90, 315
repentance, 26, 62, 171–80, 227–29, 297, 311, 319, 334–35
resurrection, 27, 47, 49, 52, 58, 60–62
revelation, 29–30, 31, 99, 110, 141, 169, 222–23, 235, 278–329, 334–36
Revelation, 27–28, 73, 114, 124, 164, 232–33, 247, 263, 315n90
Ridderbos, Herman, 54n11, 133
Rigney, Joe, 14 n. 27
Romans, 89, 133, 223, 245, 248, 282–85
Ross, Hugh, 52

Sacks, Jonathan, 44n20, 324n119, 327
sacred canopy, 146n79, 175–84, 212, 230, 346
scandal of particularity, 38n11, 95–99, 161, 165, 239, 260, 262–63, 267, 271
scapegoating, 21, 158, 219–20, 249, 254
Scheler, Max, 151, 176
Screwtape Letters, The, 2n3, 8n16, 14n26, 115–16, 258
secular liturgies, 189–92, 236
self-destruction, 10, 25–28, 71, 74, 76, 340
self-emptying, 39, 340
servant 23, 38, 58, 59, 72–78, 94, 116–17, 174, 208
sexual identity/practice, 225–37

Shoemaker, H. Stephen, 12, 20, 324–25, 327, 334n144, 342n11
Sickness Unto Death, The, 103n18, 174n6, 192, 225n115, 230n120, 330n136
sign,
    of Jonah, 3–4, 43–44, 49–51, 74–84, 89–90, 253–54, 261–63, 340–343
    perfect sign, 51, 84–86
Simpson, Christopher Ben, 293–94
sin, 12–14, 18, 19n38, 56, 58–59, 65, 67–69, 96, 111–12, 146n80, 154–55, 158–59, 180–84, 188, 226–33, 239, 254
Smith, James K. A., 18n36, 101–2, 145n77, 152n100, 177n15, 189–91, 237n139, 259n9
Snodgrass, Klyne R., 231
social justice, 69, 115–16, 120–21, 127, 150–51, 156, 206–8, 242–43
Sponheim, Paul R. 63–64
Springsted, Eric O., 28n28, 142–44, 207n77, 241n145, 263n16, 264n17, 297n45, 305n66, 308–9, 314, 316, 327n130
Sprinkle, Preston, 114
Starr, Charlie, 288n25
Steinbeck, John, 20nn40–41
stewardship,
    of creation, 244–51, 261–63
    of the gospel, 91–106, 107–251
Streett, R. Alan, 109nn2–3, 192n49
suffering, 85–86, 158, 213–15, 240–241, 245, 263–65, 307–9, 311–13, 338–39

Taylor, Charles, 18, 280n14
Teilhard de Chardin, Pierre, 343
temple, 5n7, 67, 164, 179, 245, 289, 323n116, 341–42
temptation, 46, 62, 112, 113n12, 116, 118, 198–99, 308, 342
theodicy, 29–30
Tickle, Phyllis, 196, 224nn109–110
Tietjen, Mark A., 174n7, 176n12
Till We Have Faces, 5–6, 16–18, 167–69, 204n70, 208, 256

Tillich, Paul, 7n13, 11, 107n1, 212–13, 229n119, 230n121, 341n9
timshel, 20–22, *88, 171*
tolerance, 153, 196, 242
Tolkien, J. R. R., 52, 88
Torrance, Thomas F., 22n44, 56nn13–14, 99, 133–44, 177n17, 269n4, 273n8, 310
totalitarianism, 21, 120, 150, 163, 236–37, 242–43, 338
tree,
    of knowledge of good and evil, 12–13, 65, 147n83, 229,
    of life, 20, 27–28, 264, 307–8, 315, 327, 333, 342–43
Tutu, Desmond, 240n141, 250
Twain, Mark, 141n66, 322
Tyson, Paul, 18n35, 102, 141n67, 146n79, 154–55, 190n44, 288n25

Ubuntu, 250

VanGemeren, Willem A. 72nn34–35
violence, 9, 25–33, 52, 75, 85–86, 114, 203, 214n93, 219n101, 324n119
Voegelin, Eric, 152, 242n146, 306
Vos, Geerhardus, 220n102, 282, 304n59, 323n116

Walker-Jones, Arthur, 247n159, 249
Walton, John H., 64–65, 326n126
Waltz, Kenneth W. 114n14, 258n4
Warfield, Benjamin B., 281–82
Webb, Eugene, 195n56, 219n101
Weil, Simone, 66, 151n97, 191–92, 203n69, 207, 241n145, 263–64, 296n45, 303–19, 332
Weston, Paul, 96n4, 98n5, 191n47, 204n69, 208n80, 299n47
Westphal, Merold, 12–13, 18n33, 65n24, 119–20, 141n65, 146n78, 174n4, 175–76, 187–88, 285–90, 296n44, 303, 320
White, R. E. O., 301n47
will to power, 8–9, 12–15, 18–21, 45–47, 111, 242–43, 252–59
Williams, Rowan, 196

Wilson, Douglas, 128, 130, 140, 145, 183, 294
Wilson, Gerald H., 72n34
Wood, Ralph C. 47n26, 86n53, 116–17, 153n103, 196, 234n131, 235n134, 242, 258n6
world Christians, 117–18
wrestling with God, 45–47, 77, 171, 324n119, 325–27, 331
Wright, Christopher J. H. 36–37, 218n100, 246n154
Wright, N. T., 48n29, 51–53, 55n12, 63, 111n7, 124n36, 125n42, 147–48, 179n23, 209–11, 213n90, 240, 243n151

Yong, Amos, 179n22, 194–95

Zahnd, Brian, 85n47, 125n40, 151n97, 261n15
Ziegler, Phillip G., 243n152
Zimmermann, Jens, 100n7, 120n30, 257n3

www.ingramcontent.com/pod-product-compliance
Lightning Source LLC
Chambersburg PA
CBHW070058020526
44112CB00034B/1474